THE BOOK OF
PSYCHIATRIC BOOKS

THE BOOK OF PSYCHIATRIC BOOKS

Edited by

Sidney Crown, M.D.
and **Hugh Freeman**, M.D.

JASON ARONSON INC.
Northvale, New Jersey
London

This book was set in 10 point Palacio by Lind Graphics of Upper Saddle River, New Jersey, and printed and bound by Haddon Craftsmen of Scranton, Pennsylvania.

Library of Congress Cataloging-in-Publication Data

The book of psychiatric books / edited by Sidney Crown and Hugh
  Freeman.
    p. cm.
  Includes bibliographical references and index.
  ISBN 0-87668-510-6 (hard cover)
    1. Psychiatry—Book reviews.   I. Crown, Sidney.   II. Freeman,
Hugh L. (Hugh Lionel)
    [DNLM: 1. Book Reviews. 2. Mental Disorders. 3. Psychiatry.
4. Psychotherapy.   ZWM 100 B724]
  RC454.4.B7 1993
  616.89—dc20
  DNLM/DLC
  for Library of Congress   92-49165

Manufactured in the United States of America. Jason Aronson Inc. offers books and cassettes. For information and catalog write to Jason Aronson Inc., 230 Livingston Street, Northvale, New Jersey 07647.

CONTENTS

Introduction ix

1 **Emile Durkeim:** *Suicide, A Study in Sociology* 1
Reviewed by R. L. Symonds
Selections

2 **Sigmund Freud:** *The Interpretation of Dreams* 9
Reviewed by Steven J. Ellman
Selections

3 **Karl Jaspers:** *General Psychopathology* 19
Reviewed by Michael Shepherd and Paul J. Harrison
Selections

4 **Anna Freud:** *The Ego and the Mechanisms of Defence* 33
Reviewed by Paul Kline
Selections

5 **Otto Fenichel:** *The Psychoanalytical Theory of Neurosis* 39
Reviewed by Richard Lucas
Selections

6 **H. J. Eysenck:** *Dimensions of Personality* 53
Reviewed by Sidney Crown
Selections

7 **Eugen Bleuler:** *Dementia Praecox or the Group
of Schizophrenias* 63
Reviewed by Manfred Bleuler and Rudolf Bleuler
Selections

8 **Eugene Minkowski:** *La Schizophrénie* 75
Reviewed by John Cutting
Selections

9 **John Bowlby:** *Child Care and the Growth of Love* 87
Reviewed by Ann Gath
Selections

10 W. Mayer-Gross, E. Slater, and M. Roth:
    Clinical Psychiatry   93
    Reviewed by Kenneth Davison
    Selections

11 Michael Balint: *The Doctor, His Patient and the Illness*   103
    Reviewed by Patrick C. Pietroni
    Selections

12 Joseph Wolpe: *Psychotherapy by Reciprocal Inhibition*   115
    Reviewed by Stuart Lieberman
    Selections

13 Kurt Schneider: *Psychopathic Personalities*   123
    Reviewed by Kevin Standage
    Selections

14 E. M. Jellinek: *The Disease Concept of Alcoholism*   133
    Reviewed by Brian D. Hore
    Selections

15 J. D. Frank: *Persuasion and Healing*   145
    Reviewed by Mark Aveline
    Selections

16 Thomas S. Szasz: *The Myth of Mental Illness*   163
    Reviewed by John Birtchnell and Andrew C. Smith
    Selections

17 Carl Ransom Rogers: *On Becoming a Person:*
    A Therapist's View of Psychotherapy   185
    Reviewed by Duncan Cramer
    Selections

18 F. Kraüpl Taylor: *The Analysis of Therapeutic Groups*   193
    Reviewed by Eric Crouch
    Selections

19 D. H. Malan: *A Study of Brief Psychotherapy*   203
    Reviewed by Jeremy Holmes
    Selections

20 **R. D. Laing and A. Esterson:** *Sanity, Madness
    and the Family*   215
    Reviewed by Anthony S. David
    Selections

21 **Eric Berne:** *Games People Play: The Psychology
    of Human Relationships*   225
    Reviewed by Duncan Cramer
    Selections

22 **Ilza Veith:** *Hysteria: The History of a Disease*   237
    Reviewed by H. Merskey
    Selections

23 **Sir Aubrey Lewis:** *Inquiries in Psychiatry, The State of
    Psychiatry, The Late Papers of Sir Aubrey Lewis*   249
    Reviewed by F. Kraüpl Taylor
    Selections

24 **Charles Rycroft:** *A Critical Dictionary of Psychoanalysis*   263
    Reviewed by John Birtchnell
    Selections

25 **Isaac M. Marks:** *Fears and Phobias*   275
    Reviewed by C. P. Seager
    Selections

26 **William H. Masters and Virginia E. Johnson:**
    Human Sexual Inadequacy   285
    Reviewed by R. P. Snaith
    Selections

27 **Henri E. Ellenberger:** *The Discovery of the Unconscious:
    The History and Evolution of Dynamic Psychiatry*   291
    Reviewed by D. Maediarmid
    Selections

28 **Irvin D. Yalom:** *The Theory and Practice of
    Group Psychotherapy*   305
    Reviewed by Eric Crouch
    Selections

29 **David J. Rothman:** *The Discovery of the Asylum*   315
    Reviewed by J. L. T. Birley
    Selections

30 **A. Bandura:** *Principles of Behavior Modification*   325
    Reviewed by Paul Lelliott
    Selections

31 **C. M. Parkes:** *Bereavement: Studies of Grief in Adult Life*   335
    Reviewed by David A. Alexander
    Selections

32 **Otto Kernberg:** *Borderline Conditions and*
    Pathological Narcissism   341
    Reviewed by Salman Akhtar and Alan M. Gruenberg
    Selections

33 **Edward O. Wilson:** *Sociobiology, the New Synthesis*   355
    Reviewed by Edward Hare
    Selections

34 **Robin Skynner:** *One Flesh: Separate Persons*   367
    Reviewed by Stan Ruszczynski
    Selections

35 **A. T. Beck:** *Cognitive Therapy and the*
    Emotional Disorders   379
    Reviewed by E. S. Paykel
    Selections

36 **Murray Bowen:** *Family Therapy in Clinical Practice*   389
    Reviewed by Michael E. Kerr
    Selections

37 **Alice Coleman:** *Utopia on Trial*   403
    Reviewed by Hugh Freeman
    Selections

    Credits   417

    Index   421

INTRODUCTION

At some point after the end of undergraduate study, books start to become valued in general more for their ideas than for their factual content. Most people will have a personal list of those which for them have been memorable, perhaps even mutative in influencing their thinking or clinical practice from that time on.

But in addition to the notion of individual choice, choices are also made at different times, by society in general or by the microsociety represented by any professional group. As a result, a particular book comes to be regarded for some time as the book of the moment, after which it either sinks into oblivion or passes into the respectability of acceptance as a textbook or an essential part of any list of reference. If it does survive for long, though, it will inevitably come to be seen rather differently after the passage of some years.

Because we thought it would be of interest to explore these ideas, since 1982 we have commissioned authors to contribute to a series in the *British Journal of Psychiatry*, called "Books Reconsidered." In most cases, contributors themselves have known the book over a long period, so that their own personal development as professionals will have interacted with the way the volume itself has stood up to time and circumstance.

This collection, edited at the invitation of Jason Aronson, includes all "Books Reconsidered" pieces that were published between the inception of the series in 1982 and the opening months of 1992. Although the choices of the editors must, to some extent, be limited by their personal interests and experience, we have tried to cover as many fields as possible that are relevant to psychiatry as a whole and to its subspecialities.

This selection includes many of the seminal works in psychiatry of the last few decades. We hope readers will find these critiques both interesting and stimulating—in some cases, possibly nostalgic.

S.C.
H.L.F.

1

Emile Durkheim:
Suicide, A Study in Sociology

Reviewed by R. L. Symonds

Everyone has heard of *Le Suicide*, by Emile Durkheim, but relatively few have read even its English translation. This is a pity, since it is a good read, although it may seem tasteless to enjoy a treatise on such a sad subject. French psychiatric literature has so lacked appeal for the English, that its first appearance in 1897 was not followed by an English translation until 1952. However, the English translation is vigorous, clear and vivid, capturing the spirit of the time of the original edition, an age away from the pompous and turgid sociological literature of today. Durkheim wrote the book, one of his two great works, using a social phenomenon – suicide – to investigate society itself. Psychiatrists might read *Suicide* for the breadth and depth of its social data, now of historical interest, and for his closely reasoned sociological arguments.

Most psychiatric trainees readily pair Durkheim with *l'anomie*, but few go further into the other types of suicide, and to the important implications of Durkheim's theories. Most psychiatric discussions of suicide give Durkheim at most a brief reference, whereas nonclinical writers often base their views upon Durkheim. Psychiatric reluctance to accept Durkheim may have been a reaction to his refutation of the "insanity" explanations of suicide then current. With historical hindsight, Durkheim's attack can be seen as a typically robust rebuttal of French theories that were even then beginning to sound outdated (see Berrios and Mohanna 1990).

Durkheim was a contemporary of both Marx and Freud, but although these three great thinkers overlap, Durkheim acknowledges neither of the others. Durkheim held that in simple societies, relationships between people are so intense that the concept of the self is underdeveloped relative

1

to the concept of the group, or "social solidarity." Society is then primary, Durkheim's first theorem. With the development of what Marx called "capitalist" means of production, society has become weakened by division of labor. When behavior is not governed by societal norms, Marx's "alienation" and Durkheim's "anomie," become apparent. Suicide is one such behavior, which according to Durkheim's second theorem cannot be reduced to individual psychological causes. Psychological mechanisms do not explain the variation in suicide rates, and even the most organic of psychiatrists must admit that only a minority of major depressives kill themselves. In his earlier *Division of Social Labour* Durkheim held that suicide could not be prevented by education, exhortation or repression, but only by altering the structure of society.

The book is divided into three parts, dealing with "Extrasocial Factors," "Social Causes and Social Types," and "The Social Element." The early chapters aim to weaken the prevalent notion that extrasocial factors are the sole cause of suicide. "Suicide and the Psychopathic States" describes types of suicides of the insane, from Jousset and Moreau de Tours. "Maniacal suicide" (the French *manie*), the killing of self to escape from imaginary danger or disgrace or to obey a mysterious order from on high, is probably severe depressive or paranoid psychosis. With the "Melancholic Suicide" is introduced the idea that the patient fails to realize the bonds that connect him with others and with things about him. Durkheim concludes that in spite of these prominent cases, most suicides are not associated with insanity—thus, "voluntary suicides." It is also in this chapter that he draws attention to the role of alcohol.

In the chapter "Suicide and Normal Psychological Types" there is a long digression on race, heredity, and cosmic (climatic) factors, mainly to refute them. Discussion on contagiousness and specificity of method or location is later taken up, concluding that suicide has little to do with imitation in the large numbers in which it occurs. Durkheim notes that the apparent statistics of suicide are actually the statistics of the opinions of officials concerning suicidal motives.

The typical Durkheimian analysis comes with the discussion on egoistic suicide. This starts with examination of religion, and the fact that the suicide rate for Protestants was greater than that for Catholics, which itself was greater than that for Jews. He notes that each of these religions has similar doctrinal views about suicide, but the Protestant religion allows freer inquiry, thus more cases are reported. He concludes that religion protects, not because of its religious sentiment but because it is a society within a society, and that the Catholic religion is a more integrated society than the Protestant.

Durkheim shows that nonmarriage increases the suicide rate, but early marriage also increases it, especially for men; that childlessness increases the suicide rate for women, and that there is a reduction of suicide risk until late middle age. A rather complex rule is derived, that the sex most preserved from suicide by marriage was constant for a given society. Citing two possible causes of marital protection from suicide, the domestic environment and assortative mating, he held that larger families were also more protective, and noted the then rapid increase in numbers of smaller families ("the density of a group cannot sink without its vitality diminishing").

He goes on to deal with changes in society, noting that great political upheavals do not necessarily increase suicide. The revolutions of 1830 and 1848 actually reduced the rate, and even elections have a small effect. He notes the now familiar fact that wars also decrease the rate, giving the examples of the Austro-Italian War of 1866 and the Franco-Prussian War of 1870. He rejects the common argument that civilians are drafted and statistics consequently difficult to keep, by noting that the same proportionate decrease occurs in women.

It is here we come to the main argument: wars and revolution arouse "collective sentiment" and cause stronger integration of society. More generally, suicide varies inversely with degree of integration of religious society, of domestic society and of the wider political society. Suicide varies inversely also with the degree of integration of social groups containing the individual. If society weakens, the individual has to depend only upon himself and recognizes no rules of conduct other than those that are founded on his private interests. Durkheim calls this egoism, and egoistic, the special type of suicide springing from excessive individuation. Durkheim treats society as a transcendent and superior form of human activity; in egoistic suicide, "the bond attaching man to life relaxes because that attaching him to his society is itself slack." "The individual yields to the slightest shock of circumstance because the state of society has made him a ready prey to suicide." We can find plenty of examples of egoistic suicide or failed suicide in our clinical practice.

Durkheim compiles a fascinating list of historical instances of suicide: the Vikings, the Celts, Vedic Brahmin, and South Sea Islanders. He quotes the example of suttee, when in 1817, 706 widows immolated themselves. Durkheim comments that in historical tribal societies, suicide was clearly a duty to remove the old and sick, but also notes the suicides of servants— in tribal society, master and servant were interdependent. Thus altruistic suicides are the opposite of egoistic, as in the former there is rudimentary individuation, whereas in the latter there is excessive individuation. He distinguishes also "optimal altruistic suicide," the individual who is accustomed to set no value on life, who easily renounces his personal being in order to be engulfed in something wider, especially in religious suicide, and, we may note today, in the fatal actions of terrorists.

Durkheim turns his attention to increases in suicide, associated with economic crises (e.g., Vienna 1874) when the rate increased by 45 percent. This was not simple hardship, because when the Prussian price of wheat rose considerably, the suicide rate did not. To emphasize that the mechanism is not hardship, in Italy of the 1870s, following unification, trade and industry sharply increased, by three times over ten years. The suicide rate went up by 36 percent in the same period. Thus financial crises, even those of prosperity, increase the suicide rate.

Durkheim's theory to explain this is very relevant today. Durkheim held that the increasing capacity of human production is matched by the increase of human wants, and Man's natural inability to restrain himself. Rather, society restrains and specifies the acceptable range of ambition, usually by the structure of social class. When society is disturbed by crises, presumably not revolutionary crises, it cannot operate this governing influence and the suicide rate increases. Economic disasters "declassify" individuals, "casting them into a lower state than their previous one," whereas economic booms allow "appetites not controlled by public opinion."

This "deregulation" Durkheim calls "anomy." *Anomy* in the English translation, comes originally from the Greek *anomia*, a noun of quality derived from *anomos*, meaning "lawless." It was actually an English word in 1591, meaning disregard of law, especially religious law. Durkheim is clearly talking about capitalist production when he refers to the "release of economic growth from all restraints, moral or religious," noting that "the occupations most prone to suicide are those with greatest capital, rather than the poorest occupations"—"those with only an empty space above them are almost invariably lost in it, if no force restrains them." "Anomy . . . differs . . . in its dependence, not on the way individuals are attached to Society, but how [Society] regulates them." "This third sort of suicide results from Man's activities lacking regulation and his consequent sufferings." Thus anomie and egoistic suicide are similar in Society's insufficient presence in the individual. What is often loosely called the state of anomy, usually referring to the unattached individual, is in fact egoism. However, Durkheim also described anomy in smaller groups, widowhood, for example, being "domestic anomy."

Durkheim describes individual forms of the different types of suicide. The altruistic form of suicide might arise as a passionate impulse in an individual obliged to kill himself, or might be present as a calm acceptance. He sees melancholic withdrawal as the abandonment of society, so that the contemplation of self becomes the contemplation of emptiness, and this leads to an abstention from living. Society is described as "not sufficiently integrated at the points where he contacts it." This is therefore egoistic suicide. It is not clear if Durkheim took this route to be the *cause* of this type of suicide. Durkheim outlined two forms of egoistic suicide which he calls "melancholic langor" and "epicurean indifference," the latter being those who kill themselves in a matter-of-fact way. The anomic suicide, however, is characterised by anger and "exasperated weariness" due to "unregulated emotions" and "an infinity of desires." Mixed forms also occur: between altruistic and egoistic types, the suicide of fanatics; between altruistic and anomic types, the suicides of dishonor. Further links between the social types and the individual psychologies are described.

In a much-quoted footnote (p. 276), Durkheim describes what was to him a rare type of suicide, termed "fatalistic suicide": "The opposite of anomic suicide . . . it is the suicide deriving from excessive regulation, of persons with futures pitilessly blocked and passions violently choked by oppressive regimes . . . the suicides of slaves." Shneidman (1976) held that Durkheim was referring to the suicide of the severe depressive, but this may confuse a societal with a clinical explanation. There have, unfortunately, been plenty of regimes since Durkheim's time that have provided the conditions for this type of suicide, in which an individual merely has to cease trying to survive.

In a chapter on "Relations with Other Social Phenomena," there is interesting detail on punishment and legal aspects. Durkheim noted the inverse relationship between suicide rate and property offences, and with homicide.

Durkheim is still relevant today. A recent search of the database *Sociological Abstracts* revealed Durkheim cited in 189 of 1,490 references, and 1,485 times in all. Later writers had noted that Durkheim's sociological approach was not antithetic but complementary to psychopathological approaches (Halbwachs 1930). Shneidman's modern synthesis of the sociological and psychological aspects of *Le Suicide* takes the four social types of suicide, the altruistic, egoistic, anomic, and fatalistic, and fits them to psychological models of suicidal behavior. While effective, this makes the psychiatrists' mistake of regarding Durkheim as primarily explaining suicide, when he was in fact explaining society.

Britain has just passed through a political philosophy seeking to revive nineteenth-century laissez-faire values by insisting, inter alia, that "there is no such thing as Society, only individuals and their families." Throughout this time, the United Kingdom continues to undergo a typical Durkheimian economic crisis, an economic boom (for some), even "deregulation" used as a term of approval, which should by Durkheimian laws have produced an increase in anomy. Over this period, the UK suicide rate has been increasing.

REFERENCES

Berrios, G. and Mohanna, M. (1990). Durkheim and 19th century views on suicide. *British Journal of Psychiatry* 156:1–9.

Durkheim, E. (1897) *Le Suicide*. Trans. as *Suicide: A Study in Sociology* by J. A. Spaulding and G. Simpson. London: Routledge & Kegan Paul, 1952.

Halbwachs, M. (1930). *Les Causes du Suicide*. Paris: Aican.

Shneidman, E. S. (1976). A psychological theory of suicide. *Psychiatric Annals* 6:51–66.

Selections from *Suicide*
by Emile Durkheim

REGARDING EGOISTIC SUICIDE

However individualized a man may be, there is always something collective remaining—the very depression and melancholy arising from this same exaggerated individualism. He effects communion through sadness when he no longer has anything else with which to achieve it.

Hence this type of suicide well deserves the name we have given it. Egoism is not merely a contributing factor in it; it is its generating cause. In this case the bond attaching man to life relaxes because that attaching him to society is itself slack. The incidents of private life which seem the direct inspiration of suicide and are considered its determining causes are in reality only incidental causes. The individual yields to the slightest shock of circumstance because the state of society has made him a ready prey to suicide.

REGARDING ANOMIC SUICIDE

If therefore industrial or financial crises increase suicides, this is not because they cause poverty, since crises of prosperity have the same result; it is because they are crises, that is, disturbances of the collective order. Every disturbance of equilibrium, even though it achieves greater comfort and a heightening of general vitality, is an impulse to voluntary death. Whenever serious readjustments take place in the social order, whether or not due to sudden growth or to an unexpected catastrophe, men are more inclined to self-destruction.

It is not true that human activity can be released from all restraint. . . Man's characteristic privilege is that the bond he accepts is not physical but moral; that is, social. He is governed not by a material environment brutally imposed upon him, but by a conscience superior to his own, the superiority of which he feels. Because the greater, better part of his existence transcends the body, he escapes the body's yoke, but is subject to that of society.

But when society is disturbed by some painful crisis or by beneficent but abrupt transitions, it is momentarily incapable of exercising this influence; thence come the sudden rise in the curve of suicides.

Anomy, therefore, is a regular and specific factor in suicide in our modern societies; one of the springs from which the annual contingent feeds. So we have here a new type to distinguish from the others. It differs from them in its dependence, not on the way in which individuals are attached to society, but on how it regulates them. Egoistic suicide results from man's no longer finding a basis for existence in life; altruistic suicide, because this basis for existence appears to man situated beyond life itself. The third sort of suicide, the existence of which has just been shown, results from man's activities lacking regulation and his consequent suffering. By virtue of its origin we shall assign this last variety the name of *anomic suicide*.

Certainly, this and egoistic suicide have kindred ties. Both spring from society's insufficient presence in individuals. But the sphere of its absence is not the same in both cases. In egoistic suicide it is deficient in truly collective activity thus depriving the latter of object and meaning. In anomic suicide, society's influence is lacking in the basically individual passions, leaving them without a check-rein. In spite of their relationship, therefore, the two types are independent of each other. We may offer society everything social in us, and still be unable to control our desires; one may live in an anomic state without being egoistic, and vice versa.

2

Sigmund Freud:
The Interpretation of Dreams

Reviewed by Steven J. Ellman

When Freud published *The Interpretation of Dreams*, he was "listless, moody, irritated with early readers of the dream book who pointed out minor slips instead of praising the whole" (Gay 1988, p. 133). This feeling persisted for a number of months and he was no more pleased with the subsequent reviews, which he thought "idiotic" or a " 'little flattering and uncommonly uncomprehending' " (Gay, p. 133). It should not be forgotten that after he had finished the dream book Freud pictured a plaque installed at 19 Berggasse (the address of his home and office) commemorating the site where he had discovered the secret of dreams. The dream book was perhaps his most cherished creation. To cite an example of his opinion of this work, he described it (1900) as containing "even according to my present-day judgement, the most valuable of all discoveries it has been my good fortune to make. Insight such as this falls to one's lot but once in a lifetime" (p. xxxiii). In writing the *New Introductory Lectures* (1933), he states,

> [I]t is right and fitting from more than one point of view that we should turn our attention first to the position of the theory of dreams. It occupies a special place in the history of psycho-analysis and marks a turning-point; it was with it that analysis took the step from being a psychotherapeutic procedure to being a depth-psychology. Since then, too, the theory of dreams has remained what is most characteristic and peculiar about the young science, something to which there is no counterpart in the rest of our knowledge, a stretch of new country. [p. 7]

9

This comment was made in 1933 when Freud was an international figure, widely recognized as the leader of a significant movement. It is striking that at this time, he still recognized the dream book as his most valuable contribution. Given his feeling about this work, it is no wonder that he was irritated with the reviewers of this revolutionary volume. One wonders how Freud would feel about a present-day psychoanalyst reviewing this publication. He might legitimately ask what criteria we can employ to review the creation he valued so highly.

On what basis should we, or can we even begin to review *The Interpretation of Dreams*? Since I am also a sleep researcher, I am aware that a number of authors from Dement to Hobson have maintained that they have disproven an aspect of what they believe to be Freud's theory of dream formation, or his views on an aspect of the function of sleep. Is this a place, then, to begin to look at the extent to which modern sleep research has confirmed or disconfirmed Freud's insights? Although I will briefly mention some of these issues, I believe the main import of the dream book is not based solely or even mainly on Freud's ideas of dream formation. Freud took this occasion to begin to develop his conceptualizations concerning what is often called his "Copernican Revolution." It is his ideas about the unconscious that capture our attention as we get to the penultimate and final chapters of *The Interpretation of Dreams*, but are dreams always formed by the instigation of an unconscious wish? In the way that Freud presented this formulation, it is an untestable hypothesis. Perhaps we might ask instead, are there frequently elements of a dream that we can theoretically most profitably explain in terms of unconscious processes? There are, of course, many related questions that could be asked: Does the concept of wish fulfillment enlighten our understanding of dream formation? It is possible for us to understand psychological functioning without utilizing the concept of compromise formation? Freud's conceptualization of the unconscious has changed our view of human existence, from slips of the tongue to symptom formation, to the content of at least many dreams. It is clear to me that both my research on sleep and dreams and the related ideas that I have written about would be greatly altered (indeed one might ask whether they would be present at all) if Freud's pioneering concepts had not been introduced through his psychoanalytic theory.

Freudian hypotheses have heightened our interest not only in the dream but in a host of psychological issues as well. His ideas about primary and secondary process (introduced in chapter 7, the final and most notable chapter in the dream book) have implications for many developmental concepts and theories concerning psychopathology. These ideas, along with his thoughts about transference and the workings of the unconscious, have shaped the whole way we look at the psychiatric world, as well as so much else in our cultural life. The impact of Freud's work should be indisputable: no one can reasonably doubt that he and psychoanalysis have made an indelible mark on the twentieth century. Similarly, no one can doubt that many of the central concepts of psychoanalysis are stated in *The Interpretation of Dreams*; it is in this work that Freud brings forth theoretical ideas about primary and secondary process, transference, the workings of the unconscious, and early ideas about repression or defense. Thus, in the same way that it is beyond argument that Freud is a central figure in the history of the twentieth century, there can be no debate about the fact that *The Interpretation of Dreams* is of central importance in psychoanalytic theory even today. We might ask, however, whether the book is in fact as central to psychoanalysis as Freud seemed to believe.

This is a complicated question that involves one's view of psychoanalysis. Most analysts today are moving away from large theoretical statements; indeed, many are attempting to find refuge in hermeneutic, narrative truth and action language positions. All of these views begin to consider analytic treatment in terms of literary texts and to a greater or lesser extent, divorce analytic treatment from general analytic theory. For those receptive to this trend, the dream book is probably little more than a historical curio piece, and thus probably a work that is rarely looked at or studied. However, for those who think that analytic treatment exists as an aspect of analytic theory, then some text like this is necessary for their very survival (Ellman 1991). My own personal predilection is toward the latter view, but I believe that Freud provided the theoretical scaffolding, and that is up to contemporary analysts to continue building the structure. The dream book is not a finished piece of theorizing, but rather a point at which to begin to consider the complicated issues that Freud attempted to answer. Nevertheless I find it difficult to believe that we would be considering the dream book if Freud's theorizing had not provided the beginnings of valuable explanations in a variety of areas.

There is, of course, considerably more controversy in relation to the present status of psychoanalytic theory in psychology and psychiatry. Most American psychologists would now accord little relevance to psychoanalytic concepts in their theoretical and experimental lives, though this may be a short-sighted theoretical stance. For example, I have fairly recently published an article (Ellman and Weinstein 1991) detailing the significant amount of experimental support that Freudian concepts receive from sleep and dream research. In the same vein, it seems to me that our views of childhood development are so influenced by Freudian concepts that it would take an extensive review to detail how much support his ideas have received from development research and childhood observational studies. His concepts are so imbedded in our theoretical views (whether we are psychoanalysts or not) that frequently, confirmatory observations of some of his ideas are not even noticed, but rather taken for granted. As a final point, though cognitive researchers frequently refer to the unconscious, their references are usually based on studies that in the past would have been called subliminal experiments. They are quick to state that their concept of the unconscious is different from the Freudian view, but one suspects that they make these statements without having studied Freudian theory. If they had, they might notice how at least some of them are following a similar theoretical path to the one that Freud began more than 95 years ago. My hypothesis is that few of them have read *The Interpretation of Dreams*. I hope in the future that this hypothesis is proved to be incorrect.

REFERENCES

Ellman, S. J. (1991). *Freud's Technique Papers: A Contemporary Perspective*. Northvale, NJ: Jason Aronson.

Ellman, S. J., and Weinstein, L. N. (1991). REM sleep and dream formation: a theoretical integration. In *The Mind in Sleep*, ed. S. J. Ellman and J. S. Antrobus. New York: John Wiley and Sons.

Freud, S. (1900). The interpretation of dreams. *Standard Edition* 4 and 5. London: Hogarth.

Freud, S. (1933). New introductory lectures on psychoanalysis. *Standard Edition* 22. London: Hogarth.

Gay, P. (1988). *Freud—A Life for Our Times*. New York: W. W. Norton.

Selections from
The Interpretation of Dreams
by Sigmund Freud

It may perhaps be useful[1] to continue our examination of the same question by considering how a dream behaves when the dream-thoughts present it with material which is the complete reverse of a wish-fulfilment—well-justified worries, painful reflections, distressing realizations. The many possible outcomes can be classed under the two following groups. (A) The dream-work may succeed in replacing all the distressing ideas by contrary ones and in suppressing the unpleasurable affects attaching to them. The result will be a straightforward dream of satisfaction, a palpable 'wish-fulfilment', about which there seems no more to be said. (B) The distressing ideas may make their way, more or less modified but none the less quite recognizable, into the manifest content of the dream. This is the case which raises doubts as to the validity of the wish theory of dreams and needs further investigation. Dreams of this sort with a distressing content may either be experienced with indifference, or they may be accompanied by the whole of the distressing affect which their ideational content seems to justify, or they may even lead to the development of anxiety and to awakening.

Analysis is able to demonstrate that these unpleasurable dreams are wish-fulfilments no less than the rest. An unconscious and repressed wish, whose fulfilment the dreamer's ego could not fail to experience as something distressing, has seized the opportunity offered to it by the persisting cathexis of the distressing residues of the previous day; it has lent them its support and by that means rendered them capable of entering a dream. But whereas in Group A the unconscious wish coincided with the conscious one, in Group B the gulf between the unconscious and the conscious (between the repressed and the ego) is revealed and the situation in the fairy tale of the three wishes which were granted by the fairy to the husband and wife is realized. The satisfaction at the fulfilment of the repressed wish may turn out to be so great that it counterbalances the distressing feelings attaching to the day's residues; in that case the

---

[1]This paragraph and the two following ones were added in 1919.

feeling-tone of the dream is indifferent, in spite of its being on the one hand the fulfilment of a wish and on the other the fulfilment of a fear. Or it may happen that the sleeping ego takes a still larger share in the constructing of the dream, that it reacts to the satisfying of the repressed wish with violent indignation and itself puts an end to the dream with an outburst of anxiety. Thus there is no difficulty in seeing that unpleasurable dreams and anxiety-dreams are just as much wish-fulfilments in the sense of our theory as are straightforward dreams of satisfaction.

Unpleasurable dreams may also be 'punishment-dreams'. It must be admitted that their recognition means in a certain sense a new addition to the theory of dreams. What is fulfilled in them is equally an unconscious wish, namely a wish that the dreamer may be punished for a repressed and forbidden wishful impulse. To that extent dreams of this kind fall in with the condition that has been laid down here that the motive force for constructing a dream must be provided by a wish belonging to the unconscious. A closer psychological analysis, however, shows how they differ from other wishful dreams. In the cases forming Group B the dream-constructing wish is an unconscious one and belongs to the repressed, while in punishment-dreams, though it is equally an unconscious one, it must be reckoned as belonging not to the repressed but to the 'ego'. Thus punishment-dreams indicate the possibility that the ego may have a greater share than was supposed in the construction of dreams. The mechanism of dream-formation would in general be greatly clarified if instead of the opposition between 'conscious' and 'unconscious' we were to speak of that between the 'ego' and the 'repressed'. This cannot be done, however, without taking account of the processes underlying the psychoneuroses, and for that reason it has not been carried out in the present work. I will only add that punishment-dreams are not in general subject to the condition that the day's residues shall be of a distressing kind. On the contrary, they occur most easily where the opposite is the case — where the day's residues are thoughts of a satisfying nature but the satisfaction which they express is a forbidden one. The only trace of these thoughts that appears in the manifest dream is their diametric opposite, just as in the case of dreams belonging to Group A. The essential characteristic of punishment-dreams would thus be that in their case the dream-constructing wish is not an unconscious wish derived from the repressed (from the system *Ucs.*), but a punitive one reacting against it and belonging to the ego, though at the same time an unconscious (that is to say, preconscious) one.[2]

---

[2][*Footnote added* 1930:] This would be the appropriate point for a reference to the 'super-ego', one of the later findings of psycho-analysis. A class of dreams which are an exception to the 'wish-theory' (those which occur in traumatic neuroses) is discussed in Chapter II of *Beyond the Pleasure Principle* and in the last pages of Lecture XXIX in the *New Introductory Lectures*.

I will report a dream of my own[3] in order to illustrate what I have just said, and in particular the way in which the dream-work deals with a residue of distressing anticipations from the previous day.

'Indistinct beginning. *I said to my wife that I had a piece of news for her, something quite special. She was alarmed and refused to listen. I assured her that on the contrary it was something that she would be very glad to hear, and began to tell her that our son's officers' mess had sent a sum of money (5000 Kronen?) . . . something about distinction . . . distribution. . . . Meanwhile I had gone with her into a small room, like a store-room, to look for something. Suddenly I saw my son appear. He was not in uniform but in tight-fitting sports clothes (like a seal?), with a little cap. He climbed up on to a basket that was standing beside a cupboard, as though he wanted to put something on the cupboard. I called out to him: no reply. It seemed to me that his face or forehead was bandaged. He was adjusting something in his mouth, pushing something into it. And his hair was flecked with grey. I thought: "Could he be as exhausted as all that? And has he got false teeth?"* Before I could call out again I woke up, feeling no anxiety but with my heart beating rapidly. My bedside clock showed that it was two thirty.'

Once again it is impossible for me to present a complete analysis. I must restrict myself to bringing out a few salient points. Distressing anticipations from the previous day were what gave rise to the dream: we had once more been without news of our son at the front for over a week. It is easy to see that the content of the dream expressed a conviction that he had been wounded or killed. Energetic efforts were clearly being made at the beginning of the dream to replace the distressing thoughts by their contrary. I had some highly agreeable news to communicate – something about money being sent . . . distinction . . . distribution. (The sum of money was derived from an agreeable occurrence in my medical practice; it was an attempt at a complete diversion from the topic.) But these efforts failed. My wife suspected something dreadful and refused to listen to me. The disguises were too thin and references to what it was sought to repress pierced through them everywhere. If my son had been killed, his fellow-officers would send back his belongings and I should have to distribute what he left among his brothers and sisters and other people. A 'distinction' is often awarded to an officer who has fallen in battle. Thus the dream set about giving direct expression to what it had first sought to deny, though the inclination towards wish-fulfilment was still shown at work in the distortions. (The change of locality during the dream is no doubt to be understood as what Silberer has described as 'threshold symbolism'. We cannot tell, it is true, what it was that provided the dream with the motive force for thus giving expression to my distressing thoughts. My son did not

---

[3]This paragraph and the two following ones were added as a footnote in 1919, and incorporated in the text in 1930.

appear as someone 'falling' but as someone 'climbing'. He had in fact been
a keen mountaineer. He was not in uniform but in sports clothes; this
meant that the place of the accident that I *now* feared had been taken by an
earlier, sporting one; for he had had a fall during a ski-ing expedition and
broken his thigh. The way in which he was dressed, on the other hand,
which made him look like a seal, at once recalled someone younger—our
funny little grandson; while the grey hair reminded me of the latter's
father, our son-in-law, who had been hard hit by the war. What could this
mean? . . . but I have said enough of it. The locality in a store-closet and
the cupboard from which he wanted to take something ('on which he
wanted to put something' in the dream)—these allusions reminded me
unmistakably of an accident of my own which I had brought on myself
when I was between two and three years old. I had climbed up on to a stool
in the store-closet to get something nice that was lying on a cupboard or
table. The stool had tipped over and its corner had struck me behind my
lower jaw; I might easily, I reflected, have knocked out all my teeth. The
recollection was accompanied by an admonitory thought: 'that serves you
right'; and this seemed as though it was a hostile impulse aimed at the
gallant soldier. Deeper analysis at last enabled me to discover what the
concealed impulse was which might have found satisfaction in the dreaded
accident to my son: it was the envy which is felt for the young by those
who have grown old, but which they believe they have completely stifled.
And there can be no question that it was precisely the *strength* of the
painful emotion which would have arisen if such a misfortune had really
happened that caused that emotion to seek out a repressed wish-fulfilment
of this kind in order to find some consolation.[4]

I am now in a position to give a precise account of the part played in
dreams by the unconscious wish. I am ready to admit that there is a whole
class of dreams the *instigation* to which arises principally or even exclusively from the residues of daytime life; and I think that even my wish that
I might at long last become a Professor Extraordinarius might have allowed
me to sleep through the night in peace if my worry over my friend's health
had not still persisted from the previous day. But the worry alone could not
have made a dream. The *motive force* which the dream required had to be
provided by a wish; it was the business of the worry to get hold of a wish
to act as the motive force of the dream.

The position may be explained by an analogy. A daytime thought may
very well play the part of *entrepreneur* for a dream; but the *entrepreneur*,
who, as people say, has the idea and the initiative to carry it out, can do

---

[4]This dream is discussed briefly in its possible telepathic aspect at the beginning of Freud's
paper on 'Dreams and Telepathy'.

nothing without capital; he needs a *capitalist* who can afford the outlay, and the capitalist who provides the psychical outlay for the dream is invariably and indisputably, whatever may be the thoughts of the previous day, *a wish from the unconscious.*[5]

Sometimes the capitalist is himself the *entrepreneur,* and indeed in the case of dreams this is the commoner event: an unconscious wish is stirred up by daytime activity and proceeds to construct a dream. So, too, the other possible variations in the economic situation that I have taken as an analogy have their parallel in dream-processes. The *entrepreneur* may himself make a small contribution to the capital; several *entrepreneurs* may apply to the same capitalist; several capitalists may combine to put up what is necessary for the *entrepreneur.* In the same way, we come across dreams that are supported by more than one dream-wish; and so too with other similar variations, which could easily be run through, but which would be of no further interest to us. We must reserve until later what remains to be said of the dream-wish.

The *tertium comparationis* [third element of comparison] in the analogy that I have just used – the quantity[6] put at the disposal of the *entrepreneur* in an appropriate amount – is capable of being applied in still greater detail to the purpose of elucidating the structure of dreams. In most dreams it is possible to detect a central point which is marked by peculiar sensory intensity, as I have shown. This central point is as a rule the direct representation of the wish-fulfilment, for, if we undo the displacements brought about by the dream-work, we find that the *psychical* intensity of the elements in the dream-thoughts has been replaced by the *sensory* intensity of the elements in the content of the actual dream. The elements in the *neigbourhood* of the wish-fulfilment often have nothing to do with its meaning, but turn out to be derivatives of distressing thoughts that run contrary to the wish. But owing to their being in what is often an artificially established connection with the central element, they have acquired enough intensity to become capable of being represented in the dream. Thus the wish-fulfilment's power of bringing about representation is diffused over a certain sphere surrounding it, within which all the elements – including even those possessing no means of their own – become empowered to obtain representation. In the case of dreams that are actuated by *several* wishes, it is easy to delimit the spheres of the different wish-fulfilments, and gaps in the dream may often be understood as frontier zones between those spheres.

---

[5]These last two paragraphs are quoted in full by Freud at the end of his analysis of Dora's first dream, which, he comments, is a complete confirmation of their correctness.

[6]Of capital in the case of the analogy, and of psychical energy in the case of a dream.

3

Karl Jaspers:
General Psychopathology

Reviewed by Michael Shepherd

To begin with, a few facts. Karl Jaspers's *Allgemeine Psychopathologie (General Psychopathology)* was first published in 1913. The author was then barely 30 years of age, working as a physician in the psychiatric hospital at Heidelberg. Two years later he moved away from medicine towards first psychology and then philosophy, the field in which he was to emerge as one of the outstanding figures of the twentieth century. He continued, however, to retain an interest in psychopathology, revising and expanding his book in several later editions. Within the German-speaking world it was at once recognized by leading psychiatrists as a unique achievement, a mountainous landmark in the history of the subject. If Jaspers's reputation was to decline in Germany between the two world wars, this is attributable chiefly to his outspoken, uncompromising resistance to national socialism. Philosophy for him was a public as well as a private concern, and it was his courageous political stand which led Hannah Arendt to describe him as a contemporary successor of Immanuel Kant.

Here, then, was a rare bonus for psychiatry. One of the foremost thinkers of the day, a trained physician, had spent a long enough period in the practice of the subject to write a major volume on its foundations. Nonetheless, half a century was to elapse before an English version appeared (Jaspers 1963), during which time countless inferior books had been translated from the same language. With some exceptions, furthermore, its reception in the anglophonic countries has been respectful rather than enthusiastic, and in some quarters downright hostile. Here, for example, is the verdict of one influential British textbook:

19

It is all over-simplified and though the phenomenology of psychiatric illness is described with great accuracy and detail, Jaspers fails to see that much of it is dependent on the institutional milieu in which the patients then lived. He therefore is unaware of some of the meaningful links, and "real causes" like genetics which were considered proven at the time the first edition appeared are no longer tenable. This work has however greatly influenced German psychiatric thinking and some who are unhappy over the logical inconsistencies of Freudian psychopathology or who would wish to subscribe to anything but Freud will find in Jaspers an adequate intellectual exercise. It will not help towards an apparent understanding of the apparent illogicalities and contradictions of emotionally toned behaviour and is therefore very dated and out of touch with modern advances in psychiatry.

As a former coexaminer of the author of this egregious assessment, I can testify to its impact on would-be members of the Royal College of Psychiatrists.

There would seem to be three principal reasons for the lukewarm response to the anglicization of *General Psychopathology*. In the first place, it is not an easy work to read, concentrated in argument and diffuse in form, difficult enough in the original German and often understandably opaque in another language despite the heroic efforts of the translators who were faced with what the late Professor E. W. Anderson acknowledged as "the difficulty and at times impossibility of rendering the author's subtle thought into concise and comprehensible English." Without persuasive advocates it was never likely to appeal to a wide readership.

A second obstacle to the ready acceptance of the text is embedded in the passage cited above. By 1963, when the English translation was published, the word *psychopathology* had become heavily coated with psychoanalytical encrustations. In contrast, the term is employed by Jaspers in a much wider sense. Its essence, he maintains, can emerge only from a composite framework constructed with "the viewpoints and methods that belong to the world of the Humanities and Social Studies . . . since the methods of almost all the Arts and Sciences converge on psychopathology." Further, in the later editions of his book Jaspers became increasingly critical of psychoanalysis which, he concluded, is a pseudo-faith, "an enormous process of self-deception conditioned by the age we live in, which bewitches its victims, who find in it the satisfaction of their lives." Not surprisingly, so negative a verdict has not endeared his views to the majority of psychoanalysts, whose powerful influence on psychiatric theory has rarely been challenged directly by so informed and penetrating a critic.

But perhaps the principal difficulty posed by the book for the reader is that of fitting it into a recognizable and familiar mould. *General Psychopa-*

thology cannot be classified as a textbook. Rather, it should be regarded as an intellectual map, a guide to a series of separate but related areas of knowledge identified in the list of contents as Individual Psychic Phenomena, Meaningful Psychic Connections, Causal Connections of Psychic Life, the Conception of the Psychic Life as a Whole, the Abnormal Psyche in Society and History, and the Human Being as a Whole. Within this broad topography there are large uncharted territories, and the contours of the map are undergoing constant revision. The primary purpose of the work, however, is to furnish not an ordnance survey but a general overview designed, in Jaspers' words, "to develop and order knowledge guided by the methods through which it is gained—to learn to know the process of knowing and thereby to clarify the material." The attainment of this objective depends primarily on the clarification of a host of concepts which are traditionally either ignored or oversimplified in the psychiatric literature. To do justice to such themes as the mind–body relationship, the role of scientific inquiry, the principles of classification, personality, the subjective-objective dichotomy, or the notions of health and disease calls for a familiarity with the history of ideas in other disciplines. It is here that Jaspers comes into his own, bringing a massive tradition of philosophy and social theory to bear on these perennial problems in relation to psychopathology.

To grasp the full significance of the achievement, however, the reader must be aware of the sources and the ways in which they have been adapted. The views of Kant, Kierkegaard, Nietzsche, Max Weber, and Jaspers' own later theorizing are as central to the construction of *General Psychopathology* as the work of Griesinger, Wernicke, Kraepelin or Kurt Schneider; and some of the better-known specific concepts are openly borrowed from German thinkers (e.g., the emphasis on phenomenology derives from Husserl and the distinction between understanding and explanation from Dilthey). For this reason, I always found extensive background reading essential when conducting seminars on the book.

General Psychopathology contains a complex admixture of exposition, psychological description, critique and, especially in the later editions, philosophical speculation. While the whole text is impregnated with Jaspers's holistic approach to his subject-matter, the neophyte is probably best advised to sample the text in fragments. He could, for example, profitably begin with the subsection on "Delusion and Awareness of Reality" (pp. 93–102); move on to "Pathological Psychogenic Reactions" (pp. 383–393); and, after contrasting the chapter on the "Psychology of Meaning" (pp. 301–313) with the "Characteristics of Explanatory Theories" (pp. 530–534), examine the use made of this distinction in the assessments of Kretschmer (pp. 40–41), Wernicke (pp. 534–537), von Gebsattel (pp.

540–546), and Freud (pp. 537–540). Then, lest he should regard Jaspers as a distant, impersonal figure, he should turn to the important sections on psychotherapy, which have been published separately in book form (Jaspers 1964), in order to appreciate Jaspers's clear-headed humanism and his concern for the doctor–patient relationship, well illustrated in the following paragraph:

> There are no scientific grounds for determining what kind of psychotherapist one will become nor the type which will be considered ideal. Certainly a psychotherapist should have a training in somatic medicine and in psycho-pathology, both of which have to be scientifically based. If he has no such training, he would only be a charlatan, yet with this training alone he is still not a psychotherapist. Science is only a part of his necessary equipment. Much more has to be added. Among the *personal prerequisites* the width of his own horizon plays a part, so does the ability to be detached at times from any value-judgement, to be accepting and totally free of prejudice (an ability only found in those who generally possess very well-defined values and have a personality that is mature). Finally, there is the necessity for fundamental warmth and a natural kindness. It is therefore clear that a good psychother-apist can only be a rare phenomenon and even then he is usually only good *for a certain circle of people* for whom he is well suited. A psychotherapist for everyone is an impossibility. However, force of circumstance makes it the psychotherapist's usual duty to treat everyone who may ask his help. That fact should help him to keep his claims to modest proportions.

To grasp fully the development of Jaspers's leitmotivs, however, it is necessary to become familiar with the structure of the whole text. One key example, which I have attempted to examine in detail elsewhere (Shepherd 1983), is the complex relationship between general psychopathology and the sciences. For Jaspers, "natural science is indeed the groundwork of psychopathology and an essential element in it but the humanities are equally so and, with this, psychopathology does not become in any way less scientific but scientific in another way." The psychopathologist must, he claims, employ the scientific method and the scientific attitude, even when dealing with subjective experience or meaningful connection, but then he goes on: "Only when the biological aspects have been clearly distinguished can we proceed to discuss what essentially belongs to man. Whenever the subject studied is Man and not man as a species of animal, we find that psychopathology comes to be not only a kind of biology but also one of the Humanities." From this springboard he elaborates the need for "metaphysical understanding" as a philosophical position.

To conclude, *General Psychopathology* remains the most important single book to have been published on the aims and logic of psychological medicine. Its scope and clarity, as Kurt Kolle has observed, provide nothing less than "the criterion by which the qualification for psychiatry is tested." For this reason alone it should be studied and assimilated by all psychiatrists in training. And by their teachers.

REFERENCES

Jaspers, K. (1913). *Allgemeine Psychopathologie. Ein Leitfaden für Studierende, Arzte und Psychologen*. 1st ed. Berlin: Springer.

_____ (1963). *General Psychopathology*. Trans. J. Hoenig and M. W. Hamilton. Manchester, England: Manchester University Press.

_____ (1964). *The Nature of Psychotherapy. A Critical Appraisal*. Trans. J. Hoenig and M. W. Hamilton. Manchester, England: Manchester University Press.

Shepherd, M. (1983). The sciences and general psychopathology. In *Handbook of Psychiatry*, vol. I, (ed. M. Shepherd and O. L. Zangwill, pp. 1–8. Cambridge, England: Cambridge University Press.

Karl Jaspers:
General Psychopathology

Reviewed by Paul J. Harrison

There is an apocryphal saying that in order to pass the Membership examination, Jaspers's name should be invoked at some stage, preferably being followed by a comment as to the great significance of his *General Psychopathology* (Jaspers 1963) and of how much is lost in translation. Underlying these sentiments is the suggestion that Jaspers is held by trainees in a mixture of esteem and uncertainty. Undoubtedly, although its importance is often stressed, the content of *General Psychopathology* is less widely known, with the length, complexity, and discursiveness of the book making it an intimidating work to read and to understand. However, its position as the undisputed bible of phenomenology and psychopathology means it cannot be ignored. Shepherd (1982) reconsidered *General Psychopathology* in the *Journal*, and other articles testify to the continuing interest which the book arouses among eminent philosopher-psychiatrists (e.g., Spitzer 1988, Walker 1988). In contrast, this article gives a trainee's perspective on Jaspers's work, and is intended to be of interest to others who may be reluctant to approach it.

Apart from the literary style used by Jaspers, which is complicated even allowing for the complexity of the subject matter, the other initial obstacle that confronts a reader is one of terminology. This arises partly as a result of the diverse components that make up *General Psychopathology*, and partly because of varying meanings attributed to key terms and concepts used in discussions of Jaspers's work. It is possible to make certain clarifications in this regard that may aid understanding of the text.

First, it is important to distinguish phenomenology from psychopathology. Phenomenology, the "study of lived experience," is a philosophical school that investigates and gives primacy to "things-in-themselves," in a way that avoids any preconceptions as to their nature or causation, and that undercuts the dichotomy between subjectivity and objectivity (Thines 1987). When applied to psychopathology, it entails the unprejudiced description of abnormal mental states, excluding all etiological and pathogenic considerations; thus, phenomenology is not only a *type* of philosophy, but a *method* by which mental life is to be approached. Moreover, phenomenologists believe that true understanding arises from such an analysis, provided a sufficiently detailed and "pure" theory-free study of this kind is carried out; it therefore requires an extensive inquiry into a patient's mental experiences independent of other aspects of the investigation. It is this phenomenological element that underlies the emphasis that Jaspers, and subsequently psychiatry as a whole, has placed on psychopathology as a largely circumscribed and autonomous field. A second distinction arises between phenomenology in its original philosophical meaning and that in which it is used in a Jasperian sense (Berrios 1989). This difference occurs because Jaspers drew upon a variety of philosophical and other sources and combined these with his psychiatric considerations to produce a hybrid brand of applied phenomenology (Kraupl Taylor 1967).

In contrast to phenomenology, psychopathology has no philosophical pretensions, but is simply the description and clarification of abnormal mental states, which may or may not be carried out in a phenomenological manner. Jaspers, being both a philosopher and a psychiatrist, utilizes elements of both, so that not only is *General Psychopathology* a detailed sourcebook of psychopathology, but is also a philosophical treatise in which he colors these descriptions in a phenomenological way; hence the combined term of "phenomenological psychopathology." Finally, the meaning of psychopathology must also be qualified. In a Jasperian sense, it is equivalent to *descriptive* psychopathology, and has no connection with *dynamic* psychopathology (Kraüpl Taylor 1967). The latter focuses on unconscious processes and their role in explaining conscious mental events, whereas Jasperian phenomenology and psychopathology are restricted to *conscious* experiences and exclude explanatory hypotheses.

Put together, these elements produce a philosophical rationale and method that form the core of Jasperian thought. However, the book does not proceed in any clear sequence of this kind, but consists of parts devoted to mainly philosophical matters, interspersed with descriptive passages defining and detailing psychopathological states. As a result, the best starting point from which to obtain an overview of Jaspers's work and goals is the introduction to *General Psychopathology* (pp. 1–50) and its appendix (pp. 825–859), together with the article reprinted in the *Journal* (Jaspers 1968). It is also helpful to be aware of the historical origins of phenomenology and other influences on Jaspers since they explain how he arrived at his particular stance (Berrios 1984, Hundert 1989).

Having highlighted some potential points of terminological confusion within *General Psychopathology*, we turn to an outline of its contents. One of the most important divisions made by Jaspers (both conceptually and in terms of the organisation of the book) is between explanation *(Erklären)* and understanding *(Verstehen)*. The former refers to the logical, causally directed knowledge that arises from scientific study; the latter is the empathic, subjective "understanding" of a patient's experiences that results from the detailed phenomenological analysis prescribed by Jaspers. These two approaches are considered to be fundamentally different in their justification, methodology, and end result (pp. 27-28, 301-313, 451-462), and an overall comprehension of a person's mental state requires both of these elements. Therefore, having outlined his philosophical and psychiatric position and given most of his classic descriptions of psychopathological symptoms in Part 1, *General Psychopathology* details both the *verstehende* psychology of meaningful connections (Part 2) and the *erklärende* psychology of causal connections (Part 3), before putting these together to give a "conception of psychic life as a whole" (Part 4). The book later moves on to consider historical and social factors affecting the psyche (Part 5). Only when all this has been accomplished can we tackle the "human being as a whole" (Part 6), at which point Jaspers becomes primarily philosophical — and particularly elaborate at times — as he discusses existential as well as phenomenological matters that are only of indirect relevance to modern psychiatric practice. Because of its arrangement, much of the essential text is concentrated in the early chapters, although the latter stages still contain important passages, such as Jaspers's critiques of Freud (pp. 359-363, 537-540), Kretschmer (pp. 40-41 et seq.), and Wernicke (pp. 534-537), and his contribution to classificatory schemata (pp. 604-616).

In what light should *General Psychopathology* be read by psychiatrists today? The distinctions drawn above are paralleled by a number of ways in which the text is, and is not, still valuable. First and foremost, it has never been equaled in psychiatry in terms of its breadth, depth, or philosophical sophistication. Even if its philosophical position can, with the benefit of hindsight, be criticized, the very attempt to synthesize psychiatry with philosophy has proved to be an enduring and as yet unsurpassed one. Second, Jaspers's definitions of features such as delusions (pp. 93-108), pseudohallucinations (pp. 68-75), self-awareness (pp. 121-128), and insight (pp. 419-427) remain seminal, and he takes psychopathology to its limit in terms of descriptive detail and clarity of thought. Third, his emphasis on accurate empathy and recording of mental state as a foundation of psychiatry continues to be universally accepted, as does the importance of a detailed and "meaningful" attempt at understanding a patient's subjective experience; indeed, it is hard to conceive of clinical practice without this central feature. Additionally, the Jasperian focus on the "un-understandable" nature of schizophrenics (p. 581) has been reflected in the question of the praecox feeling and the role that subjective impressions play in diagnosis and classification (Schwartz and Wiggins 1987). Other important insights and clarifications made by Jaspers concern the distinctions between primary and secondary (pp. 584–585), organic and functional (p. 460), and personality versus disease process (pp. 702–706), as well as the understanding/explanation dichotomy, which, in various guises, continues to be of interest (McHugh and Slavney 1983, Schwartz and Wiggins 1988).

Beyond these main areas, however, details of Jaspers's work may be of less relevance and permanence. From a philosophical perspective, phenomenology has always been controversial, and since Jaspers's time has diminished in acceptance; this has been due largely to the realization that theory-free observation is in practice unattainable. In addition, the validity of Jaspers's adaptation of it to psychiatry has been criticized; moreover, the extent to which everyday psychopathological descriptions are really phenomenological or Jasperian has been doubted (Berrios 1984). Recently, the whole question of the nature of mental states and their position in contemporary neuroscience has been raised by the neurophilosophers (P. M. Churchland 1984, P. S. Churchland 1986), a debate that may have profound consequences for all aspects of phenomenology and psychopathology, including the Jasperian form (Harrison 1991).

If we set aside the philosophical component of Jaspers's work, the question of its value becomes primarily a practical one: Are there other descriptions and categorizations of psychopathological phenomena that are of greater utility or validity? Several other texts of psychopathology exist (e.g., Fish 1967, Kraupl Taylor 1979, Scharfetter 1980, Sims 1987), of which Sims's is the most readable and philosophically neutral. Certainly, for an introduction to "symptoms in the mind," these later books are more accessible starting points than Jaspers's. However, the latter repays the reader's efforts and remains a reference book of unique significance, even if in the future some of its stature is lost as its component subjects—psychiatry, philosophy, and science—progress.

REFERENCES

Berrios, G. E. (1984). Descriptive psychopathology: conceptual and historical aspects. *Psychological Medicine* 14: 303–313.

―――― (1989). What is phenomenology? A review. *Journal of the Royal Society of Medicine* 82: 425–428.

Churchland, P. M. (1984). *Matter and Consciousness*. Cambridge, MA: Bradford.

Churchland, P. S. (1986). *Neurophilosophy*. Cambridge, MA: Bradford.

Fish, F. (1967). *Clinical Psychopathology*. Bristol, England: John Wright.

Harrison, P. J. (1991). Are mental states a useful concept? Neurophilosophical influences on phenomenology and psychopathology. *Journal of Nervous and Mental Disease* 179: 309–316.

Hundert, E. (1989). *Philosophy, Psychiatry and Neuroscience: Three Approaches to the Mind.* Oxford: University Press.

Jaspers, K. (1963). *General Psychopathology.* Trans. J. Hoenig and M. W. Hamilton. Manchester, England: University Press.

_____ (1968). The phenomenological approach in psychopathology. *British Journal of Psychiatry* 114: 1313–1323.

Kraupl Taylor, F. (1967). The role of phenomenology in psychiatry. *British Journal of Psychiatry* 113: 765–770.

_____ (1979). *Psychopathology,* 2nd ed. Sunbury-on-Thames, England: Quartermain House.

McHugh, P. R., and Slavney, P. R. (1983) *The Perspectives of Psychiatry.* Baltimore, MD: Johns Hopkins University Press.

Scharfetter, C. (1980). *General Psychopathology.* Cambridge, England: University Press.

Schwartz, M. A., and Wiggins, O. P. (1987). Typifications: the first step for clinical diagnosis in psychiatry. *Journal of Nervous and Mental Disease* 175: 65–77.

_____ (1988). Perspectivism and the methods of psychiatry. *Comprehensive Psychiatry* 29: 237–251.

Shepherd, M. (1982). Karl Jaspers: *General Psychopathology. British Journal of Psychiatry* 141: 310–312.

Sims, A. C. P. (1987). *Symptoms in the Mind,* London: Baillere Tindall.

Spitzer, M. (1988). Psychiatry, philosophy and the problem of description, In *Psychopathology and philosophy,* ed. M. Spitzer, F. A. Uehlein, and G. Oepen, pp. 3–18. Berlin: Springer Verlag.

Thines, G. (1987). Phenomenology. In *Oxford Companion to the Mind,* ed. R. L. Gregory, pp. 614–616. Oxford: Oxford University Press.

Walker, C. (1988). Philosophical concepts and practice: the legacy of Karl Jaspers' psychopathology. *Current Opinion in Psychiatry* 1: 624–629.

Selections from
General Psychopathology
by Karl Jaspers

The following excerpts are chosen to illustrate Jaspers's views on several areas, each of which is covered in considerable detail in the book. The topics are: a definition of phenomenology, the relationship of brain and psyche, the distinction of explanation from understanding, and Jaspers's basic definition of delusions. The first three excerpts demonstrate some of the philosophical and conceptual elements that characterize the book, while the fourth exemplifies the detailed descriptions of psychopathological phenomena for which it is also noted.

Phenomenology sets out on a number of tasks: it *gives a concrete description* of the psychic states which patients actually experience and *presents* them *for observation*. It reviews the inter-relations of these, *delineates* them as sharply as possible, differentiates them and creates a suitable terminology. Since we never can perceive the psychic experiences of others in any direct fashion, as with physical phenomena, we can only make some kind of representation of them. There has to be an act of empathy, of understanding, to which may be added as the case demands an enumeration of the external characteristics of the psychic state or of the conditions under which the phenomena occur, or we may make sharp comparisons or resort to the use of symbols or fall back on a kind of suggestive handling of the data. Our chief help in all this comes from the patients' *own descriptions*, which can be evoked and tested out in the course of personal conversation. From this we get our best-defined and clearest data. Written descriptions by the patients may have a richer content but in this form we can do nothing else but accept them. An experience is best described by the person who has undergone it. Detailed psychiatric observation with its own formulation of what the patient is suffering is not any substitute for this. . . .

The first step, then, is to make some representation of what is really happening in our patients, what they are actually going through, how it strikes them, how they feel. We are not concerned at this stage with connections, nor with the patients' experience as a whole and certainly not with any subsidiary speculations, fundamental theory or basic postulates. We confine descriptions solely to the things that are present to the patients' consciousness. Anything which is not a conscious datum is for the present non-existent. Conventional theories, psychological constructions, interpretations and evaluations must be left aside. We simply attend to what exists before us, in so far as we can apprehend, discriminate and describe it.

We are guided . . . by *the basic conception* that all causal connections and the entire extra-conscious substructure of psychic life have their foundations in somatic events. The extra-conscious element can only be found in the world as something somatic. We suspect that these somatic events take place in the brain, particularly in the cerebral cortex and in the brain stem, and we conceive them as highly complicated biological processes. We are very far removed from their discovery. We do not know a single somatic event which we could consider to be the specific basis for specific psychic events. . . .

These views . . . could be formulated as *"mental illness is cerebral illness"* (Griesinger, Meynert, Wernicke). This declaration is as dogmatic as its negation would be. Let us clarify the situation once more. In some cases we find connections between physical and psychic changes taking place in such a way that the psychic events can be regarded with certainty as consequences. Further, we know that in general no psychic event exists without the precondition of some physical basis. There are no "ghosts." But we do not know a single physical event in the brain which could be considered the identical counterpart of any morbid psychic event. We only know conditioning factors for the psychic life; we never know *the* cause of the psychic event, only a cause. So this famous statement, if measured against the actual possibilities of research and the actual findings, may perhaps be a possible, though infinitely remote, goal for research, but it can never provide a real object for investigation. To discuss statements of this sort and try to solve this problem in principle indicates a lack of critical methodology. Such statements will vanish from psychiatry all the more quickly in proportion as philosophic speculations vanish from psychopathology and give place to a philosophical maturity in the psychopathologist.

. . . we shall keep the expression *"understanding"* (Verstehen) solely for the understanding of psychic events from within. The expression will never be used for the appreciation of objective causal connections, which as we have said can only be seen "from without". For these we shall reserve the expression *"explanation"* (Erklären). These two different expressions denote something very specific which will grow clearer as the reader proceeds and the number of examples increases. In questionable cases where one or the other expression could be used interchangeably we shall use the term "*comprehend*" (Begreifen). The very possibility of any systematic study or clear-sighted research in psychopathology depends upon grasping the fact that we are dealing here with polar opposites, static understanding as opposed to external sense-perception and genetic understanding as opposed to causal explanation of objective connections. These represent totally different, ultimate sources of knowledge.

Some scientists tend to deny the validity of any psychological source of scientific knowledge. They only accept what can be perceived objectively by the senses, not what can be meaningfully understood through the senses. Their viewpoint cannot be refuted since there is no proof of the validity of any ultimate source of knowledge. But at least we might look for consistency. Such scientists should refrain from talking of the psyche or even thinking in terms of psychic events. They should give up psychopathology and confine themselves to the study of cerebral processes and general physiology. They should not appear as expert witnesses in Court, since on their own showing they know nothing about the subject-matter; they can give no expert opinion on the psyche, only on the brain. They can only help expertly with reference to physical phenomena and they should give up any pretence to history taking. Such consistency would gain one's respect and we might think it worthy of the name of science. More commonly we find, however, denials and doubts expressed in interjections such as "this is only subjective," etc. This seems a sterile nihilism shown by people who would not persuade themselves that their incompetence is due to their subject-matter, not to themselves.

Delusion manifests itself in *judgments*; delusion can only arise in the process of thinking and judging. To this extent pathologically falsified judgments are termed delusions. The content of such judgments may be rudimentary but takes no less effective form as mere awareness. This is usually spoken of as a "feeling" that is also an obscure certainty.

The term delusion is *vaguely* applied to all false judgments that share the following external characteristics to a marked, though undefined, degree: (1) they are held with an *extraordinary conviction*, with an incomparable, *subjective certainty*; (2) there is an *imperviousness* to other experiences and to compelling counter-argument; (3) their content is *impossible*. If we want to go behind these mere external characteristics into the psychological nature of delusion, we must distinguish the original *experience* from the *judgment* based on it, i.e., the delusional contents as presented data from the fixed judgment which is then merely reproduced, disputed, dissimulated as occasion demands. We can then distinguish two large groups of delusions according to their *origin:* one group *emerges understandably* from preceding affects, from shattering, mortifying, guilt-provoking or other such experiences, from false-perception or from the experience of derealisation in states of altered consciousness, etc. The other group is for us *psychologically irreducible*; phenomenologically it is something final. We give the term *"delusion-like ideas"* to the first group; the latter we term *"delusions proper."* In their case we must now try and get closer to the facts of the delusional experience itself, even though a clear presentation is hardly possible with so alien a happening.

4

Anna Freud:
The Ego and the Mechanisms of Defence

Reviewed by Paul Kline

This book was first published in English in 1937. In science fifty years is a long time, longer even than in politics, yet I can recommend psychiatrists to read this traditional psychoanalytic text for many reasons.

In the first place, for sentimental reasons. Anna Freud, daughter of the Master, is no ordinary analyst. Furthermore, her real contribution to psychoanalysis lay in her elucidation of the defenses and in the very necessary extension of the work to children. Freudian developmental theory was largely retrospective and inferential, so that the work of Anna Freud was particularly valuable. This book is concerned with both these aspects of her work.

Another reason for reading this book is that the simplicity of the style and the immediacy of the clinical material give a powerful impression of the real nature of defense mechanisms. It is a pleasure to realize that subtle and rich descriptions of largely unconscious mental events can be described without jargon in clear, ordinary, yet striking language. Every psychologist or psychiatrist who has failed to resist the temptation to yield to jargon, however learned, in his reports or papers should read this book.

The content of the book, in my view, is still valuable. It sets out clearly the main defence mechanisms and is richly illustrated with clinical material. I know of no better guide to these unconscious processes. At this juncture, however, I can hear readers' objections that surely Freudian defenses are old hat, that psychoanalysis has moved on, that modern analysts and psychiatry in general have outgrown the model of the mind implicit in the notion of defences.

This view of defenses is, I think, mistaken. Thus, experimental psychology, which has always been so strongly opposed to psychoanalytic ideas, has recently become interested in unconscious processing (of information rather than affect), and concomitantly studies of subliminal perception are now more respectable in departments of psychology and there is a considerable body of experimental work relevant to defense mechanisms. I think this experimental evidence is important because it substantiates the psychoanalytic concept of defences.

Defenses, given that they can be substantiated, are important for a variety of reasons. First, for eclectic psychiatrists and psychologists they give valuable insights into behavior. Notions such as denial and reaction formation are useful in unraveling presenting symptoms. Repression, too, is widely used even by workers who would refuse validity to anything psychoanalytic.

Furthermore, they are powerful in understanding complex attitudes and viewpoints in society, ones that often desperately require change. Thus to conceive of racism as projection helps us understand its protagonists and suggests methods of alteration. The violence of antivivisectionists, for example, and of soccer crowds, when seen as displacement becomes less strange. The savagery of those in favor of fierce punishment for sexual offenders and murderers, and the reaction-formation of those troubled by such conflicts, again makes sense.

Defense mechanisms, even for those who are cautious in accepting the concepts of psychoanalysis, have powerful explanatory force; they may be among the most long-lasting and useful ideas in psychoanalysis. Their lucid and elegant explication by Anna Freud seems to me well worthy of reading; this is a classic text.

Selections from
The Ego and The Mechanisms of Defence
by Anna Freud

Psycho-analytical theory and the mechanisms of defence. The term "defence," which I have used so freely in the three last chapters, is the earliest representative of the dynamic standpoint in psychoanalytical theory. It occurs for the first time in 1894, in Freud's study "The Defence Neuro-Psychoses," and is employed in this and several of his subsequent works ("The Aetiology of Hysteria," "Further Remarks on the Defence Neuro-Psychoses") to describe the ego's struggle against painful or unendurable ideas or affects. Later, this term was abandoned and, as time went on, was replaced by that of "repression." The relation between the two notions, however, remained undetermined. In an appendix to *Inhibitions, Symptoms and Anxiety* Freud reverted to the old concept of defence, stating that he thought it would undoubtedly be an advantage to use it again, "provided we employ it explicitly as a general designation for all the techniques which the ego makes use of in conflicts which may lead to a neurosis, while we retain the word repression for that special method of defence which the line of approach taken by our investigations made us better acquainted with in the first instance." Here we have direct refutation of the notion that repression occupies a unique position amongst the psychic processes, and a place is made in psychoanalytical theory for others which serve the same purpose, namely, "the protection of the ego against instinctual demands." The significance of repression is reduced to that of "a special method of defence."

This new conception of the role of repression suggests an enquiry into the other specific modes of defence and a comparison of those so far discovered and described by psycho-analytical investigators.

The same appendix to *Inhibitions, Symptoms and Anxiety* contains the conjecture to which I alluded in the last chapter, namely, that "further investigations may show that there is an intimate connection between special forms of defence and particular illnesses, as, for instance, between repression and hysteria." Regression and reactive alteration of the ego (reaction-formation), isolation and "undoing" what has been done are all cited as defensive techniques employed in obsessional neurosis.

A lead having thus been given, it is not difficult to complete the enumeration of the ego's defensive methods as described in Freud's other writings. For instance, in "Jealousy, Paranoia and Homosexuality," intro-jection, or identification, and projection are mentioned as important defensive methods employed by the ego in morbid affections of this type and are characterized as "neurotic mechanisms." In his work on the theory of instinct he describes the processes of turning against the self and reversal, and these he designates as "vicissitudes of instinct." From the point of view of the ego these two latter mechanisms also must come under the heading of methods of defence, for every vicissitude to which the instincts are liable has its origin in some ego-activity. Were it not for the intervention of the ego or of those external forces which the ego represents, every instinct would know only one fate—that of gratification. To these nine methods of defence, which are very familiar in the practice and have been exhaustively described in the theoretical writings of psycho-analysis (regression, repression, reaction-formation, isolation, undoing, projection, introjection, turning against the self and reversal), we must add a tenth, which pertains rather to the study of the normal than to that of neurosis: sublimation, or displacement of instinctual aims.

So far as we know at present, the ego has these ten different methods at its disposal in its conflicts with instinctual representatives and effects. It is the task of the practising analyst to discover how far these methods prove effective in the processes of ego-resistance and symptom-formation which he has the opportunity of observing in individuals.

Verification of our conclusions in analytic practice. The facts which have to be laboriously assembled and related in a theoretical exposition can fortu-nately be brought to light and demonstrated without further difficulty in the analyses of our patients. Whenever by means of analysis we reverse a defensive process, we discover the different factors which have contrib-uted to produce it. We can estimate the amount of energy expended in establishing repressions by the strength of the resistance which we encounter when we seek to lift them. Similarly, we can deduce the motive which prompted a patient's defence against an instinctual impulse from his frame of mind when we reintroduce that impulse into consciousness. If we annul a neurotic defence set up at the instance of the super-ego, the analysand has a sense of guilt, i.e. he experiences super-ego anxiety. If, on the other hand, the defence was set up under pressure from the outside world, he experiences objective anxiety. If, when analysing a child, we revive painful affects which he had warded off, he feels the same intense "pain" as forced his ego to resort to defensive measures. Finally, if we intervene in a defensive process which was motivated by the patient's dread of the strength of his instincts, precisely that occurs which his ego sought to avoid; the id-derivatives, hitherto suppressed, make their way into the territory of the ego and meet with but little opposition.

Considerations bearing upon psycho-analytic therapy. This survey of the defensive processes gives us a very clear idea of the possible points of attack for analytic therapy. In analysis the defensive processes are reversed; a passage back into consciousness is forced for the instinctual impulses or affects which have been warded off and it is then left to the ego and the super-ego to come to terms with them on a better basis. The prognosis for the solution of the psychic conflicts is most favourable when the motive for the defence against instinct has been that of super-ego anxiety. Here the conflict is genuinely endopsychical and a settlement can be arrived at between the different institutions, especially if the super-ego has become more accessible to reason through the analysis of the identifications upon which it is based and of the aggressiveness which it has made its own. Its dread of the super-ego having thus been reduced, there is no longer any need for it to resort to defensive methods, with pathological consequences.

But, even when the defence in infantile neurosis has been motivated by objective anxiety, analytic therapy has a good prospect of success. The simplest method—and that least in accordance with the principles of analysis—is for the analyst, when once he has reversed the defensive process in the child's own mind, to try so to influence reality, i.e., those responsible for the child's upbringing, that objective anxiety is reduced, with the result that the ego adopts a less severe attitude towards the instincts and has not to make such great efforts to ward them off. In other cases analysis shows that the various anxieties which have led to the defence belong to an actual situation now long past. The ego recognizes that there is no longer any need to fear it. Or again, what appears to be objective anxiety proves to have its source in exaggerated, crude and distorted notions of reality, based on primeval situations once actual but now no longer existing. Analysis unmasks this "objective anxiety" and shows that it is a product of phantasy against which it is not worth while to assume defensive operations.

When the ego has taken its defensive measures against an affect for the purpose of avoiding "pain," something more besides analysis is required to annul them, if the result is to be permanent. The child must learn to tolerate larger and larger quantities of "pain" without immediately having recourse to his defence-mechanisms. It must, however, be admitted that theoretically it is the business of education rather than of analysis to teach him this lesson.

The only pathological states which fail to react favourably to analysis are those based on a defence prompted by the patient's dread of the strength of his instincts. In such a case there is a danger that we may annul the defensive measures of the ego without being able immediately to come to its assistance. In analysis we always reassure the patient who is afraid of admitting his id-impulses into consciousness by telling him that, once they are conscious, they are less dangerous and more amenable to control than when unconscious. The only situation in which this promise may prove illusory is that in which the defence has been undertaken because the patient dreads the strength of his instincts. This most deadly struggle of the ego to prevent itself from being submerged by the id, as, for instance, when psychosis is taking one of its periodic turns for the worse, is essentially a matter of quantitative relations. All that the ego asks for in such a conflict is to be reinforced. In so far as analysis can strengthen it by bringing the unconscious id-contents into consciousness, it has a therapeutic effect here also. But, in so far as the bringing of the unconscious activities of the ego into consciousness has the effect of disclosing the defensive processes and rendering them inoperative, the result of analysis is to weaken the ego still further and to advance the pathological process.

5

Otto Fenichel:
The Psychoanalytical Theory of Neurosis

Reviewed by Richard Lucas

In the fly leaf, this book was described as a textbook of first-rate quality and a standard reference for many years to come. However, psychoanalysis is not a static subject and, as such, does not lend itself to a definitive textbook with an inbuilt rigidity.

In a way, this book was already out of date when published in 1946. Following the controversial discussions in the British Psychoanalytical Society during the war, where different factions argued their cases, the society formed three subgroups in 1946: the followers of Anna Freud; the supporters of Melanie Klein; and an independent group who worked with such famous names as Balint and Winnicott. These new developments and their subsequent ongoing scientific contributions would make the concept of creating a definitive textbook on psychoanalysis an impossibility.

The book can be looked upon as a resume of the application of the early classic Freudian concepts to all spheres of psychiatry. The title is quite misleading as, in this book, Fenichel applies his analytic approach not just to neurosis, but to psychosis, psychosomatic disorders and personality disorders. He also comments on all varieties of treatment approaches from counseling to ECT.

The book is not easy to read. When I started my psychiatric training some twenty years ago, having an interest in psychoanalysis, I bought Fenichel's book. Although I have used it in a reference sense over the years, at that time, I found myself unable to read it in a systematic way. The first consultant psychotherapist I worked for strongly felt that it was not a suitable book for a beginner in the field of analytic psychotherapy due to its style.

Yet the book carries a certain authoritative presence and has a classic, lasting quality to it. How is this to be explained? It seems that one needs to understand the man behind the book before turning to any more critical review of the contents. This information is to be found in the obituary to Fenichel given by Ernst Simmel in March 1946 to a joint memorial meeting of the San Francisco Psychoanalytical Society and the Psychoanalytical Study Group of Los Angeles, as reported in the *International Journal of Psychoanalysis*, 1946.

Fenichel was described as the truest follower and best representative of Freud's teachings. To quote Simmel: "With Fenichel's death, Freud has died once more." Fenichel was described as not praising Freud, but quoting, explaining, and defining him. At the time of writing the book, Fenichel had earned the reputation of *the* spokesman for the orthodox Freudian approach, with the facility to enumerate points in a cold and systematized way.

He was a widely read man who, even in his teens, had read some Freud, and although he had a medical training, his interest always lay in analysis. By the age of 21, he was reading his first paper as a guest speaker to the Viennese Society ("On a Derivative of the Incest Conflict"). In 1922 he moved to Berlin to complete his analytic training and by 1933, when he left Berlin with the advent of the Nazis, he had already written 108 papers and published 34. In 1924, on joining the teaching staff in Berlin, although only 26, he had such a reputation as to be referred to as "*the* Dr. Fenichel, already known in wide circles." Fenichel described his own love for teaching as his "teaching libido." This love for didactic teaching can be seen to run through his book.

In 1933 he was invited by the Norwegian psychoanalysts to Oslo, and in 1936 he went to Prague. Due to the threat of the Nazi invasion, he settled in California in 1938 and spent the remainder of his years teaching and training in San Francisco until his sudden death in 1946, shortly after the publication of *The Psycho-Analytical Theory of Neurosis*. By the end of his scientific career, he had given 200 papers, had had 72 publications, had written innumerable book reviews, but he is best remembered for the textbook under review here. The obsessional thoroughness of his approach to the subject can be appreciated by the size of the bibliography at the end of the 700-page book. It contains 1,646 references, and yet he introduces them with an apology, saying a comprehensive bibliography had been prepared but that paper shortage necessitated limitations for the time being! The book was first published in 1934, but a second edition with a new introductory outline came out in 1946.

Fenichel would have seen his role as a teacher of Freud, clarifying the work of Freud to students. Also, in the early days, and ever since, there have been those who would try to dilute or refute Freud's insights. Thus, Fenichel viewed himself as the upholder of orthodox analytic theory against erosive tendencies. It is this view, held by Fenichel and others going to the United States with the Nazi persecution, that set the attitude of American postwar analysis, namely, to uphold classical analysis, in a somewhat inflexible way, through the ego-psychology school of thought. It could be seen to uphold analysis against erosion but also to have a stultifying effect.

Freud's view was not one of a blind loyalty of theories. In his paper on narcissism Freud (1915) worried about not adopting too rigid an approach to metapsychology—this being the word used by Freud for viewing of the mind's structure in its most theoretical way. When talking of speculative theories, such as notions of the ego-libido, energy of the ego, and instincts, Freud counsels for a "preparedness to replace by other notions as we apprehend things more clearly. For these ideas are not the foundation of science, upon which everything rests; that foundation is emotion alone. They are not the bottom but the top of the whole structure, and they can be replaced and discarded without damaging it."

As already stated, the book's title is misleading as it contains Fenichel's views of every branch of psychiatry. He even addresses the issue of statistics on therapeutic results of psychoanalysis. For non-analysts this might have been felt welcome, as here was an orthodox psychoanalyst of repute, prepared to give his views on every aspect of psychiatry, from an analytic position. However, his uncompromising style leads to structured over-simplification.

Despite his having extensive chapters on psychoses, perversions and character disorders, Fenichel insists his book only addresses neuroses. In the introduction he says:

> This book is *not* a textbook of psychoanalytical psychology, it limits itself to the theory of neurosis. It is true that neuroses, for the analyst, provide the most fruitful study in the realm of mental phenomena; after having studied the neuroses, it will be easier to study other mental phenomena. In this sense, this is perhaps a first volume of a textbook on psychoanalytical psychology.

At the outset, he categorically informs the reader of his authority. To quote again from the introduction,

> We shall try to engage as little as possible in polemics, but concentrate, rather, on explaining that which already seems established. It is unavoidable

that, in the choice of the material to be presented, in the decision as to which problems should be given more space and which less, and in the arrangement of the book, the personal beliefs of the author are reflected. However, since he hopes his scientific convictions are well founded, he is of the opinion that this will not be a disadvantage.

The reader is, to a certain extent, expected to be taught as an unquestioning pupil. Yet, it is Fenichel's, over and above Freud's and others', views that are expounded. For example, Fenichel repudiates Freud's concept of the death instinct. Fenichel writes:

There are many possible objections to his new theory. Here the following will suffice. The instinctual aim of destruction is the opposite of the sexual search for an object to be loved; of this there is no doubt. Questionable, however, is the nature of this antithesis. Are we dealing with basically different instinctual qualities, or is this contrast again a matter of differentiation of an originally common road? The latter seems more probable.

While Fenichel is by no means alone in his view, Freud's insight of a primary self-destructive instinct has enormous clinical application. Anyone working in general psychiatry and having to manage psychotic patients, is only too well aware of massive, self-destructive forces in action. The concept of the death instinct was later elaborated by Klein, with envy taken as the external manifestation of the death instinct, and became one of the dividers of Kleinian and non-Kleinian theory. Bion later took the concept further, seeing the psychotic part of the mind dominated by the death instinct. He pointed out that it is at the point of being most in touch with emotional pain and needs that, in schizophrenia, the destructive forces are dangerously mobilized and can lead to a massive fragmentation of the mind and the process of thinking, in a way of which one, clinically, is so familiar.

Sometimes Fenichel's dogmatic style can be somewhat off-putting, leading to a need to hold on and digest statements further to get the substance from them. For example, talking about interpretations, he writes: "A valid interpretation brings about a dynamic change manifested in the subsequent associations of the patients and in his entire behavior." One may argue that a narcissistic patient might ignore a valid interpretation, going on in an unchanged way. However, Fenichel also is making an important point, namely, the need to look for the effects of an interpretation in the subsequent material that follows.

The more I read, the more I found myself wanting to argue against dogmatism. For example, Fenichel counsels against direct infant observation, writing: "The temptation is great to apply concepts and ideas valid for higher stages of maturation to the behavior of young children." Yet infant observation has become regarded as an important part of training for psychoanalytic and analytic psychotherapy courses, as well as child psychotherapy trainings. It enhances the capacity to observe nonverbal communications and report them, before giving consideration to their meaning. This helps toward learning the discipline of the neutral observer in analysis.

Perhaps he is most helpful in addressing the intricacies of Freud's metapsychology. With his Germanic background and thus his understanding of the original language, he conveys clear views on the meaning of instincts, drives, etc. However, the old-fashionedness of issues addressed is, at times, evident. In his chapter on mechanisms of defense he writes: "With regard to therapy, those types of actual neuroses that are due to an unfortunate sexual regimen do not need any other therapy." I don't think many analysts would think in this way nowadays.

Following a chapter on psychosomatic disorders, incorporating Alexander's well-known views of character types underlying different disorders, he turns to the psychoses. In his chapter on manic-depressive states, there is a striking omission of two classical papers written in the 1930s by Melanie Klein, although he goes out of the way, at the back of the book, to say his references were up to 1943. These papers added crucially important concepts to our understanding of the dynamics of manic-depressive states. These included the concept of the manic defense, namely, that manic states are states of denial of underlying unbearable depression and persecution, and the concept of manic reparation, in contrast to reparation proper. It would have been impossible for Fenichel not to have known these papers and their seminal importance. It is interesting that he quotes as many references to Melitta Schmideberg, as to her more eminent mother, illustrating the historical/political developments in analysis at the time, with the movement in the United States toward the ego psychology viewpoint and anti-Kleinian stance.

Paradoxically, Fenichel shows a refreshing stance toward the problem of tackling the inaccessibility of psychotic disorders. He stresses the need for pioneering work in the institutions. Freud, of course, had classified psychoses as narcissistic neuroses, namely, that the libido was turned inwards, so that with the absence of transference, analytic interpretative work was not possible. Fenichel argues that in psychoses, "the analyst has no other means than to use the non-narcissistic remainder of the personality in attempts to increase patients' object relationships sufficiently to start the analytic work."

Fenichel talked of a "modification of analytic technique" necessary for this purpose, a view shared by other American analysts, such as Jacobson and Searles, involved with psychotics. In England, Rosenfeld was later to argue that there was a psychotic transference, concrete in form, which needed analyzing by interpretation, and, in that sense, the basic analytic technique did not require modification in approaching psychotic patients.

His summarized view of schizophrenia was to contrast it to neuroses: "Neuroses represent a regression to infantile sexuality; the psychoanalysis of neuroses brought about an understanding of infantile sexuality. Schizophrenia represents a regression to the primitive levels of the ego; psychoanalysis of schizophrenics will permit understanding of the evaluation of the ego." He emphasizes Freud's concepts of regression, breakdown, and reconstitution through delusional symptoms, to describe the evolution of the psychotic process.

The chapter on character disorders reflects the classic analytic thinking in the thirties, with the description of oral, anal, urethral, phallic/narcissistic, and genital character traits. Again, Fenichel is refreshing in encouraging an approach to treatment of character disorders. He quoted Freud as saying that "a fairly reliable character" is one of the prerequisites of a successful analysis. Fenichel talks of firstly getting the patient to see that he uses his behavior for defensive purposes in a repetitive way. If this can be achieved, then one might be able to make headway with some difficult character disorders.

His final chapters are on therapy and the prophylaxis of neurosis. He clearly differentiates counseling from psychoanalysis, but is not dismissive of counselling, emphasizing the importance of the "work of learning" and the "work of adjustment." He says that the patient "must acknowledge the new and less comfortable reality and fight tendencies to regression." In a style, as if directed for students revising for an examination, he has a section on contradictions to psychoanalysis, although many of those he mentions, such as age or schizoid personality, would nowadays be disputed.

It has been interesting to reconsider this book from the historical viewpoint. It shows that psychoanalysis has not stood still, but many advances in our knowledge on fundamental concepts and technique have taken place since Freud's death. The book may also illustrate how the attitude brought by Fenichel and others, fleeing from Nazi Europe, had a strong influence on the direction of development of postwar analysis in the United States. The uniqueness and thoroughness of the quality of Fenichel, as a teacher of psychoanalysis, does guarantee this book's place as a classic and a lasting reference source on early orthodox psychoanalysis.

Selections from
The Psychoanalytical Theory of Neurosis
by Otto Fenichel

TRANSFERENCE

The repetition of previously acquired attitudes toward the analyst is but one example of the most significant category of resistance, the handling of which is the core of analysis: the transference resistance. Understanding the contents of the patient's unconscious from his utterances is, relatively, the simplest part of the analyst's task. Handling the transference is the most difficult.

It seems very natural that in the course of an analytic treatment the patient should produce powerful affects. They may appear as anxiety or joy, as an increase in inner tension beyond the point of endurance, or as a happy feeling of complete relaxation. They may also take the form of specific feelings toward the analyst: an intense love, because the analyst is helping him, or bitter hatred, because the analyst forces him to undergo unpleasant experiences. But the problem becomes more complicated when a patient's affect is in contradiction to what is happening in the analysis, as, for example, when a patient hates the analyst for helping him, or loves him for imposing an unpleasant restriction. The problem is even more complicated when the patient obviously misconstrues the real situation and loves or hates the analyst for something which, in the judgment of the analyst, is nonexistent. Such misconstruing of the actual psychoanalytic situation is a regular occurrence in almost every analysis. Freud was at first surprised when he met with this phenomenon; today Freud's discoveries make it easy to understand it theoretically. The analytic situation induces the development of derivatives of the repressed, and at the same time a resistance is operative against it. The derivatives may make their appearance as highly concrete emotional needs directed toward the person who happens to be present. Resistance distorts the true connections. The patient misunderstands the present in terms of the past; and then instead of remembering the past, he strives, without recognizing the nature of his action, to relive the past and to live it more satisfactorily then he did in childhood. He "transfers" past attitudes to the present.

In analysis, transference has a twofold aspect. Fundamentally it must be considered as a form of resistance. The patient defends himself against remembering and discussing his infantile conflicts by reliving them. Transference actions (since the object is not the right one and the situation is not fitting) serve the purpose of distorting the original connections, and the discharge thus attained is necessarily insufficient. The analysand, seeking immediate satisfaction of derivatives instead of facing his original impulses, attempts to use a short-circuit substitute for his repressed drives. On the other hand, the transference offers the analyst a unique opportunity to observe directly the past of his patient and thereby to understand the development of his conflicts.

In everyday life, too, there are transference situations. It is a general human trait to interpret one's experiences in the light of the past. The more that repressed impulses seek expression in derivatives, the more hampered is the correct evaluation of the differences between the present and the past, and the greater is the transference component of a person's behavior. However, the psychoanalytic situation in particular promotes the production of transference in two ways: (1) The environment which is reacted to has relatively uniform and constant character and therefore the transference component in the reactions becomes much more pronounced. (2) Whereas in other situations people react to a person's actions and words – thus provoking new reactions and creating new realities all of which obscures the transference character of the original action – the analyst, in contrast to this, provides no actual provocation to the patient and responds to his affective outbursts only by making the patient aware of his behavior. Thus the transference character of the patient's feelings becomes clearer. The analyst's reaction to transference is the same as to any other attitude of the patient: he interprets. He sees in the patient's attitude a derivative of unconscious impulses and tries to show this to the patient.

Practically, this task is far more difficult than any other type of interpretation. Were the analyst to behave as the patient's parents had previously done, he could not help him, for then what had occurred in the patient's childhood would merely be repeated. And were the analyst to behave in a contrary way, he would not be able to cure the patient either, for then he would only be fulfilling the patient's resistance wishes. The analyst, therefore, must do neither the one nor the other. If he were to feel flattered by the love of the patient and responded in kind, or if he were hurt by the patient's feeling of hate, in short, if he were to react to the

affects of his patient with counteraffects, he could not successfully interpret; for the patient could respond to interpretations in some such way as:
"No, I love you or hate you not because of unresolved love or hate
tendencies of my past but because you have actually behaved in a lovable
or hateful way."

There are several reasons why analytic institutes require that all analysts
themselves first be analyzed. One of the reasons is that in psychoanalytic
courses it is not possible to give clinical demonstrations, and consequently
the future analyst can learn analytic technique only by personal experience.
A second reason is that the analyst's own repressions would make him
overlook certain things in his patient, or see others in an exaggerated way
and therefore falsify their significance. Much more fundamental is a third
reason. It is not easy to face the innumerable and various affects with
which patients bombard the analyst without reacting with counteraffects,
whether conscious or unconscious. The unconscious tendencies of the
analyst to express his own unresolved love and hate tendencies by reacting
to transference with countertransference must therefore be eliminated
through a training analysis.

Systematic and consistent interpretative work, both within and without
the framework of the transference, can be described as educating the
patient to produce continually less distorted derivatives until his fundamental instinctual conflicts are recognizable. Of course, this is not a single
operation resulting in a single act of abreaction; it is, rather, a chronic
process of working through, which shows the patient again and again the
same conflicts and his usual way of reacting to them, but from new angles
and in new connections.

CRITERIA FOR THE CORRECTNESS OF INTERPRETATIONS

The problem of how the analyst knows his interpretations are correct has
been postponed until now. A familiar objection made to psychoanalysis is
that interpretations are arbitrary, that the analyst more or less projects his
own fantasies onto the patient. He is said to make things easy for himself:
if the patient says "yes" to an interpretation, that is taken as a proof of its
validity; if he says "no," he thereby shows a resistance to the interpretation, proof positive of its validity. As for scientific certainty, there simply is
no evidence of it.

What is the real situation? As a matter of fact, it is correct that a patient's
yes usually is accepted as a confirmation and that, under certain circum-

stances, a no is not regarded as a refutation. Freud very rightly called attention to an analogous situation, that of the judge. The confession of an accused person is generally valid as proof of guilt, although in exceptional cases the confession may be false; but a denial on the part of the accused is by no means proof of innocence. The difference between the accused and a psychoanalytic patient is merely that the former consciously conceals the truth, the latter unconsciously.

Hence neither a yes or a no in reply to an interpretation is a final criterion as to its validity. It is rather the manner in which the yes or no is expressed. Certainly there is a kind of no that merely represents a final attempt to maintain an attitude that has become insupportable. There are various signs by which such a patient betrays, immediately after uttering his no, that he has been inwardly affected by the interpretation and feels that what the analyst has called to his attention really exists within himself. But in general one can say that an interpretation to which the patient objects is wrong. That does not necessarily mean that it is wrong in content, that, for instance, the impulse which the analyst surmised and imparted to the patient had never been operative. The interpretation may be correct in content but incorrect dynamically or economically, that is, given at a moment when the patient could not grasp its validity or get any farther with it. Sometimes a yes may be simulated by the patient out of politeness or negligence or fear of the consequences of a contradiction or for some other reason, whereas his behavior may show that inwardly he is saying no.

To put it differently, it is not a matter of the words used by the patient in responding to an interpretation. In giving an interpretation, the analyst seeks to intervene in the dynamic interplay of forces, to change the balance in favor of the repressed in its striving for discharge. The degree to which this change actually occurs is the criterion for the validity of an interpretation. It is the patient's reactions in their *entirety* that give the answer, not his first yes or no. A valid interpretation brings about a dynamic change, manifested in the subsequent associations of the patient and in his entire behavior.

Freud once compared psychoanalysis to a jigsaw puzzle, in which the aim is to construct a complete picture out of its fragments. There is but one correct solution. So long as this is not discovered, one can perhaps recognize isolated bits, but there is no coherent whole. If the correct solution is found, there can be no doubt as to its validity, for each fragment fits into the general whole. A final solution reveals a unified coherence in which every hitherto incomprehensible detail has found its place. And, also before this happy point is reached, dynamic-economic changes in the state of the patient are decisive for determining whether or not the procedure of the analyst is adequate.

Enquiry into connections ("Understanding" or "perception of meaning"—Verstehen; "Explanation" or "perception of casual connection"—Erklären). Phenomenology presents us with a series of isolated fragments broken out from a person's total psychic *experience*. Other studies present us with data of a different order, e.g., psychological performances, somato-psychic events, expressive gestures, psychotic actions and inner worlds. How are all these various data to be related? In some cases the meaning is clear and we understand directly *how one psychic event emerges from another*. This mode of understanding is only possible with psychic events. In this way we can be said to understand the anger of someone attacked, the jealousy of the man made cuckold, the acts and decisions that spring from motive. In phenomenology we scrutinise a number of qualities or states and the understanding that accompanies this has a static quality. But in this question of connectedness, we grasp a psychic perturbation, a psyche in motion, a psychic connection, the actual emergence of one thing from another. Here our understanding has a genetic quality (a psychopathology of meaningful phenomena). Not only do we understand subjectively experienced phenomena in this way, but all the other phenomena which are directly visible to us in their objective manifestations, e.g., actual performances and the works and personal worlds of our patients, which may all have provided us with the material for our static observations.

Broadly speaking, however, "understanding" has two different meanings, according to whether it is termed *static* or *genetic*. The *static mode* denotes the presentation to oneself of psychic states, the objectifying to oneself of psychic qualities, and we shall exercise this kind of understanding when we come to the chapters on phenomenology and the psychology of expression, etc. In the second part of the book we shall occupy ourselves with the *genetic mode*, that of empathy, of perceiving the meaning of psychic connections and the emergence of one psychic phenomenon from another. The qualification of "static" or "genetic" will only be added to "understanding" (Verstehen) where there might be some confusion. Otherwise we shall use the term "understanding" according to context, implying in one chapter the static mode, in another the genetic.

In psychopathology our genetic understanding (or perception of meaningful connection) soon reaches its limits. (We can call this process "psychological explanation" if we like, but then we must keep it clearly distinct, as of a different order from objective causal explanation, which is the perception of causal connection in the strict sense.) In psychopathology psychic phenomena appear suddenly as something entirely new, in a way we cannot understand at all. One psychic event follows another quite incomprehensibly; it seems to follow arbitrarily rather than emerge. Stages of psychic development in normal people, psychic phases and episodes in abnormal people are all incomprehensible events and appear as purely temporal sequences. It is equally difficult to understand the whole range of a person's psychic development and its full meaning in genetic terms. We can only resort to *causal explanation,* as with phenomena in the natural sciences, which, as distinct from psychological phenomena, are never seen "from within" but "from the outside" only.

In order to be clear we shall keep the expression *"understanding"* (Verstehen) solely for the understanding of psychic events "from within." The expression will never be used for the appreciation of objective causal connections, which as we have said can only be seen "from without." For these we shall reserve the expression "explanation" (Erklären).

. . . the question then arises what we are to understand by the term *"biological."* Obviously it seems not to be what the science of biology takes as its subject; that is, those ever concrete and therefore particular matters which research can explore, but rather something within which all particulars occur and from which they all derive. But this whole is no object for research, it is only an idea, a philosophical concept of comprehensiveness. It seems to me that the biology of this "biological psychiatry" therefore expresses the drive of an idea, a philosophical tendency, which perhaps does not quite understand itself but as an object for scientific research it appears quite baseless.

Research when guided by an idea takes definite form only when it leaves the broad outlook and comes close to the facts. If it is true that symptom-complexes originate in disturbances of individual biological function-complexes, then the connection between the phenomena which at first sight appear heterogenous must be concievable as functionally linked in the complex. The question is: How are we to grasp the connection of the symptoms in the complex? How do they hang together? The answer is missing. The fact of their *statistical correlation*—if this indeed could be established—would only become a scientific fact if one knew the way in which the symptoms themselves cohere together.

THE BASIC PROBLEM OF PSYCHOPATHOLOGY: IS IT PERSONALITY DEVELOPMENT OR PROCESS?

The investigation of the basic biological events and the meaningful development of the life-history culminates in a differentiation of two kinds of individual life: the *unified development of a personality* (based on a normal biological course through the age-epochs and any contingent phases) and the *disruption* of a life which is broken in two and falls apart because at a given time a process has intervened in the biological happenings and irreversibly and incurably altered the psychic life by interrupting the course of biological events.

The criteria for a process in the life-history are: The appearance of a new factor which can be localised within a brief span of time; the accompaniment of this by a number of known symptoms, the absence of any precipitating cause or of any experience sufficient to explain the onset. We speak, on the other hand, of the *development of a personality* in so far as we have been able to understand what has developed within the total framework of the life-history in all its categories, always presupposing a foundation of normal biological events. The deciding factors are experiences, precipitating stimuli and events which can be adequately understood together with the absence of any known symptom-complexes belonging to a process which can be allocated to any given point in time. (p. 702).

6

H. J. Eysenck:
Dimensions of Personality

Reviewed by Sidney Crown

The immediate postwar period was an exciting time to be a psychologist at the Maudsley. With routine IQ and personality testing for both adult and childrens' departments manageable by a small, informal group of trainers and trainees who yet had time left over for research (!), an increasing number of Ph.D. students from Great Britain, Europe, Australia, New Zealand, the United States, and Canada became involved in Eysenck's "program" research—my first introduction to this term.

We were dimly aware that all that had gone on up to this point—to 21-year-olds had anything of significance gone on before?—had been written up in a book with a curious title: *Dimensions of Personality*. We learned soon enough about "dimensions" sitting long hours over noisy "calculating machines" working out the "factor saturations" of the tests we were investigating. Looking back now I realize that it was the only time in my life I have ever worked in the more intimate atmosphere of those days very near to a number of great men, of whom Hans Eysenck and Aubrey Lewis were the kingpins.

Over coffee we argued with Eysenck about the appropriateness of a title like *Dimensions* as we later argued against other titles like *Uses and Abuses* and *Sense and Nonsense*. We suggested, in our arrogance, that titles like that would never catch on! Little did we know that these, among others, would be part of the landscape of paperback displays in 1980.

Even at a period when, at every level and in all departments, the Maudsley was full of clever people (will no one document this period?) Eysenck's intellect was regarded as exceptional, and his capacity unique to write simply and clearly. His ability to think on his feet made him a formidable opponent in any academic debate, equally admired and feared. For many of us it was also to be our only experience in a lifetime of being part of a research team whose conception and direction came from one person. Eysenck exerted steady pressure on us to present papers at meetings and to publish, a pressure sometimes feared and resented but which surely might have a place in the training of psychiatrists today. It remains in my memory as an exciting time, and even now Eysenck still preserves a great deal of his eternal youth so that I find it difficult to accept that he will be retiring shortly.

While his total corpus of research and writing is considerable even by contemporary standards, my dusty and marked copy of *Dimensions* still interests and excites me and I think represents Eysenck's talents most exactly. It is impossible to assess the long-term status of one's mentors. However, *Dimensions of Personality* seemed fundamentally to advance the psychology of "personality" by extending to it the precise statistical methods that, to that time, had mainly been restricted to the field of cognition. Only R. B. Cattell's parallel work in the United States had a similar place in the development of the subject. Neuroticism and extraversion seemed an appropriate framework around which to orientate an almost infinite number of researches in an attempt to characterize the physical, emotional, and motivational aspects of personality.

"PERSONALITY" IN 1947

Personality as a concept has been so dominated by the attempt at objectivity, particularly through questionnaires, that it is hard to realize the situation in 1947. The most influential textbook was G. W. Allport's *Personality*, a thoughtful and scholarly text but much in the philosophical tradition of academic psychology. The methodology of Eysenck and Raymond B. Cattell was that of multiple factor analysis, previously used to analyse intellect on both sides of the Atlantic: in Britain stemming from Spearman and in the U.S. culminating in the work of L. L. Thurstone. (An abiding memory was a BPS meeting in Edinburgh when I found myself in a urinal with Cattell on one side and Thurstone on the other! It was a testing few minutes for my immature social skills. However, as I remember it, we chatted. . . .)

Dimensions had a Grand Design: to map out personality with the use of "objective" tests within the framework of multivariate statistical analysis. Valhalla was represented by the possibility of individuals being symbolized, through their test results in multidimensional space. The correlation of their personality attributes with the results of treatment would be known and, lo and behold, psychiatry would be made easier. It took an emotional crisis and (as they say nowadays) retraining in medicine to teach me that there are no shortcuts.

EYSENCK'S PERSONAL TOUCH

Unlike the present cool culture but like many other senior men of that time, Eysenck was always encouraging young people. Despite his theoretical preoccupation with the problems of selection and guidance, I doubt whether he felt that successful research potential could be predicted. So he took the simple step of actively encouraging anyone who wanted to do it! He was pleased with those that were successful and philosophical about those who failed. The Ph.D. ladder in his office grew and grew (I was amazed when I saw it a year or so ago).

It is sad to note, in passing, how active encouragement of people in training seems to have ceased. In preparing for one of my first research projects, Erich Guttman, one of the most respected clinicians at the Maudsley at that time, accompanied me from there to St. Bernard's Hospital, Southall, on public transport in order to introduce me to the physician superintendent, J. B. S. Lewis, whose patients I was going to test.

WHAT IS *DIMENSIONS* ABOUT?

The research program summarized in *Dimensions* follows the orthodox psychometric exploratory model of the time, developed originally by Spearman in the study of school children's intelligence. Essentially Eysenck was attempting to objectify—to define operationally was the modish phrase of the period—psychoneurosis and to show how neurotics differ from normals. The general guiding hypotheses of neuroticism and extraversion were not of course original but had a background, the first in clinical psychiatry and clinical psychology, the second in the analytical psychology of Jung. The basis of the entire edifice was an extensive statistical analysis of the Maudsley item sheet. Later from item analyses of extant personality inventories of that time the prototype of the EPI (medical questionnaire) was developed.

In the course of factorially defining these parameters many other tests came to be included, some of them quaintly non-Eysenckian, such as the attempt to objectify a group Rorschach test; the validity and use of projection tests being an area of intense argument. *Dimensions* records the investigation and use of every way of exploring possible aspects of neuroticism and introversion. Approaches varied from perception to action, from reversal of perspective, color form, and dark vision, to tests of manual dexterity, such as the Cambridge triple tester (pursuit-meter). My memory is of us as totally involved Eysenckian Ph.D. students—our attempt to establish our identity distinct from "the doctors" at that time perhaps even more favored than now. We were assigned an area to explore in our theses and were grateful to have a clear, well supervised program. Certainly, we almost all completed our projects rather than fell by the wayside, as so many seem to do today. To anyone present at that time and now middle-aged, one of the sadnesses of *Dimensions* is to remember the topics and those who worked on them, some now busy academics in their own right and others vanished from the scene. My impression of this selected group of postgraduates with a thirty-five-year follow-up is that assiduity as a personality trait is better rewarded than originality or flair.

Of the traits and tests explored in *Dimensions* many are of interest only to the psychometric historian: persistence, irritability, scatter (of test scores), level of aspiration, perseveration.

In one chapter, with the old-fashioned name of "Physique and Constitution," Eysenck anticipates a future major interest in objective tests of physiological function and psychosomatic relations. Thus body build and various aspects of autonomic activity (salivary secretion, choline esterase secretion) were investigated. One of my own memories of the period is returning from a particularly harassing talk about research with Aubrey Lewis who, staring at me coldly, had asked with mock naivete why it was I related with such certainty psychogalvanic reactivity to sweat-gland activity.

Two other broad areas Eysenck began and never followed through, although I cannot help feeling there is still much research mileage in them, were suggestibility as a personality trait and the analysis of aesthetic preferences and sense of humor. The analysis of suggestibility into primary (ideo-motor) and secondary (being influenced) and the possible relation to hypnotizability still seem interesting. Certainly, the nature of hypnosis remains a tantalizing puzzle. The matter of aesthetic preferences through art, flowers, photographs, bookbindings, and so on, and the analysis of sense of humor as a personality trait both seem ridiculously neglected areas.

Before leaving the topic of humor there is a small, if unintentional, gem for those who only know Eysenck from his interests and attitudes in later years. In the course of selecting suitable subjects for two experiments exploring the relation of hysteria and suggestibility, not only were the patients "selected very carefully by the most experienced and senior psychiatrist at the hospital" but "all the case-notes were read carefully by the writer and the crucial cases . . . were seen by the Clinical Director. . . ." The sixty patients thus selected were given eight suggestibility tests, four tests of primary and four tests of secondary suggestibility "by the experimenter in person."

A further general message from *Dimensions* relates to Eysenck's abiding view of personality as a hierarchical organization. Thus "specific responses" at the lowest level, working up through habitual responses, to traits (persistence, rigidity, etc.) and types (extraversion). Insofar as there is any flexibility for human personality in the psychometric model of man, it is surely provided for within this organizational structure.

IS *DIMENSIONS* A GREAT BOOK?

One aspect of this series might be to ask how highly a book might be regarded from the points of view of abiding originality, of style, and of something difficult to define but basically of quality.

On originality, *Dimensions* rates highly on what might be termed secondary originality but not primary. By this I mean the basic ideas of others were developed in an original way but the ideas themselves were not original. There seems no comparison in originality with either the writings of—dare I say it?—Freud as a historical figure nor—even more daring perhaps—of R. D. Laing as a contemporary person. The writings of both of these may well continue to inspire generations in a way *Dimensions* simply will not.

Comparison of style must surely be with the great textbooks compiled by those lucky few who, like Eysenck himself, are both the originators and synthesizers. In this sense *Dimensions* seems to fall considerably below the textbooks great in their specialized fields by Sheila Sherlock, Paul Wood, Avery-Jones, Zachary Cope, Russell Brain, or Gordon Holmes.

So far as deep, indefinable quality is concerned, comparisons might be with E. D. Adrian's *Physical Basis of Perception*, Durkheim on *Suicide* or F. M. R. Walshe's *Critical Essays in Neurology*. These are undeniable classics, which *Dimensions* is not.

What might therefore be the current importance of *Dimensions*? Does it repay reading for postgraduates or for the rest of us?

DIMENSIONS IN 1982

Aubrey Lewis, in a characteristically sophisticated and guarded foreword noted: "Psychiatrists concerned to understand their patient rather than to measure him are disposed to look askance at methods which could seem to them atomistic, aridly statistical and untrue to the dynamic influences which mold and determine human individuality." However he goes on to reassure the reader that this is not the whole story; that . . . "measurement may be possible and a sight obtained of the promised land where mental organization will be as well understood as the physical organization of human beings now is."

Thirty-five years later, surely a reasonable time from which to make a preliminary even if not a definitive judgment, how far has the promise of *Dimensions* been realized? Has *Dimensions* been an influential book? Obviously, it depends on what you mean by that. Certainly it has been theoretically influential for several generations of psychologists and psychiatrists. Various improved versions of the EPI are widely used in research projects. This is the practical side of things.

But there remains a profound methodological question. The dimensional approach to personality in 1947 seemed to offer a logical sequence first to describe personality in relatively simple terms and then to explore specific aspects in depth. But the depth studies elaborating the dimensional studies have been relatively disappointing. Possibly psychology as a method of studying man has a fundamental and irreconcilable problem. On the one hand, ideographic, subjective psychology, which is interesting, is inherently unprovable; nomothetic and statistical psychology, with its arbitary definition of what is scientific, limits itself to the worthy but dull. This is an old paradox recently revived and well argued by Laing. Certainly Eysenckian psychometric man as an image would, after all these years, hardly provide an absorbing hero for a novel, a play, or an opera. Man's essence still seems to be left out despite Aubrey Lewis's hopes.

Eysenck was a charismatic leader who engendered excitement in all who worked under him, and the experience makes me wonder whether research authenticated by consensus as in research committees, although understandable in today's economic climate, is ever likely to encourage originality. A charismatic research leader may be, and usually is, opinionated, has tunnel vision, and seems unpersuaded by others of the limitations of what he does, but is the sort of person that young researchers follow. Ultimately however, in terms of the long-term goals set by Eysenck himself, the final paradox seems that the gap between the qualitative, literary, and artistic view of personality and the psychometric can never be bridged by Eysenck's chosen scientific methodology.

In short, *Dimensions* makes an interesting re-read for those with a personal involvement but not really for new readers. It has undoubted historical interest as the base of one of the most elaborate programs of personality research. It does not, however, have the originality, style, or intrinsic quality to become a classic.

Selections from
Dimensions of Personality
by H. J. Eysenck

Dimensions of Personality was researched and written at the time of the post–Second World War psychometric explosion. The emphasis in the philosophy of science of the time was on the operational definition of human traits. Thus intelligence is not an abstract concept but consists of what intelligence test measure; similarly, with personality and the objectification of its measurement.

Thus, from the foreword by Aubrey Lewis, professor of psychiatry, and Eysenck's colleague:

> Personality is so cardinal a matter in psychiatry that any ambiguity in the concept or uncertainty about how to describe and measure the qualities it stands for must weaken the whole structure of psychiatry, theoretical and clinical. . . .
>
> Psychiatrists concerned to understand their patient rather than to measure him, are disposed to look askance at methods which could seem to them atomistic, aridly statistical and untrue to the dynamic influences which mould and determine human personality. It is, however, precisely in its methods that the research described in this book may be found to contribute most to the psychology of personality, and, consequently, to the theory and ultimately to the practice of psychiatry. These methods . . . aim at the analysis, by reliable statistical techniques, of experimental and clinical data so that measurement may be possible and a sight obtained of the promised land where mental organization will be as well understood as physical organization of human beings now is.

This foreword fairly represents Eysenck's psychometric and methodological challenge and also a critical skepticism, even though this doubt is hidden beneath polite encouragement.

Eysenck's own enthusiasm comes through most clearly in the introduction and conclusion of his book.

Thus, from the introduction:

The work here presented is the result of a concentrated and cooperative effort to discover the main dimensions of personality, and to define them operationally, i.e., by means of strictly experimental, quantitative procedures. More than three dozen separate researches were carried out on altogether some 10,000 normal and neurotic subjects. . . .

. . . the time has come when preliminary surveys of isolated traits, and the exploratory studies of small groups, must give way to work planned on an altogether larger scale. . . .

A wide variety of topics is covered in the researches, then described. These include neuroticism and extraversion, concepts of central and permanent importance to Eysenck; the analysis of measurements of physique and constitution; of ability and efficiency; of suggestibility and hypnosis; of aesthetic appreciation and expression.

Eysenck's conclusion as to what he had achieved at the time are represented by the following quotations from the concluding synthesis:

The isolation of a number of tests which may be used for measuring introversion and neuroticism is only the first step on a very long road. . . . We know next to nothing about the relative contribution of hereditary and environmental factors to the development of a neurotic or an introverted personality. . . . The relative fixity with which a person is likely to retain his position on the neurotic continuum or on the introverted continuum. . . . About the predictive value of these test . . . [o]nce the problems have been made amenable to quantitative treatment by the development of a sufficient number of personality tests, there is no reason why these questions should not find an answer through specially devised experiments. . . .

The researches . . . have succeeded in isolating two main personality dimensions, and in discovering a series of tests which enable us to perform quantitative investigations along these two dimensions. . . .

7

Eugen Bleuler:
Dementia Praecox or the Group of Schizophrenias

Reviewed by Manfred Bleuler
and Rudolf Bleuler

Bleuler's aim in becoming a doctor and his interest in schizophrenia are deeply rooted in his origins. He was born on April 30, 1857 (his father lived from 1823–1889, his mother from 1829–1898). All his ancestors were from Zollikon, which was, up to the end of the last century, a rural village an hour's walk from the city of Zurich. The population of Zollikon lost some of its ancient rights during the eighteenth century and had been increasingly subjected to the government of the city of Zurich. Up to 1830, an academic career was unusual and difficult for the rural population; it remained difficult during Bleuler's youth. It is astonishing, however, that in spite of the difficult access to academic education, the intellectual interest and the enthusiasm for the ideals of enlightenment grew even greater among the rural population.

It became increasingly important for the rural people to give an academic education to their young men. The hope grew: if our sons are academically trained, they will be able to perform their duties as clergymen, judges, and particularly as doctors as well, or even better, than the old aristocrats of the city. Under these circumstances, Eugen Bleuler decided to become a doctor, and he understood medicine as part of natural sciences.

The first directors of the psychiatric University Clinic Burghölzli Zurich (opened 1870) were highly qualified and internationally known professors who became famous on account of their research in neuropathology and in neurophysiology. As Zurich at this time had no academic tradition, they had been called to their chairs from Germany.

The rural population felt that these great men had no personal contact with their psychotic patients on account of their academic interests and their language (the population spoke a German dialect). Under these conditions, Bleuler conceived the overwhelming wish to become a modern doctor who lived and spoke with them in their mother tongue. He had the wish to become a psychiatrist such as the population around him had dreamed of—a psychiatrist who could help his patients both by modern medicines and by understanding them personally and being close to them.

Bleuler completed his medical studies in Zurich in 1881. In the following years, he was an assistant in the psychiatric clinics of Waldau-Bern and Burghölzli-Zurich and also studied in Paris (under Charcot), in London, and in Munich (under von Gudden). One of his first publications as a young student concerned synestesia (1880). There followed papers on cerebral anatomy, neurology, and neurophysiology.

While an assistant of Auguste Forel in the Burghölzli Clinic, Bleuler was chosen as director at the psychiatric Clinic Rheinau, at the age of 29. He stayed there from 1886 to 1898. Rheinau was at that time a small village of farms. In the eighth century, a monastery had been founded there on an island in the Rhine. In 1867, it had been turned into a psychiatric hospital. Bleuler was not yet married, and lived there alone, in contact with his patients. He worked with them (mostly in agriculture), organized their free time (for instance, hiked with them, played in the theater with them, and danced with them). He was also the general physician of the patients of the clinic and the inhabitants of the village. During his life with the patients, Bleuler had always a memo pad at hand, where he noted what touched and interested him in his patients' behavior. He frequently noted in shorthand what the patients actually said.

In 1898, the government of the canton of Zurich appointed Bleuler as Auguste Forel's successor as director of the Psychiatric Clinic Burghölzli and as professor of psychiatry at the university. He did not wish to leave his patients in Rheinau, but in his new position in Burghölzli, he was much closer to his sick parents.

In his new position, Bleuler had less time for his patients, as he had many other duties. He worked in close touch with his staff, which included Carl Gustav Jung from 1900 to 1910; they discussed (in touch with Sigmund Freud) the psychodynamic life of schizophrenics.

In the first years of this century, a group of German psychiatrists, headed by Gustav Aschaffenburg, professor in Cologne, planned to write a great *Manual of Psychiatry* (thirteen large volumes). Its main aim was the exact description of the manifold psychopathological phenomena, and an effort to outline disease entities, with specific cerebral causes. This was intended to be a continuation of what Kraepelin had inaugurated with his textbook.

Aschaffenburg knew Bleuler both on account of his contribution to the introduction of Kraepelin's conceptions and for his great but critical appreciation of Freud's concepts. Bleuler's motivation for writing the *Manual's* volume on *Dementia Praecox* clearly reflected his principal aims in life: he wanted to be a physician in the sense of his time and to contribute to the progress of medicine, and he wanted at the same time to be close to his patients and to know and study them personally. He was eager to describe psychopathology in an objective, scientific way and to suggest at the same time the importance of understanding the personal psychodynamic life of the individual patient.

THE MAIN TEXT OF THE BOOK

It commences with a short presentation of the history of the concept "dementia praecox." Bleuler introduced the term "schizophrenic psychoses" both in order to eliminate the erroneous idea that the patients become "demented" and to take into consideration that not all patients become psychotic at an early age. His designation also expressed his doubts in regard to the assumption that dementia praecox corresponds to a disease entity. The following main text, under the title "Symptomatology," describes in an exact and objective way his observations while living with schizophrenic patients in Rheinau. The chapter is subdivided into "elementary functions" (the dissociated associations and affectivity, the ambivalence) and "secondary symptoms" (as, for instance, hallucinations, delusions, morbid attitudes). All these descriptions are based mainly on Bleuler's daily notes while with schizophrenic patients. These notes filled several thousand small pages written in shorthand. This is the first and most important characteristic of the book: *it is based mainly on personal and direct observations.*

The second characteristic of the book consists *of an endeavor to discover the psychological individual background of the psychotic symptoms.* This is not done by theoretical considerations but by noting observations that concern the psychological background. From Bleuler's description of symptoms emanates his empathy for the patient to the reader. To what is such an emanation due? Certainly not by direct calls for empathy! It may be due first to the fact that Bleuler gives well-observed examples of symptoms noted in much more detail than an impersonal description. Bleuler also repeats again and again that the symptoms were observed in a patient whose emotional and intellectual inner life is essentially intact, but frequently hidden. Thus, we gain the impression that we are in duty bound to accept the schizophrenic as one of us, and as one who merits our help. The same effect is gained from the demonstration that many symptoms are symbols for emotionally laden ideas of the patients, just as the contents of our dreams are often symbols. Bleuler also describes how patients suffer from ambivalence, from contradictory emotions and impulses (due to double bind, in modern jargon). As it is true of everyone's life to overcome ambivalence, the description of the schizophrenic's difficulties suggests the idea: "He is one of us and we can feel with him."

An example: A schizophrenic woman from the Burghölzli Clinic had asked to see Bleuler. When he saw her, he found her mute and in catatonic stiffness. He suddenly noticed, however, a little movement of the patient: for a short while, she touched Bleuler's wedding ring. This movement suggests the interpretation that the patient wanted to express: "I look like a stone, but I am a woman with healthy feelings appreciating marriage." Bleuler never maintained that his impression of his patient's motivation for touching the wedding ring really corresponded to what was going on in her thoughts. The observation, however, qualified his impression as possibly realistic. And it is certain that Bleuler's impression due to objective observation aroused his empathy for a patient "looking like a stone"—and it evokes the empathy of the book's readers for catatonic patients.

CHAPTERS SUPERSEDED BY MODERN RESEARCH

While Bleuler's exact, minute descriptions of his schizophrenic patients (suggesting empathy through objectivity) are still of value and interest in modern times, the following chapters on course and outcome of psychoses and on the families of schizophrenics have lost their importance in the light of new research since 1911.

Bleuler, however, had already shown that the course of schizophrenic psychoses is extremely varied—with one exception: the schizophrenic never becomes "demented" and never loses his intellectual and emotional life, even if it is often hidden behind his dissociation of thoughts and emotions. Bleuler mentioned that many schizophrenics recover so far that they can live a healthy life outside a hospital. He hesitated, however, to speak of absolute, complete recovery. One of the reasons lies in the critical evaluation of the patient's prepsychotic personality. If prepsychotic personality difficulties continued to exist after social recovery, Bleuler asked himself critically: Was perhaps the prepsychotic personality disorder already a sign of the oncoming psychosis? He feared that the designation of complete recovery was uncertain in such a case, and was not permitted by objective, scientific thinking. Furthermore, for many years Bleuler's main duties did not allow him to follow-up the course of many patients after their discharge from hospital, particularly not during his isolation in Rheinau. Compared with his great experience with hospitalised patients, his experience was restricted with patients discharged from hospital.

THEORETICAL CONSIDERATIONS

One of Bleuler's main aims in choosing and following his career was to arrive at an understanding of the schizophrenic symptoms as expressions of an inner psychodynamic life. And one of the main aims of his book was to describe the results of these endeavors, and to introduce them into modern psychiatry. He studied the schizophrenic's inner life essentially in the same way as we study the inner life of neurotics, of healthy men, and of ourselves. He included in this study ideas of Freud, and discussed them with him.

Bleuler was successful in his endeavors to recognise schizophrenic "symptoms" as reflecting the patient's life experience, his cognition, his emotions, his fears and hopes. His way of analyzing the schizophrenic's inner life enabled him—and enables us—to feel with the schizophrenic, to acknowledge him as "one of us," a man as we are, worthy of the same social and medical care when in stress and difficulty. The great importance of this becomes evident when we realize how strong tendencies in the opposite direction have frequently existed in all cultures and at all times. All too frequently, the schizophrenic was considered to be no longer one of us, to be wracked and ruined for good, to be a demented and degenerated man, or a man possessed by evil spirits or demons. Even in the psychiatry of this century, there has been a strong trend in this direction, declaring that the inner life of the schizophrenic was incomprehensible to the healthy.

While Bleuler understood the schizophrenic symptoms as a direct or symbolic expression of the patient's inner life, he never claimed that his psychological understanding explained the patient's psychosis. In other words, he did not understand why psychologically intelligible parts of the patient's inner life lose control by experience and logic, to a degree which characterize him as a psychotic, as a man who loses his usual social position. Bleuler understood, for instance, that a schizophrenic's ambivalence is essentially of the same nature as ambivalence of the healthy, that it is due to contradictory emotionally laden life experiences, to the double bind. However, Bleuler did not understand why this ambivalence becomes overwhelming, why the patient thinks, feels, and acts in many respects as if there were different souls in him, as if he consisted of different personalities, that he becomes split to a psychotic degree.

It was logical in this situation to assume that hidden behind the schizophrenic symptoms, which are psychodynamically intelligible, is concealed a "primary disorder." Like most psychiatrists of his time, such as Kraepelin and Sigmund Freud (and many other psychiatrists of our times), Bleuler supposed that the primary disorder was a metabolic or anatomical cerebral disturbance. Bleuler mentions, however, the possibility that anomalies in personal development could be a primary cause of schizophrenic psychoses. Bleuler looked for symptoms of the primary disorder that were independent of the psychodynamic life. He suspected some physical findings to be primary symptoms, but we know today that some of them are of another nature. He believed that the splitting (the dissociation of thoughts, of emotions, of attitudes, and of acting) were close to primary symptoms, while he understood most of the other symptoms of the psychosis as due to the intrapsychic, psychodynamic life, as being secondary.

The terms "primary" and "secondary" symptoms of schizophrenic psychoses are no longer in use and sound old-fashioned. The essential content of Bleuler's theoretical conception, however, is astonishingly similar to the conception of most modern psychiatrists. They agree with Bleuler that the symptoms of the schizophrenic psychoses can be understood psychodynamically, and they agree with Bleuler that this understanding does not, as yet, answer the great question: Why has the schizophrenic lost all consideration for reality and logic in many ways during his fight to harmonize the inner disharmonies (the double bind) of his life experience? Why has he became psychotic in spite of an inner life which we feel to be near our inner life? In this regard, too, most modern psychiatrists hypothesize like Bleuler that behind the psychodynamically intelligible morbid symptoms exists a hidden morbid background of the psychosis. They no longer call it, as Bleuler did, "primary disease," but their description of "vulnerability" with regard to schizophrenic psychoses or hidden disturbances only visible by markers corresponds closely to Bleuler's conception. As Bleuler did, most modern psychiatrists suppose that this primary disease, this vulnerability, is due to an abnormal cerebral function—today, in particular, of a neurohumoral origin. As in 1911, however, up to the present time, no specific derangement such as the deepest and specific derangement of schizophrenic psychoses has been discovered.

THE CHAPTERS ON "THERAPY"
(BY RUDOLF BLEULER)

Bleuler excluded the superfluous and the questionable, and based therapy on an established effective foundation. Considering the treatment methods at the present time, we may understand his position. But this attitude explains also why Bleuler expressed himself carefully about the dialogue with his patients.

What principles are specified in his book? The symptomatology of the schizophrenic patient is essentially comprehensible. The underlying factors are the therapist's profound empathy, his sufficient knowledge of the patient's personal history and of psychodynamics, as well as his awareness of the fact that healthy, although split off or distorted parts of the personality, persist even in the most disturbed patient. Uncovering psychotherapy, as with the neuroses, helps only in the less severe cases. The therapist practises with his patient mainly reality testing and impulse control. Daily routine and living together in the clinic are aspects that should be embedded in a structured environment. Acting-out destructiveness must be prevented, but at the same time *freiraum* and tolerance should be taken into account, more so than would be possible outside the clinic. The vehicles of therapy are dialogue and an active community life.

And what if we had to summarize the bases of treatment in the present day? We would confirm the fact that therapy should be less uncovering and more structured. In our opinion, the following is true: First, the therapist is not just a good, knowing, and commenting partner in a dialogue, but is the person who fulfills the patient's desire for a parent figure and who, in certain areas of the relationship, is omnipotent and able to fuse with him. This means that the therapist expresses clearly what he thinks to be correct or incorrect. He is capable of verbalizing the unspoken feelings and thoughts of the patient, and presenting them in a framework which provides security. He makes no secret about his own feelings and associations that arise in the therapy, or about his personal gain. He confirms the experiences communicated to the patient in the dialogue in a well-defined framework on the level of action, which in the end result is more important for the patient. And, step by step, he draws himself out of his parent role, but is available to the patient if necessary for years. Second, understanding is less causal and analytical than purposive and synthetic; abnormal experience is declared as an expression of a healthy, constructive striving, and must be led out of its distorted and threatening state. Third, because anxiety-raising feelings and impulses are not repressed into the unconscious, but instead are split off into other conscious areas of the personality, it is not the task of therapy to let them become conscious, but to (re)integrate them into the whole of the personality. Fourth, disturbed functions should not just be pointed out, but also corrected and actively trained, for example, cognitive and affective control of reality, fantasizing and symbolizing, organizing and weighing of matters, coherent communication, metacommunication of contradictions, and so on. Fifth, the healthy resources of the patient and his family are not just an implicit presupposition for therapy; they should be explicitly applied and strengthened.

If we compare this description with Bleuler's basic statements of 1911, we notice that the latter have maintained their validity up to the present time, but have been developed further and made more precise. Concerning the realization of these principles in the clinic—Bleuler's main field of work—a certain loss is apparent. There was a state of distress concerning personal and financial matters; there were the difficulties of the preneuroleptic era, and the extensive relinquishment of private life. However, one cannot avoid seeing that the clinical setting at the time was more a community of life and destiny between the patients and nurses than it is today, and in this sense, it came closer to the ideal of the active therapeutic community.

CONCLUSION

The main text of Bleuler's book consists of a careful and objective description of his observations during long-term living with schizophrenics—a description that demonstrates the direct and symbolic correlation of the schizophrenic's symptoms with his inner, psychodynamic life.

It is furthermore important that he shows again and again that the schizophrenic is never demented in the sense of Bleuler's time; that he preserves in his background the intellectual abilities and emotional life of the healthy. From Bleuler's minute descriptions of what is healthy in the schizophrenic, and of the correlation of his symptoms with an inner life close to our inner life stresses, comes the conception that the schizophrenic patient is not foreign to us, that he is not unintelligible, and that we can develop empathy for him. The schizophrenic patient needs our help, as does any patient.

For the care of the schizophrenic patient, an active therapeutic community is important. It is essential in therapy that nurses, doctors, relatives, and others are in a natural way near the patient, sharing parts of life with him.

Selections from
Dementia Praecox or the Group
of Schizophrenias
by Eugen Bleuler

SYMPTOMATOLOGY

Certain symptoms of schizophrenia are present in every case and at every period of the illness even though, as with every other disease symptom, they must have attained a certain degree of intensity before they can be recognized with any certainty. Here, of course, we are discussing only the large symptom-complexes as a whole. For example, the peculiar association disturbance is always present, but not each and every aspect of it. Sometimes the anomalies of association may manifest themselves in "blocking," or in the splitting of ideas; at other times in different schizophrenic symptoms.

Besides these specific permanent or fundamental symptoms, we can find a host of other, more accessory manifestations such as delusions, hallucinations or catatonic symptoms. These may be completely lacking during certain periods, or even throughout the entire course of the disease; at other times, they alone may permanently determine the clinical picture.

As far as we know, the fundamental symptoms are characteristic of schizophrenia, while the accessory symptoms may also appear in other types of illness. Nevertheless, even in such cases close scrutiny often reveals peculiarities of genesis or manifestation of a symptom, which are only found in schizophrenia. We can expect that gradually we will come to recognize the characteristic features in a great number of these accessory symptoms.

A description of the symptoms can be based only on clear-cut cases. But it is extremely important to recognize that they exist in varying degrees and shadings on the entire scale from pathological to normal; also the milder cases, latent schizophrenics with far less manifest symptoms, are many times more common than the overt, manifest cases. Furthermore, in view of the fluctuating character which distinguishes the clinical picture of schizophrenia, it is not to be expected that we shall be able to demonstrate each and every symptom at each and every moment of the disease.

THE FUNDAMENTAL SYMPTOMS

The fundamental symptoms consist of disturbances of association and affectivity, the predilection for fantasy as against reality, and the inclination to divorce oneself from reality (autism). Furthermore, we can add the absence of those very symptoms which play such a great role in certain other diseases such as primary disturbances of perception, orientation and memory, etc.

1. The Altered Simple Functions, (a) Association

In this malady the associations lose their continuity. Of the thousands of associative threads which guide our thinking, this disease seems to interrupt, quite haphazardly, sometimes such single threads, sometimes a whole group, and sometimes even large segments of them. In this way, thinking becomes illogical and often bizarre. Furthermore, the associations tend to proceed along new lines, of which so far the following are known to us: two ideas, fortuitously encountered, are combined into one thought, the logical form being determined by incidental circumstances. Clang-associations receive unusual significance, as do indirect associations. Two or more ideas are condensed into a single one. The tendency to stereotype produces the inclination to cling to one idea to which the patient then returns again and again. Generally, there is a marked dearth of ideas to the point of monoideism. Frequently some idea will dominate the train of thought in the form of blocking, "naming," or echopraxia. In the various types of schizophrenia, distractibility does not seem to be disturbed in a uniform manner. A high degree of associational disturbance usually results in states of confusion.

As to the time element in associations, we know of two disturbances peculiar to schizophrenia—pressure of thoughts, that is, a pathologically increased flow of ideas, and the particularly characteristic "blocking."

A young schizophrenic who had first appeared as either paranoid or hebephrenic and then some years later became markedly catatonic, wrote the following spontaneously:

The Golden Age of Horticulture

"At the time of the new moon, Venus stands in Egypt's August-sky and illuminates with her rays the commercial ports of Suez, Cairo, and

Alexandria. In this historically famous city of the Califs, there is a museum of Assyrian monuments from Macedonia. There flourish plantain trees, bananas, corn-cobs, oats, clover and barley, also figs, lemons, oranges, and olives. Olive-oil is an Arabian liquor-sauce which the Afghans, Moors and Moslems use in ostrich-farming. The Indian plantain-tree is the whiskey of the Parsees and Arabs. The Parsee or Caucasian possesses as much influence over his elephant as does the Moor over his dromedary. The camel is the sport of Jews and Arabs. Barley, rice, and sugar-cane called artichoke, grow remarkably well in India. The Brahmins live as castes in Beluchistan. The Circassians occupy Manchuria in China. China is the Eldorado of the Pawnees."

A hebephrenic patient, ill for fifteen years but still able to work and still full of ambitions, gave me the following oral answer to the question, "Who was Epaminondas?":

"Epaminondas was one of those who are especially powerful on land and on sea. He led mighty fleet maneuvers and open sea-battles against Pelopidas, but in the second Punic War he was defeated by the sinking of an armed frigate. With his ships he wandered from Athens to Hain Mamre, brought Caledonian grapes and pomegranates there, and conquered the Beduins. He besieged the Acropolis with gun-boats and had the Persian garrisons put to the stake as living torches. The succeeding Pope Gregory VII . . . eh . . . Nero, followed his example and because of him all the Athenians, all the Roman-Germanic-Celtic tribes who did not favor the priests, were burned by the Druids on Corpus Christi Day as a sacrifice to the Sun-God, Baal. That is the Stone Age. Spearheads made of bronze."

These two performances indicate a moderate degree of schizophrenic association disturbance. Though they stem from two patients whose clinical picture is diametrically different, yet they are amazingly similar. In these patients, the most important determinant of the associations is completely lacking—the concept of purpose. The first patient apparently desires to describe oriental gardens, as such an odd idea for a plain, simple clerk who had never left his native land but idled in a hospital ward for years. The second patient formally adheres to the question put to him, but in fact never speaks of Epaminondas; actually he covers a much larger group of ideas.

This means that thoughts are subordinated to some sort of general idea, but they are not related and directed by any unifying concept of purpose or goal. It looks as though ideas of a certain category (in the first case pertaining to the Orient, in the second, to data of ancient history) were thrown into one pot, mixed, and subsequently picked out at random, and linked with each other by mere grammatical form or other auxiliary images.

8

Eugene Minkowski: *La Schizophrénie*

Reviewed by John Cutting

Eugene Minkowski was born in St. Petersburg, educated in Warsaw, and obtained his medical education in Munich. He moved to France in 1915. He served in the medical corps attached to the French army throughout that war and was awarded several medals for bravery. He then settled down in Paris, where he remained as a practicing psychiatrist until his death in 1972. He was never a professor, nor even a consultant in a prestigious psychiatric hospital, but he was able to command respect from all who knew him.

La Schizophrénie, subtitled *Psychopathologie des Schizoides et des Schizophrènes*, was first published in 1927 and a revised edition appeared in 1953. At the time of the original edition, Bleuler's book *Dementia Praecox oder Die Gruppe Schizophrenien* (1911) had not been translated into French and the Kraepelinian-Bleulerian notion of schizophrenia, encompassing virtually all forms of nonorganic, nonaffective psychosis, was not accepted by French psychiatrists. They subscribed to a more manifold classification of psychosis (see Pichot 1982) in which a variety of paranoid states were distinguished from hebephrenia or catatonia. It was essentially a pre-Kraepelinian classification which has persisted in attenuated form to this day.

Minkowski's aim in writing the book was to try and convince his compatriots that Bleuler was right in his overall scheme. However, Minkowski's intention was not merely to provide a synopsis of Bleuler's ideas for those compatriots who could not or would not read German. He had quite specific and unique views about the essential psychopathology of schizophrenia and it was these views which he wanted to put across, while acknowledging at the same time that "despite our divergence of opinion I am still a pupil of Bleuler. I walk in the furrow which he ploughed."

It is the nature of Minkowski's divergence from Bleuler which I want to address in this article. Until I translated one of the chapters of this book (Cutting and Shepherd 1987), Minkowski was virtually unknown to English-speaking psychiatrists. I have rarely seen any reference to his numerous publications. Laing referred to him in his *Divided Self* (1959) and he is sometimes regarded as an existential psychiatrist. However, Laing was much more influenced by Binswanger, who, in my view was more abstruse and quite wrong in his claims about the condition.

What was Minkowski's contribution to the psychopathology of schizophrenia, and why should we bother about it today? After all, what with magnetic resonance imaging, positron emission tomography, single photon emission computerized tomography, and so on, isn't the clue to the nature of schizophrenia just around the corner?

Minkowski's claim on our attention is simply that, in my opinion, he provides the most comprehensive psychological account of schizophrenia ever written. Moreover, although his scheme lacks any biological foundation, his observations are so accurate and profound that not only can they be immediately accommodated within current neuropsychological models of schizophrenia (see Cutting 1990) but they also illuminate and help to confirm neuropsychological theories of the mind that were formulated without reference to psychiatric disorders at all (e.g., Kosslyn 1987). He possessed a quite uncanny knack of appreciating how sterile the psychological theories of mind of his time were—associationism, psychoanalysis, Gestalt psychology. More striking, he had, in retrospect, the ability to leapfrog over the equally bankrupt theoretical schools that came later—behaviorism, cognitive psychology—and formulate a theory of mind that is in complete accord with current neuropsychological thinking. He was, in short, ahead of his time, but, more than this, he was the first person, to my knowledge, to appreciate that a correct understanding of the nature of schizophrenia can illuminate the nature of the normal mind. All commentators, before and since, have adopted a one-way approach, trying to explain schizophrenia in terms of some theory of normal functioning (which has invariably turned out to be false). All, that is, except Jaspers, who at least had the sense to appreciate that it was "un-understandable" according to any psychological theory or biological mechanism that he knew of. Minkowski saw schizophrenia as allowing insights into normality just as much as normality could illuminate the schizophrenic mind.

First, what did Minkowski reject of Bleuler's scheme? He disagreed with Bleuler on two points. He did not believe that a loosening of associations was an adequate explanation of the entire clinical picture, and he did not consider that emotional complexes had any specific bearing on the development of particular symptoms. It is not entirely clear why he rejected the "loosening of associations" theory, but it is probable that he simply saw his own theory as a better alternative. As we have seen, he was keen to promote the Bleulerian view of schizophrenia in France, referred to Bleuler at several points as his *maître*, and therefore probably did not want to discredit him too much. As for the influence of Freud and Jung on Bleuler's views, Minkowski is more definite. Although generally sympathetic to psychoanalytic views of normal human development, he could see no role for them in causing or even moulding any aspect of schizophrenia.

Minkowski's second acknowledged *maître* was Henri Bergson, the French philosopher whose most well known legacy is probably the concept of a stream of consciousness. A cursory acquaintance with Bergson's views on the nature of the mind is essential in order to understand Minkowski's ideas, because, if there was any theory of the normal mind which he tried to apply to schizophrenia, it was Bergson's.

Bergson believed that there were two forces that determined a normal person's mental life. One was intellect, the other instinct. These two forces were diametrically opposed to one another, in that each treated the world in completely different ways.

Intellect was the power of seeing things as separate from one another, frozen in time and separate in space—what he called the "cinematographic" representation of the world. Bergson was writing at the dawn of the silent film era, and it was not unnatural that he should have used this analogy. Another analogy for the property of intellect, used by Bertrand Russell in his commentary on Bergson (Russell 1946), is of a carver of chicken. The intellect carves up the chicken, but with "the peculiarity of imagining that the chicken always was the separate pieces into which the carving-knife divides it."

It is much harder to understand what Bergson meant by instinct. His analogies belong to the realm of poetry: it is a "cavalry charge," it is a "shell which bursts into parts," it is "life itself." Somehow, instinct represents the fluidity of things across time, blurring memory and perception. It also encompasses intuition or common sense.

The difficulty one has in grasping the essence of this worldview should not detract from its correctness, according to Bergson, because he wrote into it the proviso that intellect is inherently incapable of understanding the nature of instinct!

Minkowski certainly thought that he understood it and thought that the psychopathology of schizophrenia was a living illustration of its validity. Consider this account by one of his schizophrenic patients:

Everything is immobile around me. Things present themselves in isolation on their own, without evoking any response in me. Some things which ought to bring back a memory, or even conjure up a thought or give rise to a picture, remain isolated. They seem to be understood rather than experienced. It is as if a pantomime were going on around me, one which I cannot take part in. There is nothing wrong with my judgement but I seem to lack any instinctive feel for life. I can't change from one emotion to another; and how can you live like that? I've lost contact with all sorts of things. The value and complexity of things no longer exists. There's no link between them and me. Everything seems frozen around me. I have even less scope for manoeuvre with respect to the future than I have about the present or the past. There is, inside me, a sort of routine which makes me quite incapable of imagining the future. Any creative ability is completely abolished. I can only see the future as a repetition of the past.

Minkowski saw overwhelming evidence in this account for a deficiency in one of Bergson's two mental forces—instinct—with, at the same time, preservation of the other—intelligence. He called this deficiency "lack of vital contact with reality" (*perte du contact vital avec la rélité*). Certainly, the words used by his patient—"I seem to lack any instinctive feel for life," "Creative ability . . . abolished," "Things . . . understood rather than experienced"— fit nearly into Bergson's scheme.

The intellectual activities of the mind were not just preserved, according to Minkowski. Bereft of all those "factors relating to instinct," there was now a "compensatory hypertrophy of everything which pertained to intellect." So, for example, there could appear what Minkowski referred to as "morbid rationalisations and preoccupations with geometry" (*rationalisme et géométrisme morbides*). Consider these examples:

An obsession with pockets made its appearance. He wanted to know what difference there was between putting one's hands straight into a normal jacket pocket and putting them into the sloping pockets of an overcoat. . . . He also had the habit of standing in front of a mirror, legs together, trying to place his body symmetrically to achieve, as he said, "an absolutely perfect position."

During his military service he had once been given an injection. The idea had then grown on him that a piece of cotton wool had entered his body, along with the injected fluid. . . . The obsession grew and grew. It was no longer just cotton wool that had been inserted, it was the metal from the needle as well, the glass from the syringe; "each organ in my body was systematically affected, until my brain was involved."

I was tormented by the vaults in churches. I could not accept that all that weight could be supported by ribs, pillars and a keystone. I could not understand why it did not fall down. I could not see why the cement in the free stones did not crumble, because it must be a particularly vulnerable pressure point. I concluded that houses stayed up only through some terrestrial attraction. I came to doubt my own senses.

Minkowski regarded such preoccupations as evidence of an enhancement in these patients of all that Bergson's notion of intellect stood for.

His most ambitious proposal was then to list dichotomous properties of the mind or qualities of the world which the mind surveys, in each of which pair one element was atrophied, and the other hypertrophied.

Atrophied	Hypertrophied
Life	Planning
Instinct	Brain
Feeling	Thought
Faculty of penetration that synthesizes	Analysis of details
Impressions	Proof
Movement	Immobility
Events and people	Objects
Realization	Representation
Time	Space
Succession	Extension
End	Means

There are other elements to his theory which can only be touched on here. One is his discussion of autistic thinking. He notes that Bleuler revised his own ideas on this in 1921 by proposing that the term *dereirendes Denken* ("thinking that takes no account of reality or deviates from it") should replace *autistisches Denken*. This is closer to his own view of schizophrenia as primarily a mind turned away from reality rather than a mind primarily turned in on itself. Another profound insight is his introduction of the concept of "a pragmatic deficit" (*démence pragmatique, déficit pragmatique*) as central to schizophrenia. Not only does it show that he appreciates the difference between the intellectual deterioration of say, Alzheimer's disease and the mental deterioration in schizophrenia, but his very use of the word pragmatic antedates by decades the "discovery" of pragmatic language by linguists in the 1950s.

> A schizophrenic knows the date but this knowledge has no precise meaning for him. He can't use it in a way which is appropriate to the circumstances. The pragmatic factor of things is affected from a very early stage.

Another concern of his is the relationship between schizoid personality and schizophrenia itself. He regards the former as a *forme fruste* of the latter, in which the atrophy of instinct and hypertrophy of intellect are slight, thus allowing a relatively normal life.

I hope I have been able to give a flavor of Minkowski's ideas. The curious thing to me is why he has been neglected, certainly in the English-speaking world. Perhaps it is a consequence of the general low esteem in which psychopathology has been held since the last war. Perhaps it is the suspicion aroused by the irrationalism and poetic imagery of Bergson's philosophy that inspired him. Most likely of all, it is the fact that it is in French, and the average professional man or woman in Britain and the United States now no longer reads foreign languages.

What of the current value of Minkowski's scheme, touched upon earlier? For me, it is correct at three levels.

First, it provides convincing account of the worldview of a schizophrenia. It certainly accords well with my own records of their experience, and illuminates many observations that I had thought at the time were trivial. For example, one of my patients had spent all his days for several years before his illness was diagnosed and treated cutting out cardboard geometrical shapes of all types. After three weeks on neuroleptics this behavior completely disappeared. This was clearly an example of a morbid preoccupation with geometry.

Second, Minkowski's scheme of atrophy of certain mental functions and a compensatory hypertrophy of contrasting functions is remarkably similar to the particular pattern of deficient and overactive mental systems that I believe is the critical psychological substrate to the condition, explicable in terms of right-hemisphere dysfunction (see Cutting 1990). If we consider that it was not until the 1940s that any specific functions at all were attributed to the right hemisphere, Minkowski's prescience on this matter is all the more astounding.

Finally, his and Bergson's notion of the normal state of affairs as consisting of two opposing forces—irrational and rational—is, in my view, quite correct. This, of course, is also a core concept in psychoanalytic theory. However, the particular interaction that Minkowski and Bergson proposed as existing *between* the rational and irrational parts of the mind is, in my opinion, much superior to that formulated by Freud. The rational mind, in the former scheme, has *no* way of knowing the workings of the irrational part. No amount of dream interpretation, analysis of slips of the tongue, or years on the couch will uncover its secrets. It may set up hypotheses, but these will, except by chance, be specious.

REFERENCES

Bleuler, E. (1911). *Dementia praecox oder die Gruppe Schizophrenien.* Trans. J. Zinkin. New York: International Universities Press, 1950.
———— (1921). *Naturgeschichte der Seele und ihres Bewusstwerdens.* Berlin: Julius Springer.

Cutting, J. (1990). *The Right Cerebral Hemisphere and Psychiatric Disorders*. Oxford: Oxford University Press.

Cutting, J. and Shepherd, M. (1987). *The Clinical Roots of the Schizophrenia Concept*. Cambridge, England: Cambridge University Press.

Kosslyn, S. M. (1987). Seeing and imagining in the cerebral hemispheres. *Psychological Review* 94: 148–175.

Laing, R. D. (1959). *The Divided Self*. London: Tavistock.

Pichot, P. (1982). The diagnosis and classification of mental disorders in French-speaking countries: background, current views and comparison with other nomenclatures. *Psychological Medicine* 12: 475–492.

Russell, B. (1946). *History of Western Philosophy*. London: George Allen & Unwin.

Selections from
La Schizophrénie
by Eugene Minkowski

All these disorders seem to converge on a single and unique notion, that of *loss of vital contact with reality*.

Vital contact with reality appears to be linked with the irrational factors in life. The ordinary concepts elaborated by physiology and psychology, such as excitation, sensation, reflexes and motor reactions, continue in parallel, largely unnoticed. The blind, the mutilated and the paralysed may be able to live in even more intimate contact with their environment than individuals whose sight is intact and whose limbs are whole; schizophrenics, on the other hand, can lose this contact even with an intact sensory-motor apparatus, memory or intelligence. The vital contact with reality is in touch with the depths, with the very essence of our personality, in which it links with the world around us. And this world is not just a collection of external stimuli, of atoms, forces and energy. It is a moving stream which envelops us at all points and constitutes the milieu without which we would not know how to live. 'Events' emerge from this like islets; they penetrate the personality by disturbing its most intimate parts. And then, by making these events part of its own make-up, our personality puts its own stamp on them, not by muscular contractions but through action, feelings, joy and tears. In this way there is established that marvellous harmony between ourselves and reality, a harmony that allows us to follow the progress of the world while at the same time safeguarding the notion of our own life.

These considerations lead one to conclude that vital contact with reality concerns the intimate dynamism of our life. We can never achieve this through the rigid concepts of spatial thought. Metaphors, not definitions, hold pride of place in this sphere of our life. Only they can impart some clarity to the notion of vital contact with reality.

This notion is not new. In his theory of psychasthenia Janet talks at length about the reality function. This idea, although not quite the same as ours, has many points in common with it. And the fact that two different paths lead in the same direction suggests that we are dealing with real and important matters which are currently 'in the air'.

The notion of a vital contact with reality, and the interpretation of schizophrenia in terms of a loss of this contact, is both simple and plausible. The newcomer to psychiatry can pick it up quickly and use it without difficulty. I am tempted to say that the notion follows on naturally from the evolution of the concept of dementia praecox.

. . . First, let us compare, in this respect, the two major mental processes which psychopathology has so far separated—schizophrenia and intellectual impairment. Most writers in recent times have insisted on a fundamental difference between these two. Nonetheless, it is not easy to say precisely in what this difference consists. We can say with some certainty that intellectual impairment affects judgement and memory. But there is no such certainty about the schizophrenic deficit. The term 'dementia' provides a very poor description of its essential nature.

To quote Bleuler: 'In schizophrenia, even when well-advanced, all the simple mental functions, as far as we know, are intact. In particular, memory, unlike the case in true dementia, is unaffected . . . One may find surprisingly that under an apparent envelope of dementia the intelligence is much less affected than one might imagine, as if it were only asleep'. Or, as Chaslin noted: 'It is as if in discordant insanity (schizophrenia) the symptoms resemble those of true dementia. The cold delirious incoherence, the indifference, the bizarre acts, the complete cessation of intellectual activity and its substitution by behavior of an inferior order, the stupor and bizarre postures, and the incoherent actions all suggest this. Despite the symptomatology, however, there is rarely any sign of true intellectual impairment, such as loss of memory or errors of judgement . . . In contrast to genuine organic dementia, where the intellectual functioning is actually worse than it appears at first sight, in the discordant form of insanity nothing seems to have been irretrievably lost and only a little effort seems to be required to revive the cerebral activity'.

What, then, is lacking in schizophrenia? And what is the key to the difference between it and true dementia? It is this very difference which we will try to uncover by making use of the opposition of intelligence and instinct which we discussed earlier. As well as noting the differences in psychological *deficits* between these two conditions we shall also draw attention to differences in *intact functioning* between them.

We will begin the study of the two processes by comparing the extreme degrees of deterioration which can occur in each.

We have chosen general paralysis of the insane as a good example of intellectual impairment. For our purpose this condition has the advantage that it usually affects individuals in the prime of life. The intellectual impairment is not then complicated by other factors, such as the physiological consequences of old age, which affects senile dementia. It exists, therefore, in a relatively pure state.

If I ask someone with general paralysis: 'Where are you?' he will reply: 'Here.' Lest he is only responding in a purely verbal and automatic way, I insist: 'But where is here?' The patient taps his foot to indicate the place where he is, or points to it with his finger, or even demonstrates the room with a gesture. 'But here', he says to us, apparently surprised and annoyed by our insistence on the matter.

There is no question here of some simple semi-automatic response. This type of reply is found surprisingly often in these patients.

The schizophrenic, on the other hand, in reply to the same question, will give the name of the place quite correctly. But he will often say that, although he *knows* where he is, he does not *feel* as if he is in that place, or that he does not feel as if he is in his body. The term 'I exist' has no real meaning for him.

Two different types of factor are involved in our spatial orientation. There are those static factors concerned with the appreciation of how objects relate to one another in a geometrical space where everything is immobile, relative and reversible. But in fact we *live* in space, and we are always aware of the notion: 'I am here at this instant'. Under normal circumstances, therefore, our spatial concepts must accommodate this awareness. Our knowledge of things and our memory images come to be grouped around the notion of 'I am here at this instant'. This allows us to tell in any set of conditions where we are: in Paris, for example, or in Finland, or at our desk.

In patients with general paralysis, the static factors that I discussed earlier, the knowledge of things and memory, are impaired. Such patients are disorientated in space, in the usual sense of the word. Despite this, the structure of their notion of themselves as being 'me in this place' remains intact and active. Schizophrenics, by contrast, know where they are, but their notion of 'me in this place' has no longer its usual quality and finally breaks down.

At a less advanced stage of general paralysis we encounter reactions which are more complex, but whose general character is the same. To the question: 'Where do you come from?' the patient will reply: 'From over there, where I was before'. He is clearly disorientated in space, and unable to name the place where he came from. Nonetheless, the internal representation of a change in place—place X before and place Y now—remains intact.

The following statements belong to the same category:

Q. 'Where are you?'   A. 'Here where I was washing myself
                                     this morning' or 'Here where I have
                                     been for some time now'.
Q. 'What is this building?'   A. 'It is the building where I have been
                                     put'.
Q. 'Who is this gentleman?'   A. 'He is someone who is here'.
Q. 'What are you doing?'   A. 'At the moment I am staying
                                     here'.

If we put someone with general paralysis in front of a mirror and ask: 'Whom can you see in there?' he will reply: 'Me'. But if we continue: 'But who is me?' he will not give his name or his job. This sort of reply is much less common in schizophrenics, even in states of deterioration. They will reply: 'Me' and then 'my activity, my personality', or 'It is energy', or, abandoning their delusions, simply state 'Me, the son of Claude Farrère'. One of our patients replied: 'I know who it is' but then admitted that she no longer experienced it in the same way: 'I know who it is, but this is merely an observation, there is nothing inside; it's a queer face; it has a fixed look, oblique and cold'.

The patient with general paralysis, even in the final stages of mental deterioration, retains some sense of awareness of self. The schizophrenic, on the other hand, does not, and is always affected by a sense of depersonalisation.

A sort of commonsense and a knowledge of where to find things is also retained in general paralysis. One such patient, when asked the date, picked up a newspaper. Another very demented patient on being asked 'What day is it?' replied: 'I have no means of knowing'. Another, asked to give his date of birth, replied: 'I can't say; I haven't got my wedding ring'. On his wedding ring he would not find his date of birth but the date of his marriage [French tradition, Tr.] but that is not the point; he knew that there are ways of compensating for a failing memory and instinctively used them.

The behavior of a schizophrenic is quite different. He usually knows the date, but the knowledge has no precise meaning for him; he cannot use it in a fashion appropriate to his circumstances. The *pragmatic* use of things is affected early in this condition.

A patient with general paralysis, in a state of profound dementia was asked: 'What are you doing?' He replied: 'I am waiting for something to happen and making plans'. Another patient, although so deteriorated that he could no longer speak, still noticed that I had left my hat in his room one day and laughed about it. For the schizophrenic such events or manoeuvres would pass him by.

These various comparisons establish what is a fundamental difference between the intellectual impairment in general paralysis and schizophrenic deterioration. We must not confuse them. In the former case the deficit is in static mental functions; in the latter dynamic factors bear the brunt of the morbid process.

9

John Bowlby:
Child Care and the Growth of Love

Reviewed by Ann Gath

I now have two copies of this book: one bought in the first year of publication, the year of my matriculation at Oxford; and the second bought thirty-five years later, for the purpose of this review. It reports a study that was a major landmark, crossing the frontiers between the professions and disciplines concerned with child development and practical child care as well as psychoanalytical theory and practice. An early impression on this second reading was the appreciation of how much has happened in the intervening years. The changes are most marked in children's wards in hospitals where parents are welcomed throughout the day and often allowed to stay overnight. In the maternity wards, much emphasis is put on not just new mothers, but new fathers, being with their babies and enjoying the process of making friends with each other. The work started by Bowlby in looking at the needs of a young child for a close, loving relationship with the mother or best substitute is continued every day in innumerable case conferences and in the Family Division of the High Court.

Much, too, has happened in child psychiatry. Family therapy, now used almost to the exclusion of all other therapeutic techniques in child guidance clinics, did not then exist. A huge amount of research has followed the first appearance of this book. Discussion was plentiful, and not without controversy, as in Michael Rutter's book *Maternal Deprivation Revisited*. This book tackled the scientific evidence behind Bowlby's statements, and no attempt will be made now to repeat or add to that argument.

The changes in pediatric wards include, however, not just a greater appreciation of the needs of young children, for which Bowlby must most certainly be thanked, but the almost complete disappearance of tuberculosis and poliomyelitis which has made long stays in children's hospital wards rare.

A new look at Bowlby's original work is timely. Despite the greater interest in the mutual needs of mothers and babies, there still remain many problems, such as the rarity of successful breast-feeding in women in social classes IV and V. At times too many children seem to be taken into care on flimsy grounds, and yet there are the painful enquiries into the tragic consequences of decisions made by social workers trying to keep the family together at all cost.

Reading this book again with hindsight, there are a number of statements that are misleading or even dangerously wrong in 1988 (e.g., "Mercifully, physical cruelty is rare"). Should not the edition now selling well in the shops with its 1980s cover have something to indicate that it is thirty-five years old, that the "modern" research added in the second edition is twenty-four years old, and that much has been learned since?

A whole chapter is devoted to illegitimate children. Since that time, the Pill made its debut and abortion has become legalized. Yet still there are just as many illegitimate children. A major change is that few are nowadays available for adoption, and the emphasis has passed onto the permanent care in families of children who are handicapped, of different ethnic background, or who have had years of ill treatment or deprivation. The psychiatric centres have not found any more effective remedies than the provision of "good enough" substitute parents. The development of adoption agencies, finally leading to the formation of the British Association for Adoption and Fostering, has been a major source of encouragement of research and new ways of caring for children previously thought unadoptable.

What has happened to the "preventive mental hygiene," as described here? There is little evidence that children are less emotionally disturbed or better behaved. Is there really any evidence that the generation left to cry as advocated by Truby King, the guru of 1930s mothers, have been failures as parents? That same generation of mothers were also prevented from intimate contact with their own babies, as Sister would hand them over neatly wrapped for feeding and remove them again afterwards, leaving the mother sadly to have to take Sister's word for it that the bundle really was a boy. Were these babies really heading for emotional disaster as claimed by one media-loving pediatrician? Certainly a lot of women were made unhappy by the thought that they had missed out on bonding and thus jeopardized their child's entire life. The references to the working mother can still cause pain, despite the reassuring findings of more recent research.

Looking back over thirty-five years one can appreciate how, with the publication of Bowlby's book, thinking about and working with children took a dramatic change of direction. How few of us will have any of our work remembered in 2013?

Selections from
Child Care and the Growth of Love by John Bowlby

In the first place, there is abundant evidence that deprivation can have adverse effects on the development of children (*a*) during the period of separation; (*b*) during the period immediately after restoration to maternal care; and (*c*) in at least a small proportion of cases permanently. The fact that some children seem to escape is of no consequence. The same is true if children drink tubercle-infected milk or are exposed to the virus of infantile paralysis. In both these cases a sufficient proportion of children is so severely damaged for no one to dream of intentionally exposing a child to such hazards. Deprivation of maternal care in early childhood is a danger of the same class.

Most of the evidence in respect of long-term effects refers to certain very grave disturbances following severe deprivation; it is easiest to work from these established connexions to those which are less well understood. The evidence suggests that three somewhat different experiences can each produce the "affectionless" and delinquent character in some children:

(*a*) Lack of any opportunity for forming an attachment to a mother-figure during the first three years.

(*b*) Deprivation for a limited period – at least three months and probably more than six – during the first three or four years.

(*c*) Changes from one mother-figure to another during the same period.

Though the general results of these different experiences appear the same, it seems probable that closer study will reveal differences.

Though it may be true, as some workers believe, that children placed in institutions for short periods after the age of about two do not develop affectionless and isolated characters, we know of enough cases where children who have been handed on from one mother-figure to another during the third and fourth years have developed very antisocial characters and have been unable to make satisfactory relations with other people to make it clear that very evil results may follow even at this age. Naturally, the effects on personality development at any given age will depend on the exact nature of the experience to which the child is submitted, information about which is all too frequently missing from records. Indeed, one of the great shortcomings of present evidence is a lack of detail and precision on this point.

Though all workers on the subject are now agreed that the first year of life is of vital importance, there is at present some debate regarding the age at which deprivation has the most evil consequences. Dr. Bowlby, after reviewing his cases, noted that the separations which appeared to do harm had all occurred after the age of six months and in a majority after that of twelve months, from which he was inclined to conclude that separations and deprivations in the first six months of life were less important for the child's welfare than later ones. This has also been the view of Miss Anna Freud. It has, however, been called in question by others who attach especial importance to the first half year. Whatever the outcome of this debate, the study of Dr. Goldfarb, in which he examines the social adjustment of adolescents in relation to the age at which they were admitted to the institution, points unmistakably to the special danger in which the child stands during the first year in comparison with later ones. Other American references to children in whom the deprivation was limited to the first year, and who none the less showed retardation and personality distortion, provide further evidence regarding the first year as a whole, though they do not contribute to the debate regarding the baby's sensitiveness during the first half of it in particular.

For the present, therefore, it may be recorded that deprivation occurring in the second half of the first year of life is agreed by all students of the subject to be of great significance and that many believe this to be true also of deprivation occurring in the first half, especially from three to six months. The balance of opinion, indeed, is that considerable damage to mental health can be done by deprivation in these months, a view which is unquestionably supported by the direct observations, already described, of the immediately harmful effects of deprivation on babies of this age.

The proper care of children deprived of a normal home life can now be seen to be not merely an act of common humanity, but to be essential for the mental and social welfare of a community. For, when their care is neglected, as still happens in every country of the Western world today, they grow up to reproduce themselves. Deprived children, whether in their own homes or out of them, are the source of social infection as real and serious as are carriers of diphtheria and typhoid. And, just as preventive measures have reduced these diseases to negligible proportions, so can determined action greatly reduce the number of deprived children in our midst and the growth of adults liable to produce more of them.

10

W. Mayer-Gross, E. Slater, and M. Roth:
Clinical Psychiatry

Reviewed by Kenneth Davison

At first sight these three authors may seem an unlikely trio, but their disparate experience and personalities proved to be complementary and the end product of their labors was a coherent and harmonious whole.

Willi Mayer-Gross (1889–1961) had been a professor in Heidelberg, but came to Britain in 1933, one of several eminent continental refugees who enriched the British psychiatric scene before and after World War II. He had been a pupil of Kraepelin, Jaspers, and Gruhle, and was a leading exponent of phenomenology, the exact study and precise description of psychic events. Much of the descriptive material in the book (particularly of the psychoses), which was such an outstanding feature, emanated from Mayer-Gross but with his English text edited by Slater.

Eliot Slater (1904–1984) was a commanding figure, both physically and intellectually. His main research interest was psychiatric genetics, although he also made important contributions in neuropsychiatry and the neuroses. He first met Mayer-Gross while training in genetics in Germany, and shared his phenomenological approach and Kraepelinian stance. His style of writing was an extraordinary amalgam of richness, robustness and precision. Slater was responsible for all the genetic sections and played the major role in the writing of the controversial Introduction, with its polemical critique of psychoanalysis.

Martin Roth (b. 1917) trained initially in neurology, but developed an interest in psychiatry partly through the influence of his chief, Russell (later Lord) Brain. He attracted the attention of Slater, who was impressed by his 1948 publication in Brain on hereditary ataxia. Shortly afterwards he went to work with Mayer-Gross at the Crichton Royal Hospital, Dumfries. Mayer-Gross was invited to write a review of old age psychiatry for the 1950 *Recent Advances* series but, finding himself fully occupied in research and lecturing, he asked Roth to take on the task in his stead (from little acorns . . .). As a result, Roth was invited to write the chapter in *Clinical Psychiatry* on "Mental Disorder in Trauma, Infection and Tumor of the Brain" and "Aging and the Mental Diseases of the Aged." In addition, he contributed to the critique of psychoanalysis, and added the recommended "multi-[dimensional approach," part of the chapter on "The Epilepsies]," and the sections on anorexia nervosa, anxiety, and hypochondriasis in Chapter 4. The whole text was, however, seen and discussed by all three authors. Roth's command of language equaled that of Slater but with a style of distinctive elegance. He was the great drawer together of threads from many sources into a rich tapestry of original thinking, best exemplified in the 1954 edition by the early exposition of his then revolutionary but now commonplace separation on prognostic grounds of the different syndromes of old-age mental disorder.

The introduction, which firmly wedded psychiatry to medicine and expressed skepticism about the relevance of sociology and anthropology, aroused most controversy and not a little opposition by its critiques of contemporary schools of psychiatry, particularly those of Freud and Meyer. Comments like "support for the [Freudian] theory is won, not by producing evidence in its favour but by enlarging the circle of those who believed in it," and "Meyer's enthusiasm in the fight against Kraepelinian classification led him to throw out the baby with the bath water," were not intended to be emollient, nor were they perceived as such. To some they were a clarion call to a more scientific psychiatry, to others an unbalanced overreaction. As one reviewer remarked, the authors could not be accused of fence sitting.

There were a number of unusual features for a book of the time, including detailed case-taking schemata for ordinary psychiatric, uncooperative or stuporose, and organic patients, chapters on "Mental Deficiency," "Child Psychiatry," and "Administrative and Legal Psychiatry" (both at home and abroad), and an extensive bibliography. Chapters on "Symptomatic Psychoses" and "Chemical Intoxications and Addictions," including reference to amphetamine, morphine, cannabis, and mescaline, have a prophetic ring.

The 1954 edition is also of interest as a historical document, providing a glimpse of the practice of psychiatry before the psychopharmacological revolution. Recommended treatments now seem crude and often naive.

Thus, paranoid reactions were treated with either superficial psychotherapy or leucotomy, and depression was treated with ECT or awaited spontaneous remission. Agitation or insomnia might respond to Tinct opii. The conventional treatments for schizophrenia of insulin coma, ECT, and leucotomy were described, but the authors were clearly not happy with them, for insulin coma was called "crude and empirical" and, referring to leucotomy, they remarked "there is no case for a wholesale handing over of chronic schizophrenics to the knife of the surgeon." The 1960 edition brought the first mention of the use of neuroleptic and antidepressant drugs and lithium, and by the 1969 edition treatments of all kinds had become more numerous and sophisticated.

Successive editions saw also a toning down of the anti-Freudian polemic of the 1954 edition, and by 1969 some value was allowed to Freud's contributions in modern psychiatry. By 1969 the Schneiderian view of neuroses as developments from personality deviations, originally propounded by Mayer-Gross, was modified to a more syndrome-based approach at the hands of Roth. He also revised the section on paranoid psychosis, extended considerably Mayer-Gross's chapter on "Alcoholism, Drug Addiction and Other Intoxications," and added chapters on "Exogenous Reactions and Symptomatic Schizophrenias" and "Social Psychiatry."

It is difficult for young psychiatrists of today to appreciate the impact this novel, stylishly written textbook had on those, like myself, who were taking their first faltering steps in psychiatry in the 1950s. For the first time the written text seemed to chime with everyday clinical experience. The authors' views that psychiatry was afflicted by sectarianism and unwarranted attempts to expand its scope and was in danger of becoming isolated from medicine, and their prescription of a return to the bedside and the discipline of clinical observation, struck a chord in many contemporary seekers after psychiatric truth.

Translated into many languages, its impact overseas was no less profound. It brought succor to the beleaguered minority of biological psychiatrists in the United States, and prominent figures such as Robins, Guze, Klerman, and Spitzer have acknowledged their indebtedness. Indeed, a connection can be traced from the book's multidimensional approach to the development of modern operational definitions of mental disorder, such as the Research Diagnostic Criteria and DSM-III.

For over two decades the book was, for many, the psychiatric bible, and even today it has not lost its value as an authoritative reference work, for it is still one of the most frequently cited textbooks in scientific papers. The high esteem in which it was held is conveyed by E. W. Anderson's review of the 1969 edition: "So much praise has been justly accorded this book that there is little the reviewer can add. This is the most outstanding textbook of psychiatry in English, certainly the reviewer knows of no other English work of the kind to rank with it. The weight of scholarship behind it is in itself impressive. It may be said fairly that the book is an outstanding contribution to British psychiatry."

Dare we hope for a fourth edition? Rumor has it . . .

Selections from
Clinical Psychiatry
by W. Mayer-Gross, E. Slater,
and M. Roth

THE FOUNDATIONS OF PSYCHIATRY
(1954 EDITION)

This book is based on the conviction of the authors that the foundations of psychiatry have to be laid on the ground of the natural sciences. In it the attempt is made to apply the methods and the resources of a scientific approach to the problems of clinical psychiatry. It is obvious that in the present stage of development of our specialty such a plan can only be carried out in a partial way, and that much of our clinical knowledge today belongs more to medical art than to science. Nevertheless we have kept to this aim because we believe that it is only from an organic connexion between the natural sciences, biology, medicine and psychiatry, and from the arduous but reliable scientific methods of investigation and discussion that lasting advances can be made.

It seems necessary to make such a statement at the outset, because now, as so frequently during the hundred years of its existence, psychiatry is in danger of losing its connexion with the body of medicine. These recurrent crises can be traced to two main causes: to the influence of psychiatric practice on the knowledge and the attitude of psychiatrists, and to the peculiar position of psychiatry between medicine and neurology on the one side and philosophy on the other.

The primary concern of the practising psychiatrist, within the walls of an institution or at large, is to treat and to help patients. He must try to do this even where knowledge is inadequate and the results of past research provide him with no or an insecure foundation. He will then turn to any tool to hand. When, for instance, the discoveries in cerebral anatomy and pathology of the eighties and nineties of the last century proved of little help in the understanding of mental patients, and when at the same time

Kraepelin's nosological classification was of little use when it came to their treatment, it was natural for psychiatrists to be allured by the psychopathological theories of Freud, which promised an explanation of the whole before the details had been elaborated. Similar manifestations of impatience, attempted short cuts and deviations from the slow advance of science, have happened before and happen now. Whenever a new branch of scientific activity appears with some relevance to human behaviour, or whenever a new philosophical movement meets with a popular response, psychiatrists seize upon it and try out its implications in their own field. This also is a way of breaking new ground, which must, however, if it is to bear fruit, be worked over by the methods of science.

This instability in the attitude of psychiatrists is made all the easier by the subjectivity and the lack of precision of psychological data. Mental events can only be described in words which are themselves often open to varied interpretations. Many terms used in psychiatry are taken from everyday language and are not clearly defined. Special terms, on the other hand, have been taken over from psychiatry into ordinary speech, so that their meaning has been watered down and become ambiguous. Much of the psychiatric literature of today owes its existence to the possibility of playing with words and concepts; and the scientific worker in psychiatry must constantly bear in mind the risks of vagueness and verbosity.

The harm that these tendencies have done and may yet do to the psychiatrist and to his reputation are not to be minimized; strict attention to scientific standards in clinical work is needed now more than ever. It is well to remember that as recently as 150 years ago the treatment of mental aberrations, excepting the care of the dangerous psychotic, was regarded as the province of the philosopher and the theologian. In this country before the First World War, whoever took up psychiatry was considered a failure, a man unable to make his way in medicine or surgery. Psychotherapy was regarded as identical with charlatanry, and the institutional psychiatrist as only fitted to act as society's custodian of its degenerate or dangerous members.

That this has now changed, and that the psychiatrist is recognized as a physician of standing as well as a counsellor in social problems of general interest, is due to the cautious industry of responsible research workers and to the impartial collection of careful clinical observations. With this in mind the following critical review of present-day tendencies in psychiatry should be read.

Although practising psychiatrists of all schools share much in common, there is rather too much dissension for the present state of psychiatry to be regarded as entirely healthy. Wide differences about fundamental issues exist between what is thought and taught in different centres. These differences inspire attitudes of dogmatism, and there is not the open-mindedness there should be. Rapid advances are being made, but are judged or even ignored on the basis of preconceptions. The solid acquisitions of knowledge from the past, where they conflict with current modes of thought, are not being reformulated where necessary, but are being neglected and even forgotten. Psychiatry is not only being split into a number of schools, but is also, which is more regrettable, being divorced from the parent science of medicine. There are indeed psychiatrists who so far from regretting the split, clear-sightedly do what they can to widen it. Growth in every field, in the number of practising psychiatrists, in the amount of time given to psychiatric teaching of undergraduate and postgraduate students, in the claims made by psychiatrists to be heard in their own and in related fields, in public esteem and support, has led to a corresponding decrease of self-criticism. The normal progress of scientific advance, by which facts are first accumulated and confirmed, and then have fitted to them a theory whose critical implications are subjected to test, has been interrupted by a flight into the air. Theoretical exposition follows theoretical exposition in ever-growing complexity, and the need constantly to check theory by seeking at every point for new facts is forgotten.

The natural corrective to these unhealthy tendencies is supplied by a return to the beside, and to the discipline of clinical observation. The authors believe that, when it leaves the study of the sick patient, psychiatry ceases to be psychiatry.

PSYCHOANALYSIS (1969 EDITION)

The modern adherent of the Freudian psychoanalytic school does not accept the whole of Freud's teaching as unalterable dogma. As psychoanalytic theory changes and evolves, it may well be that a rapprochement between this and the other schools will become possible. Freud has done more than any other thinker to teach psychiatrists to look at the development of the personality historically. To this extent psychoanalytic teaching has come to stay; it has been partly integrated into psychiatric practice and has formed the starting point of a certain amount of research. However, if the remaining distance is to be narrowed, some further changes in attitudes will be essential. It must be realized that, despite its claim of comprehensiveness, the whole of the existing body of doctrine is inadequate to cover all forms of human behaviour; that psychological processes are manifestations of physiological ones in another dimension; that any kind of pathology, or disease process, introduces new factors of which not even the rudiments may be seen in the normal. On the methodological side, room must be made for scepticism, for the experimental test, and for the abandonment of what has proved fallacious. It is time that the subject should be taught as any other subject, to be accepted or doubted by the student in the light of his reason. It would be best to abandon altogether that process of indoctrination which is called a teaching analysis. There is but one truth; and in our asymptotic approach towards it the worker in the field of human psychology has to submit himself to the same disciplines as obtain in every other science. [p. 20]

THE RELATIONSHIP BETWEEN FUNCTIONAL AND ORGANIC MENTAL DISEASE IN OLD AGE (1960 EDITION)

The view that most cases of mental disorder commencing in old age with predominantly affective, paraphrenic and delirious symptoms evolve towards an organic dementia cannot be sustained. The differences in clinical picture which separate these disorders from each other and from senile and arteriosclerotic psychoses are matched by an unlikeness in course and outcome and in psychological performance among other characteristics. The delirious states are organic in aetiology though their natural history is that of the symptomatic psychoses rather than that of the irreversible cerebral degenerations. But the remaining disorders are divided by differences in prognosis into two sharply defined groups. On the one hand there are senile and arteriosclerotic psychoses with a mortality of 70–80% two years after admission; on the other hand are the affective and paranoid psychoses with a death rate of 10–25% after two years. The difference in clinical picture between the affective and paraphrenic psychoses is sharp; that between the two former groups much less so.

Evidently we are dealing in these two groups with diseases dissimilar in aetiology. The possibility that organic lesions play some part in the causation of affective disorder and paraphrenia in old age cannot be excluded, but it is much more likely that they have no more of a gross cerebral pathology than the diseases so named in earlier life.

If the mental diseases of old age can, in fact, be grouped into entities as clearly defined as those of earlier ages, the relationship between the organic and functional psychoses assumes a much more consistent pattern than hitherto. As in old age, so at all times of life there is a margin of overlap between the "functional" and "organic" types of mental illness. In most instances this is sufficiently small to be accounted for in terms of chance association. But there are some apparent exceptions. In arteriosclerotic psychosis, for example, sustained depressive symptoms probably occur rather more often than they should on chance expectation alone.

But the psychiatrist tends to see a selected population in which those with prominent psychiatric symptoms are likely to be over-represented. It would, moreover, be reasonable to expect that when cerebral disease occurs in potential manic depressives, for example, the manifestation rate of about one in three or four characteristic of the gene that is the specific cause of the disease, might be increased. Although the cerebral disease would clearly play a small part in the causation of the mixed states with both organic and endogenous depressive features that resulted, the clinical picture in such cases could be regarded as the expression of two relatively distinct processes. Whether the true incidence of depressive and manic pictures in cerebrovascular disease can be fully accounted for by such considerations remains uncertain, but it seems unlikely on the evidence available that cerebral arteriosclerosis can play more than a small part in the aetiology of affective psychoses in old age. Nor is it necessary in the case of mental disorders of senescence to think in terms of some special relationship between cerebral disease and the clinical features we associate with the "functional psychoses."

SOCIAL PSYCHIATRY—PREVENTION (1969 EDITION)

The most essential feature of any psychiatric service is that the benefit it confers should outweigh any harm or damage that it does. Since the effects of programmes of primary prevention are at present quite unknown the authors believe that in the list of priorities secondary and tertiary prevention should come before primary prevention. This means the provision of services of excellent quality to ensure early diagnosis and treatment and promote effective rehabilitation. For the present, no country in the world disposes of an adequate service for therapy. Neither the resources available for such services nor their organization in integrated entities comes up to satisfactory standards even in highly developed countries.

But in most areas the primary need is for more research. If a psychiatrist permits uncritical enthusiasm for action in the community to outweigh all other considerations he runs other risks. If he is to advance knowledge he must remain acutely conscious of the extent of his ignorance. Once he convinces himself that he knows, he will learn nothing new.

11

Michael Balint:
The Doctor, His Patient
and the Illness

Reviewed by Patrick C. Pietroni

Remembering where you were when Jack Kennedy died has become a favorite question to ask of people of an age to remember that day in November 1963. For a certain generation of general practitioners, a not dissimilar question might be, "When did you first read *The Doctor, His Patient and the Illness?*" Balint's impact on general practice is remarkable and unquestioned. His book, first published in 1957, appears among the top ten, if not the top three, that all new entrants into general practice "must read." Yet the paradox is that few, if any, trainees will actually read his book, that Balint groups have a falling membership, that the Balint Society, founded after his death by a group of GPs, is on the periphery of modern general practice thinking, and that few if any permanent developments have come from his followers. Balint might well be excused if he paraphrased the quote attributed to Jung. "Thank God I'm Balint and not a Balintian."

THE CONTEXT

To appreciate Balint's work on general practice, it is important to set it in the context not only of the state of general practice and of psychoanalysis, but of much of Balint's own background and training. He was born in Budapest in 1896. His father was a GP, an often forgotten fact, and after completion of his own medical studies Balint trained in the Hungarian Institute of Psychoanalysis and was analyzed by Ferenczi. The Hungarian system of psychoanalytic training differed in one essential form from the practice traditionally adopted in Vienna and Berlin: the supervision of the candidate's first case, or cases, was carried out by the candidate's training analyst. Balint writes in the section on training, "In the Hungarian system the interrelation of the transference of the patient and the countertransference of his analyst is in the focus of attention right from the start and remains there. In the Berlin system the countertransference of the candidate to his patient is by tacit agreement not dealt with in supervision but is left to be worked through in his personal analysis." Balint brought his experience of the Hungarian system to England and experimented with it in part in the groups he developed for GPs.

Like many of his European colleagues, Balint left Europe just before the war and eventually settled in London, where he quickly obtained a consultant post both at University College Hospital and at the Tavistock Clinic. This was in the early 1950s; the National Health Service had been launched, and the separation of general practice from specialized medicine had become organized and institutionalized. General practice as a separate discipline did not exist in any fundamental form and, for many medical students, entering general practice was seen as a failure. They had fallen off the ladder: the Royal College of General Practitioners did not yet exist, and the medical establishment, in the form of Lord Moran, was actively derogatory of general practice. When the possibility of a separate College of General Practitioners was suggested, his famous remark, "Over my dead body," still rankles with many of the active GPs of that time. General practice had to wait till the early 1960s for its renaissance. The work of Michael Balint, and the publication of the book in 1957, were critical points in the emergence of this new discipline.

Psychoanalysis in the late 1940s and 1950s had itself emerged as a clinical entity in its own right, and the Tavistock Clinic had quickly become a center of national and international excellence. The scientific basis to this new form of treatment was, and still is, disputed, but it had gained a place within the public service sector, and under the leadership of Sutherland, psychoanalysts at the Tavistock were encouraged to explore how the theoretical insights derived from their work might be applied to individuals, groups and institutions not directly involved in the practice of psychoanalysis. It is against this background that Balint, together with his wife, Enid, started the research project at the Tavistock Clinic that was to lay the foundation for *The Doctor, His Patient and the Illness*.

THE WORK AND THE IDEAS

Michael and Enid Balint had already begun to apply that psychoanalytic experience to the training of social workers involved in marital work. In

1954 they "collected" a group of GPs to take part in research seminars. Initially this focused on the drugs usually prescribed by GPs. Balint soon realized that the most frequently prescribed drug was the doctor himself, and the seminars evolved into an exploration of "the doctor as a drug." Weekly meetings followed over a number of years, and transcripts were kept of the seminars. Doctors presented cases they encountered in their daily work, and together with the Balints explored and analyzed their patterns of work. As the seminars progressed it was possible to identify recurring problems, and Balint, in the introduction to the first edition of the book, defines it thus: "Why does it happen so often that in spite of earnest efforts on both sides, the relationship between patient and doctor is unsatisfactory and unhappy? What are the causes of this undesirable development and how can it be avoided?" The chapter headings of the book are in part the responses to this particular question. Phrases such as "the apostolic function," "collusion of anonimity," "underlying diagnosis," "ticket to the door," "dilution of responsibility," and "teacher–pupil relationship" are all examples of the immense creativity present in those original research seminars. These phrases have a simplicity and depth that ensures their immortality.

However, it was not long before the flaws began to appear. Balint's enthusiasm for the psychological took over and he could not avoid encouraging the participants to develop their psychotherapeutic skills. Understandably, the model offered was psychoanalytic and psychodynamic. Many GPs began seeing patients for one hour after a busy surgery, and rather than learning from the seminars about the limitations of the psychoanalytic model, they experienced all the problems of the untrained psychotherapist. Many had learned how to start, but few had understood the importance of when to stop, or indeed, how to stop. Thus the caricature of the Balint-trained doctor as a detective-inspector ferreting around for the culprit cause also became part of the mythology of Balint groups and is, unfortunately, still present today.

Balint failed to give due emphasis to physical factors in psychotherapy as well as psychoanalysis. His closest consideration of the body was when he underlined the importance of nonverbal behavior. He rightly challenged the "elimination of the cause by appropriate physical examination," but in so doing encouraged the mind–body split that plagues both the practice of psychoanalysis and medicine. Balint focused on the psychological aspects of general practice and helped to raise the doctors' awareness of the factors involved in the complex interactions occurring in their consulting rooms. As long as he remained in the role of anthropologist his contributions were, and are, of immense value. When he crossed the boundary and became a clinician and teacher, his interventions began to have an impact which he at times denied and at times decried. Several of the original group of Balint-trained doctors left general practice and took up psycho-therapy or psychoanalysis full time. Even though he saw this development as a failure of the group work, it became very difficult to stop the trend. For the next few years, Balint experimented with the notion of focal and brief psychotherapy, and it seemed that he was developing a model of psycho-therapy more suited to the needs of general practice. However, it became clear through the work of Malan and others that it required even greater skill and experience to make the appropriate assessment necessary for short-term work. In any case, what was described as short-term work involved thirty to forty one-hour sessions, a totally impractical option for GPs to consider seriously. Nevertheless, when Balint died in 1970, his impact on general practice was assured and the work he initiated was continued by a small but loyal group of disciples.

Balint's essential contribution to general practice was to use his psycho-analytic training and knowledge to describe, explore, and illuminate the nature of general practice. Instead of the "doctor as a drug" or the "doctor's feelings," read countertransference. Instead of the "presenting symptom as the ticket to see the doctor," read "unconscious motivation." He reminded doctors trained in the medical model that psychological prob-lems can often present as physical symptoms—not a new concept, but one that freed many practitioners from the limitations of their medical educa-tion. Balint challenged the notion of the objective scientific doctor standing or sitting at a distance from his patient. He demonstrated how not only treatment but the diagnosis is formed as a result of an interaction between doctor and patient. And finally, he provided a model for training doctors to develop their psychological skills within their consulting rooms. Like all pioneers, he overstated his case, but the caveats, doubts, and cautionary comments which are to be found in his writings have only partially been explored by the majority of his followers.

Following the work Balint did on brief psychotherapy, he undertook a research study on the use of repeat prescriptions in general practice. The results of this work were published after his death in a book entitled *Treatment or Diagnosis* (Balint 1970). Further books published by his colleagues—*Patient-Centered Medicine* (Hopkins 1972), *Six Minutes for the Patient* (Balint and Norell 1973). *The Human Face of Medicine* (Hopkins 1979), and *While I'm Here, Doctor* (Elder and Samuel 1987)—have attempted to develop the work undertaken by Balint in the 1950s. While the thrust of Balint's descriptive analyses of general practice consultations still stands the test of time, there has been a recognition that the caricature of the Balint-trained doctor as a detective-inspector is all too often an accurate description. Balint's concept of "the doctor as a drug" and the role of the doctors' emotions were probably his greatest gifts to general practice. However, there is a clear danger of confusing emotional curiosity with caring, and much of the criticism leveled at Balint stems from this misunderstanding. The more recent work described in the later work by his colleagues focuses on freeing the doctor from discovering *why* so that he can observe *how* the patient talks, thinks, feels, and behaves the way he does. The patient is given permission to complain about anything, and the doctor has to learn to bear the frustration, uncertainly, and helplessness that are inherent characteristics of the human condition. This is a far cry from the "long hour" and the "focal therapy" with the notion of "selective attention" and "selective neglect" that were the hallmarks of Balint's work in the 1950s and 1960s.

BALINT SEMINARS

The second major outcome of Balint's work, which is also well described in his original book, was the method of training. Balint recognized that to suggest that all doctors, let alone health-care workers, should have a personal analysis was not only totally impractical but also likely to be laughed at. Nevertheless, he realized that for GPs to work at a psychological level with their patients required "a limited though considerable change in the doctor's personality." This statement, like the concept of "the doctor as a drug," remains as a testament to Balint's courage and genius. Psychoanalysis had for many years recognized the importance of a personal analysis as part of the training necessary for a therapist. Balint attempted to borrow from psychoanalysis and adapt to the needs of general practice. The structure of the seminars involved a group of doctors meeting weekly where cases were presented. As Balint himself wrote: "Our chief aim was a reasonably thorough examination of the ever-changing doctor–patient relationship, i.e., the study of the pharmacology of the drug 'doctor.'" Balint discouraged any preparation or formal case presentation, and through his interventions would facilitate a frank account of the emotional aspect of the doctor–patient relationship. "The doctors tried hard to entice the psychiatrists into a teacher–pupil relationship but for many reasons it was thought advisable to resist this. What we aimed at was a free give-and-take atmosphere in which everyone could bring up his problems in the hope of getting some light on them from the experience of others."

In the second half of *The Doctor, His Patient and the Illness* Balint describes this method of training, and in a further book, *A Study of Doctors* (Balint 1966), he provides the evaluation of results in much greater detail. Balint groups have continued since their development in the late 1950s. However, outside the Tavistock Clinic they have not taken root with any great success and attempts to introduce similar methods of training for medical students and general practice trainees have largely been unsuccessful. Part of the reason for this is that the leaders of Balint groups may not be explicit about their objectives. Thus members often attend with different expectations from those of the leaders and are put on the defensive: This is especially so if the leaders' expectations are kept covert. Whatever the leaders' or members' expectations may be, during the course of such groups both soon recognize that the boundary between personal issues and professional concerns is difficult to maintain. As doctors reveal information concerning their approach to their patients, they inevitably reveal and face their own values, prejudices, and belief systems. This may lead to an uncomfortable realization that the defense systems they choose to adopt in their professional lives are similar to those in their personal lives. For some, this is a new and public discovery that is nevertheless welcomed. For others it can come as an unwelcome and painful shock. Balint was aware of this problem from the outset, but was determinedly against the groups developing into therapy sessions. He attempted to select and screen out those doctors who were seeking therapy and discouraged personal revelations in the group. He did not think that the group should be a substitute for therapy, yet one of Balint's original ideas was to copy the Hungarian psychoanalytic training model. In this method the analysand receives both analysis and supervision of his first case by his analyst—that is, the supervisory (training) and therapeutic (treatment) roles are combined. The analysand is thus able to discuss his own feelings toward his patient (countertransference) with an analyst who is familiar with the analysand's interpersonal and intrapsychic problems. Balint's aim was "to help doctors to become more sensitive to what is going on consciously or unconsciously in the patient's mind when doctor and patient are together." Yet in the seminars, Balint limited himself to commenting only on the doctors' *public* and *conscious* statements. He did not comment on or interpret any covert or unconscious material that he observed. Any statements involving personal problems were actively discouraged and not taken up. In addition, Balint, although recognizing the importance of the doctor/group leader relationship and the doctor/rest of the group relationship, tried to avoid discussions of an interpersonal and intimate nature that involved these areas.

Bacal (1972) suggested that Balint training primarily affects what he has termed the "area of professional ego." He suggested that change in this area is "related to the capacity of a doctor to free up and convert enough of his preoccupation and anxiety over personal problems into what we call the therapeutic interest or curiosity, so that he is in a position to do a good professional job." Bacal went on to infer that although Balint was aware of the need to mix the training and treatment models, he did not utilize the Hungarian system to its full extent. Bacal describes the case of a young doctor who, after attending Balint seminars for three years, still experienced considerable inhibitions with his younger women patients. He attended psychotherapy for eight months and subsequently reported much improvement in his ability to work with such patients. The issue Bacal raised was whether a doctor could have derived the help he obtained from psychotherapy while attending a Balint group. To be fair to Balint, he was aware of the potential limitations of his method of training: "I am aware that by all this I have not said much about these self-imposed limitations of our interpretations, and furthermore that by this simplified description I have deliberately disregarded a number of dynamic complications. Lastly, whether or not these limitations can be adhered to in the long run, or how necessary or desirable it is to adhere to them, is another matter, and only further experience can decide." It is a sad reflection on the work of the Balint Society that few, if any, such experiments have been encouraged. The developments in general practice education in this area have largely come from other workers (Freeling 1982, Lurie and Gallagher 1972, Heron 1973, Marinker 1972, Pietroni 1984).

THE CRITICS

It is unfortunate that Balint's critics in general practice have limited themselves to his original book. Balint's psychoanalytic writings are largely ignored, and the serious attempts he made to evaluate the outcome of the training method are difficult to obtain. The criticisms have centered around the scientific/unscientific nature of psychoanalytic theories and the limited understanding Balint had of the nature and task of general practice. Sowerby (1977) provided the most cogent attack on Balint, which can be summarized as follows:

1. Balint made the irrefutable conjecture (unscientific) that a scientific understanding of human behavior was possible in theoretical terms, and believed that general practice is primarily concerned with psychological problems.
2. He believed that psychological illness should not be diagnosed by exclusion, and that the diagnostic process was one of description rather than identification.

3. He initiated a confusion of language and proliferation of jargon that privileges that verbally articulate and the emotionally demonstrative.

Sowerby's paper has itself been rightly criticized, but his views represent a major section of general practice thought and practice. It is ironic that those that disagree with Sowerby will also find Balint's ideas and training methods limited, but for very different reasons. Balint failed to give due emphasis to physical factors in psychotherapy or psychoanalysis. Ignoring the body and its effect on the mind is a fundamental omission of psychoanalytic theory, just as the omission of the mind and its importance to the body has plagued "scientific" medicine.

Balint had an enquiring and original mind. He experimented with different techniques, but largely stayed within the accepted psychoanalytic framework. This has had a stultifying influence on psychotherapeutic approaches in general practice. Behavioral approaches, the use of transactional analysis, co-counseling, and humanistic models of group psychotherapy have not had sufficient use or impact because the individually-based psychodynamic and psychoanalytic model, as practiced by Balint, has been so influential within general practice. In addition, the educative nature of the task of general practice has been overly influenced by Balint's misunderstood views of the "apostolic" function of the GP. Balint wrote: "It was almost as if every doctor had revealed knowledge of what was right and what was wrong for patients to expect and to endure and further as if he had a sacred duty to convert to his faith all the ignorant and unbelieving among his patients." It seemed that Balint was challenging the assumption that doctors should advise, reassure, direct, influence, and suggest. Under the influence of Balint training, many GPs learned "how to listen" in a particular way and how to become less intrusive and nondirective. The idea that the nondirective approach is nondirective is, of course, nonsense. Balint's views on this issue were also quite clear: "It does not matter whatsoever whether the doctor shuts his eyes and refuses to see what he is doing or accepts his role and chooses consciously what he teaches—teach he must."

Balint *was* a great teacher, although characteristically he declined to accept his undoubted charisma and influences. The mark of a truly creative and civilized mind is that it can hold paradoxically opposing viewpoints on an issue at one and the same time. Judged by this criterion, Balint showed marks of genius, and we all owe a great debt to his father, a general practitioner!

REFERENCES

Bacal, H. A. (1972). Balint groups: training or treatment. *Psychiatry in Medicine* 3:373–377.
Balint, E., and Norell, J. (1973). *Six Minutes for the Patient*. London: Tavistock.

Balint, M., ed. (1966). *A Study of Doctors*. London: Tavistock.

_____ (1970). *Treatment or Diagnosis*. London: Tavistock.

Elder, A., and Samuel, O. (1987). *While I'm Here, Doctor*. London: Tavistock.

Freeling, P. (1982). *In-Service Training - A Study of the Nuffield Courses of RCGP*. Windsor, England: NFER/Nelson.

Heron, J. (1973). *Course for New Teachers in General Practice*. Human Potential Research Project. Guildford, England: University of Surrey.

Hopkins, P., ed. (1972). *Patient Centered Medicine*. London: RDP Ltd.

_____ ed. (1979). *The Human Face of Medicine*. London: Pitman Medical.

Lurie, M. J., and Gallagher, J. M. (1972). Innovative techniques for teaching psychiatric principles to general practitioners. *Journal of the American Medical Association* 221:696–699.

Marinker, M. (1972). A teacher's workshop. *Journal of the Royal College of General Practitioners* 22:551–559.

Pietroni, P. C. (1984). Training or treatment—a new approach. *British Journal of Holistic Medicine* 1:109–112.

Sowerby, P. (1977). *The Doctor, His Patient and the Illness*: a reappraisal. *Journal of the Royal College of General Practitioners* 27:583–589.

Selections from
The Doctor, His Patient and the Illness
by Michael Balint

INTRODUCTORY

For a number of years research seminars have been organized at the Tavistock Clinic to study the psychological implications in general medical practice. The first topic chosen for discussion at one of these seminars happened to be the drugs usually prescribed by practitioners. The discussion quickly revealed—certainly not for the first time in the history of medicine—that by far the most frequently used drug in general practice was the doctor himself, i.e. that it was not only the bottle of medicine or the box of pills that mattered, but the way the doctor gave them to his patient—in fact, the whole atmosphere in which the drug was given and taken.

This seemed to us at the time a very elevating discovery, and we all felt rather proud and important about it. The seminar, however, soon went on to discover that no pharmacology of this important drug exists yet. To put this second discovery in terms familiar to doctors, no guidance whatever is contained in any text-book as to the dosage in which the doctor should prescribe himself, in what form, how frequently, what his curative and his maintenance doses should be, and so on. Still more disquieting is the lack of any literature on the possible hazards of this kind of medication, on the various allergic conditions met in individual patients which ought to be watched carefully, or on the undesirable side-effects of the drug. In fact, the paucity of information about this most frequently used drug is appalling and frightening, especially when one considers the wealth of information available about other medicaments, even those most recently introduced into practice. The usual answer is that experience and common sense will help the doctor to acquire the necessary skill in prescribing himself. The shallowness of this self-reassuring advice becomes apparent when it is compared with the detailed instructions based on carefully controlled experiments with which every new drug is introduced into general practice.

When the seminar realized this disquieting state of affairs, our mood changed, and we decided forthwith that one of the aims, perhaps the chief aim, of our research should be to start devising this new pharmacology.

The importance of a study of this kind is perhaps much greater nowadays than ever before; but the reason is only partly inherent in medicine. Particularly as a result of urbanization, a great number of people have lost their roots and connexions, large families with their complicated and intimate interrelations tend to disappear, and the individual becomes more and more solitary, even lonely. If in trouble, he has hardly anyone to whom to go for advice, consolation, or perhaps only for an opportunity to unburden himself. He is more and more thrown back on his own devices. We know that in many people, perhaps in all of us, any mental or emotional stress or strain is either accompanied by, or tantamount to, various bodily sensations. In such troubled states, especially if the strain increases, a possible and in fact frequently used outlet is to drop in to one's doctor and complain. I have deliberately left the verb without an object, because at this initial stage we do not know which is the more important, the act of complaining or the complaints that are complained of. It is here, in this initial, still "unorganized" phase of an illness, that the doctor's skill in prescribing himself is decisive. We shall discuss presently the unexpected consequences that may be brought about by the doctor's response to his patient's complaints. Before doing so I propose to say something about our methods and the general set-up of our research.

Our work has been carried out exclusively in the form of discussion groups, consisting of about eight to ten general practitioners and one or two psychiatrists. The groups met once a week for two to three years, though some went on longer. The meetings were held on the early afternoon of the free half-day usually taken by general practitioners. This enabled them to attend without serious interference with their practice; in fact, this arrangement worked so well that even in the busiest months of general practice, from December to March, the attendance was very good — averaging for the whole year from ninety to ninety-five per cent of the possible total.

Our venture was a mixture of research and training. At the outset I had some idea that, psychologically, much more happens in general practice between patient and doctor than is discussed in the traditional text-books. If my ideas were correct, the events that I wanted to get hold of could be observed only by the doctor himself; the presence of a third person, however tactful and objective, would inevitably destroy the ease and intimacy of the atmosphere. Such a third person would see only an imitation, perhaps a very good imitation, but never the real thing.

Thus, the research could be conducted only by general practitioners while doing their everyday work, undisturbed and unhampered, sovereign masters of their own surgeries. But general practitioners are entirely untrained for this task; this is a matter to which we shall have several occasions to return in the following pages. Moreover, when we started, no established method was in existence, so far as I am aware, for training general practitioners in psycho-diagnosis and psychotherapy. Thus we were faced with three different though interlinked tasks. The first was to study the psychological implications in general practice; the second to train general practitioners for this job; and the third to devise a method for such training. . . .

The uncertainty caused by the complex structure of our venture is reflected in our terminology. The mainstay of our research-cum-training will be referred to in this book as group discussion, case conference, research seminar, discussion seminar, discussion group, etc.; all meaning the same but describing it from different angles.

As will be seen, the doctors tried hard to entice the psychiatrists into a teacher–pupil relationship, but for many reasons it was thought advisable to resist this. What we aimed at was a free, give-and-take atmosphere, in which everyone could bring up his problems in the hope of getting some light on them from the experience of the others. The material for our discussions was almost invariably provided by recent experiences with patients reported by the doctor in charge. The continuity of the course enabled us to follow the development of the patients' problems for two or three years—occasionally even longer—and thereby to examine how far our ideas, diagnoses, predictions, therapeutic attempts, etc., were correct and useful or otherwise.

Our chief aim was a reasonably thorough examination of the ever-changing doctor-patient relationship, i.e. the study of the pharmacology of the drug "doctor." In order to obtain reliable data for this study we tried to restrict to a minimum the use of written material in our discussion groups. There was no reading of prepared reports or manuscripts; the doctors were asked to report freely on their experiences with their patients. They were allowed to use their clinical notes, but only as an *aide-mémoire* and not as a *précis*. From the beginning our intention was that a doctor's report should include as full an account as possible of his emotional responses to his patient, or even his emotional involvement in his patient's problems. A frank account of this, the emotional, aspect of the doctor–patient relationship can be obtained only if the atmosphere of the discussion is free enough to enable the doctor to speak spontaneously. Any prepared manuscript or written report would of necessity involve a good deal of secondary elaboration of this spontaneous material, which was exactly what we wished to avoid.

12

Joseph Wolpe:
Psychotherapy by Reciprocal Inhibition

Reviewed by Stuart Lieberman

I first came across this particular book during my training at Boston City Hospital in 1970. It was by that time 12 years old. Skinnerian operant conditioning was the rage in the psychological and psychiatric circles; reciprocal inhibition seemed at the time to be considered passé. The psychoanalysts had already discounted any suggestion that the only effect of insight-oriented therapy was to provide a therapeutic setting in which reciprocal inhibition took place. Behaviour therapists were busy working out complex positive and negative reinforcement schedules for illnesses as diverse as schizophrenia and alcoholism. Dr. Laing put in an appearance in Boston at that particular time, extolling the virtues of the existential benefits of madness. But, I imagine that in its day, this book was highly controversial, since it challenges the central premise of psychoanalysis—that the essence of psychotherapy is uncovering and expression of the repressed.

Wolpe presented a new theory of psychotherapy based on learning theory: neurotic behaviour is presented as originating in learning, and the theory predicts that its elimination is a matter of unlearning. Thus, the gauntlet was thrown down and psychoanalysis challenged. Wolpe introduces his ideas with experimental observations which were made on cats in which lasting neurotic states had been induced. Should anyone doubt that cats can be made neurotic, they need only discuss their current doubts with our sister profession, The Pet Psychiatrists. An antagonism between feeding responses and anxiety was found to occur.

It is this finding that was transposed into the realms of psychotherapy with humans. The therapeutic principle of reciprocal inhibition is as follows: "If a response antagonistic to anxiety can be made to occur in the presence of anxiety-evoking stimuli, so that it is accompanied by a complete or partial suppression of the anxiety responses, the bond between these stimuli and the anxiety responses will be weakened."

Wolpe's basic method was simple. An anxiety hierarchy was constructed with patients, and the patient was then made to relax (reciprocally inhibited), while imagining items in the anxiety hierarchy. A 90 percent cure was claimed with neuroses from simple phobias through to character neuroses, which were believed to consist of intricate systems of phobias. The reciprocal inhibition which was used ranged from assertive responses, sexual responses, relaxation responses, respiratory responses, "anxiety-relief" responses, conditioned motor responses, "pleasant" responses in the life situation [with drug enhancement], and interview-induced emotional responses. These were the responses at the disposal of the therapist by which therapeutic change may deliberately be brought about.

Justification for this method is coherent and logical. A background explanation of the relationships between anatomical structures in behaviour, discussion about the making and unmaking of functional neural connections, in other words—learning and unlearning, are followed by a definition of neurotic behaviour—"any persistent habit of unadaptive behaviour acquired by learning in a physiologically normal organism."

My main criticism of *Reciprocal Inhibition* is that it oversimplifies the method by which human beings acquire neurotic illnesses. This oversimplification leads to a blinkered epistemology of the totality of human experience. Psychotherapy by reciprocal inhibition attempts to break the links between the person and extrapersonal stimuli. The mistake of psychoanalysis initially was to ignore this very important area. The mistake in psychotherapy by reciprocal inhibition is to ignore the fact that human beings can create within themselves a world whose inner reality and experience bears little resemblance, if any, to the outer reality of the world within which that person lives. Hence, people have strong beliefs in religion, strong cravings for and addictions to various forms of art and culture; they also can internally (intrapsychically) create and maintain belief which leads to neurotic behaviour. Looking at a systemic level, the theory of reciprocal inhibition bypasses the power inherent in a system. Systems may condone certain types of symptoms, but condemn others. For example, one family may consider it is perfectly permissible for the entire family to bathe together in the nude, while another family exists in which such behaviour would be cause for instant referral to the nearest psychiatrist. In one therapeutic group it is permissible to stand up, shout, move about, roll on the ground, and regress to birth while in another therapeutic group, any such movement could lead to instant dismissal from the group.

But where is the strength of this book? I believe it lies in the systematic way that innovative, interesting, and successfully used therapeutic techniques and methods of treatment are presented. Why should it be reread? In much of psychiatric practice, there remains extreme ignorance about creative ways of working with people. Psychotherapy using reciprocal inhibition actually includes the therapeutic relationship itself. I regret that much of the ignorance is within the psychiatric profession, while much of the psychological work is being done by psychologists, nurses, social workers, and occupational therapists. Many of them will already have absorbed the principles of psychotherapy by reciprocal inhibition, and because they are unable to prescribe and use drugs, they have forged ahead in their abilities to use their relationship with patients in an effective way.

When the Royal College of Psychiatrists feels that psychotherapy training of any sort should not be made mandatory for junior psychiatrists, it will not surprise me that recommendations that this book be read by every junior psychiatrist would also fall on deaf ears. Nevertheless, I would make this recommendation. It is a book well worth reading and was written well before the polemics about behavioral therapy versus "analytical psychotherapy" destroyed any concordance that could have occurred within the psychiatric profession.

Selections from
Psychotherapy by
Reciprocal Inhibition
by Joseph Wolpe

RECIPROCAL INHIBITION AS A
THERAPEUTIC PRINCIPLE

Chapter 4 described how neurotic cats were treated by getting them to eat in the presence of small and then gradually increasing "doses" of anxiety-evoking stimuli. The treatment was uniformly successful and I gave reasons for concluding that this was so because the anxiety responses were inhibited by the eating, which resulted on each occasion in setting up a measure of conditioned (learned) inhibition of the anxiety responses to whatever stimuli had evoked them. With repetition more and more conditioned inhibition was built up, so that the anxiety-evoking potential of the stimuli progressively diminished—eventually to zero.

The observations led to the framing of the following general principle:

> If a response antagonistic to anxiety can be made to occur in the presence of anxiety-evoking stimuli so that it is accompanied by a complete or partial suppression of the anxiety responses, the bond between these stimuli and the anxiety responses will be weakened.

This hypothesis does not deny the possibility that these bonds may be weakened by other means too; but the only other known process by which habits are broken down—experimental extinction—is singularly ineffective when it is anxiety that has to be extinguished. Certainly neurotic anxiety responses are not often extinguished by repeated evocation. Even with mild degrees of anxiety the ineffectiveness of the extinctive mechanism is striking. Miller, for example, found that a fear-accompanied motor habit required hundreds of trials to be extinguished. If there had been only a conditioning of fear, and no motor habit, the process would probably have taken even longer, since the motor activity itself would tend to inhibit anxiety (see below). The poor extinction of anxiety responses is apparently due to (a) the small amount of reactive inhibition generated by autonomic responses, and (b) the reinforcement of the anxiety responses by anxiety drive reduction when the organism is passively removed from anxiety-evoking stimuli.*

When the reciprocal inhibition principle was first formulated about ten years ago on the basis of the experiments on cats, the possibility of its clinical use hinged on the answers to two closely interrelated questions: (a) Were there other responses besides eating by which anxiety responses could be inhibited and could have their habit strength weakened? (b) Would it be possible to apply the findings to the treatment of human neurotic states? An attempt was made to answer both questions simultaneously by experiments on neurotic human subjects, employing responses other than feeding in the presence of anxiety-evoking stimuli. It was hoped that some of these responses would prove to be antagonistic to the anxiety responses, would inhibit the latter and thereby decrease their habit strength.

In selecting responses to oppose the anxiety responses I was guided by the presumption that responses that largely implicate the parasympathetic division of the autonomic nervous system would be especially likely to be incompatible with the predominantly sympathetic responses of anxiety. Although there is evidence strongly suggesting that sympathetic and parasympathetic responses are usually synergic, in many circumstances they are by and large opposed and one or other clearly dominant.

In the first three classes of responses that I came to use in clinical therapy—(a) assertive responses, (b) sexual responses, and (c) relaxation responses—there are, as far as the autonomic system is concerned, persuasive indications of parasympathetic ascendancy. A good deal of the evidence in favor of this with regard to assertive (angry) responses has been summarized by Arnold. Ax has questioned Arnold's position, but his own observations reveal a tendency for the pulse and respiratory rates to be raised in fear and lowered in anger. In the realm of sexual responses, erection is subserved by the *nervus erigens* which emanates from the sacral parasympathetic plexus. This plexus also supplies part of the innervation of the female sex organs. Parasympathetic responsiveness during sexual excitement is not confined to the sex organs, being manifested, for example, in increased gastric secretion. Sympathetic responses, such as raised pulse rate, are also present, but in the genital organs they become

---

*Nevertheless reactive inhibition can have a therapeutic role, typified by Dunlap's "negative practice." A very well worked out case has . . . been reported by Yates.

prominent only in relation to ejaculation. The parasympathetic effects of muscle relaxation are easily observed in anxious subjects trained in relaxation. In the course of a few minutes I have known the pulse rate to drop 30 beats or more, breathing to become slower, and sweating palms to become dry or nearly dry. Decrease in blood pressure as well as pulse rate has been shown by Jacobson to accompany relaxation.

Parasympathetic dominance also seems to characterize the emotional responses (evoked during an individual's ordinary day-to-day commerce with the world) that have been held to account for the beneficial fluctuations in neurotic reactivity referred to in Chapter 6. However diverse their details may be, the responses concerned appeared to have a pleasantness of tone in common. The correspondence of feelings of pleasantness with parasympathetic effects on the circulation is evident from Leschke's review of the work of numerous investigators. The rate of the pulse drops and its amplitude usually rises, in contrast with a constant increase in rate and decrease in amplitude accompanying unpleasantness, pain, or fear. To the same effect is Gellhorn's statement that pleasurable emotions induced by gustatory and olfactory stimuli cause parasympathetic excitation. Similarly, while exciting or disturbing music raises both blood pressure and pulse rate, calm or heroic music has the opposite effect. But it would be a mistake to assume that unless an emotional response constellation manifests parasympathetic dominance, it is incapable of inhibiting anxiety. Just as, in the motor sphere, to walk and to jump are mutually antagonistic, although they may utilize many muscle elements in common, an emotional response that utilizes many elements in common with anxiety may be antagonistic to the total anxiety response. The central nervous system is the fountainhead of emotional excitation, and the distribution of responding elements depends upon previously organized complex units of neural organization. Thus it is essentially a *pattern* of emotional responses that is excited or else inhibited.

About four years ago I made an effort to procure a response that was theoretically the diametric opposite of anxiety, in the hope that this would be a particularly effective therapeutic instrument. The method used was to present a word stimulus at the moment of cessation of an uncomfortable electric shock in order to condition to this word the bodily changes that ensued upon its cessation. These, presumably, would be the negative of such anxiety responses as the shock had evoked. In a few cases the expected conditioning was successfully accomplished.

It seemed reasonable to look in other directions too. There was no a priori reason for assuming that inhibition of anxiety could be accomplished only by responses that were themselves physiologically opposite to anxiety. Evidence is available that there are arrangements in the nervous system which make it possible for motor responses also to produce inhibition of anxiety. Freeman and Pathman found that the galvanic skin response (GSR) to disturbing stimuli reverted to its initial level most rapidly in subjects responding with overt muscular action, even if this took such apparently unadaptive forms as squirming and giggling. Haggard and Freeman subsequently found that motor activity directed to a relevant problem leads to subsidence of the GSR to its pre-existing level more rapidly than activity consisting of nondirected restless movements. It is doubtless in consequence of this ability to inhibit anxiety responses that motor responses can diminish the habit strength of anxiety responses. This has been illustrated in the clearest way by an experiment by Mowrer and Viek which led directly to the use of a new therapeutic method.

Probably just such a mechanism accounts for the fact that in the learning of a fear-connected activity (e.g., the learning by a young child to cross a street) the fear that is present during early performances disappears after repeated practice. It is also quite possible that in some instances of the therapeutic use of assertive behavior the motor responses play as important a part as the aggressive emotional responses in inhibiting anxiety responses.

Intense respiratory responses such as produced by single deep inhalations of 50–70 per cent carbon dioxide have also turned out to be anxiety-inhibiting, although in themselves these responses seem in no way to be physiologically opposite to anxiety.

As will be shown in detail below, success has attended the therapeutic use of each one of the above-mentioned classes of responses (although in the vast majority of cases two or more are used, and relaxation is nearly always one of them). . . . The three classes mentioned as the earliest to be tried—assertive responses, relaxation responses, and sexual responses—have had by far the widest application, and I refer to them with good reason as my "bread and butter" responses.

In addition to the responses whose evocation is deliberately planned, and undoubtedly of foremost importance in some cases, are the interview-induced emotional responses. These arise in some patients in response to the very presence of a situation in which they entrust their happiness to the special knowledge and skill of another human being. There is reason to believe that these responses, in so far as they are anxiety-inhibiting, are the cause of the remarkably uniform proportion of satisfactory results (about 50 per cent apparently cured or much improved) that are yielded by a variety of older methods of therapy ranging from reassurance to psychoanalysis.

Of course the use of techniques based on the reciprocal inhibition principle does not preclude the evocation of these nonspecific interview-induced emotional responses. They presumably occur as frequently as in any other kind of therapy; with effects as desirable. But in order to meet any suggestion that the reciprocal inhibition techniques themselves also have as little real effect as the special methods that other therapists use and regard (mainly erroneously) as having special virtues—in other words, that the therapeutic success that follows the use of reciprocal inhibition techniques is also entirely or mainly due to nonspecific emotional responses—the following facts must immediately be stated:

1. Out of a total of 210 patients who have had these techniques applied to them, nearly 90 percent have been either apparently cured or much improved, in contrast with a percentage not exceeding 60 in almost all other reported series.

2. The average number of interviews per patient is low (mean = 31).

3. Patients frequently improve rapidly in a small number of interviews after having had prolonged psychoanalytic or other therapy with little or no success.

4. There is almost always an obvious direct relationship between the amount of application of a given procedure and the amount of improvement. This is especially clear with the desensitization technique based on the use of relaxation.

13

Kurt Schneider:
Psychopathic Personalities

Reviewed by Kevin Standage

The first edition of *Psychopathic Personalities* appeared in 1912, roughly ten years after Jaspers's *General Psychopathology* and the last edition of Kraepelin's *Textbook of Psychiatry*. Schneider's role in applying Jaspers's method of psychopathological study to Kraepelin's classification of psychiatric disorder has been seen as an important aspect of his work (Hoenig 1982) and is evident in his own *Clinical Psychopathology* (Schneider 1959). However, his study of the classification of psychopathic personalities, an area that Kraepelin never succeeded in delineating clearly (Lewis 1974), is regarded as his most important contribution (Anderson 1959, Hoenig 1982).

When I began to study Schneider's work, about fifteen years ago, I was encouraged by my mentors to use the term "personality disorders" rather than "psychopathic personalities," and this has become a habit, so that in what follows I have used the two terms as if they were synonymous. Having no German, I am naïvely unaware of any nuances which may have been lost in the process and can only hope that I am not doing Schneider a disservice. I have been unable to discover when, or by whom, the substitution was first made. Certainly, the term "psychopathic personality" is obsolescent in English, its use now being more or less confined to mental health legislators and to psychologists working in the forensic field. Even among these groups, there is growing opposition to its use (Blackburn 1988).

Werlinder (1978) has provided an account, in English, of the first edition of *Psychopathic Personalities*. The ninth edition (Schneider 1950) was translated by Marion Hamilton. The two presentations are similar, suggesting that Schneider's views did not alter much during the lifetime of the work.

Furthermore, Hamilton acknowledged the help she received from W. Mayer-Gross and E. W. Anderson, both of whom were familiar with Schneider's teachings. Therefore, it is likely that her translation of the ninth edition provides a representative account of the views which Schneider expressed during his career. Werlinder reveals that some criticisms of Schneider were made in the interval between the publication of the ninth edition and the appearance of Hamilton's translation. Although the criticisms were sufficiently serious to prompt a response from Schneider (1958), who by then had retired, they are not often discussed in English texts.

Psychopathic Personalities is in two sections. The first deals with issues of general importance, including definitions of key concepts, while the second provides descriptions of what Schneider considered to be the important types of personality disorder which were encountered in clinical practice.

To Schneider, "personality" was a word used to convey someone's uniqueness, including his or her individual feelings and goals. It should be described in psychological terms, although it does not include the attributes usually referred to as "intelligence." Personality was normal if the subject was more or less average in comparison with others with the same cultural background. So-called abnormal personalities, by contrast, were variations on this "broadly conceived range of average personality" (p. 3). Such variations represented excesses or deficiencies in a statistical sense, and judgment of good or bad was "immaterial."

This definition of abnormal personality enabled Schneider to achieve his objective of introducing a way of describing personality disorders that was not judgemental. However, Schneider's critics claimed that he returned to a judgmental position when he went on to define such (personality) disorders as those "abnormal personalities who either suffer personally because of their own abnormality or make the community suffer because of it." Such criticism was unfair, because Schneider left no doubt that he believed that "psychopathy lies in the degree to which the abnormality of personality afflicts the individual, not in the amount of social friction which may be engendered around him" (p. 3).

Schneider's definition of personality disorder was intended to establish which area, in what would otherwise be a very large field, was of concern to psychiatry—a gesture that would surely be appreciated by today's politicians and managers of mental health services! On a more serious note, I wonder whether it holds the key to understanding the discrepancy between the rates of psychiatric disorder (including personality disorders) that are reported by clinicians and researchers using structured interviews.

In both sections of *Psychopathic Personalities*, Schneider discussed at length the relationship between personality disorder and other forms of mental illness. He confessed to finding it difficult to apply the medical model to *any* psychiatric disorder, since patients are often unperturbed by their experiences. However, it seemed reasonable to him that the concept of illness be introduced if mental changes occurred which could best be explained by a disease process. He thought it inappropriate to refer to psychopaths as "ill," because they did not meet this criterion, although to buttress this argument he removed from the category patients with disturbed behavior resulting from diseases such as encephalitis.

It is often overlooked that Schneider emphasised the limitations of the diagnosis of a personality disorder. Typologies of such disorders were, he claimed, no more than descriptions of people, conceived within a professional relationship and inevitably incomplete. He was also strongly opposed to attempts at classifying personality "systematically," by referring to structural models. In his opinion, such classifications failed to depict the types of patients encountered in the clinical setting.

Nevertheless, Schneider believed that it was important for psychiatrists to take into account those stable characteristics of patients that were conveyed by concepts such as personality and personality disorder, especially in cases of neurosis. While not liking the term "neurosis," he paid considerable attention to individual neurotic symptoms which, to a greater extent than most modern psychiatrists, he saw as intrinsic features of personality disorders.

In the second section of the book, Schneider presented his own, unsystematic, typology of personality disorders. The equivalent terms in English for his ten types are (following Hamilton's translation): hyperthymic, depressive, insecure (with sensitive and anankastic subtypes), fanatic, attention-seeking, labile, explosive, affectionless, weak-willed, and asthenic. For each type he provided a description and a background review, including such things as genetic studies, differential diagnosis, and social impact. There is a high degree of internal consistency in these accounts.

Although it has been difficult to devise an approach to diagnosis which does justice to Schneider while at the same time addressing present-day concerns about reliability, some evidence of the validity of the typology has been found (Standage 1977). It was also observed that there were relationships between diagnoses made within Schneider's classification and *DSM-III* (Standage 1986).

The most frequently expressed criticism of Schneider is that he negated the role of psychotherapy. However, this is not apparent on reading *Psychopathic Personalities*. There, he simply commented that psychotherapy might not be very effective for patients with personality disorders and that such disorders should be taken into account when treatment was undertaken—not a very contentious opinion by today's standards! A more valid criticism might be that he underestimated the role of intrapsychic and interpersonal factors as determinants of the behavioral patterns that are implied by the term "personality disorder." In particular, I am surprised that he paid so little attention to concepts of self, which I would have expected to emerge in a phenomenologically oriented review of such disorders.

In fact, when I read the descriptions of the various personality types, I do not derive a strong sense of what it is like to be labile, affectionless, weak-willed, and so on, and I can only speculate on the reasons for this, which must include my own defensiveness and lack of sophistication in phenomenology. I have to search for the phenomenological elements in the work, and I find it in such things as the attempt to distinguish form from content, the emphasis on individual, meaningful data being required to put flesh on the skeletal typological diagnosis, and the need for the clinician to question the ways in which, say, an attention-seeking personality seeks attention.

Schneider appreciated that his personality types overlapped, but he did not recognize that the reliability of such a method of diagnosis would be low. If he had access to the modern literature, which indicates that there is a strong affinity between psychometric measures and clinical concepts, in spite of the efforts of psychiatrists and psychologists to prove otherwise, I wonder whether he would be quite so negative about systematic classifications, which lead naturally to a dimensional approach and thus to improved reliability? Such an approach would be consistent with his definition of abnormal personality.

Another criticism which might be made of Schneider today is that, although he paid a lot of attention to the relationship between personality disorders and the endogenous psychoses, he did so only in terms of either/or. It has now become conventional to consider these conditions on *separate* diagnostic axes, as exemplified in *DSM-III*. It may be that Schneider wanted to promote the view that, in general, personality disorders and psychoses are qualitatively distinct from one another, in contrast to that which sees them as intermediaries between the latter and "normality."

Perhaps the most remarkable thing about *Psychopathic Personalities* is that the issues presented in it are still the major ones in the field of personality disorder. This makes it an excellent postgraduate text.

As criticism continues to be expressed about the diagnosis of personality disorders, it is salutary to remind oneself that Schneider set out to replace Kraepelin's socially valuing descriptions of such patients with a classification which was nonevaluating, psychological, and clinically relevant. Much work is still needed to determine the importance of personality in general psychiatry. Certainly, the treatment provided for patients with personality disorders needs to be improved—an undertaking that will derive little impetus from Schneider's rather sardonic comments (my favorite is the advice to stay out of the way of labile personalities on their bad days!). However, those who follow Schneider's approach to the definition and description of such disorders should at least remain free of allegations of prejudice.

REFERENCES

Anderson, E. W. (1959). Preface. In *Clinical Psychopathology*, by K. Schneider, trans. M. W. Hamilton. New York: Grune & Stratton.

Blackburn, R. (1988). On moral judgments and personality disorders. The myth of the psychopathic personality revisited. *British Journal of Psychiatry* 153: 505–512.

Diagnostic and Statistical Manual of Mental Disorders (1980). 3rd ed. Washington, DC: American Psychiatric Association.

Hoenig, J. (1982). Kurt Schneider and Anglophone psychiatry. *Comprehensive Psychiatry* 23:391–400.

Lewis, A. (1974). Psychopathic personality: a most elusive category. *Psychological Medicine* 4:133–140.

Schneider, K. (1950). *Die Psychopathische Personlichkeiten*. 9th ed. Wien: Franz Deuticke.

_____ (1958). Der psychopath. *Fortschritte der Neurologie-Psychiatrie* 26:1–6.

_____ (1959). *Clinical Psychopathology*. Trans. M. W. Hamilton. New York: Grune & Stratton.

Standage, K. (1977). The diagnosis and classification of personality disorders. Ph.D. dissertation. Memorial University of Newfoundland, Newfoundland.

_____ (1986). A clinical and psychometric investigation comparing Schneider's and the *DSM-III* typologies of personality disorders. *Comprehensive Psychiatry* 27:35–46.

Werlinder, H. (1978). Psychopathy: a history of the concept. (Uppsala Studies in Education.) *Acta Universitatis Upsaliensis*, 6.

Selections from
Psychopathic Personalities
by Kurt Schneider

GENERAL PRINCIPLES

A host of separate elements constitute one human individual, but three distinct and complex structures—intelligence, personality and the physical organism—may be isolated in theory though they are intimately inter-related in fact. A certain degree of intelligence, Jaspers says, is a necessary condition for personality to develop at all but intelligence devoid of personality is a very blunt tool. Closer still is the relationship between personality and physical impulse, but for purposes of discussion it is not difficult to discriminate between all three and treat personality as a separate subject matter.

Abnormal Personality

Investigation of psychopathic personality not only involves some defini-tion of personality but some understanding of what is meant by abnormal personality.

Norms may be of two kinds. In the first place normal may mean the factual average. In the second place there may be a subjective element, the implication of some personal standard. Norm then comes to mean what is judged normal and gains a regulative force. In this sense Goethe, Bismarck, St. Francis might all represent a regulative norm or standard. However, if norm is taken in the first sense, abnormal simply means what is not the average and involves no element of depreciation. If norm is taken in the second sense, then deviation into abnormality implies the transgression of some standard. Psychiatry is only concerned with norms in the first sense as factual averages. Mezger points out that no hard and fast distinctions of this sort could be made when assessing what is meant by normal behaviour, but to our mind it is essential that any discussion on abnormal personality should keep these two types of norm clearly separate.

Our psychological norms are general guides rather than exact percentages, which will dispose of W. Stern's objection that on the basis of "counting heads" a state of mass-hysteria might be regarded as normal. Normal behavior springs from the people of our own day and culture and therefore may have some relativity but it is never so transient a phenomenon as Stern's example.

The definition of abnormal personality which we shall use is therefore as follows: abnormal personality is a variation upon an accepted yet broadly conceived range of average personality. The variation may be expressed as an excess or deficiency of certain personal qualities and whether this is judged good or bad is immaterial to the issue. The saint and the poet are equally abnormal as the criminal. All three of them fall outside the range of average personality as we conceive it so that all persons of note may be classes as abnormal personalities.

Psychopathic Personality

Abnormal personalities are then very numerous, but among them we find two well-defined groups to which we have given the title psychopathic personality. These contain abnormal personalities who either suffer personally because of their own abnormality or make the community suffer because of it.

This is hardly a scientific definition but it is a practical one and covers all the abnormal personalities that psychiatrists encounter. For this reason it is an improvement on a previous definition which in some ways was more accurate but applied only to the first group—those who suffer personally from their own abnormality. Koch however used to distinguish between his psychopathic patients according to whether they were an affliction to themselves alone or to other people or indeed to both. Many psychopaths in the first sense may become delinquent and many delinquents may also happen to be psychopaths in the first sense, suffering acutely from their own abnormality. But the point we wish to make is that the psychopathy lies in the degree to which the abnormality of personality afflicts the individual, not in the amount of social friction which may be engendered around him.

Psychopathic personality may easily be confused with ordinary delinquent personality as indeed they may both be with other abnormal personalities. Individual behavior varies enormously and sometimes it seems to earn the title psychopathic while at others it might be better termed abnormal. The amount of suffering which any community considers it is undergoing can only be a very rough criterion of psychopathy and its obvious subjectivity hardly needs to be pointed out. The abnormal individual who leads a revolution will be called mad by some and a hero by others, but might or might not be a psychopath. The definition therefore which holds that psychopathic personality not only suffers from its own abnormality but makes the community suffer has certain social implications and needs to be very carefully applied. It does however meet the need for a working definition as long as it is remembered that from the strictly scientific point of view it is the abnormal quality of the personality alone which is of consequence.

SOMATIC FACTORS IN PSYCHOPATHIC PERSONALITY

In our opinion personality and even more so abnormal (psychopathic) personality are both essentially the innate constitution, though Koch and Ziehen would disagree. Constitutional factors are practically synonymous for genetic ones but factors environmental to the foetus or the baby have a share in building up personality, and in the process the specifically innate elements become effaced, but these exogenous or pseudo-psychopathies cannot be distinguished from the real endogenous ones. Environmental factors are universally recognised as of far-reaching importance in feeble-mindedness, but we do not agree with Raecke that external factors play so important a part in contributing to abnormal (psychopathic) personality. The primary aetiology is a genetic one and on the whole in Germany there is little opposition to this view.

Every personality develops. We agree with Jaspers in regarding this development as a maturation or an unfolding of inborn characteristics, a product of living and experiencing in the widest sense. Though in our view the organism's basic characteristics and general potential is a constitutional factor well-established from the start, we do not under-estimate the influence of environment on development. Education, personal history and events must be taken into account and have their effect in turn on potentiality and basic characteristics.

SELECTING A TYPOLOGY—ITS USE AND LIMITATIONS

Individual personality is rich and complex so that any one characteristic is scarcely likely to represent the whole person, though perhaps when several type descriptions and subtypes are combined in the one portrait this is sometimes very nearly accomplished. In actual practice therefore these type-descriptions are not very useful. A depressive psychopath or a weak-willed psychopath with affectionless traits rarely presents himself so clearly as this in the clinic and because of the complexity of personality factors and the actual blending of types we are mostly reduced to the simple use of the description "psychopath". If we were to try to allot the psychopaths admitted during one clinical year into their respective types we would find we could only do this with a relative few. The hundred and one idiosyncrasies of human nature do not lend themselves readily to methods of clinical diagnosis nor to any attempt to reduce them into pathological categories.

Any satisfactory description of psychopathic qualities should denote some characteristic constitutional anomaly exhibited with some relative continuity. A confirmed hyperthyme will remain one throughout his life though there may be some long or short term modifications, and this is probably true of the affectionless type. With the other types there may be loss continuity. Many may be insecure and attention-seeking when young and later on lose such qualities or carry only very slight traces of them. Age may create an asthenic type of failure in people otherwise robust. Few adults appear weak-willed and the characteristic wavering and impulse to wander tends to develop below the surface, determining constant shifts in their behaviour. Significant experiences and circumstances will also affect changes in the presented picture and too little attention has been paid in the past to the way in which personality traits are moulded by experience. Some are reinforced and some are weakened, while others will resist all influences. Neither the hyperthymic nor the affectionless types are readily influenced, but traits of insecurity, depression, asthenic self-concern and hypochondria are all modifiable. If however the qualities are very pronounced, limits will be encountered; experience will either count for very little or for only a limited period. Where the qualities are less well defined, the possibilities for modification widen. Duehrssen referred in this respect to Schultz-Hencke who classified our types into two groups, constitutional and neurotic. Kahn also has commented on the fact that both endogenous and reactive psychopathic episodes occur. Psychotherapy may offer some circumscribed help with the first, but with the second it is really in its element. If any experience can take effect, psychotherapy has a chance, since it is itself an experience. Reactively modifiable or unmodifiable states correlate fairly exactly with psychotherapeutic possibilities and their opposite.

Clinical labels have of course practical implications. No experienced clinician will content himself with mere type-description, but beginners, whether doctors or welfare personnel, are easily misled by typology to rely on such descriptions too much, and once the patients have been labelled psychopaths, it may be felt there is no further problem to solve. It is unfair to charge psychiatrists as a whole with the practice of labelling a patient a psychopath and then withdrawing with an air of resigned fatalism, but typology is abused in this way by some and a real danger exists that patients will be seen only in this formal way while psychological content, motivation, personal history and the possibilities of psychotherapeutic influence are all overlooked. There is usually scope for modification in the complexities of psychopathic personality, however typical or well-labelled this may be in the first place. On the other hand the opposite error also needs watching. We may get lost in all the personal conflicts of our patient and overlook the inborn disposition and the vulnerable personality, hidden reefs on which our therapy may founder. There is no need for fine differentiation of what is constitutional; it is only necessary to be aware of that something which precedes experience and gives to each individual his specific quality. Neuroses, apart from psychosomatic disturbances, flourish in constitutionally abnormal psychopathic personalities in which they find at least one essential condition for their existence. It is remarkable how often this is overlooked, particularly among psychotherapists, who sometimes show a quite astonishing blindness to facts of innate disposition. In infectious illness we consider the constitution as fully as the precipitating agents. Should not the same principle hold for the neuroses? This is only an analogy as there is no question of illness with the neuroses but the question of constitution seems equally important. The hereditary occurrence of psychopathic qualities is already established; psychopaths do exist. If we conceive psychopathic personality to be solely the consequence of early childhood conflict and try to understand it in these terms alone, we shall end in confusion and unreality. On the other hand we ourselves have never maintained that the psychopathies are to be ascribed wholly to hereditary disposition.

The whole concept of types should be kept plastic and their relative permanency remembered. Experiences, circumstances, life history need all to be taken into account and there is no bar to psychotherapy. Indeed it is better for therapists and educators not to overestimate the disposition and underestimate psychological influences or the practice of their art might suffer. Yet those with a critical mind will see the constant need to try to establish the type of personality and the non-reactive factors, the endogenous somatic fluctuations. Otherwise disillusionment may set in or too naïve an assessment be made of the situation and what has been accomplished. Psychologists often have a very difficult task and are prone to believe in their achievements but in fact sometimes only organic and unpsychological factors are at work or there have been other psychological influences independent of the therapist; such situations have their psychological complexities as well!

14

E. M. Jellinek:
The Disease Concept of Alcoholism

Reviewed by Brian D. Hore

Concern over those individuals who drink alcohol to excess goes back many centuries, this concern being directed at the effect alcohol has on the individual and on society. Levine (1978) pointed out that the idea of alcoholism as a progressive disease with the key symptom of "loss of control" did not simply start with the foundation of Alcoholics Anonymous or the publication of Jellinek's monograph. Such a concept is, in fact, at least 200 years old.

During the last century there was much debate on whether alcoholism was a *disease* or a form of *deviance* as well as on the issue of *control of drinking*. Levine (1978) emphasizes that alcohol was regarded as an addictive substance long before opium was. The Temperance Movement, the main body concerned with alcohol problems during the nineteenth century, accepted the concept of addiction, but emphasized *alcohol* as being the addictive agent. However, following Prohibition, the disease model of alcoholism came more to the fore, stressing that the cause of addiction related to the individual host and not to alcohol itself.

Such an idea of alcohol as a disease had been advanced long before Prohibition. Rush (1814), for example, designated intoxication a disease of the will which resulted in increasingly frequent bouts of drinking. However, others in the nineteenth century such as Todd (1882; cited by Jellinek) argued that the individual did not lose control but rather chose to drink— "the man drinks simply because he likes to drink or because he likes to be drunk."

THE CONTRIBUTION OF JELLINEK

Jellinek's publication was the principal landmark in the field of alcoholism this century. Jellinek, through a variety of methods including obtaining information from members of Alcoholics Anonymous and extensive reading of the literature, attempted to extract a disorder called alcoholism from a variety of drinking patterns that were known to occur. Together with the views of Alcoholics Anonymous, the academic support of the Yale School of Alcohol Studies and the development of the National Council of Alcoholism, this led to an almost universal acceptance of the disease concept in the United States for many years.

In Britain the reaction was more ambivalent. Although the *British Journal of Addiction* (formerly the *British Journal of Inebriety*) was first published in 1892, the majority of physicians in the United Kingdom did not believe in the disease concept. The traditional British view was that alcoholism was nothing but drunkenness and bad behavior which just did not occur among decent people. This ambivalence toward the disease concept is probably the prime reason why there have been relatively few specialized facilities provided to help people with alcohol problems over the last thirty years.

Jellinek defined alcoholism as "any use of alcoholic beverages that causes any damage to the individual or society or both." He particularly stressed two types of alcoholism (gamma and delta) which showed clinical features he considered indicative of a disease.

Features included in both types were acquired tissue tolerance to alcohol, adaptive cell metabolism, withdrawal symptoms on cessation of alcohol intake, craving for alcohol, and either the loss of control drinking pattern (gamma) or the inability to abstain (delta). In gamma alcoholism individuals would lose control immediately once they started drinking, the ingestion of one drink leading to a chain reaction (i.e., drinking would occur in a mechanistic way), while in delta alcoholism the individual was unable to abstain even for a day or two from alcohol.

Jellinek was fully aware of cultural and economic factors that influence alcohol consumption, and was also concerned that an exclusive emphasis on the disease concept of alcoholism (gamma and delta alcoholism) would exclude many other problems related to alcohol. He also considered that certain other patterns of drinking were symptomatic, that is, carried out to relieve underlying symptoms, and that these were therefore not illnesses since they lacked the features of the gamma and delta patterns. Alcohol was an agent capable of inducing addiction, and in those with gamma or delta alcoholism it was likely that there would be a progression from psychological to physical addiction.

To Jellinek, adaption of cell metabolism to alcohol was a feature that indicated physiopathological changes in body cells analogous to those changes believed to occur in drug addiction. While being aware of their theoretical (nonfactual) nature, he extensively lists the different theories of such changes. He seemed to draw close parallels between patterns of behavior in the gamma and delta subjects with those among individuals addicted to opiates. He also regarded opiate addiction as a disease and believed that just because an individual had such a disease that was a form of addiction, it was not outside his or her powers to do something about it. Such as individual was, therefore, responsible for taking the necessary steps to deal with it.

It is worth stressing the latter point as recent critics (e.g., Heather and Robertson 1981) have discussed how labelling individuals as alcoholics may exclude them from responsibility and will also stigmatize them. These critics have also emphasized how such labelling may exclude others with drinking problems from attending treatment centers and deter individuals in the early stages of alcohol problems from attending for help. Furthermore, it may encourage the perpetuation of an irreversible drinking pattern and would thus be self-fulfilling.

Jellinek separated those factors responsible for drinking before the onset of the disease from the disease itself. He agreed that learned behavior may be an important factor in predisease drinking, but while understanding psychological formulations which saw drinking as a symptom of underlying disorders, did not consider these formulations themselves explained the process of alcoholism. Essentially, Jellinek's theory involves seeing an individual drinking for a variety of reasons (including social, psychological, and cultural), and in certain individuals this leads to a process (of as yet unknown physiological and pathological change) which explains the key features described above. Although genetic factors might be important, Jellinek suggested that any individual, however healthy or well organized, who drinks heavily enough for long enough may become addicted. The marker of physical dependence was the presence of withdrawal symptoms, and here Jellinek drew on the experimental work of Isbell and colleagues (1955; cited in Jellinek), particularly those experiments in which former morphine addicts were given large amounts of alcohol and subsequent withdrawal symptoms were assessed on cessation of alcohol intake.

The World Health Organization (WHO 1952) described addictive drugs as falling into three types: those where pharmacological properties of the drug were of primary importance (e.g., opiates); those habit-forming drugs in which the psychological reaction of the user was of primary importance; and those of an intermediate category where both factors were important. Alcohol was considered as a drug in the intermediate category: its pharmacological action was important but addiction could only occur in those individuals whose makeup led them to seek an escape in alcohol.

Adaptation of cell metabolism, one of the key features of alcoholism, was thought to be indicated by the presence of withdrawal symptoms. Another key feature, increased tissue tolerance, had been clearly demonstrated by tests which measured the threshold of blood concentration at which performance deteriorated. These showed that in heavy drinkers a higher blood alcohol level was required to produce this deterioration. Increased tolerance was regarded as a changed physiological response to alcohol, and it was suggested that this would also be combined with the inability of individuals to compensate for this, particularly on individual tasks. Physiological experiments on people had already demonstrated that tolerance could be induced, and it was known that alcohol was cross-tolerant with other drugs such as general anesthetics—higher levels of anaesthetics were needed in alcoholics or heavy drinkers. It was also known that changes in tolerance could not be explained by the change in the rate of absorption of alcohol from the gut or increase in oxygenation or excretion.

Craving was regarded by Jellinek as being of two types: a psychological type that occurred between bouts of drinking and accounted for relapse after abstinence, and a physiological or potential physiological type that occurred during the time that people were drinking. These related to delta and gamma alcoholism respectively. It should be emphasized that loss of control to Jellinek, apart from meaning the loss of freedom following the first ingestion of alcohol in a new bout of drinking, was "characterized by minor withdrawal symptoms in the presence of alcohol in the blood stream and the failure to achieve the desired euphoria for more than a few minutes."

IMPLICATIONS OF THE DISEASE CONCEPT

In discussing the attitudes of the WHO, Jellinek argued that whether alcoholism was regarded as an illness or not was not crucial; what was important was where it was placed. He also stated that there were many conditions that medical men legitimately claimed as their own which did not constitute diseases.

Although there were inherent difficulties in labelling a disorder as a disease, placing it within the sphere of health rather than that of morality was of major importance in helping alcohol abusers, particularly in the United States. Jellinek reviewed the attitude of the federal government and different states within the U.S. toward the concept of alcoholism as a disease. In one state, Rhode Island, alcoholism was *not* seen as a public health problem but rather was related to a legal act covering chastity, morality, and decency! Jellinek stressed that the attitude of the public was crucial in helping to provide incentives for the rehabilitation of the alcoholic.

CRITICISMS OF THE DISEASE CONCEPT

Before the onslaught of criticism by behavioral psychologists (e.g., Heather and Robertson 1981), there were two other important developments. First, there was Keller's (1972) comment that while a loss of control and the fact of one drink leading to continuous drinking could clearly happen in an individual, not all individuals lost control on every occasion and, in fact, many controlled their drinking for certain periods. Second, there was Edwards and Gross's (1976) description of the alcohol dependence syndrome, which was clearly influenced by Jellinek, but different in that the syndrome was regarded as a collection of signs and symptoms, and was graded (i.e., it was not an "all or none phenomenon"). Individuals could be at different levels of dependence and move in either direction. Edwards and Gross also considered that biochemical factors as well as psychological ones were important in describing the syndrome. However, as Heather and Robertson (1981) pointed out, particularly with the emphasis on the immediate loss of control of drinking after a period of abstinence, in many ways the alcohol dependence syndrome was a more socially acceptable form of the disease concept. They criticise both Keller (1972) and Edwards and Gross in their suggestion that "concepts which do not qualify as scientific propositions are those which are not falsifiable. The conception of impaired control is not falsifiable because it cannot specify the conditions under which controlled drinking will occur and the conditions under which it will not and for the purposes of scientific discourse, is strictly meaningless."

Jellinek's concepts have been most critically analyzed by Heather and Robertson (1981) using a behavioral psychology perspective and a knowledge of statistics. They drew attention to important experimental evidence which had developed after Jellinek's book was published, including studies which attempted to determine the environmental correlates of designated behavioral responses in an individual. By changing environmental consequences, changes in responses were recorded. In relation to abusive drinking, the experiments involved alcoholics carrying out spontaneous tasks, the reward of which would be money or alcohol; in general, the harder the individual worked, the more reward he/she obtained. In this situation (which of course is different from that outside the laboratory) individuals did not drink rapidly and consistently to high levels of intoxication, and they frequently chose not to work harder to obtain more alcohol.

Heather and Robertson (1981) concluded therefore that in those individuals labelled alcoholics there was clearly the ability to control their drinking behavior. In clinical experience, of course, many experienced doctors would agree that individuals diagnosed as alcohol addicts or suffering from the alcohol dependence syndrome do abstain for periods, and on some occasions only drink to moderate levels of intoxication. It is also clear that environmental factors, for example being in a group of other men who are drinking heavily, may govern the amount that the individual drinks. For Heather and Robertson (1981) alcoholics certainly did not show mechanical drinking to the extreme degrees of intoxication predicted by Jellinek's theories (i.e., "one drink leads to a drunk"), nor did they always show an inability to abstain.

A second group of experiments quoted by Heather and Robertson showed what happened to individuals when they were given priming doses of alcohol or when they thought they had received alcohol but had not. As with experiments on aggression and alcohol, these found that whether an individual craved alcohol or not was much more a function of if they believed they had received it rather than if they had actually done so. This would support a psychological rather than a physiological explanation of craving.

Heather and Robertson (1981) concluded that "the issue of impaired control in alcoholics may be profitably explored in psychological, sociopsychological or broad sociological terms and need not be confined to physiological or other internal events. The important implications of these alternative explanations are that none of them rest on a strict separation of alcoholics from non-alcoholics and that none of them would entail any suggestion of an irreversible process."

BIOLOGICAL ASPECTS OF ALCOHOLISM

Jellinek placed great emphasis on biological processes responsible for the behaviour of an alcoholic, although he had no understanding, in terms of scientific facts, as to what these were. Behavioral critics of the disease concept, however, do not really explain how these types of phenomena, particularly changes in functional tolerance and the presence of withdrawal symptoms, can be explained in psychological terms.

Gross and his colleagues (1977) developed a method of quantifiably measuring the alcohol withdrawal syndrome, and also subjected the pattern of withdrawal symptoms to factor analysis. Their work suggested that, in an uninterrupted episode of drinking, critical cumulative blood alcohol concentrations rather than quantities or days of alcohol intake were related to the development of most features of the withdrawal syndrome. During a period of four to six days of alcohol intake in alcoholics, significant levels of the withdrawal syndrome tended to occur after drinking episodes in which the average daily peak concentration was greater than approximately 200 mg per 100 ml, and the average daily minimal concentration was greater than about 50 mg per 100 ml.

Gross (1977) stated that "the withdrawal syndrome may be viewed as an indirect toxic effect of the sustained critical concentrations of alcohol, presumably a consequence of the underlying changes which produce physical dependence during the intake period. With a sufficient number of such episodes or prolongation of drinking over a sufficient period of time and an insufficient number and duration of nondrinking periods which could presumably permit recovery, there is evidence that some residual manifestations of withdrawal may persist for months and might even become irreversible."

Particularly important to Gross's view was thus that physical dependence once it has been induced can be more easily reintroduced. This "carryover" of physical dependence suggests the persistence of physical changes, perhaps in the brain. Functional tolerance, defined by Gross (1977) "as the diminished effect of the same blood alcohol concentration on neurophysiological and behavioural responses was also shown, once it has been acquired, to be more readily reacquired." Again, this carryover of functional tolerance suggests long-lasting changes.

Trachtenberg and Blum (1987) have suggested that the physiological craving for alcohol may be the result of naturally occurring deficits of opiate-like substances as well as other neurochemicals. These deficits may occur genetically or as a result of long-term drinking, and further psychological factors such as stress can produce a chronic deficiency of naturally occurring enkephalins and endorphines. These theories would link genetic, psychological and biological factors in a theory of alcoholism. At present, these theories cannot be proven, although there seems to be growing evidence of biochemical changes in fundamental areas of cerebral functions (e.g., levels of neurotransmitters and opioid-like substances in animals and maybe humans) after regular alcohol use. This, together with the carryover of functional tolerance and physical dependence would suggest that in those that consume alcohol over a prolonged period there are long-lasting biological changes. This links with Jellinek's view that some biological process was occurring in the body cells of alcoholics.

CONCLUSIONS

There is no doubt that Jellinek's book was of major importance in establishing abnormal drinking as a matter that lay within the sphere of health rather than deviance. It set the tone and continues to do so for the illness concept of alcoholism, particularly in the United States. The criticisms and research studies have suggested, however, that some of the more simplistic concepts (e.g., immediate loss of control) have had to be modified. Nevertheless, the recent increase in interest of a biological process underlying dependence and the studies of Gross and colleagues would suggest that a biological factor is involved, particularly in the carryover of physical dependence and functional tolerance. Jellinek believed strongly in such an underlying biological process. Finally, as his critics have pointed out, Jellinek's views have been largely incorporated into the alcohol dependence syndrome, which is the predominate model used by workers in the alcohol field, particularly in Great Britain.

REFERENCES

Edwards, G., and Gross, M. M. (1976). Alcohol dependence, a provisional description of a clinical syndrome. *British Medical Journal* 1:1058–1061.

Gross, M. M. (1977). Psychobiological contributions to the alcohol dependence syndrome, a selective review of recent research. In *Alcohol Related Disabilities*, eds. G. Edwards, M. M. Gross, M. Keller, et al., Geneva: WHO.

Heather, N., and Robertson, I. (1981). *Controlled Drinking*. London: Methuen.

Keller, M. (1972). On the loss of control phenomenon in alcoholism. *British Journal of Addiction* 67:153–166.

Levine, H. G. (1978). The discovery of addiction, changing conceptions of habitual drunkenness in America. *Journal of Studies of Alcohol* 39:143–174.

Rush, B. (1814). An inquiry into the effect of ardent spirits. In *A New Deal in Liquor, a Plea for Dilution*, ed. Y. A. Henderson, pp. 185–227. New York: Doubleday, 1934.

Trachtenberg, M. C., and Blum, K. (1987). Alcohol and opioid peptides, neuropharmacological rationale for physical craving of alcohol. *American Journal of Drug and Alcohol Abuse* 13:365–372.

World Health Organization (1952). Expert committee on drugs liable to produce addiction (3rd report). WHO technical report series no. 57. Geneva: WHO.

Selections from
The Disease Concept
of Alcoholism
by E. M. Jellinek

In speaking about the species of alcoholism and alcoholics I shall give brief descriptions and attach labels to them without any pretension to formal definitions. Only those species of alcoholism will be described and labeled here that may come at all into consideration as disease processes or symptoms of disease processes.

Gamma alcoholism means that species of alcoholism in which (1) acquired increased tissue tolerance to alcohol, (2) adaptive cell metabolism (see below), (3) withdrawal symptoms and "craving," i.e., physical dependence, and (4) loss of control are involved. In gamma alcoholism there is a definite progression from psychological to physical dependence and marked behaviour changes such as have been described previously by Jellinek.

This species produces the greatest and most serious kinds of damage. The loss of control, of course, impairs interpersonal relations to the highest degree. The damage to health in general and to financial and social standing are also more prominent than in other species of alcoholism.

Gamma alcoholism is apparently (but not with certainty) the predominating species of alcoholism in the United States and Canada, as well as in other Anglo-Saxon countries. It is what members of Alcoholics Anonymous recognize as alcoholism to the exclusion of all other species. Of course they use loss of control and "craving" as the criteria par excellence but these necessarily involve the other characteristics of gamma alcoholism mentioned above.

Delta alcoholism shows the first three characteristics of gamma alcoholism as well as a less marked form of the fourth characteristic—that is, instead of loss of control there is inability to abstain.

In gamma alcoholism, the adaptation of cell metabolism and the other characteristics mentioned above indeed represent physiopathological changes analogous to those in drug addiction as well as psychopathological conditions which differ from those of any possible pre-alcoholic psycho-pathology. With the exception of the psychological changes and the loss of control, which is replaced by the inability to abstain, the same changes are involved in delta alcoholism.

If it should be conceded that morphine, heroin and barbiturate addiction involve grave physiopathologic processes which result in "craving", then they may be designated as diseases (and they are included in the American Medical Association's nomenclature of diseases). The gamma and delta species of alcoholism may be regarded so by the same tokens (and alcoholism is included, too, in the list of the American Medical Association). Of course it is a matter of opinion whether or not such processes are designated as diseases. On the other hand, the presence of the physiopa-thological changes leading to craving cannot be denied in the addictions, whether to narcotic drugs or to alcohol. The current majority opinion to which the present writer subscribes, and subscribed before it was a majority opinion, is that anomalous forms of the ingestion of narcotics and alcohol, such as drinking with loss of control and physical dependence, are caused by physiopathological processes and constitute diseases.

If at this point, before starting another bout, he is placed in a situation in which he has no access of alcohol, he will not show any of those behaviours that the absence of alcohol brings forth during the state of intoxication. He may stay in an institution for many months without showing any distress, even if no therapy is being carried out. Here one certainly cannot speak of an irresistible craving or a physical demand for alcohol, even though on leaving the institution he may immediately turn to alcohol.

The loss of control has been aptly designated by Stewart as loss of freedom. This loss of freedom follows the first ingestion of alcohol in a new bout. The choice of the expression is felicitous as it reflects the despair that the alcoholic feels. Moreover it perhaps brings home to the nonspecialized physician, psychologist and social worker the idea that he is not dealing with a free agent and that it is futile to suggest to the patient that he "cut down on his drinking".

The loss of control which is described by members of Alcoholics Anonymous as well as by students of alcoholism as the inability to stop after one or two glasses, and is sometimes referred to as the insatiability of the alcohol addict (e.g., Straus and McCarthy, Vogel), seems to be characterized by minor withdrawal symptoms in the presence of alcohol in the blood stream and the failure to achieve the desired euphoria for more than a few minutes. These symptoms explain superficially the behavior observed in the so-called loss of control and they suggest a combination of short-range accommodation of nervous tissue with long range acquired increased tolerance.

A Working Hypothesis. The various psychological and psychiatric etiologies of alcoholism may fully explain the heavy drinking which paves the way for addiction, but they do not explain the great changes, the progressions, and the loss of control as they occur in gamma alcoholism. The same is true of sociocultural etiologies, although some drinking patterns inherent in certain sociocultural constellations play a role in the conditioning of the cell metabolism (particularly in the genesis of delta alcoholism).

As far as America is concerned, where the therapist is predominantly concerned with the gamma alcoholic, I would suggest that the main structure around which research should center is the pharmacological process of addiction.

15

J. D. Frank:
Persuasion and Healing

Reviewed by Mark Aveline

Jerome Frank, notable psychotherapy researcher, emeritus professor of psychiatry at Johns Hopkins, and persistent campaigner for nuclear disarmament, published the first edition of *Persuasion and Healing* in 1961. The revised edition, extensively rewritten, and the focus of this appraisal, came out in 1973.

I have particular affection for this book, it being the first psychotherapy text that made any sense to me. Here was a writer that described the healing processes common to all successful psychotherapy—an integrationist after my own heart, a man who wrote common truths which felt intuitively right. What did he say, how have his insights stood the test of time, and did he neglect important areas of the psychotherapy process?

As the title suggests, Frank is concerned with the process of healing in which he sees acts of persuasion as central: psychotherapy is viewed as an example of person-to-person influence. Writing now, the word "influence" is likely to raise hackles in certain psychodynamic circles. Perhaps as a dialectic reaction to the rise of the directive behavioral therapies some propose an ideal that psychotherapy is nondirective, simply a "being with" while creative resolutions emerge within the patient. Frank takes an equally hopeful but more pragmatic view. His hypotheses are (1) "a major source of the distress and disability of persons who seek psychotherapeutic help is demoralization, a sense of failure or of powerlessness to affect oneself and one's environment" and (2) common to all types of psychotherapy are features that combat demoralization by alleviating specific symptoms of distress or disordered behavior and, more importantly, restoring self-confidence and promoting a sense of mastery through successful experiences.

Frank recognizes that each school of psychotherapy has its own conceptual schemes and practices, and that therapists, not surprisingly, emphasize the value of their own schools of working. His argument is that what they have in common is more important in healing than what divides them. His thesis is not, as some have deemed, an assault on the effectiveness of psychotherapy, rather a homing-in on essentials.

Each chapter is headed by a quotation from *Alice's Adventures in Wonderland*. Says the Dodo, "Everybody has won and all must have prizes." This is all too true of psychotherapy. Smith, Glass, and Miller (1980) demonstrated with their meta-analysis of effect size in 375 studies involving 25,000 subjects that indeed psychotherapy is effective. The average patient is 80 percent better off than the untreated control. However, their studies and many others have failed to show a clear lead in effectiveness of one system of dynamic psychotherapy over the rest. Type of therapy probably accounts for less than 25 percent of the outcome variance.

THE ASSUMPTIVE WORLD

In Chapter 1, which places psychotherapy in its American context, three key elements enter into Frank's characterization of the subject. First, there is a trained, socially sanctioned healer to whom, second, a sufferer comes seeking relief and, third, that jointly the healer and the sufferer, often with the aid of the group, participate in a circumscribed more or less structured series of emotionally charged words, acts and rituals that mediate the healing influence. So far, so good. The comparison is then drawn with primitive healing, religious conversion and even so called *brainwashing* (my emphasis); these themes are explored in Chapters 3, 4, and 5.

For me, Chapter 2 is of prime importance. Building his conceptual framework, Frank suggests that the protean problems for which psychotherapy is sought or offered can be viewed as temporary or persistent unsuccessful adaptations to stress. These failures are determined by personal inadequacies arising from important early life experiences (and it is recognized from constitutional factors, both in-born and acquired). Were Frank to be writing now, I hope he would give greater emphasis to the third dimension of interactions within the systems in which the individual lives now. In order to function it is imperative for everyone to impose an order on the welter of experiences impinging upon him. "To do this, he develops out of his personal experiences a set of more or less implicit assumptions about himself and the nature of himself and the world in which he lives, enabling him to predict the behavior of himself and others and the outcome of his own actions. The totality of each person's assumptions may be conveniently termed his assumptive world."

The concept of an assumptive world is close to George Kelly's view of man as a scientist actively construing his world and in quite different language the complex inner world of object relations developed by Fairbairn, Guntrip, Winnicott and Klein in this country and Kohut and Kernberg in the United States. These latter therapists describe distorting inner maps of psychological reality, developed as the self fragments or fails to integrate in the face of frustration and disappointment in early childhood. While not being a richly worked concept, it has the merit of being easy to understand. To function and enjoy life, a person's assumptive world must correspond to conditions as they actually are. The validity of assumptions can be checked against experience. As man is a social creature, his attitudes and values are formed and validated in interactions with others. For example, between husband and wife the mutual expectation of a chain of rewarding interactions, alternating the roles of listener and supporter, is confirmed and strengthened when that happens, but disrupted when it does not occur. What expectations are brought, whether they be positive or negative and how these expectations link with childhood transactions is of special interest in psychotherapy. The child's view is based on his experience of his environment and the reference groups he has encountered. This may be unrepresentative, or lacking in some crucial aspect, or may be ambiguous or inconsistent. Deficiencies in the assumptive world ill-equip the individual to cope with stress and adapt; change is felt as threatening; the old structure is held onto; regressive patterns of coping are deployed. The necessity for change is minimized by avoidance of the facts from within and without (repression and denial), and by seeking false confirmations.

The aim of psychotherapy, then, is to help the patient correct the attitudes causing him trouble. It will be difficult to alter major assumptive systems. Modestly, and probably realistically, Frank sees the changes produced by psychotherapy as minor; however, this is often sufficient. A change in one assumptive system initiates a chain of events which alters other systems. Frank sets up his argument in the next three chapters by suggesting that altering the general attitude to changing, or more specifically inducing a move from demoralization to hope, is the key element of the healing process, and that two elements strengthen the therapist's position—power and similarity.

THE PSYCHOTHERAPIST AS SHAMAN, PERSUADER, AND PLACEBO AGENT

Chapters 3 to 6 cast the net widely. Western industrial societies view illness essentially as a malfunctioning of the body to be corrected by appropriate medical and surgical interventions. Nonmedical practitioners, who in the world treat many more sufferers than do physicians, "see illness as a disorder of the total person, involving not only his body but his image of himself and his relations to his group. Instead of emphasizing conquest of the disease they focus on stimulating or strengthening the patients' natural healing powers." The healer enters into an intense emotional relationship with the patient.

To illustrate, but not, as he acknowledges, to prove his theme, Frank describes the practices of shamans in primitive cultures. Special feelings of hopelessness such as death curses are countered by involvement in powerful rituals staged by the healer. The shaman knows his culture well, occupies a position of respect in it (and is careful to select cases that will respond!). The shaman encourages catharsis, is confident of success, and prescribes vivid, impressive activities, often publically performed, for the patient to undertake; these activities tap shared assumptive beliefs of the patient, healer and that society. The self-worth of the patient is heightened by being the focus of attention; the confession of secrets helps to make sense of his condition, counters his sense of sin and brings him into a closer relationship with the group and the shaman. Religious healing as at Lourdes affords another example of soul medicine.

One result of successful psychotherapy often is a more optimistic attitude to the meaning of existence. In a most uncomfortable comparison, the active ingredient in religious revivalism and thought reform are seen as relevant to change in psychotherapy. Frank puts on one side questions of desirability and moral validity. He focuses on the demoralization that usually characterises the preconversion state, on the emotional approach of the converter who is in the ascendent position and the sense of inner joy that follows conversion to the other's viewpoint. In brainwashing personal humiliation and invasion of privacy feature. Self-accusation and group accusation play their part. Participation and repetition pave the way to the desired end. ESP and the Jones catastrophe in Guyana are contemporary examples of the misuse of psychological power. Rereading Chapter 4 was a salutary experience; the familiar face of interpretation, disclosure, feedback and working through in regular sessions took on a new cast. Psychotherapy is undoubtedly powerful and a little of that power resides in the mystique of the situation. It must not be forgotten that the patient is in a vulnerable state and is open to abuse. I was reminded once more of the importance of the therapist having the highest ethical standards and of the robust self-preserving attitudes that Strupp and his colleagues (1977) urge patients to adopt.

Chapters 5 and 6 are easier to take. Experimental studies on persuasion, while limited in their generalizability are illuminating if, in a controlled setting, a clinical effect can be reproduced. In summary, aroused subjects seek reasons for their state and readily adopt explanations proffered by the experimenter. Active participation fosters change in opinion. Opinions held by the group tend to be adopted by the individual. Submissive individuals with low self-esteem, lacking in self-confidence and prone to anxiety are especially susceptible to persuasion; as is readily apparent, this profile characterizes many of those who seek psychotherapy. Demand situations, such as hypnosis, provide cues as to what is expected of the subject, cues of which the experimenter may be unaware. The higher the power, prestige or status of the experimenter, the greater is his biasing effect. Operant conditioning has been shown to be a powerful source of human learning and as an unconscious and occasionally conscious force, has to be considered by the proponents of nondirective psychotherapy. These studies identify processes that may well occur in therapy interactions. Whether their result is compliance alone, or the beginning of internalization and enduring change has yet to be decided.

In Chapter 6, Frank reviews the evidence of the effects of placebos and the importance in psychotherapy of bringing the patient's expectations into line with what they will actually experience. Many of the studies reviewed have been carried out by Frank and his team of researchers over a twenty-five year period. The work of the team is described at greater length in Frank (1974). The team, which has included Morris Parloff, Barry Gurland, Rudolf Hoehn-Saric, Stan Imber, Bernard Liberman, and Anthony Stone, is now, sadly, dispersed and, such is the transient nature of even solid achievement, not replaced.

Freud (1905), recognized the fact that "expectation coloured by hope and faith is an effective force with which we have to reckon . . . in all our attempts at treatment and cure." Frank found that mean personal discomfort scores fell dramatically in outpatients given placebo medication described as being a helpful preparation for their complaints; significantly, much of the improvement occurred before commencing the medication. The patients appeared to be responding to the increased interest and enthusiasm of the staff. Other studies underline the power of favourable expectations in the physician and that the placebo response is particularly a function of current mental sets and less so of enduring personality traits.

Of course, what is being described is change in symptoms and not the attitudinal change sought by psychotherapy. Mobilizing hope, it may be said, gets the process going.

An important comparison of outcome in patients with neuroses randomly assigned to minimal, individual, or group therapy showed an equal and sustained drop in personal discomfort. Decrease in social ineffectiveness was most apparent in the group treatment and especially in those who stayed in the group for at least six months. No improvement was seen in the minimal therapy group. The key ingredient in change in social ineffectiveness appears to be contact with people in which some form of learning takes place. It must be said that five years later there was no significant difference between all three groups. I interpret this as meaning that psychotherapy is one of a variety of influences that people may be exposed to in their lives and that when it works, it does so by catalysing changes that were awaiting favorable circumstances.

The findings of experimental research coincide with simple observation of the ways in which therapists strengthen patients' expectation of help and shape the way in which this is to be received. For example, psychoanalysts are prone to reinforce their status as help giver and authority figure by use of culturally established symbols. "They include heavily ladened book cases, couch with easy chair, and usually a large photograph of the leader of their particular school gazing benignly, but impressively on the proceedings." The fact that role orientation figures large in early therapy sessions led Frank to devise and demonstrate the beneficial effect of pretherapy role induction procedures. This finding has influenced clinical practice and similar procedures are in standard use in many individual and group therapy centers.

THE THERAPIST AND THE EVOCATIVE AND DIRECTIVE PSYCHOTHERAPIES

Not only is the patient prepared for his role but the training institutes have a similar socialization function for the therapist. For example, in analytic training, the analysand immerses himself in the training program and develops his self-confidence through group identification. The language he learns is arcane and only understood by initiates. His personal analysis requires full participation and confers mastery of the technique and theory. The real sacrifices in terms of family life and interests are rewarded by high prestige and, at least in the United States, financial security. However, arrival at the status of Member of the Institute depends on the "candidate" completing his training analysis to the satisfaction of the senior analysts. As Frank comments, the incentive to conform is great and the whole process resembles indoctrination. Like Frank, I feel the same analysis could be applied to many trainings.

The purpose of training analysis is to foster self-knowledge, thereby freeing the therapist of certain conflicts and vulnerabilities, and to develop greater objectivity so that the therapist will be more sensitive to and tolerant of the attitudes and feelings of his patients. Expert therapists are more able to establish and maintain therapeutic relationships than nonexperts, but there is clearly a fine line between objectivity and coldness, and self-awareness and morbid introspection. Harking back to an earlier theme, cultural, social, and attitudinal similarity between therapist and patient are favourable prognostic indicators but what counts at the end of the day is the nature of the relationships that they form. David Malan (1963) concluded in his study of brief psychotherapy that "prognosis is best when there is a willingness on the part of the patient and the therapist to become deeply involved and . . . to bear the tension that inevitably ensues."

The remaining chapters describe individual group and residential therapies. The last is a particularly fine account of the traditional mental hospital and ways in which the therapeutic community may mobilize helpful forces.

All forms of psychotherapy can be placed on an evocative-directive continuum.

Evocative therapies such as psychoanalysis and Rogerian client-centered therapy aim to promote the patient's total personality development. The therapist is facilitative and permissive, and provides the patient with experiences that will enable him to overcome his fears, abandon his defenses and realize his potential for self-actualization, joy and harmonious relationships with others. The assumption is that this potential is stymied through hurtful experiences in childhood which led to the development of self-protective and self-limiting defences. Increased maturity, creativity, spontaneity are the benchmarks of success. Analysis, which is especially suitable for patients with the ability to describe their inner world, is itself, like everything else, subject to influence. The European context shaped the Freudian model of the therapist as an aloof parent to whom secrets are confided; in less hierarchical America, a more comradely model prevails. Also American action-orientated pragmatism gave a major push to the directive therapies.

In what ways can evocative therapies be viewed as methods of persuasion? Taking again the paradigm of analysis, the patient is encouraged to express himself in complete freedom, but, often with little overt encouragement that he is doing well. From a position of dependence, he struggles with upsetting feelings sustained by his belief that benefit will accrue and that in this his therapist, despite his ambiguous social behaviour, is an expert guide. For him modeling or identification is a potent source of covert influence. The therapist's flexibility and tolerance may be adopted into his own nature, likewise open acceptance of limitations will help the patient to feel less threatened by his own shortcomings. In theory the therapist is neutral but in practice subtle cues influence what material the patient produces. These productions are then taken as confirmations of prestigious theory and as marks of progress. The very ambiguity of the situation fosters a wish, mixed with resentment and other important emotions, to get it right. Exploration of the past and disclosure of guilt is met with impartial interest that implies forgiveness. Interpretations make sense of current feelings, often in terms of past experience. What was inexplicable becomes explicable; and the explanation gains in power as the patient discovers its utility in everyday life. Furthermore the dramatic quality of Freudian images of battling drives and Jungian timeless archetypes has its own appeal.

Directive therapies reduce ambiguity to the minimum and structure the therapy situation as much as possible. Exhortation, advice, instruction, and providing a good example, the familiar forms of persuasion, all feature. The aim is to help the patient gain or regain his sense of control. The therapist builds up faith by demonstrating his skill in a particular technique, and the patient consolidates this by active participation. The persuasive element (reinforcement, modeling and counterconditioning) are given open recognition in theory and practice. Inspired, the patient enters states of great emotional arousal in which he is more open to change, as through, for example, flooding he is confronted with situations and inner feelings previously avoided. A sense of mastery follows success.

COMMENTS

Frank stands squarely in the nonspecific camp of therapeutic factors: these are held to be of overwhelming importance in the healing processes of psychotherapy. His position is strongly buttressed, on the one hand, by the lack of evidence that certain forms of psychotherapy are significantly better than others, and on the other by the finding that benefit undoubtedly does accrue from therapy, personal distress is reduced, and social effectiveness is increased. His insights have stood the test of time and therefore one might have expected the multitude of different psychotherapies to diminish in number as a common, empirically based therapy came into being. Yet new hordes have emerged to swell the considerable body of the host. How can this be?

Psychotherapists at one end of the spectrum are uncomfortable with any notion that they influence, worse still manipulate their patients; their work, though informed by complex theory and prescription of technique, is closer in its imaginative and creative aspects to art than science. Their opposites embrace science and a vocabulary of goals, methods and objective behavior. Both are aware that the effectiveness of their approaches leaves much to be desired. Also if theory is as good as it is made out to be, accurate prediction of outcome should be easy. It is not. There is a gap between idealized theory and reality. Doubt, however, may be reduced by conviction and narrowing of focus to eliminate dissonant facts. This, I hasten to concede may be true of the "nonspecific therapist" as well as the "schools man." New schools represent new hope—and advances in knowledge too! A further element in the continuation of schools is simple human needs to be different or special and to belong. A final factor, and one, which in view of the individual and enormously varied nature of the subject is luckily irradicable, is personal preference itself. Having been fortunate to meet many therapists of different persuasions, I conclude that they adopt approaches which they are comfortable with and which make sense to them in some personal way. The combination is generally beneficial.

Frank would be the first to acknowledge that his account is partial, both in focus and in bias. Describing the common elements in psychotherapy means giving less emphasis to the unique aspects of the different systems. For example, he neglects to report the value demonstrated in Malan's study and the Menninger Psychotherapy Research Project on analytically orientated psychotherapy of focusing on transference, particularly negative transference, and termination and loss. Here therapy and research combine to identify an important specific element in one kind of practice.

Persuasion and its servants have star billing in some therapies, and, superficially, a walk-on role in others. Frank has performed a most valuable service in his overview by reframing hallowed practices and forcing therapists to consider what are the effective ingredients in their approach: refinement may follow. At the very least nonspecific factors are crucial in initiating change, fostering hope and countering demoralization. Also it is unlikely that therapists will be effective unless they provide some form of success experiences. In my judgement they are necessary and almost sufficient causes of change.

Truth has yet to be mentioned. In the text various theories of development and personality structure are referred to as appealing and plausible, and the point is well made that a theory does not have to be true to be influential. Nevertheless, aspects of the truth are there to be discovered and rediscovered; and an accurate theory is much better than a plausible one. The early work of Laing and the observation-based deductions of Bowlby and Mahler, to mention but two, have special relevance for certain problems of self relationships and of failures of development. Not only do they fit the facts but they help the therapist by providing a structure to support him against the cold winds of confusion and doubt.

By taking such a dispassionate anthropological view of healing, Frank does not do justice to the positive elements in psychotherapy. Psychotherapy is a special kind of healing for emotional hurts; "thou shalt not exploit" is fundamental to its ethics. Persuasion is a poor description of the sustained effort needed to undo fundamental damage to self-esteem and trust. If psychotherapy is persuasion, then it is a benevolent form. Modern psychotherapies emphasize personal responsibility and choice: indeed special care is taken not to foster excessive dependence; ideally the patient is enabled to leave therapy as an equal. Freedom, not conformity is their aim.

Lucid, literate and persuasive, *Persuasion and Healing* was a classic then, and remains one now.

REFERENCES

Frank, J. D. (1974). Therapeutic components of psythotherapy. A 25 year progress report of research. *Journal of Nervous and Mental Disease* 159: 325–342.
Freud, S. (1905). Physical (or mental) treatment. *Standard Edition*.
Malan, D. H. (1963). *A Study of Brief Psychotherapy*. London: Tavistock.
Smith, M. L., Glass, G. V., and Miller, T. I. (1980). *The Benefits of Psychotherapy*. Baltimore, MD: Johns Hopkins University Press.
Strupp, H. H., Hadley, S. W., and Gomes-Schwartz, B. (1977). *Psychotherapy for Better or Worse*. New York: Jason Aronson.

Selections from
Persuasion and Healing
by J. D. Frank

THE ASSUMPTIVE WORLD

In order to be able to function, everyone must impose an order and regularity on the welter of experiences impinging upon him. To do this, he develops out of his personal experiences a set of more or less implicit assumptions about himself and the nature of the world in which he lives, enabling him to predict the behavior of others and the outcome of his own actions. The totality of each person's assumptions may be conveniently termed his "assumptive world."

This is a short-hand expression for a highly structured, complex, interacting set of values, expectations, and images of oneself and others, which guide and in turn are guided by a person's perceptions and behavior and which are closely related to his emotional states and his feelings of well-being.

FORMATION OF THE ASSUMPTIVE WORLD

For a person to be able to function successfully and enjoy life, his assumptive world must correspond to conditions as they actually are. For it is only to the extent that a person can successfully predict the results of his acts that he can behave in such a way as to maximize chances for success and minimize those for failure. Thus everyone is strongly motivated constantly to check the validity of his assumptions, and every act is both a consequence of a more or less explicit expectation and a test of its validity. If the consequences of the act fail to confirm the prediction, the person is in trouble. He must either modify his expectations and the corresponding behavior or resort to maneuvers to conceal their incorrectness and evade their unfortunate consequences. This process for the most part goes on automatically and outside of awareness.

The validity of some aspects of the assumptive world can be checked against experiences unmediated by other persons. For example, the test of the assumption that a glowing poker is hot is to touch it. But since man is a social creature, his most significant experiences are with other persons, and those aspects of his assumptive world most essential to his functioning—his attitudes and values—can only be validated through his interactions with others, individually or in groups. An example of an interaction chain between two persons, which is guided by, and helps to form, the attitudes of each, is the following:

A man comes home late for supper after a hard day at the office and greets his wife with a warm kiss. She responds in kind and makes a sympathetic remark about his work load as they go in to supper. This encourages him to tell her about the events of the day. She shows interest, so he continues until he has gotten everything off his chest. Then he is prepared to listen to his wife's account of her doings, which he encourages with appropriate signs of interest, and so they have a pleasant chatty meal. Such an interactional chain is based on mutual expectations of affection and understanding and, in turn, strengthens these expectations, increasing the likelihood of similar mutually gratifying behavior on subsequent occasions. Thus the favorable behavior and assumptive systems of each member of the couple with respect to their relationship continually reinforce each other.

Starting the same way, the interaction might run quite a different course. The wife does not return her husband's kiss, but says coldly that he is late for supper again. As they go in to dinner he makes an angry rejoinder to which she responds in kind. He picks up the paper and buries himself in it while he eats. She does the same with a book. Here the husband's initial favorable expectations, which he expressed by a warm kiss, are disappointed by his wife's coolness. This leads him to alter his assumption about his wife's attitude and to change his behavior correspondingly. The subsequent interactions lead to a progressive breakdown of communication, confirming the unfavorable mutual expectancies of each spouse and increasing the likelihood that future interactional chains will run the same unsatisfactory course. This example illustrates how interactions between two persons form a mutually regulative system in which the behavior of each influences the other and simultaneously helps each to form his own psychic life.

The development of the assumptive world starts as soon as the infant enters into transactions with his environment. These generate experiences leading him to form assumptions about the world in which he finds himself. These coalesce into generalizations, whose validity depends on two factors: the representativeness of the sample on which they are based, and the accuracy of the information it gives him.

The infant, of course, has only very small samples to go on. This does not matter too much with respect to the inanimate world because its features are relatively homogeneous and supply clear, unambiguous information. One does not have to experience many chairs or shoes to reach valid generalizations about chairs and shoes, and a single experience with a lighted match suffices to reach a valid conclusion about the properties of fire.

This does not hold true in the world of people. Their messages are often ambiguous and complex, and the child's sample—his own family in the first instance—may be far from typical. If the family group provides a rich repertory of adaptive skills, and if his parents make him feel loved and wanted and treat him as if he is capable and good, then he comes to see himself as a well-equipped, competent, lovable person in a friendly, secure universe. The world is his oyster. He welcomes new experiences, tackles them with confidence, and easily modifies his behavior and assumptive world according to the outcome. Thus he readily learns and develops.

The family environment may fall short of this ideal in many ways. It may be lacking in opportunities for certain experiences. For example, there may be no adequate father figure or inadequate opportunity to play with other children. Thus the child may grow up lacking certain important assumptive systems simply for want of a chance to develop them. More serious difficulties occur if the child is unfortunate enough to have unloving or inconsistent parents. If they are profoundly inconsistent, he may become so confused that he loses all confidence in his ability to interpret experience. This may contribute to a schizophrenic breakdown in later life. Parental rejection may lead him to see himself as unlovable, in a hostile world: "I a stranger and afraid. In a world I never made." If he has been constantly belittled, he may grow up feeling inadequate to deal with many situations. Assumptive systems like these obviously tend to cause a person to avoid new experiences since he fears the worst from them.

THE STABILITY OF THE ASSUMPTIVE WORLD IN RELATION TO PSYCHOTHERAPY

According to the formulation offered here, the aim of psychotherapy is to help a person to feel and function better by enabling him to make appropriate modifications in his assumptive world. What helps or hinders such changes? Assumptive systems, once established, tend to resist change for a variety of reasons. One is that with increasing age new experiences lose their power to produce changes in established patterns. This may be partly because of physiological changes concomitant with maturation and also because, as life goes on, new experiences are increasingly outweighed by the accumulation of previous ones. . . .

Since a person relies on his assumptive world to create a predictable universe, anything that casts doubt on any part of it is a threat to his personal security. An experience that is inconsistent with a person's expectations arouses a feeling of surprise. This may be tinged with fear or other unpleasant feelings if the person doubts his ability to make the necessary adjustment, or exhilaration if he is confident he can cope with the situation. That is, the emotional impact of an experience seems related to the extent to which it implies the necessity of a change in the assumptive world. It seems as if the emotional upheaval is greater the more crucial to the person's security the attitude is and the greater the change required. Contrast the emotions accompanying the discovery that what one took to be a robin is really a bluebird with those accompanying a religious conversion involving far-reaching changes in the convert's values.

. . . the aims of all [psychotherapy's] forms are to help the patient correct the attitudes causing him trouble. These may be quite circumscribed and specific, such as a fear of snakes, or very general, such as a sense of alienation or despair; but in all cases success in psychotherapy depends, in the first instance, on combating the more general attitudes that hamper the patient's ability to change. Thus success in therapy depends in large part on its ability to combat the patient's demoralization and heighten his hopes of relief. All forms of psychotherapy do this implicitly, regardless of their explicit aims. Progress in therapy, in turn, further shifts the balance toward the "welfare emotions," such as love, joy, and pride, so that, with luck, the process becomes self-enhancing.

Major assumptive systems, especially unhealthy ones, are resistant to change, and in most cases the changes produced by psychotherapy are minor. Fortunately, this often suffices. Many maladaptive patterns can be improved without extensive changes in the patient's assumptive world. Much psychotherapy consists of supporting patients through crises until they can regain their previous state of equilibrium. Small changes produced by psychotherapy in one assumptive system may initiate a train of events that eventually produce changes in many others. By enabling a patient to gain a more favorable perception of his boss, for example, psychotherapy may lead him to treat the boss differently. This may evoke changes in the boss' behavior that heighten the patient's self-confidence, initiating a widening circle of beneficial changes in his assumptions about himself and other people. . . .

AMERICAN PSYCHOTHERAPY IN PERSPECTIVE

Human beings spend most of their lives interacting with each other. In the process they influence one another powerfully for good or ill. This book

has singled out for study one particular class of influencing procedures—
the psychotherapy of adults. . . .

Common Features of Psychotherapy

Four shared features of all psychotherapies seem distinguishable. The first
is a particular type of relationship between the patient and a help-giver,
sometimes in the context of a group. The essential ingredient of this
relationship is that the patient has confidence in the therapist's competence
and in his desire to be of help. That is, the patient must feel that the
therapist genuinely cares about his welfare.

Caring in this sense does not necessarily imply approval, but rather a
determination to persist in trying to help no matter how desperate the
patient's condition or how outrageous his behavior. Thus the therapeutic
relationship always implies genuine acceptance of the sufferer, if not for
what he is, then for what he can become, as well as the therapist's belief
that the patient can master his problems.

The therapist's acceptance, based on empathic understanding, validates
the patient's personal outlook on life. The patient's sense that he is
understood and accepted by someone he respects is a strong antidote to
feelings of alienation and is a potent enhancer of morale. . . .

The patient's faith in the therapist's competence is enhanced by the
latter's socially sanctioned role as a help-giver, evidenced by the fact that
he has had special training and, in therapy, by his mastery of a special
technique. The success of relatively untrained therapists, however, is
evidence that this is not always necessary.

A second common feature of all psychotherapies is that their locales are
designated by society as places of healing. Thus the setting itself arouses
the patient's expectation of help. . . . Protected by the setting, the patient
can concentrate on the prescribed therapeutic activities. He can participate
in complex, emotionally charged rituals, suspend his critical faculties,
freely express his emotions, indulge in leisurely self-exploration, day-
dream, or do whatever else the therapy prescribes, secure in the knowledge that no harm will come to him during the session and that he will not
be held accountable in his daily life for whatever he says or does during it.
By thus freeing him to experiment, the combination of healer and setting
create favorable conditions for change.

Third, all psychotherapies are based on a rationale or myth which
includes an explanation of illness and health, deviancy, and normality. If
the rationale is to combat the patient's demoralization, it must obviously
imply an optimistic philosophy of human nature. This is clearly true of the
rationales underlying most American psychotherapies, which assume that

aggression, cruelty, and other unattractive forms of human behavior result from past hurts and frustrations and that, as the person progressively frees himself from these and achieves fuller self-awareness, leading him to feel more secure, he will become kinder, more loving, more open to others, and more able to reach his full potential. . . .

The fourth ingredient of all forms of psychotherapy is the task or procedure prescribed by the theory. Some therapeutic procedures closely guide the sufferer's activities, others impel him to take the initiative; but all share certain characteristics. The procedure is the means by which the sufferer is brought to see the error of his ways and correct them, thereby gaining relief. It also affords the patients a face-saving device for relinquishing his symptoms when he is prepared to do so. The procedure demands some effort or sacrifice on the patient's part, ranging all the way from collaborating in hypnosis to undergoing repeated painful shocks. . . .

The central point is that the therapeutic efficacy of rationales and techniques may lie not in their specific contents, which differ, but in their functions, which are the same. The therapeutic relationship, setting, rationale, and task in conjunction influence patients in five interrelated ways which seem necessary to produce attitude change and therapeutic benefit. First, they provide him with new opportunities for learning at both cognitive and experiential levels. Cognitively the therapist may help the patient to clarify sources of his difficulties in his past life, or the contingencies in his environment that maintain his distress. The therapist and other members of a group in group therapy also serve as models of alternative ways of handling problems. But the most important learning in therapy is probably experiential and is provided by confronting the patient with discrepancies or contradictions between his assumptive world and actuality. Insight-oriented therapies confront him with discrepancies between his self-image and his own hidden feelings; group methods face him with discrepancies between his assumptions about others and their actual feelings or between the impression he thinks he is making and his actual effect. Awareness of these dissonances creates a powerful incentive to change in directions suggested by the cognitive insights the patient is gaining simultaneously.

Second, all therapies enhance the patient's hope of relief. This hope rests in part on the patient's faith in the therapist's and the treatment method. Experienced therapists in early interviews explicitly try to strengthen the patient's favorable expectations and to tailor them to the therapeutic procedure.

A more enduring source of hope deserves a heading of its own because it includes other components. This is, third, the provision of success experiences which enhance the sufferer's sense of mastery, interpersonal competence, or capability. The detailed structure of behavior therapies, the objective measures of progress, and the emphasis on the patient's active participation virtually assure that he will experience successes as treatment progresses.

Unstructured, open-ended procedures like psychoanalysis also provide success experiences. These therapies seem ideally suited for intelligent, verbally adept patients who rely heavily on words to cope with life's problems. The patient experiences a feeling of mastery when he gains a new insight or becomes aware of a hitherto unconscious thought or feeling. The therapist enhances the patient's sense of achievement by maintaining that all progress is due to the patient's own efforts. Thus all successful therapies implicitly or explicitly change the patient's image of himself as a person who is overwhelmed by his symptoms and problems to that of one who can master them.

Fourth, all forms of psychotherapy help the patient to overcome his demoralizing sense of alienation from his fellows. Through his interactions with the therapist and the group (if there is one) within the framework of a shared conceptual scheme, he discovers that his problems are not unique and that others can understand him and do care about his welfare. . . .

In short, when successful, all forms of psychotherapy relieve dysphoric feelings, rekindle the patient's hopes, increase his sense of mastery over himself and his environment, and in general restore his morale. As a result, he becomes able to tackle the problems he had been avoiding and to experiment with new, better ways of handling them. These new capabilities decrease the chance that he will become demoralized again and, with good fortune, enable him to continue to make gains after psychotherapy has ended.

16

Thomas S. Szasz:
The Myth of Mental Illness

Reviewed by John Birtchnell

Thomas Szasz is one of the most disliked names in contemporary psychiatry, and *The Myth of Mental Illness* is one of the most disapproved of books. It was Szasz's contention that illness can affect only the body and that there can be no such thing as an illness of the mind. He described mental illness as a metaphorical illness, maintaining that one can speak of a "sick" mind only in the same way as one can speak of a "sick" joke or a "sick" economy. He went on to argue that, if there is no mental illness, there can be no treatment for it, and no cure of it. There was, for him therefore, no medical, moral, or legal justification for involuntary psychiatric intervention or hospital admission. Such actions he considered to be crimes against humanity. He believed, after John Stuart Mill, that a man's body and soul are his own and not the state's, and that each individual has the right to do with his body whatever he pleases so long as it does not harm anyone else or infringe on anybody else's rights.

Szasz's respect for human liberty may, in part, be the result of his youth being spent in an increasingly threatened part of Europe. In 1938, following the Nazi occupation of Austria, his family, who lived in Budapest, left Hungary for America. He was aged 18 and, shortly afterwards, entered the University of Cincinnati, from which he graduated with honors in physics. He is now almost 70, but still speaks with a Hungarian accent. In his book he observed that speaking a language with a foreign accent is like having a transference reaction. In such a reaction one person behaves towards another as though he were someone else previously familiar to him. His move from Hungary to America, at this critical time, may account for his subsequent preoccupation with language and with communication.

Szasz moved progressively further away from physics, the study of inert objects and natural laws, to a concern with what he termed man's sign-using behavior. He qualified in medicine at the age of 24, entered psychiatry two years later, and between the ages of 27 and 30 underwent psychoanalytic training. It is important to understand that, although he is often critical of Freud, he is seriously committed to psychoanalysis and has always maintained a private practice for voluntary fee-paying patients.

His contention was that what psychoanalysts and other psychosocially orientated psychiatrists do is communicate with patients by means of language, nonverbal signs, and rules. Beyond this, they analyze, by means of verbal symbols, the communicative interactions which they observe and in which they themselves engage. For this reason he believed that psychiatry has much in common with the sciences concerned with languages, sign-using, and communication. There is, in Szasz, a polarization between his first love, physics, and his later preoccupation with communication. It is this which lies at the heart of his distaste for the medical model of psychiatry. In fact, it was his enthusiasm for such disciplines as symbolic logic, semiotics, and sociology that caused him to deplore the reliance of psychiatry on what he considered to be the outmoded conceptual framework of organic medicine. The conceptual scaffolding of medicine, he argued, rests, quite reasonably, on the principles of physics and chemistry; but these have no relevance for his behavioral or interactional conception of psychiatry.

The Myth of Mental Illness, Szasz's first book, was written with great passion, and the ideas expressed in it were clearly pressing to be let out. He began it at the relatively early age of 34, when he was called to active duty in the U.S. Navy and when he was relieved of the burden of a full-time psychoanalytic practice. He was appointed to the chair of psychiatry at the Upstate Medical Center of the State University of New York in Syracuse, at the age of 36, before he submitted the book for publication. Within a year of its publication, the Commissioner of the New York State Department of Mental Hygiene demanded, in a letter which specifically cited the book, that Szasz be dismissed because he did not "believe" in mental illness. He survived, although some of his supporters were less fortunate. In an interview in 1972 he confessed that he continued to teach orthodox psychiatry to his students in much the same way as an atheist might teach comparative religion (Sabbagh 1972).

It is useful to draw parallels between Szasz and the psychologist Timothy Leary, whose seminal work, *The Interpersonal Diagnosis of Personality,* was published in 1957. Within Leary's book there were remarks which were every bit as contentious as those of Szasz, but either because his book had a more respectable title, or because he was a professor of psychology and not of psychiatry, he was able to get away with them. In the end, however, he suffered a worse fate than Szasz: he was expelled from his post at Harvard for continuing to advocate the use of psychedelic drugs. Szasz and Leary had both been influenced by the psychoanalyst Harry Stack Sullivan, whose own book *The Interpersonal Theory of Psychiatry* was published in 1953. Szasz drew freely on Sullivan's game model in explaining hysterical behavior. The inspiration for much of Leary's research derives from Sullivan's belief that the field of psychiatry is the field of interpersonal relations. Leary considered that Sullivan had convincingly buried the much-berated remains of descriptive, Kraepelinian and negatively value-toned psychiatry, but had provided no substitute system of classification. He devoted himself to rectifying this omission and predicted that "within a few decades" direct interpersonal terms would replace what he called "the disorganized nosology of present day psychiatry."

There is clearly an antiauthoritarian component to the personalities of both Szasz and Leary, and both have a need to challenge the established order of things. At the same time, both have a redeeming, constructive side to them. Szasz's criticisms of orthodox psychiatry feature mainly at the beginning and the end of his book. Once he had got these off his chest, he settled down to a sober and serious account of various alternatives to the medical model. It is not widely known that the book carries the subtitle *Foundations of a Theory of Personal Conduct*. Like Leary, he stated that he had two objectives. The first was what he called a "destructive" analysis of the concept of mental illness, and of psychiatry as a "pseudo-medical enterprise." The second, and to my mind by far the more important, was the presentation of a "constructive" synthesis of the knowledge which he had found useful in filling the gap created by the shedding of the "myth of mental illness."

The theme which runs throughout the book is Szasz's struggle to come to terms with the diagnosis of hysteria. In fact, had his iconoclastic zeal been less fervent, a more suitable title for the book might have been "Problems in the Diagnosis of Hysteria." This would have won him more friends and gained him less notoriety. He referred to hysteria as a paradigm of mental illness, and maintained that everything he said about hysteria would, in principle, equally apply to all other so-called mental illnesses. In fact, hysteria is a most unusual condition, and is far from what one might select to represent a typical mental illness. It belongs to a kind of no man's land between a physical and a mental condition, for although the patient presents with physical symptoms he does so for psychological reasons. The condition was deliberately chosen by Szasz because it so admirably suited his purpose, and the book is, I think, one of the best accounts of the possible mechanisms which lie behind the hysterical process.

One of Szasz's most consistent and compelling arguments is that an illness is something that happens to someone (i.e., something that one has). The illness takes over or inhabits the person's body. The function of the clinician is to work on this thing inside the person, to dispel it or to bring it under control. What disturbed Szasz about orthodox psychiatry is that it induces in the patient a passive attitude—that he simply lets the doctor get him better. This also applies, he felt, to classical psychoanalysis. In his opinion, most so-called mental illnesses are not something which one has, but something which one does. This distinction is perhaps not always as clear cut as he would have us believe. Many who suffer from recurrent, severe affective disorders would be in no doubt that these are things which happen to them, although it must be conceded that, whatever it is which does happen to them, it in turn causes them to do things, such as hide themselves away from others or give their possessions away. There are, of course, physical illnesses that cause patients to do things (the choreas, for example), although what they cause them to do are not of an interpersonal nature. The principle, however, has considerable relevance for psychiatry, for it implies that patients are, to a large extent, responsible for their thoughts, words, and actions, and therefore should play a more active and responsible part, with the support of the therapist, in resolving their problems. It has especial relevance for hysteria, in which the patient presents himself or herself as being helplessly in the grip of some physical condition but is, in fact, actively deciding to take on the condition, that is, he or she is actively deciding to be passive!

Szasz laid great emphasis on the fact that the hysteric chooses to play the role of a sick person because sick people get looked after in our society. Like the infant's cry, the message, "I am sick" is exceedingly effective in mobilizing others to some kind of helpful action. In the hysterical transaction, disability is used as a coercive tactic to force others to provide for one's needs. The hysteric would not adopt his particular posture if there were not those who are prepared to respond to it in a helping way. The helpers thus hasten to the side of the helpless. In the wild, the animal who pretends to be sick is either attacked or ignored. Szasz argued that within civilized societies there are understandings that it is acceptable to be weak and needy. One such understanding derives from religion. Should man be sick, help-seeking, poor, and humble, God will care for him and protect him: God will forgive him, help him, love him, and allow him to be passive and incompetent. Also, there are people within society who derive satisfaction from helping the needy. The parent who rewards his child's persistent helplessness and dependency in order to enhance his own importance and self-esteem is one such person.

Szasz considered that the physicians follow in the footsteps of their predecessors, the priests, in responding to the call of the sick. What passes for medical ethics, he claimed, is a set of paternalistic rules, the net effect of which is the persistent infantilization and domination of the patient by the physician. He accused Freud of a similar attitude, maintaining that he insisted that the psychoanalytic relationship between analyst and analysand must be that of a superior and a subordinate. He did not seem to regard genuine cooperation between equals as either possible or desirable. One suspects, therefore, that what lies behind Szasz's objection to psychiatric conditions being called illnesses is that this induces a one-down, helpless attitude in patients and a one-up helping attitude in psychiatrists. His inclination is clearly towards a cooperative endeavor between patient and therapist that maximizes the patient's choices in the conduct of his life.

What many psychiatrists find so confusing about Szasz is that he appears to be denying the existence of what so obviously do exist, namely mental illnesses. In fact, he does not deny the existence of the various diagnostic conditions, and quite freely writes of them. He simply chooses not to call them illnesses. Psychiatrists then counter with: if he acknowledges their existence, what does it matter what he calls them? It matters a great deal, because what one calls something is an indication of what class of phenomenon one considers it to belong to, and this determines how one responds to it. Quite early in the book Szasz made it clear that he considers diagnostic categories to be forms of communication, similar in certain respects to languages. Here again, hysteria fits into this class of phenomenon more easily than do certain other diagnostic categories. He maintained that it is pointless to think in terms of a cause or a treatment for a language. Instead, it is necessary to understand why the person chooses to speak in such a language and what he is trying to say in it. What makes hysteria such a challenge for Szasz is that the language the patient chooses to speak in is what he calls "the language of illness." Although he chooses to speak in the language of illness, he clearly is not ill.

For Szasz, interpreting the language of hysteria is similar to Freud's method of interpreting a dream. The choice of symptom is important, since this may be a clue to what the patient is trying to say. Szasz warned against trying to render the symbolism of the hysterical symptom into the more concrete form of ordinary language. There is a parallel here with Freud's distinction between the primary process of dreams and the secondary process of grammatical, logical speech. Szasz further warned that the hysteric's message may have been intended for an internal object, and not for the person who actually receives or tries to interpret it. A further feature of hysterical communications is that, like dreams, they may have a number of meanings all condensed into one.

The important question to ask about the communication of the hysteric is why does he not say what he needs to say straight out; why does he have to resort to such a roundabout form of communication? There are two obvious answers to this. The first is that indirect messages permit communicative contact when, without them, the alternative would be total inhibition, silence, and solitude; the second is that more direct communication might be offensive or forbidden. The indirect communication therefore has a protective function. By being ambiguous, the communicator is only hinting at a delicate issue, and may be able to disown both to the recipient or to himself the true content of the message. It could be said that the hysteric cannot afford to be aware of what he is doing, for if he were he could no longer allow himself to do it.

Considerations such as these led Szasz to describe the hysteric as both a liar and a cheat. He observed that psychiatrists are reluctant to use such blunt terms; once a person is called a patient, the psychiatrist somehow is unable to think in terms of deception or mendacity. This he believed is regrettable since it signifies the contemporary psychiatrist's sentimentalising attitude toward those they consider to be mentally ill. Szasz would insist that it is essential to be clear about the hysteric's intention to deceive before it is possible to understand and subsequently to help him. While it does not seem that the hysteric carefully plans his strategy, it is a mistake, he contended, to emphasise the unwitting quality of his behavior. "Conscious" and "unconscious" are terms with which Szasz is never comfortable, since they detract from the principle that, at all times, the patient is aware of, and carries responsibility for what he is doing.

In order to explain why the hysteric needs to resort to lying and cheating, Szasz drew upon games theory. In fact, as the book progressed he moved away from considering mental illness as languages toward considering them as forms of game playing. This set them more into a social context, and implied that psychiatric patients have motives for their actions, (i.e., that there is method in their madness). It is here that he felt that Sullivan had the edge on Freud, for Freud largely continued to relate to the patient as though he were ill, to consider that the pathology resided within him, and to encourage the patient to adopt a passive, regressive attitude. Phrased in terms of game-playing, the hysteric is someone who would gladly take advantage of cheating if he believed he could get away with it. He plays at being sick because he is afraid that if he tried to participate competently in certain real-life activities he would fail. His cheating is so staged as to lead those around him to interpret it not as a selfish stratagem but as unavoidable suffering. Viewed as a game, hysteria is characterized by the goal of domination and interpersonal control. The typical strategies employed in pursuing this goal are coercion by disability and illness.

One important feature of game playing is that it takes more than one person to play a game. A patient cannot continue to play his particular game unless the significant others with whom he interacts play the same game by the same rules. In one illustrative case, Szasz described a woman who found that the simplest and most effective way that she could cope with her oppressive, unreasonable, and intrusive mother was by lying. The discovery that her mother would accept her lies without openly challenging them encouraged her use of this strategy, and eventually lying became established as characteristic features of her personality. Szasz wrote, "As both she and I familiarized ourselves with the type of game she was playing, it became increasingly evident that the people to whom she lied knew, most of the time, that she was lying. And of course, she did too." He went on, "Her husband ostensibly accepted her lies as if they were truths and then used his knowledge that they were falsehoods to manipulate her in his own interests." Ideas such as this are very much a part of the theory of present-day family therapy.

Viewing mental illness, and in particular hysteria, as a form of game playing has considerable implications for therapy. By adopting a particular symptom, or complex of symptoms, the patient has adapted as best he can to his particular life situation. It is important to be respectful of this, and to appreciate the usefulness of the symptom for him. The psychiatrist whose sole aim is to free the patient of his symptom may be ignoring any consideration of how this might affect his adjustment to life. It could equally be argued that a patient may not be prepared to relinquish his symptom unless he can see a way of adapting to his circumstances without it. Szasz suggested a number of possible directions in which the hysteric might move. These include more effective coercion or domination of others; greater submission to others and increased preoccupation with suffering; or withdrawal from the struggle over interpersonal control by progressive isolation from real life relationships.

These last suggestions bear a striking resemblance to the kind of thinking that lay behind Leary's interpersonal classification of behavioral styles. Since, in their separate books, Szasz and Leary made no reference to each other, it seems likely that, although both were inspired by Sullivan, they reached their respective positions via independent routes. Adams (1964) effected a useful synthesis of the two approaches. Starting from the premise that mental illness is not a health or medical problem but a phenomenon involving interpersonal behavior, he proposed that programs of alleviation and prevention must rest on a systematic understanding of interpersonal conduct. He then drew attention to a body of recent research which indicated that all interpersonal behavior, whether adaptive or maladaptive, could meaningfully be categorized within one systematic frame of reference. This was organized around Leary's two dimensions of dominance-submission and affection–hostility. Fifteen years later, McLemore and Benjamin (1979) made a further significant contribution by proposing a general method for translating traditional diagnostic categories into psychosocial terms that avoided what they termed "continued endorsement of a disease conceptualisation of abnormality by being explicitly constructed in terms of psychosocial behaviors." Over the past decade, research in the interpersonal field has made considerable progress, and Kiesler (1986) concluded a comprehensive review with the statement, "Systematic interpersonal diagnosis is an increasingly viable and practicable option."

There was therefore in Szasz's book the germ of an idea, which, had it been more modestly presented, would have contributed to an interesting debate. He tended to spoil his case by being such a mischief maker. It seems likely that there was something of the mischiefmaker in Leary, too. Between them, they may have held back progress in the interpersonal field. Hopefully, more sober researchers are now making up the lost ground.

REFERENCES

Adams, H. B. (1964). Mental illness or interpersonal behavior. *American Psychologist* 19:191–197.
Kiesler, D. J. (1986). Interpersonal methods of diagnosis and treatment. In *Psychiatry, Vol. 1,* ed. J. O. Caveman, pp. 1–23. New York: Lippincott.
Leary, T. (1957). *The Interpersonal Diagnosis of Personality.* New York: Ronald.
McLemore, C. W. and Benjamin, L. S. (1979). Whatever happened to interpersonal diagnosis? *American Psychologist* 34:17–34.
Sabbagh, K. (1972). The boy from Syracuse. *World Medicine.*
Sullivan, H. S. (1953). *The Interpersonal Theory of Psychiatry.* New York: W. W. Norton.

Selections from
The Myth of Mental Illness
by Thomas Szasz

HYSTERIA AS A GAME

By slightly modifying Piaget's scheme of the development of the capacity to follow and to be aware of rules, I propose to distinguish three stages, or types, of mastery of inter-personal processes: coercion, self-help, and co-operation. This series constitutes a developmental sequence. Coercion is the simplest rule to follow, the easiest game to play; self-help is the next most difficult; and co-operation is the most demanding of them all.

Coercion, Self-Help and Co-operation in Hysteria

The hysteric plays a game in which there is an unequal mixture of coercive, self-helping, and co-operative strategies. While coercive manoeuvres predominate, elements of self-help and co-operation are not completely lacking. A distinct achievement of this type of behaviour is a synthesis of sorts among three separate and to some extent conflicting games, values, and styles of life. In this lies its strength as well as its weakness.

Because of this inner contradiction in the hysteric's life-game, he fails to play well at any one of three games. To begin with, the hysteric places a high value on coercive strategies. True, he may not be aware that he has made a choice between coercion and other strategies. His wish to coerce others may be 'unconscious'. Usually, however, it is not so much unconscious as it is in-explicit. In psychotherapy, it is generally recognized by the therapist and readily acknowledged by the patient. The point to be emphasized here is that although the hysteric espouses the value of coercion and domination he cannot play this game in a skillful and uninhibited manner. To do so requires two qualities he lacks: a relatively indiscriminating identification with the aggressor, and a large measure of insensitivity to the needs and feelings of others. The hysteric has too much compassion to play the game of domination openly and successfully. He can coerce and dominate with suffering, but not with "selfish" will.

To play the game of self-help well requires committing one's self to it. This often leads to isolation from others: human relationships are not strongly cultivated. Religious, artistic, or other work investments displace interest in personal relationships. Playing well at this game is highly rewarded in our culture. Preoccupation with one's body or with suffering and helplessness interferes, of course, with one's ability to concentrate on the practical tasks that must be mastered to play such games well. Moreover, the tactic of dominating others by displaying helplessness cannot be maintained unaltered in the face of a high degree of demonstrable competence in important areas of life. The aim of coercing others by exhibiting helplessness may still be retained but the tactics by which this goal is pursued must be modified. The proverbial absent-minded professor is a case in point. Here is a composite of the famous scientist, highly skilled in his complex work performance, who is at the same time as helpless as a child when it comes to feeding himself, putting on his boots, or paying his income tax. Exhibitions of helplessness in these areas invite help in exactly the same manner in which bodily complaints invite medical attention.

Finally, the game of co-operation implies and requires a value which the person exhibiting hysterical symptoms may not share at all. I believe that in hysteria, we are confronted with a genuine class of values—namely, between equality and co-operativeness on the one hand, and inequality and domination—submission on the other. This conflict of values actually takes place in two distinct spheres: in the interpersonal system of the patient and in the interpersonal system of therapy.

In psychiatry, the problem of hysteria is not formulated in this way. Psychiatrists prefer to operate with the tacit assumption that whatever their values are they are the same values that their patients hold and their colleagues share! Of course, this cannot always be the case. If, however, value conflicts of this sort are as important in psychiatry as I am suggesting why are they not made explicit? The answer is simple: because doing so threatens the cohesion of the group—that is, the prestige and the power of the psychiatric profession.

Hysteria as a Mixture of Conflicting Values and Disparate Games

The idea that hysterical symptoms (as well as other neurotic symptoms) are compromises is a cornerstone of psychoanalytic theory. Early in his work, Freud thought in terms of compromise formations between instinctual drives and social defences, or between selfish needs and the requirements of communal living. Later, he asserted that neuroses were due to conflicts and compromises between id and ego, or id and superego. I now want to describe hysteria as still another compromise, this time among three different types of games.

Typical of the coercive game we call "hysteria" is the powerful promotive impact of iconic body signs on those to whom they are directed. The patient's relatives, for example, tend to be deeply impressed by such communications, often much more deeply than they would be by similar statements framed in ordinary language. The display of sickness or suffering is thus useful for coercing others. This feature of hysteria, more than any other, accounts for its immediate and immense practical value to the patient.

The game of self-help is also present in most cases of hysteria. Classically, hysteria patients were said to exhibit an attitude of indifference towards their suffering. This manifest indifference signifies, firstly, a denial that the patient has in fact made a coercive communication and, secondly, and affirmation that the patient aspires to a measure of self-sufficiency. Hysterics are thus not wholly coercive in their relationship to others but are, to some extent, self-reliant and self-sufficient. However, they can attend to their self-helping strategies only half-heartedly, being ready to coerce by means of symptoms should other methods of mastery fail. Learning new tactics of self-help or co-operation is difficult for them and is often not encouraged in the social setting in which they live.

Hysterics play the co-operative game very imperfectly. This is to be expected, as the games requires and presupposes a feeling of relative equality among the players. Persons employing hysterical methods of communication feel—and often are—inferior and oppressed. In turn they aspire to feeling superior to others and to oppressing them. But they also seek equality of sorts and some measure of co-operation as potential remedies for their oppressed status.

Hysteria is thus mainly a coercive game, with small elements of self-help and still smaller elements of co-operation blended in. This view implies that the hysteric is unclear about his values and their connection with his behavior.

We might again note here that several of the patients reported in the early psychoanalytic literature were young women who became "ill" with hysteria while caring for a sick, usually older, relative. This was true in the case of Breuer's famous patient, Anna O.:

> In July 1880, the patient's father, of whom she was passionately fond, fell ill of a peripleuritic abscess which failed to clear up and to which he succumbed in April 1881. During the first months of the illness Anna devoted her whole

energy to nursing her father, and no one was much surprised when by degrees her own health greatly deteriorated. No one, perhaps not even the patient herself, knew what was happening to her; but eventually the state of weakness, anaemia and distaste for food became so bad that to her great sorrow she was no longer allowed to continue nursing the patient.

Anna O. thus started to play the hysterical game from a position of distasteful submission: she functioned as an oppressed, unpaid, sick-nurse, who was coerced to be helpful by the very helplessness of a (bodily) sick patient. The women in Anna O.'s position were—as are their counterparts today, who feel similarly entrapped by their small children—insufficiently aware of what they valued in life and of how their own ideas of what they valued affected their conduct. For example, young middle-class women in Freud's day considered it their duty to take care of their sick fathers. Hiring a professional servant or nurse for this job would have created a moral conflict for them, because it would have symbolized to them as well as to others that they did not love (care for) their fathers. Similarly, many contemporary American women find themselves enslaved by their young children. Today, married women are generally expected to take care of their own children; they are not supposed to delegate this task to others. The "old folks" can be placed in a home; it is all right to delegate their care to hired help. This is a complete reversal of the social situation which prevailed in upper- and middle-class European circles until the First World War and even after it. Then, children were often cared for by hired help, while parents were taken care of by their children, now fully grown.

In both situations, the obligatory nature of the care required generates a feeling of helplessness in the person from whom help is sought. If a person cannot, in good conscience, refuse to provide help—and cannot even stipulate the terms on which he will supply it—then truly he becomes the help-seeker's slave. Similar considerations apply to the relationship between patients and physicians. If physicians cannot define their own rules—that is, when to help and in what ways—then they, too, are threatened with becoming the hostages of patients (or their representatives).

The typical cases of hysteria cited by Freud thus involved a moral conflict—a conflict about what the young women in question wanted to do with themselves. Did they want to prove that they were good daughters by taking care of their sick fathers? Or did they want to become independent of their elders, say, by having a family of their own, or in some other way? I believe it was the tension between these conflicting aspirations that was the crucial issue in these cases. The sexual problem—say, of the daughter's incestuous cravings for her father—was secondary (if that important); it was stimulated, perhaps, by the interpersonal situation in which the one had to attend to the other's body. Moreover, it was probably easier to admit the sexual problem to consciousness and to worry about it than to raise the ethical problem indicated. In the final analysis, the latter is a vastly difficult problem in living. It cannot be "solved" by any particular manoeuvre but requires rather decision-making about basic goals, and, having made the decisions, dedicated efforts to attain them.

A SUMMING UP

Viewed as a game, hysteria is characterized by the goal of domination and interpersonal control. The typical strategies employed in pursuing this goal are coercion by disability and illness. Deceitful gambits of various types, especially lies, also play a significant part in this game.

If we wish to address ourselves to the problem of the "treatment" of hysteria (and of other "mental illnesses"), we must first clearly face the question: In what directions—that is, towards what types of games—should the behaviour of the patient change? The word "therapy"—in contrast to the word "change"—implies that the patient's current behavioral state is "bad" and that the direction in which the therapist wishes the patient to move is "good," or at least "better." What is "bad," "better," and "good" are here defined by the physician. Person-oriented psychotherapy requires, however, that patients be assisted in defining their own conceptions of psychosocial "illness" and "health." This implies that a patient might set himself goals at variance with the values of his therapist: the patient may change in ways not specifically intended by the therapist, and indeed contrary to the therapist's personal preferences. In a sensible scheme of the psychotherapeutic interaction there must be room for this contingency.

Descriptions of therapeutic interventions and of modifications in patients' life activities might better be framed in terms of changes in the patients' game-orientations and strategies. In the case of the hysteric, for example, changes which might be labelled "improvements" or "cures" by some may occur in any one of the following directions: more effective coercion and domination of others; greater submission to others and increased preoccupation with suffering; withdrawal from the struggle over interpersonal control by progressive isolation from real-life relationships; and finally, learning the goals and strategies of other games and becoming invested in some of them.

Thomas S. Szasz:
The Myth of Mental Illness

Reviewed by Andrew C. Smith

The *Myth of Mental Illness* was never reviewed in this *Journal*. It was its author's second book, and has been followed by over sixteen others, of which eight are in print in this country at the moment. It became a staple in the reading lists of critics of psychiatry, who appear to find it, (especially in conjunction with *The Manufacture of Madness*, 1971), a convincing demolition of much of the basis of our work. It is anathema to psychiatrists, so although our critics read it, we rarely do. What does it say?

The main burden of the book is a discussion of hysteria and its meaning, the references to "mental illness" being in fact off the main track, and mentioned *en passant*. Nine out of the sixteen chapters even carry the word "hysteria" in their titles.

After introductory polemic fireworks (e.g., "I believe that we are in danger of purchasing superiority and power over non-psychiatrists and patients at the cost of scientific self-sterilization and hence ultimate professional self-destruction," p. 4), and the first appearance of the remark that hysteria will do as a paradigm for all mental illness (on pp. 8 and 9), the argument starts with Charcot and hysteria. The author says that this is because "it marks the beginning of the modern study of so-called mental illness" (p. 26), but we may think that it is because hysteria is his subject and more amenable to his theme than nineteenth-century descriptive psychiatry. He maintains that Charcot and Freud relabeled hysterics as helplessly disabled and thus not suitable to be condemned as malingerers. Thus they made not a scientific discovery but, Szasz points out repeatedly, a moral and political shift, concerned with the doctor–patient relationship, the question of who is entitled to the consideration accorded to the genuinely sick, and the desirability of encouraging dishonesty, semi-honesty, and helplessness.

Many subjects of interest, especially moral and political interest, to Szasz, are touched upon, not all of them sufficiently relevant to warrant mentioning if they cannot be discussed fully: for example, whose advocate is the doctor when the patient is paying privately? When the doctor is paid by state insurance? In Soviet Russia? The attitudes of Christianity and Judaism to helplessness are discussed; witchcraft is mentioned briefly (it will of course figure more fully in *The Manufacture of Madness*); there are four pages on Piaget's work, and a discussion of the logic of signs and Bertrand Russell's theory of logical types. But these are digressions, and the main interest is the development of discussion of conversion hysteria in terms of role-playing (of the helpless and ill patient), communication of "problems in living" in a language of gestures indicating illness or helplessness, and a discussion of games, cheating, lies, and mistakes. The theory of the patient's attitude is best given briefly in Sullivan's words, cited largely with approval by Szasz: "The hysteric might be said in principle to be a person who has a happy thought as to a way by which he can be respectable even though not living up to his standards. That way of describing the hysteric, however, is very misleading, for of course the hysteric never does have that thought. At least it is practically impossible to prove that he has had that thought." (Sullivan 1956, quoted on p. 267). Conversion is seen not as a mysterious quasi-neurological process, as so often seems to linger in psychiatric grappling with it, but as "translation . . . from personal problems to bodily problems, while the form changes from verbal (linguistic) language to bodily (gestural) language" (p. 90). This model of hysteria is surely in the mainstream of psychiatric and psychoanalytic development, but Szasz's treatment, although lengthy, is unfortunately narrow, with no adequate discussion of the overlap with actual organic disease.

There is much demand for clarity and science, an epigraph from Popper and many references to Bertrand Russell, but it must be pointed out that the Szasz himself fails to be clear and unambiguous on the central subject that fascinates him — are hysterics malingering? There appears to be conflict between his psychoanalytic background (he was a psychoanalyst and sometimes uses psychoanalytic terms such as "superego" (p. 127) and "significant objects" (p. 238n.) — both omitted in the 1972 edition) according to which he might be expected to be deterministic about the patients, and his interest in the moral nature of human communications. Whole chapters expound how the hysterical patients are sending untruthful messages that they are ill, and Szasz seems to have grasped the nettle and said that they are glorified malingerers. And yet, it turns out that he does not see everything in black and white terms, and he fudges the issue, using the concept of unconscious cheating, and is just as vague and benighted as the rest of us unclear psychiatrists. Thus, "mental illnesses can be understood only if they are viewed as occurrences that do not merely happen to a person but rather are brought on by him (perhaps unconsciously) . . . (p. 59); "the hysteric . . . must lie both to himself and to others" (p. 248); "cheating of the type called hysteria" (p. 248; "mendacity and cheating" in the 1972 edition). Where he has been discussing games and role playing, "by and large, persons called 'mentally ill' impersonate the roles of helplessness, hopelessness, weakness, and often of bodily illness—when, in fact, their actual roles pertain to frustrations, unhappiness, and perplexities due to interpersonal, social and ethical conflicts." But he inserts a footnote after "impersonate": "I do not wish to imply that this impersonation is a consciously planned strategy, arrived at by deliberate choice among several alternatives" (p. 254); this footnote is slightly different in the 1972 edition: ". . . that this impersonation is always a consciously planned strategy . . . although, sometimes, it clearly is."

Again, the hysteric "may not be aware that he has made a choice between coercion and other human values ["strategies" in the 1972 edition]. His wish to coerce may, in other words, be unconscious [This word is in quotation marks in the 1972 edition]. Usually, however, it is not so much unconscious as it is inexplicit" (p. 260). He leaves the reader tantalised, saying only that the ridicule of how conscious is a given mental act is a pseudo-problem, the answer not being fixed, but depending on the social situation under consideration. As often, his discussion fascinates, and may infuriate, but is not completed. Some of the space spent on digressions could have been used in clearer conclusions.

What of mental illness, which figures in the title of the book; the so-called mental illness on which antispychiatrists take Szasz to be so illuminating? Here he argues very poorly and largely deserves the angry dismissal he usually gets from psychiatrists. For not once but repeatedly he makes a point by reference to hysteria and then says that it thereupon applies to mental illness in general because he chose hysteria initially as his paradigm of mental illness. This breathtaking extrapolation is never justified, and is, to borrow a moral term from our moralist author, dishonest.

He will be "using conversion hysteria as a paradigm of the sort of phenomena to which the term 'mental illness' may refer" (p. 8), and "everything that will be said about hysteria pertains equally, in principle, to all other so-called mental illnesses and to personal conduct generally" (p. 9). "We may dispense with considerations of the physiochemical causes or mechanisms of hysteria (and of other mental illnesses too), since there is neither observational evidence nor logical need for them" (p. 82—omitted in the 1972 edition). Then in the closing chapters of the book he repeatedly uses the phrase "hysteria and mental illness" as if this coupling had been fully discussed and justified.

Yet in fact there is no discussion of major mental illness, nothing on severe depression with its physical changes and cognitive disability, only brief nods at schizophrenia (e.g., bodily delusions are "consciously unrecognized impersonations of bodily illness" [p. 249]); nothing on heredity; nothing on delirium, hallucinogenic drugs, and the riddle of amphetamine, alcohol and cannabis psychoses; nothing on trying to understand puerperal psychosis with explosive onset a few days after childbirth. His example of psychosis (p. 131) is morbid jealousy in a wife, not described but used in a vignette to illustrate the labelling and confinement of inconvenient people. There is nothing to suggest any thoughtful familiarity with general acute psychiatry as it encounters and tries to deal with what is usually called severe mental illness.

He is a gadfly to the psychiatric profession. He writes pungently, but argues misleadingly. He crusades and provokes, and takes the opportunity to end his updating summary written for the 1972 paperback edition with the statement that involuntary psychiatric interventions are crimes against humanity. (This is not expounded in the book itself—perhaps its appearance was irresistible to the author after the success of *The Manufacture of Madness* in 1971?). I find he stimulates thought, and forces me to think in combating him. He says the psychiatric emperor has no clothes at all. I know he has some, but I look and find they are tattered in places.

REFERENCES

Sullivan, H. S. (1966). *Clinical Studies in Psychiatry*. Ed. II. S. Perry, M. L. Gawel, and M. Gibbon. New York: Norton.

Szasz, T. S. (1962). *The Myth of Mental Illness*. London: Seeker and Warburg.

Further Selections from
The Myth of Mental Illness

PSYCHIATRY AS SOCIAL ACTION

The thesis that psychiatric operations constitute types of social action has been well documented. Although more obvious in the case of such occurrences as involuntary hospitalization or commitment than in psychoanalysis, the idea that psychiatric activity of any sort is, among other things, a form of social action must be taken as our point of departure for what follows. I propose to distinguish three classes of action patterns, more or less distinct and separate from each other, according to the psychiatrist's position vis-à-vis the games which he encounters in his patients, their families, and the society in which they and he live.

The psychiatrist as theoretical scientist is an expert on game-playing behavior and shares his knowledge of this subject with those who hire him as expert, or who wish to learn from him as a scientist who makes his knowledge public.

The psychiatrist as applied scientist or social engineer sorts out players and assigns them to the games which they can, or ought to, play.

The psychiatrist as social manipulator of human material punishes, coerces, or otherwise influences people to induce them to play, or to cease to play, certain games.

The first type of psychiatric activity is such as to make the work of the psychiatrist virtually indistinguishable from the work of the anthropologist, the social psychologist, the sociologist, or the so-called behavioral scientist. Psychiatry, so conceived, is a branch of social science. It must, nevertheless, remain of interest and significance to medicine—even if it ceases to parade as a biological science—unless the scope of medical activities be restricted to confines much narrower than it presently occupies. Insofar as medicine must assist persons who are in distress—rather than merely repair biophysical bodies that are deranged—it seems inconceivable that it should be able to function without knowledge concerning man as a social being. The psychoanalytic therapist's social role, although not exactly that of theoretical scientist, comes close to it. This is because his direct social impact is restricted to those who are prepared to be exposed to it of their own volition. Psychoanalytic treatment, properly conceived, is not forced on anyone, any more than information or knowledge is forced on anyone in a democratic society.

The psychiatrist as social engineer, sorting out players for their "proper" games, is encountered in the military services, marriage counseling, psychiatric hospitals, courts, and elsewhere. In the military services, for example, the psychiatrist's role is to determine who can play being soldier and who cannot. Those who cannot are punished and/or released from the game. Similarly, the state hospital psychiatrist's job, perhaps a bit over-simplified, is to ascertain who must play the game of "mental illness." Those who cannot play the game of "social normality" are assigned to the game of "psychiatric illness." In effect this means that they must take the role of mental patient and all that it embraces. Moreover, they are deprived of the opportunity to change games, so to speak. They can get out of the mental illness game only if they are willing and able to play at being normal, or if they die.

The third type of psychiatric activity—the active manipulation of persons, families, groups, and so forth—is not clearly demarcated from the second type. The main distinction between the two is that in the former the psychiatrist's activity is limited, by and large, to sorting, classifying, or role-assigning, whereas in the latter it proceeds to molding the "patients" into the forms or roles that have been chosen for them. For instance, a psychiatrist who merely advises a married couple not to get a divorce has done a job of classifying or sorting. He decided to sort the two people into the class of marriage partners (to each other). If, however, he does not stop there but proceeds to "treat" both husband and wife, with the explicit aim of helping the marriage to succeed, then he is also acting as a source of influence to bring about the desired role-playing in the patients. Shock therapy, psychotherapy with children, and many other psychiatric inter-ventions illustrate activities of this kind. The activities of the psychiatrist as social engineer, sorting people into the pigeonholes of "identity" in which they "belong" and making sure that they will fit by exerting the "right" kinds of influence on them, have not passed unnoticed by some astute literary and philosophical observers. Needless to say, I think we ought to have serious reservations concerning psychiatric activities of the second and third types. My considerably greater satisfaction with the first type of psychiatric activity, however, must not be construed to mean that I believe all is well with it. It would be desirable to keep an open and critical mind toward it as well.

EPILOGUE

In Pirandello's play, *The Rules of the Game*, the following conversation takes place:

> LEONE: Ah, Venanzi, it's a sad thing, when one has learnt every move in the game.
> GUIDO: What game?
> LEONE: Why . . . this one. The whole game—of life.
> GUIDO: Have you learnt it?
> LEONE: Yes, a long time ago.

Leone's despair and resignation come from believing that there is such a thing as *the* game of life. Indeed, if mastery of *the* game of life were the problem of human existence, having achieved this task, what would there be left to do? But there is no game of life, in the singular. The games are infinite.

Modern man seems to be faced with a choice between two basic alternatives. On the one hand, he may elect to despair over the lost usefulness or the rapid deterioration of games painfully learned. Skills acquired by diligent effort may prove to be inadequate for the task at hand almost as soon as one is ready to apply them. Many people cannot tolerate repeated disappointments of this kind. In desperation, they long for the security of stability—even if stability can be purchased only at the cost of personal enslavement. The other alternative is to rise to the challenge of the unceasing need to learn and relearn, and to try to meet this challenge successfully.

The momentous changes in contemporary social conditions clearly forewarn that—if man survives—his social relations, like his genetic constitution, will undergo increasingly rapid mutations. If this is true, it will be imperative that all people, rather than just a few, *learn how to learn*. I use the term "to learn" rather broadly. It refers, first, to the adaptations that man must make to his environment. More specifically, man must learn the rules that govern life in the family, the group, and the society in which he lives. Further, there is the learning of technical skills, science, and learning to learn. Clearly, there is no "objective" limit to learning. The limiting factor is in *man*—not in the challenge to learn. Leone's dilemma is the dilemma of a man so far withdrawn from life that he fails to appreciate, and hence to participate in, the ever-changing game of life. The result is a shallow and constant life which may be encompassed and mastered with relative ease.

The common and pressing problem today is that, as social conditions undergo rapid change, men are called upon to alter their modes of living. Old games are constantly scrapped and new ones started. Most people are totally unprepared to shift from one type of game-playing to another. They learn one game or, at most, a few, and desire mainly the opportunity to live out life by playing the same game over and over again. But since human life is largely a social enterprise, social conditions may make it impossible to survive without greater flexibility in regard to patterns of personal conduct.

Perhaps the relationship between the modern psychotherapist and his patient is a beacon that ever-increasing numbers of men will find themselves forced to follow, lest they become spiritually enslaved or physically destroyed. By this I do not mean anything so naive as to suggest that "everyone needs to be psychoanalyzed." On the contrary, "being psychoanalyzed"—like *any* human experience—can itself constitute a form of enslavement and affords, especially in its contemporary institutionalized forms, no guarantee of enhanced self-knowledge and responsibility for either patient or therapist. By speaking of the modern psychotherapeutic relationship as a beacon, I refer to a simpler but more fundamental notion than that implied in "being psychoanalyzed." This is the notion of being a *student of human living.* Some require a personal instructor for this; others do not. Given the necessary wherewithal and ability to learn, success in this enterprise requires, above all else, the sincere desire to learn and to change. This incentive, in turn, is stimulated by hope of success. This is one of the main reasons why it is the scientist's and educator's solemn responsibility to clarify—never to obscure—problems and tasks.

I hope that I have been successful in avoiding the pitfalls of mysticism and obscurantism which, by beclouding the problems to be tackled and solved, foster feelings of discouragement and despair. We are all students in the school of life. In this metaphorical school, none of us can afford to become discouraged or despairing. And yet, in this school, religious cosmologies, nationalistic myths, and lately psychiatric theories have more often functioned as obscurantist teachers misleading the student, than as genuine clarifiers helping him to help himself. Bad teachers are, of course, worse than no teachers at all. Against them, skepticism is our sole weapon.

17

Carl Ransom Rogers:
On Becoming a Person:
A Therapist's View of
Psychotherapy

Reviewed by Duncan Cramer

Carl Rogers, who died in California in 1987 at the age of 85, was ranked in a late-1970s survey of American clinical psychologists and counselors as being the psychotherapist who most influenced them, surpassing such stalwarts as Sigmund Freud and Joseph Wolpe. This book was the fourth one that he published and is reputedly the most renowned. In the United Kingdom it is his best-selling book, being reprinted on average every eighteen months and having sold about 4,000 copies in the last two years.

This book consists of twenty-one papers written between 1951 and 1961 while Rogers was responsible for first the University of Chicago Counseling Center and subsequently the Psychotherapy Research Section of the Wisconsin Psychiatric Institute, which he joined in 1957. Many of the papers were presented to general audiences that Rogers had been invited to address, and all are written in a nontechnical style that is easily understood. While most of the contributions had already been published elsewhere, they were generally not readily available to those who wanted to follow Rogers's thinking more closely. Gathering the papers together in one place meant that his ideas could reach a wider readership.

Incidentally, a more accurate subtitle for the book would have simply been *A Therapist's View*, since some of the later papers in this volume are concerned with issues that go beyond psychotherapy to include education, creativity, the growth and use of knowledge in the behavioral sciences, and intergroup tension. Indeed, one of these papers was contributed not by Rogers but by an academic educationalist who attended one of his short courses and who wrote an appreciative letter on his reactions to this immediately after the course as well as a year later. The majority of the papers, however, are concerned with psychotherapy and with what it means to be psychologically healthy.

There are three basic assumptions which seem to run through these papers and through his writings generally, and which may be used to illustrate his ideas. First and foremost is his optimistic belief that people will live a constructive and fulfilling life provided they are fully aware of their own feelings and experiences and use this knowledge to guide their behavior. This point of view is most clearly and convincingly argued in chapter 9, entitled "A Therapist's View of the Good Life: The Fully Functioning Person." In this paper he suggests that if we are alert to all our feelings, then the expression of negative acts will be tempered by our awareness of positive experiences. In addition, being fully sensitive to our feelings will provide us with greater information on the most appropriate course of action for us to take and will also give us more feedback on where we may have gone wrong.

Rogers's own therapeutic way of working, which he did not recognise constituted a new, personal and distinctive approach to therapy until 1940, is described in the first chapter of the book in an autobiographical piece, unpretentiously entitled "This Is Me". It grew from his realization that the diagnostic, psychoanalytic and rather mechanistic approach that he had at first adopted in the treatment of delinquent and underprivileged children at the Rochester Guidance Center, where he initially worked, was not always successful. He somewhat cryptically recounts in this chapter one incident in particular that led him to question the value of this approach and to develop a more satisfying way of working.

During the course of many interviews with an intelligent mother, he had been sensitively trying to point out to her, but with little success, that the unruly behavior of her child was due to her early rejection of the boy. After they had both agreed that, since they did not seem to be making any progress, treatment should be terminated, she then asked Rogers whether he counseled adults. Since he did, she asked for help and began to talk about the unsatisfactory nature of her relationship with her husband, and her own sense of failure and confusion. Although Rogers does not explicitly state that the boy's behavior improved, he does write that therapy was ultimately successful.

Such events as these gradually convinced him that it was the patient or client who knew what the problems were and that the role of the therapist should be to provide a conducive atmosphere in which clients could direct their own therapy. He came to call this approach client-centered therapy. Later the word "client" tended to be substituted with that of "person" to emphasize that his ideas were not confined to what constituted successful therapy but could also be applied more generally to facilitate constructive behavior in other spheres of life, as illustrated in the later chapters of this book. Although not happy with the term "client," he preferred it to that of "patient," which had adverse connotations of dependence and passivity.

One notable implication of this philosophy for the training of therapists, which is not always readily appreciated or understood, is that his style of working is not necessarily the approach which should be adopted by every clinician. In fact, therapists should be encouraged to develop their own therapeutic outlook based on their own experience of helping others. Consequently, Rogers was opposed to setting up organizations that would teach his own mode of working, since this would contradict his fundamental belief that we should trust and be guided by our own experiences. It is worth stressing, however, that it does not necessarily follow from client-centered theory that such organizations would subvert rather than propagate this central teaching. Despite Rogers's skepticism, a number of national and international associations concerned with the development of the client-centered approach have been running for some years, although it is not yet clear whether his forebodings have been confirmed.

Inextricably related to Rogers's belief in the potentially positive nature of human beings is his view that this aspect will only predominate and flourish if a person's feelings are genuinely understood and accepted, even if they are not allowed to be acted on, should they be seen as being socially destructive. Rogers thought that the acknowledgement and acceptance of such harmful urges should help to defuse them. It is somewhat surprising then that Rogers did not include in this collection his paper entitled "The Necessary and Sufficient Conditions of Therapeutic Personality Change" (1957), in which he succinctly laid down the three therapeutic attitudes that were necessary and sufficient for therapeutic improvement to occur. Although the theoretical position in this paper is described in chapter 14, "Significant Learning: In Therapy and in Education," the original exposition would have provided a useful summary for the lay reader and would have considerably enhanced the value of this collection.

The most concise statement of Rogers's view of the process of therapy is to be found in a paper called "The Process Equation of Therapy," which, although published at the same time as this book in the *American Journal of Psychotherapy* (1961), was also unfortunately not included in it. In this paper, he proposes that this equation can be crudely and tentatively expressed as: "The more the client perceives the therapist as real or genuine, as empathic, as having an unconditional regard for him [sic], the more the client will move away from a static, unfeeling, fixed, impersonal type of functioning and the more he will move toward a way of functioning which is marked by a fluid, changing, acceptant experiencing of differentiated personal feelings" (p. 40). This neatly captures the three essential therapeutic or core conditions of genuineness, empathy, and unconditional positive regard, as well as the kind of changes that can be observed taking place in the client. A more detailed explication of these changes, which were based on trying to listen as naively as possible to many hours of recorded therapy sessions, can also be found in chapter 7 entitled "A Process Conception of Psychotherapy."

The third main assumption underpinning Rogers's approach is his belief in the importance of endeavouring to empirically test ideas. In chapter 10, "Persons or Science? A Philosophical Question," he reconciles what he previously thought was the incompatible nature of objective science and his highly subjective approach to therapy by recognizing the essentially personal character of the creative process of scientific thinking. When first studying an unfamiliar phenomenon such as psychotherapy, he believed it necessary for scientists to immerse themselves in their relevant experience, from which may emerge tentative hypotheses concerning its structure and the underlying processes that determine it. Consequently, in his attempt to understand and objectify the process of psychotherapy, Rogers was the first therapist to systematically record electrically what took place. The earliest verbatim account of a complete case of therapy ever published is that of Bryan in Rogers's *Counseling and Psychotherapy* (1942). His theory of therapy was based on listening to and trying to understand cases such as these.

Client-centered theory generated a considerable amount of research up until the mid-1970s, much of which was carried out by Rogers and his associates. A highly commendable characteristic of this work was its attempt to examine the client-centered theory of the relationship between the process and outcome of therapy, a feature that current psychotherapy research would do well to emulate. Enticing but largely uncritical snippets of this imaginative research are presented in chapters 11 and 12, respectively entitled "Personality Changes in Psycho-Therapy" and "Client-Centered Therapy in the Context of Research." The most detailed review of research on the therapeutic effectiveness of the three core conditions as viewed from a strictly client-centered perspective is, however, to be found elsewhere in Gurman's chapter "The Patient's Perception of the Therapeutic Relationship" in *Effective Psychotherapy*, edited by himself and Razin (1977).

Perhaps the less than positive results of later studies on the therapeutic role of these therapist's attitudes and the decreasing youthfulness of the original workers led to the decline of research in this area. However, more recently there has been a resurgence of empirical interest in the role of the therapist–client relationship by both behavior therapists and empirically minded psychodynamic clinicians, and which hopefully may help to resolve the inclusive nature of previous research. Although Rogers drew attention to this point in his earlier book *Client-Centered Therapy* (1951), there is a surprising dearth of research by client-centered workers on the therapeutic process as seen by the client. If clients know what the problems are initially, then presumably they are also in a better position to realize how these problems were overcome. It may be unrealistic, however, to expect people who are psychologically distressed to be able, or to be particularly interested in trying, to understand in detail their own therapeutic process. Nonetheless, clients' reflections on their own treatment may provide useful leads in furthering our knowledge of psychotherapy.

While *On Becoming a Person* may serve as an overview of the client-centered theory of human behavior, people who are principally interested in how Rogers actually carried out therapy, particularly as reflected in the verbal exchanges which took place between him and his clients in recorded sessions, would do better to turn to his two previous volumes *Counseling and Psychotherapy* and *Client-Centered Therapy*, which contain many examples of such interchanges with indispensable annotated comments. Although Rogers claimed to have been more directive in those earlier days, there are fewer published verbatim illustrations of his later less directive approach. One highly commendable exception is the filmed half-hour demonstration session with Gloria, which has been fully transcribed in Rogers's chapter in Burton's *Operational Theories of Personality* (1974). However, it should be borne in mind that at present there is little evidence to suggest that the client's increasing self-awareness of feeling, which Rogers focuses on as being indicative of and necessary for therapeutic improvement, is related to outcome, let alone a determinant of it.

Hopefully, the more popular appeal of *On Becoming a Person* will continued to promulgate Rogers's belief in the trinity of subjective experience, objective scrutiny and the essentially positive nature of humanity in helping us, not only to further understand the process of psychotherapy, but also to lead more fulfilling lives.

REFERENCES

Rogers, C. (1942). *Counseling and Psychotherapy*. Boston: Houghton Mifflin.

_____ (1957). The necessary and sufficient conditions of therapeutic personality change. *Journal of Consulting Psychology* 21:95–103.

_____ (1961). The process equation of therapy. *American Journal of Psychotherapy* 15:27–45.

Selections from
On Becoming a Person:
A Therapist's View of
Psychotherapy
by Carl Ransom Rogers

I might start off these several statements of significant learnings with a negative item. *In my relationships with persons I have found that it does not help, in the long run, to act as though I were something that I am not.* It does not help to act calm and pleasant when actually I am angry and critical. It does not help to act as though I know the answers when I do not. It does not help to act as though I were a loving person if actually, at the moment, I am hostile. It does not help for me to act as though I were full of assurance, if actually I am frightened and unsure. Even on a very simple level I have found that this statement seems to hold. It does not help for me to act as though I were well when I feel ill.

What I am saying here, put in another way, is that I have not found it to be helpful or effective in my relationships with other people to try to maintain a façade; to act in one way on the surface when I am experiencing something quite different underneath. It does not, I believe, make me helpful in my attempts to build up constructive relationships with other individuals. I would want to make it clear that while I feel I have learned this to be true, I have by no means adequately profited from it. In fact, it seems to me that most of the mistakes I make in personal relationships, most of the times in which I fail to be of help to other individuals, can be accounted for in terms of the fact that I have, for some defensive reason, behaved in one way at a surface level, while in reality my feelings run in a contrary direction.

A second learning might be stated as follows—*I find I am more effective when I can listen acceptantly to myself, and can be myself.* I feel that over the years I have learned to become more adequate in listening to *myself*; so that I know, somewhat more adequately than I used to, what I am feeling at any given moment—to be able to realize I *am* angry, or that I *do* feel rejecting toward this person; or that I feel very full of warmth and affection for this individual; or that I am bored and uninterested in what is going on; or that I am eager to understand this individual or that I am anxious and fearful in my relationship to this person. All of these diverse attitudes are feelings which I think I can listen to in myself. One way of putting this is that I feel I have become more adequate in letting myself *be* what I *am*. It becomes easier for me to accept myself as a decidedly imperfect person, who by no means functions at all times in the way in which I would like to function.

This must seem to some like a very strange direction in which to move. It seems to me to have value because the curious paradox is that when I accept myself as I am, then I change. I believe that I have learned this from my clients as well as within my own experience—that we cannot change, we cannot move away from what we are, until we thoroughly *accept* what we are. Then change seems to come about almost unnoticed.

Another result which seems to grow out of being myself is that relationships then become real. Real relationships have an exciting way of being vital and meaningful. If I can accept the fact that I am annoyed at or bored by this client or this student, then I am also much more likely to be able to accept his feelings in response. I can also accept the changed experience and the changed feelings which are then likely to occur in me and in him. Real relationships tend to change rather than to remain static.

So I find it effective to let myself be what I am in my attitudes; to know when I have reached my limit of endurance or of tolerance, and to accept that as a fact; to know when I desire to mold or manipulate people, and to accept that as a fact in myself. I would like to be as acceptant of these feelings as of feelings of warmth, interest, permissiveness, kindness, understanding, which are also a very real part of me. It is when I do accept all these attitudes as a fact, as a part of me, that my relationship with the other person then becomes what it is, and is able to grow and change most readily.

I come now to a central learning which has had a great deal of significance for me. I can state this learning as follows: *I have found it of enormous value when I can permit myself to understand another person.* The way in which I have worded this statement may seem strange to you. Is it necessary to *permit* oneself to understand another? I think that it is. Our first reaction to most of the statements which we hear from other people is an immediate evaluation, or judgement, rather than an understanding of it. When someone expresses some feeling or attitude or belief, our tendency is, almost immediately, to feel "That's right"; or "That's stupid"; "That's abnormal"; "That's unreasonable"; "That's incorrect"; "That's not nice." Very rarely do we permit ourselves to *understand* precisely what the meaning of his statement is to him. I believe this is because understanding is risky. If I let myself really understand another person, I might be changed by that understanding. And we all fear change. So as I say, it is not an easy thing to permit oneself to understand an individual, to enter thoroughly and completely and empathically into his frame of reference. It is also a rare thing.

To understand is enriching in a double way. I find when I am working with clients in distress, that to understand the bizarre world of a psychotic individual, or to understand and sense the attitudes of a person who feels that life is too tragic to bear, or to understand a man who feels that he is a worthless and inferior individual—each of these understandings somehow enriches me. I learn from these experiences in ways that change me, that make me a different and, I think, a more responsive person. Even more important perhaps, is the fact that my understanding of these individuals permits them to change. It permits them to accept their own fears and bizarre thoughts and tragic feelings and discouragements, as well as their moments of courage and kindness and love and sensitivity. And it is their experience as well as mine that when someone fully understands those feelings, this enables them to accept those feelings in themselves. Then they find both the feelings and themselves changing. Whether it is understanding a woman who feels that very literally she has a hook in her head by which others lead her about, or understanding a man who feels that no one is as lonely, no one is as separated from others as he, I find these understandings to be of value to me. But also, and even more importantly, to be understood has a very positive value to these individuals.

18

F. Kräupl Taylor:
The Analysis of Therapeutic Groups

Reviewed by Eric Crouch

Frederick Kräupl Taylor came to Great Britain in 1939 at the age of 34 as a refugee from Czechoslovakia, where he had specialized in internal medicine. He could not initially gain medical registration here, but worked for a period in the pathology laboratory at the York Retreat and, in his spare time, studied mathematics, statistics, philosophy, and psychology. Later, he trained as a psychiatrist and was invited by Sir Aubrey Lewis to the Maudsley Hospital, where he was a consultant from 1948 until 1971.

These, and further details of his career, can be found in two articles in *Psychiatric Bulletin*—his "Perspective" article, published in January 1982, and the obituary that appeared in July 1989, following his death earlier that year. He remained intellectually active into old age, as I discovered when in 1986 he published a very sharp review in *Psychological Medicine* of the book I wrote with Sidney Bloch on group therapy.

In the "Perspective" article, Kräupl Taylor described three main areas in which he was interested. These were psychotherapy, descriptive psychopathology, and the concept of illness. His three principal published works, *The Analysis of Therapeutic Groups*; *Psychopathology, Its Causes and Symptoms*; and *The Concepts of Illness, Disease and Morbus*, arose from these three areas of interest.

His work on psychopathology derived originally from Jaspers; the book is full of detail and very readable. His ideas about the concept of illness combined philosophical sophistication with common sense—recognizing, for example, that we use pragmatic rather than absolute criteria in classifying illness, and that the identification of what is morbid may be influenced by cultural trends.

His obituary stressed his individuality, the warmth of his personality, and the breadth of his interests, though it is perhaps difficult for me (lacking a Maudsley background) to judge exactly where he fitted into British psychiatry. Nevertheless, it seems clear that his ideas about psychotherapy developed over the whole of his career and were influenced both by his research and by his own experience of conducting psychotherapy. His theoretical development started with Freudian analytic ideas, but moved steadily away from them in the direction that led others eventually toward more cognitive behavioral approaches to psychotherapy.

Having started a training analysis and attendance at discussion groups at Anna Freud's house, he moved on to work with S. H. Foulkes, the pioneer of group analysis. However by 1961, when *The Analysis of Therapeutic Groups* was published, he had moved far enough away from his analytic background for the title to be a pun. The "analysis" referred to is in fact his sociometric study of the processes occurring in his groups, and the book makes very little except critical reference to specifically psychoanalytic concepts.

Beginning with his observations on psychotherapy as a mode of treatment and a general discussion of group psychotherapy, the book has five main chapters. The longest is a consideration of the way in which he thought group psychotherapy could be subjected to scientific study, illustrated by the results of his own research. This is followed by a narrative account of one of his groups and, lastly by evaluation of the results of group therapy—both in the one previously dissected and in others he studied.

The opening "General Evaluation of Psychotherapy" reflects his disillusionment with psychoanalytic therapy and his doubts that psychotherapy in general can be anything other than a palliative. Kräupl Taylor suggests that therapists are misled by paying more attention to positive than to negative outcomes, so that accounts of psychotherapy always contain generalisations from unrepresentative results. He makes points that are now common currency—that the therapist's genuine belief in his theory and the patient's trust in the therapist are powerful medicine in themselves, whereas the nature of the theory may be less important. In addition, the actual procedures that take place in the therapy room may be very similar, despite wide theoretical differences between therapists. Conversely, adherents of the same theoretical school may differ widely in technique.

He goes on to list four ingredients of analytic group psychotherapy that he regards as age-old in their application.

The first is a temporary reduction in social restrictions. In most societies, there are festivals in which the usual social decorum may be abandoned and reversal of social roles or social status may occur. He compares this with the lifting of restrictions on verbal communication in psychotherapy and reversal of the usual doctor–patient relationship, so that the patient becomes the active partner and the doctor much more a passive confidant. He felt this reversal to be one Freud's most significant innovations.

Second, there is the confession of sins (self-disclosure). Confessional arrangements in religious practice have ancient links with the supposed causation of disease. The "cleansing" effect of confession and the relief that follows it (in all but the severely depressed) are seen as an important part of psychotherapy.

Third, emotional excitation (catharsis). He sees evidence that the therapeutic power of emotional arousal has long been recognized in religious ceremony, while in psychoanalytic therapies, this factor appears as the cathartic expression of pent-up emotions.

Finally, interpretation of the meaning of illness and symptoms gives the sufferer some rationale for what is happening to him. In ancient cultures, these depended mostly on religious belief. Interpretation gives a comforting feeling of insight, but also provokes an emotional reaction that may itself be of benefit.

Chapter 2 is entitled "Methods of Group Therapy," but consists in fact mainly of Kräupl Taylor's own views about the running of groups. He draws attention to the range of educative, suggestive, and inspirational group therapies that were fashionable at that time, and contrasts them with analytic ones. The customary role of the doctor in giving advice is contrasted with the passive stance of the group analyst. He is critical of some therapists who, he says, neglect their duty to elicit a full psychiatric history and make a diagnosis, and expresses concern at the tendency for nonmedical therapists to run groups without medical backup.

Kräupl Taylor goes on to suggest that therapists are blinded to their actual role in the group by analytic theory, which dictates they should be passive and noncommittal. Thus, the passivity of the therapist prompts his patients to search for indications of his instructions to them in the little he does say and in his body language. His own actions in a group were based on telling the patient the truth, but his comments were timed and phrased with an eye to the responses he hoped to elicit.

A brief section on selecting patients for group therapy makes use of the uncontroversial "group balance" approach, and this is succeeded by a section on group tasks. In this, he reveals himself as an early exponent of explicit instruction to patients about their role and behavior in the group (most often given today as pregroup instructions). He expects group members to accept that their tasks are candid self-revelation, disclosure of significant life experiences, and a search for interpretations that will make neurotic responses seem intelligible. For his part, the therapist needs to take on the role of regulating the emotional tension in the group, though a raised emotional tension is needed for change to occur. He suggests that the optimal size for a group is five to eight, mentions the merits of "closed" rather than "open" groups, warns against attrition, and proposes the addition of a limited number of new patients to replace dropouts.

Chapter 3, where he drops the pun, contains what Kräupl Taylor must have seen as the "meat" of the book. With its title of "The Study of Therapeutic Groups," it tries to get at a scientific method for studying the phenomena of the therapy group. He sets out some of the pitfalls—the mass of data generated by recording their sessions, the subjectivity involved in condensing the material, and the remoteness from the clinician's focus of interest of objective measurements.

He discusses content analysis of group therapy and early studies of the relative importance of various topics of discussion: a number of studies of verbal interaction are reviewed. He elects to simplify some earlier work of Chapple and to measure temporal characteristics rather than content of verbal interaction in groups: a way of measuring the distribution among group members of verbal interaction was devised.

Developing Moreno's sociometric methods, the professed feelings of group members for each other are studies, as are the two phenomena of popularity and dominance: he finds that group members show greater concordance in judging dominance than in judging popularity. He had noted that group members who are especially dominant but at the same time unpopular tend to drop out of therapy prematurely, and suggests that this knowledge is clinically useful.

A contrast is drawn between public and private popularity, the former expressed openly in the group and the latter in dyadic interactions or via questionnaires. He explores discrepancies between publicly and privately expressed feelings, noting that these are less in all-female than in all-male groups: unpopular group members tend to be emotionally isolated. While men tended to be more dominant in the groups he studied, they were not necessarily more popular. Observations about the level of verbal interaction include the point that interaction builds to a peak as the group proceeds, tends to fall off somewhat, and then rises again once the subject of termination has been introduced.

Chapter 4 gives an account of a group Kräupl Taylor himself conducted and also studied. He provides a thumbnail sketch of each member, comments on the pattern of their individual involvements in the group, and reproduces some characteristic slices of discussion, focusing particularly on sexual topics, which he regards as particularly important. In the next chapter, Kräupl Taylor examines the outcome for each of the patients in the group, and makes some general comments about the outcome of group therapy. Citing Eysenck's well-known (and contentious) statement that two-thirds of neurotic patients improve with time, with or without psychotherapy, he notes that the proportion of improvers in this group is indeed around two-thirds. Nevertheless, his conclusion is that group therapy does have an effect in palliating symptoms and in sustaining the patient, so that curative processes may in time occur, much as a plaster cast supports a broken leg.

How does one see the book at this distance in time? Kräupl Taylor exercised a degree of intellectual honesty and scientific rigor that has not always been common among psychotherapy writers, and the book is valuable for that. He became skeptical, perhaps realistically so, about what group therapy can achieve, and came up against the frustrating complexity of studying groups scientifically.

His comments on the nature of psychotherapy arose from his observations as a therapist rather than from his scientific studies, and the links he made between psychotherapy and older cultural and religious traditions are important. Despite his sociometric studies of group interaction, the ingredients he regarded as important in groups are essentially intrapersonal factors, and he seems to have dismissed interpersonal factors, especially interpersonal learning. His scientific results, though set out in detail, are sadly disappointing: not much of direct clinical importance arises from them.

Kräupl Taylor made some important critical comments about the practice of group analysis: some therapists did not individually examine their patients and some nonmedical therapists worked without medical cover. It is notable that this criticism has been taken on board by the largest organization of group analytic practitioners in Britain, where the importance of individual formulations is stressed and specific medical cover is arranged for lay therapists.

Another change, judging by the account of his own group, is the wider range of therapies now available, which allows group therapists to be more selective. Today's therapists would almost certainly have guided at least three of his patients in the direction of behavioral or cognitive therapies.

Overall, this is not one of the classics of the group therapy literature. The first two chapters are a good read as a critique of psychotherapy, but the later ones are likely to attract only those with a specialized interest in research in the subject. Those who are interested in Kräupl Taylor and his ideas should rather look at his other two books, which are much more important works and better deserve to be remembered.

Selections from
The Analysis of
Therapeutic Groups
by F. Kräupl Taylor

F. K. Taylor's opening words illustrate his skeptical attitude toward psychotherapy:

> Many modern forms of psychotherapy have found wide acceptance because they promised not just alleviation of symptoms but radical cures of neuroses and other psychiatric diseases.
>
> Psychoanalytic theory originally postulated that neurotic symptoms had their origin in emotional complexes formed in infancy and retained as permanent but unremembered sources of trouble in the unconscious mind. The aim of treatment was to make unconscious complexes accessible to conscious memory and thus enable incarcerated emotions to find nonneurotic outlets.
>
> This theoretical model was modified and refined until psychoanalytic therapy was often presented as a procedure undermining unconscious resistance to self-knowledge by gradually increasing tolerance of guilt-charged and tabooed desires. Nevertheless it remains doubtful how far psychotherapy can achieve radical cures. Some forms of treatment may have a specific effect on certain neurotic conditions, if administered to the right kind of patient at the right time. Unfortunately, as next to nothing is known about how to choose the right psychotherapy for the right patient at the right time, assertions about the specificity of any method have little practical value, and published results show that, whatever the method, about two-thirds of neurotic patients report at least some improvement. We cannot escape the conclusion therefore that psychotherapy, like many other forms of medical and surgical treatment, is for most patients a palliative procedure whose aim is to relieve suffering and allow time for remedial adjustment.
>
> Psychotherapy is sometimes defined as any procedure in which a therapist relies exclusively on psychological influences in treating his patients. In practice, this definition restricts the term to techniques which use only words and gestures, and avoid physical or chemical applications.

Such a narrow definition applies only to specialized psychotherapies. Psychological effects cannot be excluded from any interaction between patient and doctor, and indeed, many therapeutic procedures, ostensibly based on physical or chemical applications, are effective only in so far as they have a psychological influence on the patient. There is no therapeutic regime in which psychological forces are not active, to enhance or reduce its intrinsic value.

It is misleading to consider the psychotherapeutic situation purely from a clinical viewpoint. This has of course been, and still is, the traditional medical approach, but has led to misconceptions arising from the tacit assumption that observations made on patients will be duplicated by observations of colleagues on other patients of the same diagnostic category. Clinicians have been unaware of an elementary fact of sampling statistics: that patients with the same diagnostic label need not be otherwise comparable. Their own patients might be a sample so biased as to be unrepresentative of the total class of patients with the same disease. Yet they generalize from their sample without hesitation or suspicion that this is scientifically unsound.

A passage from Chapter 3 gives a taste of his approach to the scientific study of groups:

I have made use of a very simple way of measuring these verbal interactions in therapeutic groups. The number of times a person speaks without being interrupted by another person or stopping spontaneously, are counted. This disregards subject matter and the length of utterances and silences. Whether it is a half-sentence or a long and uninterrupted speech, the score is always one.

The number of scored utterances is the higher the more a person excites others to respond to him. A high score of individual interactions indicates frequent verbal exchange with other group partners. A person with a low individual interaction score either said little or, if he spoke for any length of time during the session, his remarks must have fallen flat and not been taken up by others.

The sum of interaction scores in a session is the total interaction score which indicates the liveliness of the verbal exchange. If everybody is reticent or disinclined to talk, there will be a low score of total interactions. A group with members eager to join in discussion will have a high score.

My original plan to score every utterance in a group proved difficult to execute and reduced the reliability of scoring lively group sessions when emotions ran high.

People may show agreement or disagreement by gestures, exclamations or brief commentaries which accompany rather than interrupt a main speaker's contribution. Some do nothing but play this kind of second fiddle. To score all such verbal and non-verbal activities in a session gives an exaggerated impression of the extent to which some people interacted with others.

It was decided therefore to score only the utterance of a speaker who captured the group's predominant attention at any time during a session. This excluded both 'second fiddle' remarks and asides which did not affect the central stream of talk.

The absolute value of the total verbal interactions in a session could not be reliably scored. Investigators differed in their judgement of what was the central stream of talk. Some habitually returned high values of total verbal interactions in all the sessions they scored, others low values.

Because of the relative consistency of high and low scoring investigators the changes of total verbal interactions between sessions ran almost parallel with different investigators. Three observers, scoring the same group independently, had an average correlation coefficient of $+0.92$ for the distribution of total verbal interaction scores over a whole range of sessions. Therefore, with only one observer, the absolute value of total verbal interaction scores which he records in any session is not exact, though his scores of the variations of these absolute values between sessions (i.e., his relative scores) can be accepted as reliable.

The same is true of individual verbal interaction scores. The absolute value of an individual score is not reliable because of the differing scoring standards of observers, but the distribution of individual scores in any session (i.e., relative individual scores) can be accepted as very reliable. The three observers mentioned had a median and modal correlation coefficient of $+0.99$ between the distributions of individual interaction scores, recorded in 27 sessions.

The value of individual verbal interaction scores is influenced also by three group characteristics, not solely by differences in scoring habits. These three influences are: (1) liveliness of discussion, (2) gradient of group participation, and (3) group size.

The liveliness of discussions is indicated, as already mentioned, by the total verbal interaction score in a session. Let us consider two sessions with only three members, i.e., a group size of three. In the first session, the total verbal interaction score is, say, 150, indicating average conversational liveliness. In the second session, the group is twice as lively and the total verbal interaction score is therefore 300.

An individual verbal interaction score of 50 in the first session is an average value denoting an average part in discussion. The same score in the livelier second session falls far short of the average, which is now 100. Thus, the same individual score indicates different degrees of verbal interaction in sessions with different degrees of conversational liveliness.

The gradient of group participation signifies whether members take an equally active part in discussion or differ widely. If they are approximately equal, individual scores will be about the same and the gradient rather flat. If some talk frequently and others are almost silent, the gradient will have a steep slope.

A section in Chapter 5 reveals his views about interpretation:

In psychoanalytically oriented treatment, explanations and interpretations of symptoms and behaviour are often regarded as the main curative measures as they impart insight into the unconscious origin of the neurosis and facilitate emotional reorientation. I consider it their function to elicit emotional reactions which the therapist believes to be therapeutically useful. Clearly, desired reactions can be obtained by interpretations varying widely in intellectual content, timing and phrasing. Thus, interpretations will be correct if they achieve the intended response. They should also be subjectively true in the sense that the therapist believes in them, even if he knows that to make them will falsify what they assert. In the tenth session, for instance, I interpreted certain phenomena as indicating that Faidoon was an outsider. This interpretation was made to challenge the group and Faidoon to alter the situation so that what I had pointed out would no longer be correct.

The reaction to challenging interpretations is not always immediate. When I told Barbara in the third session that her headaches were a neurotic reaction to the arrival of a female competitor, the immediate and only result was an annoyed rejection of my remarks. In the sixth session, in a similar situation, when a third woman arrived, Barbara had no headaches, and went all out to prove me wrong by taking an active and spirited part in the conversation.

Another challenging remark which had the desired effect of inspiring a wish to prove me wrong happened six years after the end of the group, when I doubted Henry's ability to overcome his neurotic fears of marriage. I think my doubt was justified, but when I communicated it to Henry the dynamic situation was altered and his determination stimulated to succeed in spite of his fears.

Interpretations are not always so challenging, though many psychoanalytic interpretations felt by the patients to be disparaging are of this kind. Other interpretations in therapeutic groups may be given to regulate the emotional intensity of discussions; intellectual interpretations to reduce excitement; disturbing interpretations to enliven discussions which are in the doldrums.

Finally, a passage from his summary chapter illustrates the detailed way in which he laid out his results:

14. The differential dyadic feelings of group members in relation to each colleague have two components:
(a) dyadic love–hate feelings varying from colleague to colleague,
(b) dyadic self-appeal feelings assumed to vary from colleague to colleague.
15. There was a frequent assumption that one's dyadic love–hate feelings were reciprocated in kind and degree by most colleagues. This strong dyadic reciprocity bias probably had its origin in the uncertainty many group members felt about their dyadic self-appeals.
16. People who were good judges of their dyadic self-appeals (i.e., who had high scores of awareness of dyadic self-appeal) tended to form dyadic

relations in which positive and negative feelings were each reciprocated (i.e., they had high scores of dyadic mutuality). The correlation between awareness of dyadic self-appeal and dyadic mutuality was +0.68 (N = 158), suggesting that the dyadic reciprocity bias also operated in reverse so that people tended to requite the feelings they believed to have aroused. If this belief was correct, a high degree of dyadic mutuality followed.

17. People who ostentatiously showed whom they liked and whom they disliked (i.e., who had high scores of display of dyadic feelings) also tended to form dyadic relations of high emotional mutuality because their colleagues tended to reciprocate the kind and degree of feeling which they so ostentatiously received. The correlation between dyadic display and dyadic mutuality was +0.35 (N = 158).

18. Dyadic mutuality, therefore, seemed to have its main roots in two personality traits: the tendency to display dyadic feelings and the ability to judge correctly one's dyadic appeals.

19. These traits were uncorrelated when the effect of emotionally mutual dyadic relations was excluded. When the effect was taken into account, the two personality traits seemed to be correlated (N = 158, r = +0.23).

20. People who were unpopular in a group tended to be emotionally isolated in that their scores of dyadic mutuality, or awareness of dyadic self-appeal, or dyadic display were significantly less than the scores of people with medium or high popularity.

21. The longer and the better group members knew each other, the higher were their average scores of dyadic mutuality, awareness and display.

22. Men and women did not differ in respect of their average scores of dyadic mutuality, awareness and display.

19

D. H. Malan:
A Study of Brief Psychotherapy

Reviewed by Jeremy Holmes

Paraphrasing Philip Larkin (1974), it might be said that British psychotherapy research "began/In nineteen sixty three"—the year of publication of *A Study of Brief Psychotherapy*—"Between the end of the *Chatterly* ban/And the Beatles' first LP."

Stimulated by his "mentor, and opponent in many controversies," Michael Balint, David Malan set out in the 1950s to establish the importance, efficacy, and feasibility of brief psychoanalytical psychotherapy in the treatment of neuroses. The social context for this project was the incorporation of the Tavistock Clinic within the NHS, and the need to find forms of psychotherapy relevant to an egalitarian service, free at the point of delivery. The intellectual context required Malan to fight on two fronts. The first was the psychoanalytical establishment which, despite early enthusiasm among the pioneers, including Ferenczi (Balint's analyst), tended to see brief psychotherapies as unsuitable for any but the most mildly disturbed, incompatible with the fundamental psychoanalytical tools of transference and deep interpretation, and in general mere palliatives compared with the benefits offered by full, and necessarily prolonged, analyses. Malan's second battle was to establish scientific validity for psychotherapy in the face of opponents like Eysenck who, using superficial outcome measures and a certain amount of prestidigitation, questioned the entire basis of psychoanalysis, claiming that it produced results no better than those achieved by spontaneous remission. Unlike some of his psychoanalytical colleagues, Malan did not respond to this challenge by turning his back on science, but rather by looking for ways in which the deep changes sought by psychoanalysis could be quantified and studied.

Malan's methodology was that of "action research," a mixture of clinical self-scrutiny and statistical rating that would, by today's standards, be criticised for its use of participant observation by the researcher, unwarranted inference from scanty data, and primitive rating methods. Nevertheless, as a pilot project it was a great advance on previous work, managing to be both clinically meaningful and to have some statistical validity.

The book is based on a study of nineteen patients treated with brief psychotherapy—ranging from four to forty sessions, with a median of fifteen. Outcome was rated on a four-point scale: 3 = substantial resolution of the main problem, 2 = limited resolution, 1 = symptomatic improvement or valuable false solution, 0 = no change; and was assessed one to three years after therapy was completed. Malan was extremely stringent in his outcome assessments, which were based on psychodynamic criteria. Balint (1959) had defined psychological health in terms of the resolution of the Oedipus complex, reflected in the capacity to form loving heterosexual relationships based on genital satisfaction. This yardstick can be felt as a powerful influence on Malan, but he also emphasized the importance of "translation of symbols," albeit in sexual terms. For instance, in order to score 3, a patient would have to have a good orgasmic heterosexual relationship, and also to have resolved and achieved insight into guilt about mistakes at work as representing "guilt in relation to male authority about homosexuality." The latter without the former would get a 2, since Malan regarded resolution of problems with the same sex as being prior to, and easier than, heterosexual resolutions. This attempt to find one fundamental outcome measure contrasts with contemporary approaches, which tend to use a battery of tests designed to pick up different aspects of social and psychological function. Malan's measure is relatively insensitive, and might also be criticized because of its strong implicit value judgment about what constitutes psychological health. In our more pluralistic, postsexualist era the pursuit of heterosexual genital satisfaction seems too narrow a goal. It would be impossible for a celibate to score 3 on Malan's criteria. However, most people would probably accept that the achievement of satisfying intimate relationships *is* of overwhelming importance as a mark and buttress of psychological health, and the value of Malan's classification is that it does not flinch from this.

Malan first established a method for scoring outcome. He then divided his sample into two roughly equal halves: ten who scored 0; nine who scored 1 or more (only five—about 25 percent—achieved 3). He was then in a position to consider his first question: In general, what are the selection criteria for brief therapy, and in particular, is it true that it is only the less disturbed, with illnesses of recent onset, who are likely to benefit? His answer to the latter is an unequivocal no: some of the most long-term and "disturbed" patients had the best outcome, while several with only mild difficulties of recent onset did poorly. This important, and possibly counterintuitive, result is particularly relevant in the face of current charges that psychotherapy is mainly of value to the "worried well." Malan appears to show that the "walking wounded" can also benefit. His result has to be qualified by his failure to develop a consistent rating scale for severity, and by the "ecology" (Malan's term) of patients referred to the Tavistock Clinic, none of whom were psychotic, and all of whom were in work (this was the 1950s) or running a home. Subsequent research on this point has on the whole confirmed Malan's results (Garfield 1986): Some evidence of previously successful adjustment ("ego strength") is correlated with good outcome in psychotherapy, but within that broad category quite disturbed patients can have good outcomes, a point established in a British context by Ryle and his collaborators (Brockman et al. 1987).

Malan's next question was a simple one, although the answer was not. If severity is not a good guide to selection, what is? Here he highlighted that most elusive of psychological entities, motivation. No formal attempt to rate motivation was made, but cases were divided into those with "high" and "low" motivation based on a variety of criteria, including whether the patient contacted the clinic after assessment asking for help, whether they altered or failed to turn up to appointments, and the therapists' assessment of their capacity for insight. On this basis he found that 85 percent of those with good outcomes had high motivation, and nearly half of those with low motivation scored 0 on outcome. The importance of motivation as a predictor of outcome has been confirmed by later studies (e.g., Keithly et al. 1980). As always, Malan was not satisfied by superficial correlations and tried to discover deeper meaning behind them. For him, motivation is an aspect of the therapeutic alliance that is a precondition of successful therapy. The best outcomes are likely where the patient is well prepared for therapy, knows in advance what is entailed, feels it is likely to help, and is seen by the therapist to be open to the technique he has to offer. While resistance later in therapy may be a healthy antidote to idealization, initial resistance, especially if manifest in lateness or missed appointments, is likely to predict therapeutic failure.

The third part of Malan's project shows him at his most ambitious and innovative. It is a process/outcome study looking at the relationship between therapeutic interventions and outcome, based on therapists' detailed case reports (rather than, as would now be required, recordings of sessions). As a psychoanalyst, he is particularly interested in the relationship between transference interpretations and outcome. From the case reports he derives a number of measures: (a) overall transference score, depending on whether transference was judged to be an important issue in therapy; (b) a transference ratio, the ratio between the number of transference interpretations and the total number of interventions of any kind made by the therapist; (c) the proportion of these interpretations linking the patient and therapist; and (d) an assessment of whether negative transference, especially feelings of grief and anger about termination, was an important feature of the therapy. These four measures were then correlated with the overall outcome score, and also with a new measure, "behavior at follow-up," which is classified on a three-point scale as "optimum" (gratitude and cooperation with a follow-up study and occasional letters to the therapist), "overdependent" (requests for more treatment, etc.), and "disturbed" (breaking off therapy, refusal of further contact).

The limitations of the method were considerable: small numbers, nonblind ratings, arbitrary rating scales, and therapist distortion. Nevertheless, the results were striking: high transference ratios were correlated with good outcome, albeit weakly ($P = 0.15$), but patient/therapist transference interpretations were strongly correlated with good outcome ($P = 0.03$), and patients in whom negative transference was explored had better outcomes and more optimal behavior at follow-up than those in whom it was not. Subsequent, more methodologically rigorous, studies have confirmed these conclusions (Marziali 1984).

This last section of the book is presented with a feeling of gathering excitement as the story unfolds, showing Malan's skills of clarification and timing at their best, leading to his triumphant vindication of the psychodynamic dogma that it is transference interpretations that are "mutative" in psychoanalytical psychotherapy.

But Malan was a scientist as well as a psychoanalyst, and was not content to let matters rest there. Although the use of transference interpretations is correlated with good outcome in psychotherapy, this does not establish a necessary causal relationship. Malan acknowledged that client-centered and forms of therapy other than psychoanalytical may also achieve good results. He therefore suggested that what is needed for good outcome is "deep involvement" between therapist and patient, and that transference interpretations are likely both to heighten this deep involvement and to be a manifestation of it. For successful therapy there has to be an emotional and theoretical congruence between patient and therapist, and a high transference ratio is, in psychoanalytical psychotherapy, a good indicator of this.

Subsequent research has on the whole confirmed much of Malan's work. Orlinsky and Howard (1981) identified five process factors that are consistently found to correlate with good outcome: adequate preparation of the clients so that they know what to expect in therapy; a strong therapeutic bond that may in part be manifest in the therapist's assessment of the patient as being well motivated; the capacity and skill of the therapist, which, in analytical psychotherapy, could well be shown by a high transference ratio; the expression of affect in session; and the number of sessions, where it appears that the more the sessions the better the outcome. Only the latter is at variance with Malan's results, but since at the Tavistock brief therapy may mean up to 40 sessions, it might be concluded that one man's brief therapy may be three times another man's maximum (Brockman et al. 1987).

What then, a quarter of a century later, is our evaluation of Malan's work? Perhaps the most outstanding feature is his style. There is a clarity and succinctness in his writing, an ability to crystallize concepts, to simplify without being simplistic, and to summarise complex clinical material in a vivid and jargon-free way that sets him apart from almost every other psychoanalytical author since Freud. His second great strength is a benign skepticism which frees him from slavish adherence to any but the most fundamental of psychoanalytical tenets, and leads him to question the paraphernalia of psychoanalysis without discarding its essential truths and techniques. Fundamentalists may resist his revisionism, just as many true believers find the bishop of Durham's quasi-agnosticism unacceptable. Other practitioners may resist even his clarity, which inevitably does some violence to the inherent opacity of the psyche, which Coltart (1986) calls "the sheer unconsciousness of the unconscious." Doing psychotherapy can never quite be like playing chess, and sometimes Malan makes it seem almost too simple. As a researcher and scientist Malan's work is unrivalled, especially in Britain, and much of what has followed has served merely to confirm his hypotheses. As a clinician one senses how deeply influenced and impressed Malan is by Balint, and how at times he uses science to resist this influence. In his next, and in my view most original and successful book (Malan 1973) this tension has gone and he finds his own unique voice, but in later years once again he fell under the spell of another powerful and charismatic figure, Habib Davanloo (1978). A final twenty-five-year outcome for Malan's therapeutic work might therefore be rated somewhere just short of 3, but how many therapists would not be content to settle for that?

REFERENCES

Balint, M. (1959). *Thrills and Regressions*. London: Hogarth.

Brockman, B., Poynton, A. Ryle, A., and Watson, J. P. (1987). Effectiveness of time-limited therapy carried out by trainees: comparison of two methods. *British Journal of Psychiatry* 151:602–610.

Coltart, N. (1986). Slouching towards Bethlehem. In *The British School of Psychoanalysis*, ed. G. Kohon. London: Free Association Books.

Davanloo, H. (1978). *Basic Principles and Techniques in Short-Term Dynamic Psychotherapy*. New York: Spectrum.

Garfield, S. L. (1986). Research on client variables in psychotherapy. In *Handbook of Psychotherapy and Behaviour Change*, ed. S. L. Garfield and A. E. Bergin. Chichester, England: Wiley.

Keithly, L. J., Samples, S., and Strupp, H. H. (1980). Patient motivation as a predictor of process and outcome in psychotherapy. *Psychotherapy & Psychosomatics* 33:87–97.

Larkin, P. (1974). *High Windows*. London: Faber.

Malan, D. (1973). *Individual Psychotherapy and the Science of Psychodynamics*. London: Butterworth.

Marziali, E. (1984). Three viewpoints on the therapeutic alliance: similarities, differences and association with psychotherapy outcome. *Journal of Nervous & Mental Disease* 7:417–423.

Orlinsky, D. E., and Howard, K. I. (1981). Process and outcome in psychotherapy. In *Handbook of Psychotherapy and Behaviour Change*, ed. S. L. Garfield and A. E. Bergin. Chichester, England: Wiley.

Selections from
A Study of Brief Psychotherapy
by D. H. Malan

RECAPITULATION AND CONCLUSION

General Statement Of The Characteristics of Patients, Therapists, And Technique

1. All patients were adults; were thought to be highly suitable for psychotherapy; were willing and able to explore their feelings; gave the impression that they could work in interpretative therapy; and gave material at interview which was understandable in psycho-analytic terms and which enabled psycho-analysts to formulate some kind of limited therapeutic plan.
2. All therapists were psycho-analytically oriented, and were willing to employ a relatively "active" technique which was entirely interpretative, was highly selective ("focal"), and in which emphasis was laid on "objective" emotional interaction with the patient.

Hypotheses And Conclusions Already Presented

1. *Therapeutic results*
   Under the above conditions it is possible to obtain quite far-reaching improvements not merely in "symptoms" but also in neurotic behaviour patterns, in patients with relatively extensive and long-standing neuroses.
2. *Length of therapy*
   These can be obtained in ten to forty sessions.
3. *Selection criteria*
   (a) The hypothesis that it is the patients with "mild" illnesses of recent onset who give the best results (Hypothesis A) is not supported.
   (b) Our results suggest that—when the patients have already been selected as described above—an important criterion indicating a good prognosis is concerned with a high motivation for insight therapy.

4. *Characteristics of technique regarded as the result of interaction between patient and therapist*
There is strong evidence:
(a) that thorough interpretation of the transference plays an important part in leading both to favourable outcome and to an optimum relationship with the therapist after termination;
(b) that important subdivisions of transference interpretation are (i) the negative transference, and (ii) the link between the transference and the relation to one or both parents; and
(c) that those therapies tend to be more successful in which transference interpretations become important early, and/or in which interpretations of the patient's grief and anger at termination are a major issue.
(d) our work provides some slight evidence that therapists tend to be more successful early in their experience of this kind of therapy, when (presumably) their enthusiasm is highest.

A Unifying Factor

The essence of most of these hypotheses may now be repeated in the following words:

> Prognosis seems to be most favourable when the following conditions apply: the patient has a high motivation; the therapist has a high enthusiasm; transference arises early and becomes a major feature of therapy; and grief and anger at termination are important issues.

Suddenly there crystallizes, from all the complexity of this long exposition of evidence, a single unifying factor of extraordinary simplicity:

> That the prognosis is best when there is a willingness on the part of both patient and therapist to become *deeply involved*, and (in Balint's words) to bear the tension that inevitably ensues.

Obviously this must be qualified. Each must become involved in a special way: the patient must bring to the therapy his intense wish for help through insight, and to the relation with the therapist both his neurotic difficulties and some of his dependence—but dependence that is neither too intense nor too primitive; while the therapist must bring his human sympathy, his therapeutic enthusiasm, and his willingness to interact "objectively," and he obviously must not become so involved that—for instance—he is resentful if therapy fails, and still less must *his* involvement be seriously complicated by unconscious reverberations from the past.

This willingness to become involved may well be an important "non-specific" factor in psychotherapy, which our particular kind of therapy shares with many others. That such factors are needed to explain the apparently good therapeutic results obtained by such a large variety of techniques is becoming increasingly widely realized. This is worth supporting by quotations:

From the transcript of the patient's first mention of the subject of termination (from the case of "Mrs. Oak," published by Rogers and Dymond [1954]):

> Yes I feel this dependency . . . it's comparable to the feeling you get when you're just finishing a very meaningful book, and have only a few pages left— a sort of wishing that you could prolong it. And there's regret, but still it's still with you, and you can still have it and touch it, and even give it away, and yet if need be go back to it.

From the author's comments on the therapy (from the case of "Mrs. Oak," published by Rogers and Dymond [1954]):

> . . . for her, one of the deepest experiences in therapy . . . (was) the realization that the therapist *cared*, that it really mattered to him how therapy turned out for her. . . .

The "specific" factor in our kind of therapy seems to be a special variety of this involvement on the part of the patient, together with insight into its meaning; i.e., the transference experience accompanied by transference interpretation, and particularly the experience and interpretation of the negative transference and of the therapist-parent link.

Selection Criteria

Now it is tempting to draw, from these hypotheses, certain conclusions about *technique*: that the therapist should start making transference interpretations as soon as possible, should take every opportunity of making the therapist-parent link, and should always devote the last third or quarter of therapy to making interpretations about termination. Whereas I certainly agree that the therapist should be aware of these factors in technique as general principles, I suspect that there is implied here a mistaken judgment about the causal relations involved. It must be remembered that the hypotheses reached in the present work—whether by clinical judgment or statistically—are all based essentially on correlations. It is a characteristic of correlations that they give no information about causal relations—a positive correlation between two factors may occur if one causes the other, or vice versa, or if both are the results of a common cause. When this consideration is applied to the present data, it will become clear that the development of transference, and hence whether transference is interpretable, presumably depend more on factors in the therapist. There is plenty of evidence from our cases that the therapist is unable not only to prevent the development of transference, but also to make use of transference interpretations unless the patient is willing and ready to hear them. If the patient has no grief about leaving therapy (e.g., the Pilot's Wife), there is no point in interpreting it. In other words, the characteristics of successful therapy that have been described are at least as much concerned with selection criteria as with technique. This view, reached by myself after such laborious study of the data, has already been expressed intuitively in the Workshop:

PINES: "If we say this is the aim in short-term therapy—dealing as soon as possible with termination and breaking off dependency—we should take on patients who can quickly enter into relationship. We should say that this man was unsuitable because it took him a long time to reach this point."

This suggests a new group of selection criteria:

1. the early development of transference, especially of a difficulty in the transference, and excluding, certain kinds of transference.

2. the capacity to mourn (already postulated by Dicks in the preliminary discussions). It seems possible that this might be judged from projection tests.

Now it will be remembered that one of our original selection criteria was a "history of real and good relationships," and two of the criteria used throughout this work by the psychologists in projection tests were the "ability to tell stories about real people" and the "ability to face emotional conflict." Obviously all these criteria are closely related to the "willingness to become involved and to bear the tension that ensues" which crystallizes from the present data. Yet none of these criteria proved of much value in predicting outcome. The question is, why?

The only tentative answers that I can give are, first, that the emphasis on "real" may be mistaken. The relation with the therapist is of a unique kind, in which phantasies derived from the past are allowed free play, and it seems to be the willingness to express these in this relation which leads to a favorable outcome. Second, the judgements of the psychologists, like those of all of us, were always overshadowed by Hypothesis A, against which our data have provided such strong evidence. There is a great need for a reexamination of the material given by these patients in projection tests, to see if some factor connected with "willingness to become involved" can be identified.

Because the patients in the present study represent such a highly selected population, there are certain selection criteria which may well be extremely important, but which have not been put to the test in our work at all. . . . If they are regarded, once more, as products of the interaction between patient and therapist, they may be re-stated in the following way:

1. The patient's willingness and ability to explore feelings;
2. The patient's ability to work within a therapeutic relationship based on interpretation;
3. The therapist's ability to feel that he understands the patient's problem in dynamic terms; and
4. The therapist's ability to formulate some kind of circumscribed therapeutic plan.

Here one can only say that undocumented experience and intuition both suggest that these four criteria may well come near to being necessary conditions to successfully focal therapy.

A Possible Future Selection Procedure

The following procedure is now tentatively suggested as a way of making practical use of all the above considerations concerning selection criteria:

1. It is essential that partial interpretations should be made in the psychiatric interview. The purpose of this is (a) to make plain to the patient that he will be offered interpretative therapy and very little else; (b) to gauge his ability to explore his feelings and his capacity for insight; and (c) to see what effect interpretations have upon his motivation.
2. For those patients who seem to be suitable, I would be inclined to recommend a second exploratory interview about a week later. The purpose of this is to give the patient a longer period during which his reactions to interpretative therapy can be studied.
3. The projection test is then given, about a week later than the second exploratory interview.
4. If (a) it is clear that the patient can be offered treatment of some kind, and (b) there is any doubt about his wish to come during this initial

period, I would suggest that he should now be asked to think the situation over and write, saying whether he would like another appointment. If he does not write, or if there is a long delay before he does so, the prognosis is automatically regarded as bad.

5. The therapist and psychologist (and the group, if they are working in a group) confer, and see if they can understand the patient's problem and formulate a therapeutic plan.

6. Careful note is made of all fluctuations in motivation and all manifestations of transference during this period. Indications of a good prognosis would then be: (a) The material is understandable; (b) A therapeutic plan can be formulated; (c) There is some indication that the patient is beginning to work with interpretations; (d) There are signs of developing transference—though, obviously, of a not too dependent or demanding kind; and (e) Motivation either starts high or shows a rapid increase during this whole period.

The hypothetical working of this procedure may be illustrated by one of the cases in the present study, the Pilot's Wife (though the uncertain influence of the endocrine factor on this patient's prognosis introduces a complication). Her complaint was frigidity, her emotional problem an intense resentment against men, and she started to *interact* with her (male) interviewer before she ever saw him, demanding to be seen by a woman doctor. At interview and at test she presented the whole of her psychopathology; and consequently there would have been no difficulty in formulating a therapeutic plan: to assign her to a male therapist, to interpret her resentment against men in the transference, and to relate this both to her frigidity and to a (presumed) highly ambivalent relation with her father. So far, all the signs were favourable. Nevertheless, her motivation was clearly ambivalent—on the one hand she said that she did not believe in psychiatry, and on the other she seemed prepared to go to some trouble to come. For this she should have been given the benefit of the doubt. When she was asked in the second interview to talk about whatever she liked, however, and she spent the whole session chatting about trivialities, the prognosis would become more doubtful. When she rang up five minutes before the third interview, wanting to put off treatment indefinitely because her husband had got into trouble, the prognosis would become very bad; and when, finally, six months later, she asked for treatment again, she either would have been referred elsewhere, or would have been accepted with the firm prediction that treatment would fail. In fact she was taken on and, in spite of a therapy of intense interaction throughout, she remained quite unchanged.

20

R. D. Laing and A. Esterson:
Sanity, Madness and the Family

Reviewed by Anthony S. David

In this series, Andrew Smith (1982) reconsidered R. D. Laing's *The Divided Self* (1960). In his sensitive, wideranging review of Laing's first book, he added to the growing weight of opinion in some psychiatric circles that it is a major though idiosyncratic contribution to our understanding of schizophrenic psychopathology. It is after all on the Royal College of Psychiatrist's current psychotherapy reading list. *Sanity, Madness and the Family*, first published in 1964, and the work which accompanied it, remains outside mainstream psychiatry yet I will argue has had an impact exceeding that of *The Divided Self* on today's practice.

The first Tavistock publication was subtitled, *Volume 1, Families of Schizophrenics*, with the implication that further volumes would deal with families of other psychiatric patients or normals. The preface to the second Penguin edition (1970) explains that on reflection the use of a control group would not help the authors answer *their* question, namely, "Are the experience and behavior that psychiatrists take as symptoms and signs of schizophrenia more socially intelligible than has come to be supposed?" (p. 12). The term "intelligible" replaces "comprehensible," as in *The Divided Self*—and is crucial. It is a term borrowed from Sartre meaning the making sense of that which is between "what is going on (process) and who is doing what (praxis)" (p. 22). We will come back to whether or not this question was answered or indeed whether it was a useful question to ask in the first place. Pausing to examine the preface itself reveals that it is its stridency and vituperation which incensed reviewers and perhaps discouraged them from reading further. The late Eliot Slater (1971) reviewed the second edition for the *British Journal of Psychiatry* (the first was not submitted) and stated that "to formulate this question involves a hypothesis regarding schizophrenia" despite the authors disclaiming any intention to propose such a hypothesis, indeed the word schizophrenia is isolated in parentheses hoping perhaps it would wither and die. Slater's answer to the authors' question was an emphatic no, and he went on to describe the whole enterprise as "irrelevant" and "disingenuous." Disingenuous it may have looked, being bereft of reliable measurers, controls and unbiased sampling, but irrelevant it certainly was not. In a review of *The Self and Others* (Laing 1969) Professor J. K. Wing (1971), though describing Laing's observations on families of schizophrenics as "subjective and partisan" goes on to confirm his importance to psychiatry if only as a curious social phenomenon.

R. D. Laing and Aaron Esterson, a contemporary from Glasgow University, set about elucidating the context of behaviors and experiences in order to make schizophrenia intelligible, comprehensible, meaningful and understandable. Following on from earlier work, it challenges the notion that the quintessence of schizophrenia is its un-understandability Jaspers 1963). This meaningfulness is seen as residing in the family "nexus" with the implication that "the schizophrenia" somehow exists only within the shared experience of a family "system," a concept derived from cybernetics and sociology and brought to bear upon families by the influential Bateson group (Bateson et al. 1956). Laing and Esterson did this by exhaustive interviews, often totaling fifty hours, with eleven female schizophrenic patients both when well and psychotic, alone and with family members in all combinations. So rich in detail were their observations that one family case history, the Danzigs, was expanded into a book (Esterson 1970). This appreciation for the subtle nuances of communication, verbal and nonverbal, and the realization that the interaction between a patient and his or her family may be infinitely more revealing than individual interviews was ahead of its time. Such concern for detail and recording belies the charge that Laing and co-workers were less than serious students of interpersonal relationships. The question of whether this effort answered their hypothesis is largely in the eye of the beholder. The data presented are of necessity highly selective. For example, does the repeated invalidation of patient Maya Abbott's feelings/beliefs/desires by her parents such as "You don't really think that," explain her ideas that her thoughts are being taken away or controlled? Does the fact that a mother listens to her daughter's telephone calls render intelligible her delusion that people listen to her telephone calls? Is Clare Church's impoverished affect explicable in the light of her parents' inconsistent and contradictory attitudes to Clare's affection for others? For most psychiatrists, the provision of context is insufficient to explain the form that a patient's experiences take, which is recognizable as pathological. Indeed the authors acknowledge that to understand fully Lucie Blairs' "phenomenology" they have to invoke "internalization and re-projection" (p. 74). The meaning which Laing and Esterson ascribe to "content" is ingenious and in itself a valuable contribution since many of the phenomena they examine are undoubtedly schizophrenic, frequently Schneiderian symptoms. If we allow a qualified "yes" to their question it still leaves many of ours, perhaps more important, untouched. Contemporary researchers were left to discover whether families of schizophrenics are more disturbed than families of other psychiatric patients (see Hirsch and Leff 1975, Rund, 1986). Does this reflect a shared genetic constitution (see Wender 1977) or the nonspecific effects on parents of having a disturbed child (see Wynne et al. 1976)?

The anti-intuitive finding that schizophrenics discharged from hospital fared worse when they returned to their parents (Brown et al. 1962) led to a substantial body of influential work from the Institute of Psychiatry reviewed recently by Hooley (1985). The techniques used for inferring family interaction from interviews with one or other parent were crude in comparison to Laing and Esterson's. The highly sensitive dissection of intrafamilial communication cannot easily be rated reliably so cannot be taken into account when measuring expressed emotion (EE). This work has been extended by psychologist Michael Goldstein and his team, who have used EE and other measures called communication deviance and affective style to examine interaction directly and in more detail. If it were possible to rate Laing and Esterson's recordings and transcripts they would almost certainly be found to be heavy with all these parameters. It seems that the authors were grappling with the same abnormalities that have provided others with a venerable area of research. Their mistake was to claim more for their studies than the methodology allowed. For instance, their statement that all families of schizophrenics are seriously disturbed is clearly an overstatement which can be explained by the fact that their objects were chronic and frequently relapsing and so were likely to come from high EE families. By sticking to the issue of relapse, workers at the Institute of Psychiatry have avoided such accusations. The Goldstein group have been more ambitious and have tried to address etiological issues in a family study follow-up of disturbed adolescents (Goldstein 1985). Twenty years after Laing, and with a host of collaborators, the same questions remain substantially unanswered.

One area in which *Sanity, Madness and the Family* has been particularly influential is family therapy in that the book linked schizophrenia with family pathology in a way that was vivid and convincing, especially to those practitioners without medical training. This was probably unintentional, as the authors object to the notion of "family pathology" as strongly as they do to neuropathology, arguing that this "biological analogy" has no place in a "social phenomenological" perspective. This major theoretical difference does little to disguise the similarity between the processes they describe and those described by family therapists—such as enmeshment, disqualification, collusion, and so on. Family therapy is an anathema to Laing and his colleagues, as is physical treatment. David Cooper (1967) quipped that "curing" is something one does to bacon and not people called schizophrenic. For Laing and Cooper, the only "treatment" was to get the patient out of the home and into an environment free from coercion. This was based presumably on the assumption that patterns of interaction cannot be changed, a view certainly not shared by family therapists (e.g., Fallon et al. 1985; Minuchin 1974). Simply reducing face to face contact may be protective (Leff et al. 1982). The experimental ward, Villa 21, at Shenley Hospital, in which Cooper managed schizophrenic patients, may have served this purpose among others. Patients could come voluntarily and refuse treatment if they wished. They had a close one-to-one relationship with a staff member from a multidisciplinary team. The ward was run democratically with patients holding communal responsibility. The doctor relinquished his white coat. This "daring" setup does not sound the least revolutionary now. Indeed, the District Services Center at the Maudsley Hospital and many other places like it, provides continuing care for chronic psychiatric patients along very similar lines. The efficacy of this sort of program was assessed in comparison to the standard treatment of the time and published in a little known paper in the *British Medical Journal* (Esterson et al. 1965). The authors could be said to be advocates of asylum in its broadest sense (as in the Philadelphia Association) and not community psychiatry or, for that matter, antipsychiatry, which seeks to destroy all such institutions and which Laing decries (McGinley and David 1985).

The most trenchant accusation made of Laing and *Sanity, Madness and the Family*, is the crime of parent blaming. It is difficult to find an explicit example of this in any of Laing's writings. Nevertheless, whether it was his intention or not, his tone and posture at times leads the reader inevitably to this conclusion. There can be no victim without a victimizer. The review from *New Society* quoted on the cover of the Penguin edition talks unabashedly of the "ugly sight of children being brainwashed by parents." Families too have inferred an attack, as shown by many heartfelt essays collected by the National Schizophrenia Fellowship (1974). It is not enough *not* to blame them; families must be supported and actively encouraged (Berkowitz et al. 1981). In the terminology of family therapy, their attitudes and actions must be "positively connoted" if any change is sought and a therapeutic alliance is to be maintained.

In conclusion, *Sanity, Madness and the Family* may be judged more favorably in hindsight than it was when first published. In an effort to give method to extreme forms of madness, it has helped to deflect the psychiatrist's microscope toward examining social interaction in a naturalistic way rather than in the sterile confines of the laboratory. It reminded us that "those psychiatrists who are not prepared to get to know what goes on outside their clinics and hospitals simply do not know what goes on" (p. 13). It has encouraged family approaches even in psychotic disorders and the growth of family therapy, unwittingly perhaps. Unfortunately, it probably alienated some families in the process. By virtue of its appeal to public and hence patient opinion, and influence on nonmedical and some medical staff, it has contributed to an atmosphere whereby less formal, more eclectic care for severely disturbed psychiatric patients could flourish.

REFERENCES

Bateson, G., Jackson, D. D., Haley, J., and Weakland, J. H. (1956). Toward a theory of schizophrenia. *Behavioural Science* 1:251-264.

Berkowitz, R., Kuipers, I., Eberlein-Fries, R., and Leff, J. (1981). Lowering expressed emotion in relatives of schizophrenics. In *New Directions for Mental Health Services: New Directions in Interventions with Families of Schizophrenics*, ed. M. Goldstein. San Francisco: Jossey-Bass.

Brown, G. W., Monck, E. M., and Carstairs, G. M. (1962). Influence of family life on the course of schizophrenic illness. *British Journal of Preventive and Social Medicine* 16:55-68.

Cooper, D. (1967). *Psychiatry and Anti-Psychiatry*. London: Tavistock.

Esterson, A. (1970). *The Leaves of Spring: A Study in the Dialectics of Madness*. Harmondsworth, England: Penguin.

Esterson, A., Cooper., D. G., and Laing, R. D. (1965). Results of family-oriented therapy with hospitalized schizophrenics. *British Medical Journal* 2:1462-1465.

Fallon, I. R. H., Boyd, J. L., McGill, C. W., et al. (1985). Family management in the prevention of morbidity of schizophrenia. *Archives of General Psychiatry* 42:887-896.

Goldstein, M. J. (1985). Family factors that antedate the onset of schizophrenic and related disorders: the results of a fifteen year prospective longitudinal study. *Acta Psychiatrica Scaninavica* 71:7-18.

Hirsch, S. R., and Leff, J. P. (1975). *Abnormalities in Parents of Schizophrenics*. London: Oxford University Press.

Hooley, J. M. (1985). Expressed emotion: a review of the critical literature. *Clinical Psychology Review* 5:119-139.

Jaspers, K. (1963). *General Psychopathology*. 7th ed. Trans. J. Hoenig and M. W. Hamilton. Manchester, England: Manchester University Press.

Laing, R. D. (1960). *The Divided Self*. London: Tavistock.

——— (1969) *The Self and Others*. Harmondsworth, England: Penguin.

Laing, R. D., and Esterson, A. (1964). *Sanity, Madness and the Family*. London: Tavistock.

Leff, J., Kuipers. L., Berkowitz, R., et al. (1982). A controlled trial of social intervention in the families of schizophrenic patients. *British Journal of Psychiatry* 141:121–134.

McGinley, E., and David, T. (1985). Sanity, madness and R. D. Laing: interview. *Maudsley and Bethlem Gazette* 32:21–24.

Minuchin, S. (1974). *Families and Family Therapy*. London: Tavistock.

National Schizophrenia Fellowship (1974). *Living with Schizophrenia—by the Relatives*. Surrey, England: NSF Publications.

Rund, B. R. (1986). Communication deviances in parents of schizophrenics. *Family Process* 25:133–147.

Slater, E. (1971). Book review. *British Journal of Psychiatry* 118:111–112.

Smith, A. C. (1982). Books reconsidered. R. D. Laing: *The Divided Self*. *British Journal of Psychiatry* 140:637–642.

Wender, P. H., Rosenthal, D., Rainer, J. D., (1977). Schizophrenics adopting parents. *Archives of General Psychiatry* 34:777–784.

Wing, J. K. (1971). Book review. *British Journal of Psychiatry* 118:360–361.

Wynne, L. C., Singer, M. T., and Toohey, M. T. (1976). Communication of the adoptive parents of schizophrenics. In *Schizophrenia 75 Psychotherapy, Family Studies, Research*, ed. J. Jerstad and E. Ugelstad. Oslo: Universitets Forlaget.

Selections from
Sanity, Madness and the Family
by R. D. Laing and A. Esterson

Our interest is in persons always in relation either with us, or with each other, and always in the light of their group context, which in this work is primarily the family, but may include also the extra-familial personal networks of family members if these have a specific bearing on the issues we are trying to illumine. In other words, we are interested in what might be called the family *nexus*, that multiplicity of persons drawn from the kinship group, and from others who, though not linked by kinship ties, are regarded as members of the family. The relationships of persons in a nexus are characterized by enduring and intensive face-to-face reciprocal influence on each other's experience and behaviour.

We are studying the persons who comprise this nexus, their relationships, and the nexus itself, in so far as it may have structures, processes, and effects as a system, not necessarily intended by its members, nor necessarily predictable from a knowledge of its members studied out of context.

If one wishes to know how a football team concert or disconcert their actions in play, one does not think only or even primarily of approaching this problem by talking to the members individually. One watches the way they play together.

Most of the investigations of families of "schizophrenics," while contributing original and useful data to different facets of the problem, have not been based on direct observation of the members of the family *together* as they actually interact with each other.

The way in which a family deploys itself in space and time, what space, what time, and what things are private or shared, and by whom—these and many other questions are best answered by seeing what sort of world the family has itself fleshed out for itself, both as a whole and differentially for each of its members.

We are concerned with persons, the relations between persons, and the characteristics of the family as a system composed of a multiplicity of persons. Our theoretical position with particular respect to our method, is as follows.

Each person not only is an object in the world of others but is a position in space and time from which he experiences, constitutes, and acts in his world. He is his own centre with his own point of view, and it is precisely each person's perspective on the situation that he shares with others that we wish to discover.

However, each person does not occupy a single definable position in relation to other members of his or her own family.

The one person may be a daughter and a sister, a wife and a mother. There is no means of knowing a priori the relation between: the dyadic set of reciprocals she has with her father, the dyadic set with her mother, and the triadic set she has in the trio of them all together; and by the same token, she may be a sister to her brother, and to her sister, and, in addition, she may be married with a son or daughter.

Let us suppose that Jill has a father and mother and brother, who all live together. If one wishes to form a complete picture of her as a family person, let alone as a person outside the family, it will be necessary to see how she experiences and acts in all the following contexts:

Jill alone
Jill with mother
Jill with father
Jill with brother
Jill with mother and father
Jill with mother and brother
Jill with father and brother
Jill with mother, father, and brother.

One sees that it is a fairly crude differentiation of the various positions that Jill has to adopt to characterize them as daughter or sister.

Samples of behaviour require to be taken of each person in the family in turn in the same way. People have identities. But they may also change quite remarkably as they become different others-to-others. It is arbitrary to regard any one of these transformations or *alter*ations as basic, and the others as variations.

Not only may the one person behave differently in his different alterations, but he may experience himself in different ways. He is liable to remember different things, express different attitudes, even quite discordant ones, imagine and fantasize in different ways, and so on.

Within the terms of phenomenology itself, this study is limited methodologically and heuristically.

Most of our data is in the form of interviews. Despite the relatively systematic nature of our sampling of the family by such interviews, our study of these families is of course far from complete, in that, firstly, the majority of these interviews were conducted in our own consulting-rooms, and not in the family homes, and second, and more serious, and interview is itself not a naturally occurring family situation.

We are also dissatisfied with our method of recording. Its main limitation is that all our permanent records are restricted to the auditory transactions of the family members in our presence. Although such a permanent library of magnetic recordings is an advance on clinical notes made during or after interviews, it can be regarded only as a stepping-stone to permanent audio-visual records.

Our findings are presented with very few interpretations, whether existential or psychoanalytic. Psychoanalysis has largely concerned itself with the relation of the unconscious to manifest behaviour. The psycho-analyst frequently makes attributions about the analysand's motives, experiences, actions, intentions, that the analysand himself disavows or is unaware of. The reader will see that we have been very sparing about making attributions of this kind in respect to the members of these families.

Undoubtedly, in our view, in all these families the fantasy experiences of the family members and the motives, actions, intentions, that arise on the basis of such experience, are mostly unknown to the persons them-selves. Thus, it is not possible to deal adequately with such a central issue, for instance, as sexuality in these families without being prepared to attribute to the agents involved fantasies of which they are themselves unconscious. However, in this volume, we have not undertaken to do this.

Our discussion and comments on each family are pared down to what seems to us to be an undeniable bedrock.

Inferences about experiences that the experiencers themselves deny, and about motives and intentions that the agent himself disavows, present difficulties of validation that do not arise at that phenomenological level to which we have restricted ourselves.

It has seemed to us on the whole desirable to limit this volume in this way, even sometimes at the price of not being able to state what we regard as basic elements of the family dynamics.

Here, then, the reader will find documented the quite manifest contra-dictions that beset these families, without very much exploration of the underlying factors which may be supposed to generate and maintain them. Subsequently we hope to go much further in interpreting data.

Another limitation, and one that we feel is necessary in the transition from a clinical to a social phenomenological perspective, is that our *totalization* of the family itself as a system is incomplete. Our account of each family is to a considerable degree polarized around the intelligibility of the experience and behaviour of the person who has already begun a career as a schizophrenic. As such, the focus remains somewhat on the identified patient, or on the mother-daughter relationship, on the person-in-a-nexus, rather than on the nexus itself. This we believe to be historically unavoidable. That this study is transitional is both its weakness and its strength, in that we hope it will constitute a bridge between past and future efforts in the understanding of madness.

In this book, we believe that we show that the experience and behaviour of schizophrenics is much more socially intelligible than has come to be supposed by most psychiatrists.

We have tried in each single instance to answer the question: to what extent is the experience and behaviour of that person, who has already begun a career as a diagnosed "schizophrenic" patient, intelligible in the light of the praxis and process of his or her family nexus?

We believe that the shift of point of view that these descriptions both embody and demand has a historical significance no less radical than the shift from a demonological to a clinical viewpoint three hundred years ago.

21

Eric Berne:
Games People Play: The Psychology of Human Relationships

Reviewed by Duncan Cramer

Games People Play is the second of four major books written by Berne describing his theory of psychotherapy, which is called transactional analysis. The other three are *Transactional Analysis in Psychotherapy* (1961), *Principles of Group Treatment* (1966), and *What Do You Say After You Say Hello?* (1972). Berne himself was an American psychiatrist, who although he was trained as a psychoanalyst was never accepted as one. Since his death in 1970, transactional analysis, or TA as it is colloquially called, has continued to flourish with its own organization, the International Transactional Analysis Association, and quarterly periodical, the *Transactional Analysis Journal*. There is usually a chapter devoted to it in most textbooks of psychotherapy, such as Corsini's (1973) exemplary *Current Psychotherapies*. Consequently, it is important to bear in mind that this book is part of a corpus of ideas and of a movement that seems to be maintaining its influence. However, as a theory it appears as yet to have generated very little empirical research concerned with testing its underlying assumptions.

Transactional analysis consists of four kinds of analyses: structural, transactional, game, and script analysis. This book describes the first three of these, but devotes most of its time to game analysis. In fact, it was written in response to requests for lists of and further information about transactional games that people play. It still provides the fullest and most detailed account of games that has yet appeared in expositions of transactional analysis, although Berne recognized that many of his descriptions were incomplete. Consequently, there is no better source to turn to for a comprehensive treatment of games. Although some other ways of looking at games have been subsequently proposed, later accounts of transactional analysis do not seem to emphasize the importance of games as a means for understanding human behavior.

In order to comprehend what Berne means by a game, it is helpful to outline a few of the main ideas of transactional analysis that are pertinent to it. According to Berne, two of the more basic psychological needs people have are first to receive recognition from other people and second to structure their time. An act of recognition is colloquially known as a stroke, and these strokes may lead to either positive or negative feelings. While Berne does not always appear to be consistent in the way that he categorizes phenomena, there seem to be six main short-term ways in which people can structure their time when with others. These, in order of their increasing complexity and their increasing potential to provide strokes, are: (1) withdrawal (e.g., daydreaming); (2) rituals (e.g., greetings); (3) activities (e.g., problem-solving); (4) pastimes (e.g., discussing holidays); (5) games; and (6) intimacy. Intimacy is the highest and most satisfying form of social interaction and perhaps may be best described as the open and honest expression of spontaneous feelings. Unfortunately, it would appear that many people are brought up to believe that playing games is being intimate, and thereby deprive themselves of experiencing more fulfilling personal relationships.

Although it is possible to describe games without a knowledge of structural and transactional analysis, the formal analysis of a game as it is usually presented in this book employs such analyses. However, it would seem that the validity of this concept does not depend on these analyses also being valid. In other words, the idea of a game may be of value outside this particular theoretical context. Structural analysis involves determining which one of three phenomenological or ego states a person is in. These three states are colloquially and most simply referred to as the Parent, the Adult, and the Child. The Parent represents the behavior (in the broadest sense) of other important people that the person has adopted, the Child consists of those behaviors that the person showed up until what may be seen to be the arbitrary age of six, and the Adult, theoretically somewhat simplistically and implausibly, is supposed to cover the objective analysis of data. Functionally, the Child may be thought of as consisting of two parts: the Natural Child, and the Adapted Child. The Adapted Child is the way that the six-and-under-year-old reacts to important others, while the Natural Child constitutes the child's true nature, which may be seen as being analogous to the Rogerian notion of the actualizing tendency. Intimacy, then, is a function of the Natural Child.

A transaction is an exchange of strokes between two people. Three kinds of transactions have been distinguished and each of these has a rule of communication associated with it which predicts what is likely to happen. The simplest transaction is called a complementary one and only involves two ego states (such as Parent and Child). The rule associated with this type of transaction is that communication will proceed smoothly on the issue being discussed. Communication will break down if the second type of transaction, a cross-transaction, occurs. This involves a transaction between three or four ego states, where the ego state that the stroke comes from is not addressed. Complementary and crossed transactions take place most frequently in rituals, pastimes and activities. The third kind of transaction, an ulterior transaction, occurs at two levels and forms the basis of games. At the social level there is an overt message (e.g., "Will you help me with my work?") which is somewhat different from that at the psychological covert one (e.g., "I want to be alone with you"). The rule of communication accompanying ulterior transactions states that the outcome of such an exchange will be determined by the psychological rather than the social level. The analysis of single transactions is called transaction analysis proper, to distinguish it from the theory of transactional analysis.

A game, then, consists of a set of ulterior transactions. This distinguishes it from rituals, pastimes, and activities. However, this statement does not constitute a sufficient definition of a game. It is also necessary that none of the players are fully aware of what they are doing. If one of the players is conscious of what is happening, then it becomes a maneuver or ploy. Games are played to obtain certain feelings and to confirm particular attitudes about oneself or others. These feelings and attitudes can be either positive or negative, but since people seek psychotherapeutic help primarily for personal difficulties, most of the games that Berne has identified have negative outcomes. They can be recognized by their repetitive nature and the consistent feelings that they evoke, and can take place over varying lengths of time. In general, people who are psychologically disturbed play games more intensely, although it is not clear whether this manifests itself in how frequently they are played or in how intense the feeling or payoff is. Despite this, however, Berne strongly implies that most people play games and that game-playing may be more common than intimacy in close relationships. Pastimes, in fact, are used to find people who will make the most compatible players, since a game involves two or more people enacting complementary roles.

The two games that were first discovered and are most fully described are colloquially called "Why don't you?—yes but" and "If it weren't for you." "Why don't you—yes but" is most commonly played at parties and in all kinds of groups, including psychotherapy groups. It can be played by a number of different people. The protagonist or agent, sometimes called "White," starts by presenting a problem. The respondents suggest possible solutions to the problem, perhaps beginning with a "Why don't you . . .?" To each of these the agent objects with a "Yes, but . . ." At the overt social level the agent seems to be requesting help on an Adult-to-Adult basis. However, at the ulterior psychological level, the agent's Child is challenging the respondent's Parent to provide an answer to an insoluble problem. The payoff for the agent in this game is being reassured that other people cannot be of help. "If it weren't for you" is the most common game played between spouses. The agent complains that the other person prevents them from doing what they want to do. At the overt, social level the respondent's Parent tells the agent's Child what they must do, while the agent's Child complains of being restricted. At the ulterior, psychological level, however, this is a Child-to-Child interaction in which the agent wants to be protected from some frightening situation.

For these, and some of the other games described, Berne tries to provide a formal or theoretical analysis, which includes the following features: (1) a general description of the game (the thesis); (2) the way in which it can be thwarted (the antithesis); (3) its aim; (4) the roles that it requires; (5) its underlying psychodynamic motivation; (6) an example of a childhood and adult form; (7) a transactional analysis of a typical situation; (8) the minimum moves involved; (9) its biological, existential, internal and external psychological and social advantages; and occasionally (10) examples of other related games. The antithesis, for example, of "Why don't you?—yes but" is to concur with the difficulty of the problem, while that of "If it weren't for you" is to allow the other person to do what they want to do. After describing in some detail what a game is, Berne outlines a number of games that have been discovered in terms of the situations that they are most likely to be found. These are: Life games (e.g., "Alcoholic"), Marital games (e.g. "If it weren't for you"), Party games (e.g, "Why don't you?—yes but"), Sexual games (e.g., "Rapo"). Underworld games (e.g., "Cops and Robbers"), Consulting Room games (e.g., "I'm only trying to help you"), and Good games (e.g., "Cavalier").

After more than twenty years, *Games People Play* remains a highly provocative and original book. Although game analysis does not seem to play a large role in the therapeutic practice of transactional analysis, this has been Berne's most popular book. The Penguin edition of it has sold more than 470,000 copies, compared with over 157,750 copies of the Corgi edition of *What Do You Say After You Say Hello?* Although it is frequently cited, it has stimulated little research. One of the more enticing aspects of the concept of a game is that it draws attention to what may be recurring patterns of social interaction. A weakness of Berne's own analysis is that he does not generally provide a satisfactory account of what the payoff is for the respondent in a game. Since games involve at least two players, it should be possible to describe the transaction in terms of the two complementary games that are enacted. While the number of games that are covered may appear daunting, a simpler method for discovering games has been proposed by James (1973), which he calls the *game plan*. It consists of asking the following questions: (1) What keeps happening over and over again?; (2) How does it start?; (3) What happens next?; (4) What happens after that?; (5) How does it end?; and (6) How do you feel after it ends? This method could be profitably used to determine the extent and kind of games that are most commonly played. For those, however, who are more interested in transactional analysis as an approach to therapy, Berne's best book on this subject is *Transactional Analysis in Psychotherapy*. A more recent and up-to-date text which provides an account of later developments in transactional analysis is Woollams and Brown's (1979) *TA: The Total Handbook of Transactional Analysis*.

REFERENCES

Berne, E. (1961). *Transactional Analysis in Psychotherapy*. New York: Grove Press.

_____ (1966). *Principles of Group Treatment*. New York: Grove Press.

_____ (1972). *What Do You Say After You Say Hello?* New York: Grove Press.

Corsini, R. J., ed. (1973). *Current Psychotherapies*. 2nd ed. Itasca, IL: F. E. Peacock, 1979.

James, J. (1973). The game plan. *Transactional Analysis Journal* 3:194–197.

Woollams, S., and Brown, M. (1979). *TA: The Total Handbook of Transactional Analysis*. Englewood Cliffs, NJ: Prentice Hall.

Selections from
Games People Play
by Eric Berne

THE FUNCTION OF GAMES

Because there is so little intimacy in daily life, and because some forms of intimacy (especially if intense) are psychologically impossible for most people, the bulk of the time in serious social life is taken up with playing games. Hence games are both necessary and desirable, and the only problem at issue is whether the games played by an individual offer the best yield for him. In this connection it should be remembered that the essential feature of a game is its culmination, or payoff. The principal function of the preliminary moves is to set up the situation for this payoff, but they are always designed to harvest the maximum permissible satisfaction at each step as a secondary product. Thus in "Schlemiel" (making messes and then apologizing) the payoff, and the purpose of the game, is to obtain the forgiveness which is forced by the apology; the spillings and cigarette burns are only steps leading up to this, but each such trespass yields its own pleasure. The enjoyment derived from the spilling does not make spilling a game. The apology is the critical stimulus that leads to the denouement. Otherwise the spilling would simply be a destructive procedure, a delinquency perhaps enjoyable.

The game of "Alcoholic" is similar: whatever the physiological origin, if any, of the need to drink, in terms of game analysis the imbibing is merely a move in a game which is carried on with the people in the environment. The drinking may bring its own kinds of pleasure, but it is not the essence of the game. This is demonstrated in the variant of "Dry Alcoholic," which involves the same moves and leads to the same payoff as the regular game, but is played without any bottles.

Beyond their social function in structuring time satisfactorily, some games are urgently necessary for the maintenance of health in certain individuals. These people's psychic stability is so precarious, and their positions are so tenuously maintained, that to deprive them of their games may plunge them into irreversible despair and even psychosis. Such people will fight very hard against any antithetical moves. This is often observed in marital situations when the psychiatric improvement of one spouse (i.e., the abandonment of destructive games) leads to rapid deterioration in the other spouse, to whom the games were of paramount importance in maintaining equilibrium. Hence it is necessary to exercise prudence in game analysis.

Fortunately, the rewards of game-free intimacy, which is or should be the most perfect form of human living, are so great that even precariously balanced personalities can safely and joyfully relinquish their games if an appropriate partner can be found for the better relationship.

On a larger scale, games are integral and dynamic components of the unconscious life-plan, or script, of each individual; they serve to fill in the time while he waits for the final fulfillment, simultaneously advancing the action. Since the last act of a script characteristically calls for either a miracle or a catastrophe, depending on whether the script is constructive or destructive, the corresponding games are accordingly either constructive or destructive. In colloquial terms, an individual whose script is oriented toward "waiting for Santa Claus" is likely to be pleasant to deal with in such games as "Gee You're Wonderful, Mr. Murgatroyd," while someone with a tragic script oriented toward "waiting for *rigor mortis* to set in" may play such disagreeable games as "Now I've Got You, You son of a Bitch."

It should be noted that colloquialisms such as those in the previous sentence are an integral part of game analysis, and are freely used in transactional psychotherapy groups and seminars. The expression "waiting for *rigor mortis* to set in" originated in a dream of a patient, in which she decided to get certain things done "before *rigor mortis* set in." A patient in a sophisticated group pointed out what the therapist had overlooked: that in practice, waiting for Santa Claus and waiting for death are synonymous.

CONSULTING ROOM GAMES: I'M ONLY TRYING TO HELP YOU

Thesis

This game may be played in any professional situation and is not confined to psychotherapists and welfare workers. However, it is found most commonly and in its most florid form among social workers with a certain type of training. The analysis of this game was clarified for the writer under curious circumstances. All the players at a poker game had folded except two, a research psychologist and a businessman. The businessman, who had a high hand, bet; the psychologist, who had an unbeatable one, raised. The businessman looked puzzled, whereupon the psychologist remarked facetiously: "Don't be upset, I'm only trying to help you!" The businessman hesitated, and finally put in his chips. The psychologist showed the winning hand, whereupon the other threw down his cards in disgust. The others present then felt free to laugh at the psychologists's joke, and the loser remarked ruefully: "You sure were helpful!" The psychologist cast a knowing glance at the writer, implying that the joke had been at the expense of the psychiatric profession. It was at that moment that the structure of this game became clear.

The worker or therapist, of whatever profession, gives some advice to a client or patient. The patient returns and reports that the suggestion did not have the desired effect. The worker shrugs off this failure with a feeling of resignation, and tries again. If he is more watchful, he may detect at this point a twinge of frustration, but he will try again anyway. Usually he feels little need to question his own motives, because he knows that many of his similarly trained colleagues do the same thing, and that he is following the "correct" procedure and will receive full support from his supervisors.

If he runs up against a hard player, such as a hostile obsessional, he will find it more and more difficult to avoid feeling inadequate. Then he is in trouble, and the situation will slowly deteriorate. In the worst case, he may come up against an angry paranoid who will rush in one day in a rage, crying: "Look what you made me do!" Then his frustration will come strongly to the fore in the spoken or unspoken thought: "But I was only trying to help you!" His bewilderment at the ingratitude may cause him considerable suffering, indicating the complex motives underlying his own behavior. This bewilderment is the payoff.

Legitimate helpers should not be confused with people who play "I'm Only Trying to Help You" (ITHY). "I think we can do something about it," "I know what to do," "I was assigned to help you" or "My fee for helping you will be . . " are different from "I'm only trying to help you." The first four, in good faith, represent Adult offers to put professional qualifications at the disposal of the distressed patient or client; ITHY has an ulterior motive which is more important than professional skill in determining the outcome. This motive is based on the position that people are ungrateful and disappointing. The prospect of success is alarming to the Parent of the professional and is an invitation to sabotage, because success would threaten the position. The ITHY player needs to be reassured that help will not be accepted no matter how strenuously it is offered. The client responds with "Look How Hard I'm Trying" or "There's Nothing You Can Do to Help Me." More flexible players can compromise: it is all right for people to accept help providing it takes them a long time to do so. Hence therapists tend to feel apologetic for a quick result, since they know that some of their colleagues at staff meetings will be critical. At the opposite pole from hard ITHY players, such as are found among social workers, are good lawyers who help their clients without personal involvement or sentimentality. Here craftsmanship takes the place of covert strenuousness.

Some schools of social work seem to be primarily academies for the training of professional ITHY players, and it is not easy for their graduates to desist from playing it. An example which may help to illustrate some of the foregoing points will be found in the description of the complementary game "Indigence."

ITHY and its variants are easy to find in everyday life. It is played by family friends and relatives (e.g., "I Can Get It For You Wholesale"), and by adults who do community work with children. It is a favorite among parents, and the complementary game played by the offspring is usually "Look What You Made Me Do." Socially it may be a variant of "Schlemiel" in which the damage is done while being helpful rather than impulsively; here the client is represented by a victim who may be playing "Why Does This Always Happen To Me?" or one of its variants.

Antithesis

There are several devices available for the professional to handle an invitation to play this game, and his selection will depend on the state of the relationship between himself and the patient, particularly on the attitude of the patient's Child.

1. The classical psychoanalytic antithesis is the most thoroughgoing and the most difficult for the patient to tolerate. The patient then tries harder and harder. Eventually he falls into a state of despair, manifested by anger or depression, which is the characteristic sign that a game has been frustrated. This situation may lead to a useful confrontation.

2. A more gentle (but not prim) confrontation may be attempted on the first invitation. The therapist states that he is the patient's therapist and not his manager.

3. An even more gentle procedure is to introduce the patient into a therapy group, and let the other patients handle it.

4. With an acutely disturbed patient it may be necessary to play along during the initial phase. These patients should be treated by a psychiatrist,

who being a medical man, can prescribe both medications, and some of the hygienic measures which are still valuable, even in the day of tranquilizers, in the treatment of such people. If the physician prescribes a hygienic regimen, which may include baths, exercise, rest periods, and regular meals along with medication, the patient (1) carries out the regimen and feels better (2) carries out the regimen scrupulously and complains that it does not help (3) mentions casually that he forgot to carry out the instructions or that he has abandoned the regimen because it was not doing any good. In the second and third case it is then up to the psychiatrist to decide whether the patient is amenable to game analysis at that point, or whether some other form of treatment is indicated to prepare him for later psychotherapy. The relationship between the adequacy of the regimen and the patient's tendency to play games with it should be carefully evaluated by the psychiatrist before he decides how to proceed next.

For the patient, on the other hand, the antithesis is, "Don't tell me what to do to help myself, I'll tell you what to do to help me." If the therapist is known to be a Schlemiel, the correct antithesis for the patient to use is, "Don't help me, help him." But serious players of "I'm Only Trying to Help You" are generally lacking in a sense of humor. Antithetical moves on the part of a patient are usually unfavorably received, and may result in the therapist's lifelong enmity. In everyday life such moves should not be initiated unless one is prepared to carry them through ruthlessly and take the consequences. For example, spurning a relative who "Can Get It For You Wholesale" may cause serious domestic complications.

Analysis

Thesis

Nobody ever does what I tell them.

Aim

Alleviation of guilt.

Roles

Helper, Client.

Dynamics

Masochism.

Examples

(1) Children learning, parent intervenes. (2) Social worker and client.

Social Paradigm

Parent–Child.
Child: "What do I do now?"
Parent: "Here's what you do."

Psychological Paradigm

Parent–Child.
Parent: "See how adequate I am."
Child: "I'll make you feel inadequate."

Moves

(1) Instructions requested–Instructions given. (2) Procedure bungled–Reproof. (3) Demonstration that procedures are faulty–Implicit apology.

Advantages

(1) Internal Psychological–martyrdom. (2) External Psychological–avoids facing inadequacies. (3) Internal Social–"PTA," Projective Type; ingratitude. (4) External Social–"Psychiatry," Projective Type. (5) Biological–slapping from client, stroking from supervisors. (6) Existential–All people are ungrateful.

22

Ilza Veith:
Hysteria:
The History of a Disease

Reviewed by H. Merskey

I only bought my own copy of this book in 1969, four years after publication. It was first offered at $7.95 and the penciled price of my copy was £3.12, a bargain by present standards for any book. It was already then the standard work on the history of hysteria. References to that history can probably be found in nearly every author since Hippocrates who has ever touched upon hysteria yet surprisingly, Veith noted, no single historical account of the subject had appeared. (This was true for English. Histories of hysteria did exist, to my knowledge, in French and Italian).

The book immediately filled a gap and was warmly welcomed. Crown (1966) said that it was "learned, well documented and extremely well written. . . ." He recommended it highly for those who like to mix pleasurable with "required" reading. The reviewer in the *Journal of Nervous and Mental Diseases* (Leavy 1966) gave a detailed report of its themes and called it "a fascinating study." In the *American Journal of Psychiatry* (1966) "F.J.B." (presumably Francis Braceland) called it "the first major history of the disorder . . . all inclusive, fascinating . . . an excellent work in all respects by a highly respected medical historian." The *Archives of General Psychiatry* (Bailey 1966) provided a detailed and slightly inaccurate account of its contents and arguments, missing out some of the most important changes in the sixteenth to eighteenth centuries, but concluding with the comment that the reader would nowhere "find the information more eloquently described than in this scholarly study." An enthusiastic supporter can never be wholly unwelcome even if the quality of his approval is sometimes slightly flawed.

One reviewer struck a dissentient note. The late Richard Hunter (1966), the greatest psychiatric historian of our time, said in *Brain* that it was "a popular illustrated account of . . . the wandering womb." He thought it attempted too much and that it was not easy reading and was not intended to serve as a work of reference. He picked out the error that Dr. Veith had dated the first edition of Robert Burton's *Anatomy of Melancholy* to 1628, observing that it coincided with the appearance of Harvey's *De Motu Cordis*, while in fact, Burton's first edition was in 1621 and his third in 1628. Nevertheless, Veith's book, as Crown remarked, has certainly served for pleasurable reading and as a prime source book. It remains a landmark perhaps even more for its clinical implications than for its historical scholarship. The implications are that it has given us an enduring perspective on the concept of hysteria as a disease. The weakness of scholarship is that some chapters (as Hunter no doubt realized) are not very original and essentially provide links between sections which represent fundamental scholarly work. The strength of the scholarship is that there is so much which is important, original, perceptive, and justified from primary sources.

The first part of the book takes us through the history of the ancient Egyptian papyri with the first recorded comments on the wandering womb to the Greek and Roman periods and into the Middle Ages. The Egyptian and Greek descriptions seem to depend on secondary sources or on translations from Greek into French. The Latin references, both classical and at later periods, seem to be handled by Dr. Veith as if she was fully in charge of that material in the original language. She shows us how Hippocrates and Galen both recognised the influence of the mind upon the body, and notes other relevant authors. She then goes on to present in some detail, the writings and views of St. Augustine. This is important because Augustine's works conditioned attitudes to demonic possession and views of illness throughout the medieval and even renaissance periods.

There is a brief but cogent reference to the rest of the medieval period, particularly the writings of Trotula of Salerno, author of *A Mediaeval Woman's Guide to Health*. A discussion of witchcraft provided by Dr. Veith also seems to me to be original and impressive. Earlier authors had dealt with the European material. Veith relates from primary—or at least contemporary—sources the development of the epidemics of witch hunting and the persecutions of witches which also prevailed in North America. She gives a particularly graphic account of the issue as it emerged in Massachusetts.

The discussion of the sixteenth- and seventeenth-century publications on hysteria is substantial and very well informed. I have always thought this the most useful and most authoritative section, dealing with Ambroise Paré and Charles LePois (Piso) in France, and Jorden, Willis, Sydenham, and others of some importance in England. Denis Leigh made a useful start on some of those writers in his good, but neglected book, on *The Historical Development of British Psychiatry* (Leigh 1961). However, I do not know of any single source in which most of this section could have been found prior to the appearance of Dr. Veith's work.

There is an excellent section based upon Dr. Veith's own scholarly knowledge of Chinese and Japanese medicine. It is valuable as a parallel to what was happening, in those ancient cultures, contemporaneously with the European themes. They did not have the idea of the wandering womb to work upon, but in some respects their notions of magic, spells, and possession are much like those of Europe. Arabic and Persian medicine is touched upon, but only briefly.

Further chapters chronicle the eighteenth and nineteenth centuries including major contributors in those periods, and then pass on to the work of Charcot and Freud, which she presents carefully and well, but not necessarily originally. (That would have been very difficult.) The well-known story of Mesmer and other hypnotists is also retold clearly.

There are no bad sections. There are good sections and some less good sections, but as a source book and as a user-friendly guide to an incomputable topic, Veith remains unchallenged. Did she do anything else? She did not define hysteria. She spoke of definition, but then glided away to a discussion of the deletion of hysteria from *DSM-II*. Thereafter, she stuck to a policy of talking of hysteria "as the various authors understood it." She did, however, tackle the broad implications of the term. She recognised that for Sydenham and others of his generation, it included many things that we would now class under other segments of psychiatric diagnosis. Indeed, it is probable that in the seventeenth and eighteenth centuries and on many occasions prior to those times, hysteria simply represented a general term for neurosis, reactive depression, and some types of personality disorder. She did not recognise so well, however, that Sydenham had included amongst the symptoms of hysteria, many disorders that we would now consider to be organic (including, for example, dropsy).

Dr. Veith describes very well the way in which different authors espoused theories for different parts of the body. She recognises the fact that in the fifteenth and sixteenth centuries when Weyer, Pare and Jorden were ascribing a uterine cause to hysteria, their work represented progress since it was returning the topic to medicine and taking it out of demonology. Thus, she noted how Jorden's arguments were used in a trial as a defence against a charge of witchcraft, an observation that Richard Hunter had previously made, but for which unaccountably she did not give him credit.

The change of view which ascribed hysteria to psychological or brain disturbances seems to date from LePois in France and Willis and Sydenham in England. Dr. Veith describes this very well and then points out how Cullen in the eighteenth century reverted back to the uterine theory. She does not explain why Cullen went backwards in this fashion nor does she follow through in all the other literature of the late eighteenth century and early nineteenth century to discuss additional authors who took the same position. Dubois d'Amiens (1833) and Landouzy (1846) both notably followed the uterine theory in that period. Perhaps no one in fact has adequately explained why they abandoned the "neurological" viewpoint for the gynecological one. Hollender (1972), however, has pointed out that in the nineteenth century it was the gynecologists who stayed longest with the uterine theory, perhaps understandably. If Dr. Veith does not highlight or explain these differences, it is perhaps partly because the job of explanation has still to be completed.

Dr. Veith discusses with much sympathy the ideas of Baglivi (seventeenth century) and of Robert Whytt (eighteenth century) who clearly seemed to relate psychological causes to physical symptoms. They were concerned to explain how these bodily changes could be produced by mental phenomena. She recognises their inability to provide a complete explanation but does not herself, in that discussion, distinguish between psychophysiological mechanisms and conversion ones. Likewise, she does not discuss Sir Benjamin Brodie (1837). Walters (1969) pointed out after Veith's work had appeared that Brodie and the early nineteenth-century anatomists and physiologists provided a foundation from which it began to be possible to see that hysterical symptoms diverged from expectations founded on a knowledge of bodily function and organic disease. Once it was possible to recognize that hysterical symptoms did not conform to anatomy and physiology, the next advance could occur through the recognition of the importance of the patient's ideas in the production of symptoms. The man who did this most definitely was Dr. J. Russell Reynolds (1869) of University College Hospital and also of the National Hospital for Nervous Diseases (Merskey 1983). Charcot (1885) acknowledged the work of Russell Reynolds and then adopted the theme and added to it the observation that hypnosis served as a means of implanting ideas which then produced hysterical patterns of symptoms. Others, incidentally, have recognised that the production of symptoms as a result of ideas was thought of before the nineteenth century. My former colleague from the Department of the History of Medicine at this University, Dr. John Wright (1980), pointed out how Boyle and Descartes did this and Blackmore (1725) also.

Arguments like the above were developed, for the most part, after Veith had completed her book. Perhaps such a dissection could only have been achieved by a clinician. However, clinicians need the scholarly base which Veith has provided in order to find their way through this material.

There are some other, smaller points that a historian might reasonably have been expected to include. Dr. Veith missed out Erasistratus who before Galen, in a famous story reported in Plutarch's Life of Demetrius, showed the influence of the mind upon the body. She is weak on English titles, misspelling Russell Brain with only one *l* several times and calling him Lord Russell Brain. She also suggests in a throwaway line that Sydenham might have taken his medical degree at Cambridge at the age of 53 (although he was an Oxford graduate) because he felt his education was not complete. Latham (1848) who produced the standard nineteenth-century translation of Sydenham's works, observes in his preface that it had been pointed out to him that Sydenham's son had become a pensioner at Pembroke College and that Sydenham took his degree from the same College. An alternative explanation might have to do with Cambridge giving Sydenham some honorary recognition or acknowledgment of his status, or else with Sydenham securing the degree in order to support his son in some fashion. Laycock (1840), an interesting and significant author, is listed in the bibliography but not in the index and the same applies to Brachet and Pomme. Laycock is particularly interesting because he gives a clear list of those who have attributed hysteria to the brain and those who attribute it to other origins or causes. Briquet is only admired in passing, on the basis of a reference by Janet. Still, at that time, his name was little regarded by anyone, and it was only later that the St. Louis school revived his reputation by giving his name, in part erroneously, to one pattern of multiple hysterical complaints.

Dr. Veith is extremely good in picking up the hints of recognition of unconscious mechanisms in Paracelsus and also in R. B. Carter, an English nineteenth-century general practitioner who was later both a correspondent to the *Times* and the *Lancet*, as well as a distinguished consultant ophthalmologist to St. George's Hospital and to the National Hospital. Carter only died in 1918 at the age of 89 after a life full of contributions both to the art and science of medicine and also to medical affairs. Unfortunately, Dr. Veith missed or did not include the significance of the discussions of railway spine and accident neurosis in the second half of the nineteenth century, which were very relevant to understanding the notion of male hysteria and the relationship of thoughts and bodily symptoms.

On the other hand, there are a number of references to the personality traits of patients with hysteria in the writings of Carter and Janet which she describes, and in her quotations from Griesinger. There are, further, some particularly interesting passages from Falret in 1866 and 1890 in which the egotism, duplicity and histrionic abilities of the patients are emphasized. Dr. Veith does not examine the development of the notion of hysterical personality during the nineteenth century and that is a topic that deserves attention, but it would have been a major additional theme.

It is also a pity that Dr. Veith stopped at Freud. The history of combat neurosis, the concept of shell-shock, and the influence of wartime experience upon notions of hysteria have been of great importance subsequent to Freud. It would have been asking too much to expect her to take into account the growing interest in the contribution of organic brain lesions to the production of hysterical symptoms since that was really only put forward strongly about the same time that her book appeared, as by Eliot Slater in 1965.

If there were faults of omission and a few minor slips, these are as nothing to the success of Dr. Veith in giving unity to a field of thought. The American reviewers and Hunter noted that hysteria had gone from *DSM-II* and was replaced by "conversion symptoms." We can now observe that hysterical personality has been cloaked as histrionic personality in *DSM-III*. These changes were in the same vein as Slater's Shorvon lecture (Slater 1965), apparently marked by some wish to deny hysteria as a substantive element in medical consideration. Veith restored to hysteria its own name and its complex, intricate, elusive, mercurial, and enduring qualities.

So long as doctors remain interested in the mind–body relationship and in understanding their patients, these phenomena will be part of their thoughts and their experiences.

REFERENCES

American Journal of Psychiatry (1966). Book review: *Hysteria: The History of a Disease* 122:1069–1070.

Bailey, P. (1966). Book review: *Hysteria: The History of a Disease. Archives of General Psychiatry* 14:332–333.

Blackmore, R. (1725). *A Treatise of the Spleen and Vapours: Or, Hypochondriacal and Hysterical Affections.* London: J. Pemberton.

Brodie, Sir B. C. (1837). *Lectures Illustrative of Certain Nervous Affections.* London: Longman.

Charcot, J. M. (1885). Clinical Lectures on *Diseases of the Nervous System.* Vol. III, trans. I. Savill. Delivered at the Infirmary at La Salpetrière. London: The New Sydenham Society.

Crown, S. (1966). Book review. *Hysteria: The History of a Disease. Brain* 89: 616.

Dubois D'Amiens (1833). *Histoire Philosophique ed L'Hystérie.* Paris: Deville Cavellin.

Hollender, M. H. (1972). Conversion hysteria – a post-Freudian reinterpretation of 19th century psychological data. *Archives of General Psychiatry* 26: 311–314.

Hunter, R. (1966). Book review: *Hysteria: The History of a Disease*. *Brain* 89:616.

Landouzy, H. (1846). Traité Complet de L'Hystérie. Paris: Ballière.

Latham, R. G. (1848). The life of Sydenham. In *The Works of Thomas Sydenham*, vol. 1, p. XIV. London: The New Sydenham Society.

Leavy, S. A. (1966). Book review. *Hysteria: The History of a Disease*. *Journal of Nervous and Mental Disease* 142:491–492.

Leigh, D. (1961). *The Historical Development of British Psychiatry*. London: Pergamon.

Merskey, H. (1983). Hysteria: the history of an idea. *Canadian Journal of Psychiatry* 28: 428–433.

Reynolds, J. R. (1869). Remarks on paralysis and other disorders of motion and sensation, dependent on idea. *British Medical Journal* 11:483–485.

Slater, E. (1965). Diagnosis of "hysteria." *British Medical Journal* 1:1395–1399.

Walters, A. (1969). Psychogenic regional sensory and motor disorders alias hysteria. *Canadian Psychiatric Association Journal* 14: 573–590.

Wright, J. P. (1980). Hysteria and mechanical man. *Journal of the History of Ideas*. 41: 233–247.

Selections from
Hysteria:
The History of a Disease
by Ilza Veith

ON GREEK IDEAS

In Greek literature the term "hysteria" is more frequently used in its adjectival form and is applied to such conditions as certain forms of respiratory difficulty in which the choking sensation was believed to be due to the pressure of the displaced uterus. Similarly, the *globus hystericus* could be explained on the basis of such organic malposition. This phenomenon was thought to occur primarily in mature women who were deprived of sexual relations; prolonged continence was believed to result in demonstrable organic changes in the womb. The thinking ran that in such situations the uterus dries up and loses weight and, in its search for moisture, rises toward the hypochondrium, thus impeding the flow of breath which was supposed normally to descend into the abdominal cavity. If the organ comes to rest in this position it causes convulsions similar to those of epilepsy. If it mounts higher and attaches itself to the heart the patient feels anxiety and oppression and begins to vomit. When it fastens itself to the liver the patient loses her voice and grits her teeth, and her complexion turns ashen. If the uterus lodges in the loins, the woman feels a hard ball, or lump, in her side. But when it mounts as high as the head, it causes pains around the eyes and the nose, the head feels heavy, and drowsiness and lethargy set in. Beyond these specific symptoms, the movement of the womb generally produces palpitations and excessive perspiration and convulsions similar to those observed in epilepsy.[1] The anatomical difficulties in the way of such free and extensive migrations were apparently of no concern to these writers. This may in part

---

[1] Authors's Note: This discussion is primarily based on the Hippocratic text *On the Diseases of Women*, i.e., *Des maladies des femmes in Oeuvres complètes d'Hippocrate*, trans. E. Littré (Paris: Baillière, 1851), Vol. VIII: Book I, paragraphs 7 and 32; Book II, paragraphs 123–27.

be due to an overwhelming ignorance of bodily structure and particularly that of the female generative system.

Such conditions were to be treated in the following manner. The physician was to undertake a manual examination to search for the dislodged uterus taking special care to avoid touching the liver; also a bandage was to be applied below the hypochondria to prevent further ascension of the womb. Into the forcibly opened mouth of the patient the physician was to pour strongly perfumed wine. Fetid fumigations for the nose and aromatic ones for the uterus were to help return the organ to its normal abode.

The great Galen of Pergamon (A.D. 129–99) also denied the ability of the uterus to wander about.[2] He too related hysteria to the womb; yet he developed his own etiological theories, which drastically diverged from all other current opinions, although they were in fact rooted in ancient physiological concepts.

ON WITCHCRAFT

No man thought himself, his family, or his possessions secure from the machinations of the devil and his agents. Every disaster that befell him was attributed to a witch.

In both England and Scotland the detection of witches became a lucrative vocation. Those so employed traveled about testing suspects for anesthetic areas. Pitcairn related that in the trial of Janet Peaston in 1646 the magistrate of Dalkeith caused John Kincaid of Tranent, the common pricker, to exercise his craft upon her. He found two marks of the devil's making; for she could not feel the pin when it was put into either of the said marks, nor did the marks bleed when the pin was taken out again. When she was asked where she thought the pins were put in her, she pointed to a part of her body distant from the real place. They were pins of three inches in length.[3]

Although these "common prickers," as they were officially called, aroused a great deal of resentment among the population, their expert

---

[2]Author's Note: Although Galen was familiar with the writings of Soranus, his reasoning concerning hysteria differed radically from that of Soranus. See George Sarton, *Galen of Pergamon* (Lawrence: University of Kansas Press, 1945), p. 97.

[3]Author's Note: Charles Mackay, *Extraordinary Popular Delusions and the Madness of Crowds* (New York: L.C. Page & Co., Inc., 1932), p. 513.

testimony was accepted without question. Towards the end of the seventeenth century, however, the fury abated somewhat, the number of witch trials decreased and some of the intellectual leaders even expressed their disbelief of "modern witchcraft." Among the most influential of these writings was John Webster's *The Displaying of Supposed Witchcraft. . . .*[4]

THE SUFFOCATION OF THE MOTHER

Jorden wrote *A Briefe Discourse* to acquaint the public as well as the medical profession with diseases of this nature so that they would never again be mistaken for bewitchment, although they appear to have some features in common. His introductory arguments were largely concerned with establishing that only a physician was qualified to deal with maladies such as Mary Glover's. Thus, though it was presumably a certain sign of sorcery, if the affected woman failed to feel the pricking of a pin and the burning by fire, Jorden maintained that this "is so ordinary in the fits of the Mother," as he "never read any author writing of this disease who does not make mention thereof."[5]

Equally firmly he refuted the following as signs of devilry: insensibility, convulsions, periodicity of the fits, the choking sensation when eating, and the commencement of fits at the sight of specific persons. All of these, he contended, were signs of disease, and, if cure was ever to be achieved through fasting and prayers it was only due to the "confident perswasion of the patient to find release by that means." He devoted the rest of his treatise to a description of the origin and nature of hysteria. His initial remarks on the subject, restating the uterine theory, show little promise of new revelations:

> This disease is called by diverse names amongst our Authors, *Passio Hysterica,*
> *Suffocatio, Praefocatio,* and *Strangulatus uteri, Caducus matricis, &c.* In English
> the Mother, or the Suffocation of the Mother, because most commonly it
> takes them with choaking in the throat: and it is *an effect of the Mother or wombe*
> *wherein the principal parts of the bodie by consent do suffer diversely according to the*
> *diversitie of the causes and diseases wherewith the matrix is offended.*[6]

But out of this traditional exposition Jorden developed new ideas which involved other organs beyond the uterus as the primary site of hysteria. To be sure, he persisted in terming it a uterine disorder, but he remarked that other parts of the body suffer "by consent." This may occur, he said, in two

---

[4]Authors's Note: London, 1677.
[5]Author's Note: *Ibid.,* "The Epistle Dedicatorie," p. *iv.*
[6]Author's Note: *Ibid.,* chap. 2, p. 5.

ways: either some noxious substance, such as "vapors,"[7] may reach the secondary organ from the afflicted womb; or there may be a sympathetic interaction between the two organs which makes the second one a "partaker of grief."

Jorden's transfer of the seat of all hysterical manifestations from the uterus to the brain constituted a major turning point in the history of hysteria. His conversion, however, was not entire. He added to the traditional factors of interrupted menstruation and sexual abstinence the idea that "the perturbations of the minde are oftentimes to blame for this and many other diseases."

WILLIS AND SYDENHAM

. . . the Distemper named from the Womb is chiefly and primarily Convulsive, and chiefly depends on the Brain the nervous stock {system} being affected.[8]

In general, however, most of Willis' arguments were designed to disprove the role of the uterus in hysteria. His practice furnished him the necessary support for his arguments, since his patients included women of every age and condition—"rich and poor, Virgins, Wives and Widows"—who were susceptible to hysterical diseases. He observed symptoms "in Maids before ripe age, also in old women after their flowers have left them; yea, sometimes the *same kind of Passions infest Men.*"[9]

Sydenham stated that he had been led to the treatment of hysteria because he had observed that next to fever it was the most common of diseases.[10] This statement may have astounded even the seventeenth-century physicians who wrote so much about hysteria, but had not learned to recognize it except in its convulsive or paroxysmal forms. Astonishing also must have been his assertion that not only women but men, too, could be counted

---

[7]Author's Note: The term "vapors" originated about this time and referred to emanations from a disordered uterus which might ascend and produce symptoms in other parts of the body. This belief gained such credence that subsequently, particularly in the English literature, the term not only became synonymous with hysteria but was also descriptive of many lesser and insubstantial female behavioral problems.

[8]Author's Note: Thomas Willis, *An Essay of the Pathology of the Brain and Nervous Stock in which Convulsive Diseases are Treated of,* trans. S. Pordage (London: Dring, Leigh, and Harper, 1684), p. 71.

[9]Author's Note: *Ibid.,* p. 69. (Italics mine.)

[10]Author's Note: *The Works of Thomas Sydenham, M.D.,* trans., and with a "Life of the Author" by R. G. Latham (London:1848), pp.11, 54.

among its victims, for it was much more emphatic than any previous statement. The following sentences are quoted verbatim, for no paraphrase could do justice to their clarity of definition and their sagacity of observation:

> Of all chronic diseases hysteria—unless I err—is the commonest; since just as fevers—taken with their accompaniments—equal two thirds of the number of all chronic diseases taken together, so do hysterical complaints (or complaints so called) make one half of the remaining third. As to females, if we except those who lead a hard and hardy life, there is rarely one who is wholly free from them—and females, be it remembered, form one half of the adults of the world. Then, again, such male subjects as lead a sedentary or studious life, and grow pale over their books and papers, are similarly afflicted; since, however much antiquity may have laid the blame of hysteria upon the uterus, hypochondriasis (which we impute to some obstruction of the spleen or viscera) is as like it, as one egg is to another. True, indeed, it is that women are more subject than males. This, however, is not on account of the uterus, but for reasons which will be seen in the sequel.[11]

Despite Sydenham's insistence on the sanity of the hysterical patient, he nevertheless recognized the manifestations to be of mental origin. Jorden had believed them to have their origin in the head, and Willis, in the brain; and both authors were aware of the frequent association of emotional disturbance with hysterical phenomena. *Yet the definite inclusion of hysteria itself among afflictions of the mind was the contribution of Thomas Sydenham.*

FREUD

From the preceding accounts, it can be seen that Charcot's influence extended to a group of brilliant pupils who inherited their master's interest in hysteria. They included Janet and Babinski in France and, especially, Freud in Austria. Beyond this, however, Charcot's tremendous renown gave the subject of hysteria a dignity that resulted in the publication of voluminous treatises not only by Charcot's disciples but also by such famous authorities as Kraepelin, Moebius, and Kretschmer in Germany, and Daniel Hack Tuke in England. While their ideas quite naturally varied to a considerable degree, there is recognizable a consistent pattern that marks the further evolution of the theories of Charcot. This unifying belief lies in the acceptance of suggestion as the governing aspect of hysteria at this phase of it history, both in its etiology and, in reverse, in its treatment.

---

[11]Author's Note: *Ibid.*, p. 85. All of Sydenham's subsequent quotations are taken from the *Epistolary Dissertation, loc.cit.*

23

Sir Aubrey Lewis:
Inquiries in Psychiatry, The State of Psychiatry, The Later Papers of Sir Aubrey Lewis

Reviewed by F. Kräupl Taylor

In 1966, Sir Aubrey Lewis retired from the Maudsley Hospital. To mark the occasion, the postgraduate students at the Bethlem Royal and Maudsley Hospitals published a selection of his writings, which appeared in 1967. But the flow of papers from his pen continued unabated until his death in 1975. Michael Shepherd was thus enabled to bring out a further volume in 1979, containing some of these "later papers."

The three books enjoyed an appreciative welcome from reviewers which was almost unanimous. A partly dissenting note came, however, from Erwin Stengel (1968, 1969). He had found that "sometimes Lewis's logic is difficult to follow and his premises are unacceptable." As an example of an unacceptable premise he mentioned remarks on suicide which were made in an address on "Health as a Social Concept," such as: "No one, I think, disputes that it can be the act of a healthy person, if it occurs in a society which sanctions suicide in given circumstances, as ours does. . . . In such a case, suicide is regarded like marriage or any other isolated but decisive act of choice which is socially approved." Stengel objected because "our society has never sanctioned suicide, although it has condoned it under exceptional circumstances while it holds up marriage as one of its most important institutions." Stengel certainly scored a verbal point here in preferring "condoning" to "sanctioning" in this context. He was also aware that the juxtaposition of suicide and marriage could have been one of Lewis's humorous quips. Yet in the end he came to this conclusion: "At any rate, all students of suicide hold that in our kind of society it is always an abnormal response, irrespective of whether or not the individual is mentally ill at the time." With this conclusion Lewis would obviously have agreed, having been at pains to distinguish social abnormality and deviance from the concept of mental illness and having argued that suicide need not to be due to the latter.

Stengel also complained that Lewis's "polished and restrained" style of writing was depressing. There is no doubt that Lewis was meticulous in his formulations, even if he, like Homer, nodded occasionally, and he was restrained in the sense of being reserved and guarded in the face of incontinent psychiatric theory-building and any messianic claims made for the powers of modern psychiatry. Was Stengel's depressive reaction to this style of writing a widespread phenomenon or merely a personal idiosyncrasy shared by few?

Yet the gravamen of Stengel's grievance was with Lewis's "preoccupations with the shortcomings and the ignorances of psychiatry and his disinclination to dwell on its achievements." He therefore stated it as his considered opinion that "one could not recommend a young doctor who thinks of taking up the discipline to read *The State of Psychiatry* (Aubrey 1976b) as an introduction. It might put him off for two hundred years." This conclusion about a long-living candidate gave rise to several letters, some in support and some in opposition, in the *British Journal of Psychiatry*, in 1968.

It seems clear from this controversy that Stengel and Lewis wished to attract different aspirants to the field of psychiatry. Stengel appears to have had in mind candidates who longed for a profession which holds out the glitter of success, respect and repute, which enthusiastically opens a door to promising knowledge, therapeutic power, worldly wisdom, and a life of work gratification. Such siren songs, however, even in diluted form, were alien to Lewis. He wished to gather around him disciples of a different caliber, disciples with a mind and a heart that longed to savor the challenges of a territory which is as yet only sparsely explored and still riddled with unsolved doubts, problems, and even crass ignorance.

Lewis spelled out some of his program in the first paragraph of his Bradshaw lecture that was published under the title "Between Guesswork and Certainty in Psychiatry." "It is," he said, "the common state of reflective and inquiring minds to be somewhere between untrammeled guesswork and certainty. It would be discreditable if psychiatrists were huddled at either extreme, wholly engaged in guessing or ignorantly certain." He went on to remark that psychiatry "is like the rest of medicine, combining moral and personal principles of action with those arrived at by the methods of science." In all sciences, whether physical, biological, or social, "there is the same essential passage from untested guess to tenable, unfalsified conclusion—which may be, rather loosely, called a confirmed conclusion or a certainty, in the sense in which the circulation of the blood is a certainty." He then considered the heuristic role which hypotheses play in all scientific activities, but warned that they can be "an impediment to knowledge when they are so loosely formulated that we cannot deduce their logical consequences and therefore cannot make predictive statements which could be verified or refuted; the systematists of the eighteenth century exemplified this in medicine." He admitted that many present-day psychiatric and psychoanalytic hypotheses are still of this flawed kind, but added consolingly that "psychiatry is not the only branch of medicine—or of knowledge—to be pilloried for lax thinking and complacent dogmatism." The value of psychiatric therapies came under scrutiny next and this involved him in an examination of the uncertainties which cling to the judgment of clinical change and the reasons for any such change by physical or psychological therapies. Though there is no escape from these uncertainties, "the doubts which attend physical methods of treatment are dwarfish alongside the giant misgivings and disputes which envelop psychotherapy in dust and fog. . . . Here then is a great domain of psychiatric practice in which there has been an excessive proportion of guesswork and rather a lot of subjective certainty. More doubt might have been salutary. [Unfortunately,] psychiatry suffers much from hopeful illusions and clichés used as incantations, just as a few decades ago it suffered even more from pessimistic and resigned inertia."

Yet Lewis was not a man of one-sided judgments. After a long litany of uncertainties and shortcomings, he confidently restored the balance in the end by turning to

the attainments of psychiatry, its solid groundwork of detailed, minute, and orderly observations, its empirical successes, its accretions through application of the basic medical sciences to clinical problems. There are large textbooks and innumerable monographs, compilations and symposia, setting forth this stock of knowledge which stands to the credit of psychiatry. It is because of it that the psychiatrist, even the self-critical psychiatrist, feels no need to beat his breast and recite penitential psalms when he meets other doctors.

In this Bradshaw lecture we have, as it were, the testament of Lewis's unflinching academic stance which seeks to steer a middle course between the Scylla of guesswork that is unchecked by fact and the Charybdis of certainty that is undented by analytic thought. He saw the spinning of irrefutable theories as an unacademic exercise, even when the theories gained far-flung fashionable repute. He distributed censure impartially, however, wherever he spotted shoddy or evasive arguments. Blinkered clinicians and erring academics were equally taken to task. Psychotherapists of analytical or other persuasions often felt unjustly singled out. But academics were not spared. Thus, when Lewis reviewed Eysenck's book on smoking, health and personality, he reproached him, saying that "partisan fervour gets the better of him, and the advocate elbows the judge out of the way." The reason was Eysenck's reference to a particular study, favorable to his argument, as "extremely careful" and "methodically far superior to the studies usually cited." Yet Lewis frostily remarked: "In fact, the defects of the study, for which it has been arraigned by several authorities, are gross." Just for once, Eysenck took it on the chin without defending himself.

Outstanding among the early papers of Lewis was his study of melancholia, and he did not shrink from using this often tabooed term. He scrutinized its meanings both historically and clinically. In his historical survey, he collated views that ranged through the course of medical history from early Greek and Roman times through the Middle Ages, the Renaissance, the eighteenth and nineteenth centuries to the opinions of Kraepelin, Adolf Meyer, Freud, Abraham, Mapother, and so many others that the references ran to 193 items. The clinical observations depicted the symptomatology and prognosis of sixty-one patients in detailed length and with many revealing quotations from patients, a feat that can hardly be repeated today, when journal editors have to be so niggardly with their space that accounts of phenomenological experiences receive rather short shrift in modern psychiatric literature. Other early papers were also phenomenological in their approach; they dealt with time experience, insight, and obsessional illness.

But in the 1930s, and even more during the war, Lewis turned his attention increasingly to the interrelations between social factors and mental illness. Papers dealing with these topics eventually culminated in the monumental lecture, "Health as a Social Concept," given to the British Sociological Association. Its closely argued content should be obligatory reading matter for psychiatrists because Lewis was here at his most illuminating best. He started with the admission that the concepts of health and disease are no more than "fictions [which] serve a useful intellectual purpose, though we know they refer merely to uplands and lowlands in a continuously graded and terraced country." In his attempt to delineate these "fictions," he was soon forced to the recognition that "there are no positive indications of health which can be relied upon and we consider everyone healthy who is free from any evidence of disease or infirmity."

What then are the available guidelines? Taking physical health first, he remarked that its diagnosis depends on the establishment of norms. There are such norms for the functions and structures of bodily organs and systems. But there are no norms for the psychological and social influences that doctors also have to consider.

The difficulties mount when we turn to mental health and illness. Lewis argued that here "we may be inclined to think that . . . the concept of 'mental illness' is essentially a social, rather than a clinical or pathological, one." Indeed many people regard as the chief yardstick of mental health the adequacy of a person's social adaptation. Yet there are no norms to provide guidance. Their place is usually taken by value judgments with their inherent pitfalls. "An adaptation is distinguished from maladaptation according as a particular valued state is favoured or jeopardized [by a person's behavior]. . . . Consequently mental health cannot be equated with good social adaptation, as many have proposed, without risk of tautology: the valued and desired state which adaptation is to attain or maintain may itself turn out to be health." Often social disapproval is regarded as indicating a person's social maladaptation. Yet Lewis pointed out that "it cannot be accepted as a satisfactory criterion varying as it does according to the group of people who express the disapproval. . . . [Therefore] we are hardly in a position to examine whether such maladaptation bespeaks disease or delinquency or (passing from medicine and law to theology) sin."

Another and apparently more objective criterion of maladaptation then came under scrutiny, namely "non-conformity to the institutions, the mores, the verbal and other customs prevailing in [an individual's] society." In particular, "a person is maladapted when his own version of his [dominant] social role is not in conformity with society's version [of it]." Such discrepancies can, of course, be due to mental illness, but it can also have its roots in misfortunes and upheavals leading to an objective decline of a person's social status which then can be at variance with the conception he still has of his own social role. It can even happen that nonconformity is valued as "a good and admired thing." Thus, maladaptation can be sociopathic without being psychopathic. This has not been generally appreciated by sociologists. "Sociological attempts to state the denotative characteristics of mental illness . . . [have been] too vague to differentiate psychopathic from other forms of social adaptation . . . [Such attempts] do not stand on their social legs, but are propped up by medical struts and stays." Those medical "struts and stays" have their basis in three criteria: "(1) the patient feels ill—a general subjective datum; (2) he has disordered functions of some part of him—a restricted objective datum; (3) he has symptoms which conform to a recognizable clinical pattern—a typological datum. . . . The truth is that, though the social effects of disease, like the social causes, are extremely important, it is impossible to decide from them whether a condition is healthy or morbid. The concept of disease, then, – and of health – have physiological and psychological components but no essential social ones."

This lecture of Lewis's has been deliberately presented in condensed detail to show the force of his reasoning. It obviously was not to the liking of many sociologists. Yet, as a reviewer in *The Times Literary Supplement* (1967) remarked, "his arguments [were] of such cogency that even the redoubtable Baroness Wootton proved subsequently entirely unable either to refute or even seriously to question their validity."

The essentially medical nature of psychiatry was a theme to which Lewis returned again in his Linacre lecture. "This view," he said, "of the medical nature of psychiatry may be contested from several directions – wrongly, I think. There are those who maintain that there is nothing properly medical about mental disorders which do not spring from recognizable physical disease. Others, [however] . . . would bring in larger battalions to supplement the medical contribution." Lewis agreed with the latter. He instanced the sciences of psychology, sociology, and anthropology, as well as the humanities which, however, "cannot, by definition, be classed as sciences. But history and ethics, and, in the long run, philosophy are branches of knowledge from which medicine draws sustenance." When we delve into the history of medicine, we see that philosophical doctrines have always had their often covert influence. Even at the time of Galen and his predecessors, doctors were divided into the opposing camps of empirics and rationalists. Lewis saw a similar cleavage between the psychiatrists of today, "between, on the one hand, those who made it their business to observe, with the utmost fullness, all the relevant morbid phenomena and to clarify them, and, on the other hand, those who wanted to go behind the phenomena, to make out the pathology, without being delayed or misled by surface appearances. The former, empirics to a man, fell into the pit of overconcern with classification, degenerated into labeling and sorting; the latter, rationalists of undoubted lineage, devised systems and hypostatised forces, sometimes without appreciating how easily closer observation could stultify their misconceived explanations of imperfectly studied behaviour." In the end, Lewis quoted with approbation the Roman encyclopaedist Aulus Cornelius Celsus who antedated Galen by over 100 years. He had urged the adoption of views that "are neither wholly in accord with one opinion or another, but hold a sort of intermediate place between [the] diverse sentiments [of the empirics and rationalists]." Lewis concurred wholeheartedly. "It is, I believe, the judicious position likely to be taken up by prudent 'discreet, groundedly learned' men of today as they comtemplate those twentieth-century psychiatric disputations which reflect the ancient contention between tough-minded and tender-minded, the empirics and the rationalists."

Lewis's great interest in men and their ideas led him to write biographical appreciations of such psychiatrists as Reil, Pinel, Maudsley, Mapother, Freud, Jung and Mayer-Gross. But the thoughts, deeds, and theories of many other men flit through his pages. They are often quoted verbatim in their untranslated languages, teasing the linguistic talents of his readers. His deep erudition and extraordinary memory enabled him to survey from a far flung compass of historical, scientific, and philosophical thought the psychiatric problems of today, weighing them in his mind that was given to scepticism and circumspection rather than ready assent or enthusiastic advocacy. When considering *Research and Its Application in Psychiatry*, he spelled out his credo that "informed criticism [is] as valuable, or indispensable, in the advancement of psychiatry as in any other field of knowledge . . . [though] by criticism I do not mean fault-finding but expert judgment and appraisal."

At the early age of 15, Lewis already showed his mettle. He then gave an address to the literary society of the Catholic school he attended in Adelaide. His teachers commented: "Mr. Lewis's discourse on the origin and history of words was instructive from a philological point of view, but rather too technical for the occasion" (Shepherd 1976).

Philology and onomastics (to use a suitably bookish term which Lewis would have appreciated) were thenceforth always close to his heart. After his retirement he could indulge this hobby. He then dissected philologically some psychiatric terms, such as, for instance, *hysteria* and *paranoia*, terms with histories "going back two and a half millennia which have had sentence of death passed upon them more than once, yet they obstinately survive . . . to outlive [their] obituarists." Among other words scrutinized were *endogenous-exogenous, psychogenic* (which he suggested "should be decently buried"), and *anxiety* (which has been the bugbear of translators because its synonyms in Latin, French, German, Italian and Spanish have their vernacular shades of meaning and can never be made quite congruent semantically). It was one of Lewis's laments that "the words of psychiatry are often unjust stewards, sorry guardians of meaning, workers of deception." What was required were definitions or glossaries which could reach across linguistic frontiers and thus bring order to the babel of weasel words and chameleon concepts. Lewis exerted himself greatly in this direction, successfully steering the British and WHO Glossaries of Mental Disorders to their completion, thus providing psychiatrists throughout the world with a common terminology. He was helped in this task by his wide knowledge of languages and his acquaintance with writers of the past. He could thus trace the path of psychiatric words and ideas as it weaved through the centuries in verbal and semantic gyrations.

Lewis had a very characteristic style of writing which has not had a universal appeal. Some seem to have found it too artificial and therefore irritating, though Stengel's "depressive" response must have been a personal peculiarity. Others have been able to enjoy its scholarly phrasing which marks it off happily from the frequent dreariness of psychiatric prose. It could even occasionally soar to belletristic heights as can be gleaned from some of the quotations in this essay. But Lewis made no allowance for those whose vocabularies were not as well stocked as his, who therefore had to suspend their reading from time to time in order to search for enlightenment in a dictionary. Yet even this resource can be of no avail, since there are many allusions that need a wider search. To give just one example: In his historical review of melancholia, he referred to Thomas Sydenham as "an ardent phlebotomist, a Sangrado of the gloomy." Sangrado? Who was he? Biographical dictionaries proved useless. The required information was eventually tracked down in a Companion of English Literature. Sangrado was a fictional physician in Le Sage's picaresque romance "Gil Blas of Santillane" and he was famed for mercilessly subjecting his patients to copious bloodlettings.

There is another stumbling-block in his style, especially for hasty readers. Lewis had to tackle each problem from every conceivable angle, leaving no facets untouched. He thus let his arguments meander through all the tributaries of his theme before he reined himself in and returned to the main current. By that time, an inattentive reader could have lost the tenor of the reasoning. This urge to be thoroughgoing was an impediment to Lewis himself, when he had to prepare a lecture. He always found that he had too much script on his hands. There was then a need to thin it out with the help of Miss Helen Marshall, his secretary for many years. Even so, he was always left with more material than could be comfortably squeezed into the time allotted to the lecture. In delivering it, he therefore had to race through his pages at breakneck speed, leaving most of his listeners, and perhaps all of them, far behind.

No such handicap is faced by the reader. He can take his time and even browse, if he feels so inclined. He will be rewarded, not by being taken on a flight of fancy that loses sight of empirical brass tacks, but by a panoramic and meditative view of the state of psychiatry and of psychiatric problems. The quality of many of the papers in the three books reconsidered here seems so timeless that one can venture to predict that perceptive readers will continue to derive benefit and enjoyment from communion with the knowledge, prudence, wisdom and humanity of Lewis's mind.

REFERENCES

Anonymous (1967). The man at the Maudsley. *The Times Literary Supplement*, December 14, p. 1213.

Letters, (1968). *The British Journal of Psychiatry*, 114:355–356, 920–921.

Lewis, Sir A. (1967a). *Inquiries in Psychiatry, Clinical and Social Investigations*. London: Routledge & Kegan Paul.

_____ (1967b). *The State of Psychiatry. Essays and Addresses*. London: Routledge & Kegan Paul.

_____ (1979). *The Later Papers of Sir Aubrey Lewis*. Oxford: Oxford University Press.

Shepherd, M. (1976). *The Career and Contributions of Sir Aubrey Lewis*. London: The Bethlem Royal and Maudsley Hospitals.

Stengel., E. (1968). Review. *British Journal of Psychiatry* 114:127–36.

_____ (1969). Review. *British Journal of Social and Clinical Psychology* 8:297–8.

Selections from the
Works of Sir Aubrey Lewis

The concept of disease, then–and of health–has physiological and psychological components, but no essential social ones. In examining it we cannot ignore social considerations, because they may be needed for the assessment of physiological and psychological adequacy, but we are not bound to consider whether behaviour is socially deviant: though illness may lead to such behaviour, there are many forms of social deviation which are not illness, many forms of illness which are not social deviation.

It is necessary at this point to draw a distinction between illness and what doctors treat. If the view were taken that everyone who goes to the doctor and receives treatment is ill, we would have a simple operational criterion, but its defects are obvious: it will fluctuate enormously from place to place and from time to time, it will depend on an attitude by the patient towards his doctor, and it will certainly fail to indicate many people whom, by any common-sense standard, one must call ill.

Moreover it must be remembered that the doctor is not necessarily acting outside his proper scope if he attends to people who are not ill. Congenital defects of bodily structure and function (e.g., malformations and benign metabolic anomalies) are not strictly illnesses but they are the concern of doctors. Pregnancy and childbirth, after all, are not illnesses either. Extension of the doctor's province has gone very far in psychiatry. The psychiatrist learns a great deal about normal and abnormal psychology which is relevant to the treatment, or the prevention, of some non-pathological states that are socially deviant. He is nowadays often, and quite properly, asked to investigate and treat disturbances of behaviour in children which can hardly be included within any warranted conception of illness (though of course they may be the prelude to illness). He may likewise investigate or treat criminals, drug addicts, prostitutes and sexual perverts. It may be that there is no form of social deviation in an individual which psychiatrists will not claim to treat or prevent–the pretensions of some psychiatrists are extreme. That time has not come, fortunately. Nevertheless it is clear that psychiatrists, and other doctors, look after plenty of people who are not ill: and conversely that there are many sick people who think as Montaigne did and would hold it absurd to commit themselves to the mercy and government of the doctors – at any rate for a nervous illness. Psychiatrists in our day are much exposed to strictures and suspicions like those which Montaigne expressed against the doctors of the sixteenth century.

Suicide illustrates the problem in deciding between social deviation and illness. No one disputes that suicide is often an outcome or symptom of illness; no one, I think, disputes that it can be the act of a mentally healthy person. If it occurs in a society which sanctions suicide in given circumstances, as ours does, and if the circumstances of the act are the approved ones, it is assumed that the act does not bespeak mental illness nor, of course, social deviation. That is, socially approved behaviour is not usually reviewed to see if it evinces mental illness; and in such a case, suicide is regarded like marriage, or any other isolated but decisive act of choice which is socially approved. But even in a society which does not disapprove of suicide, the act may be a sign of mental illness; and it may be suspected to be such for two reasons: because of the circumstances in which it occurs, and because of the disorder of psychological functions which the person displays, apart from his suicidal behaviour. When the circumstances indicate that the act is not in conformity with the social roles which the person is required to enact, this is not sufficient to denote illness, though it excites inquiry into the matter. The decision about illness must be made in the light of a further inquisition, into psychological functions. If these are found disordered, then the suicidal act may be assumed to have been also an evidence of mental illness – but even this would not be true unless the suicidal act fitted into the total pattern of disordered function which the person displayed. A person may be mentally ill, yet his suicide may be extrinsic to this, or represent, so to speak, a normal and even healthy response to the situation in which he finds himself. It may seem absurd to talk of suicide as in any circumstances a healthy response, but it is absurd only if one holds to the opinion that biological adaptation is the true and final criterion of health. By any biological standard the suicide of a person who has not reproduced is surely a supreme instance of maladaptation.

The psychoanalytical concepts of mental health and illness call for special consideration. Though there is no unanimity among psychoanalysts on the matter, they concentrate on inner psychological criteria, and some of the terms they use for definition would make it impossible to tell whether an individual is mentally healthy unless he has been psychoanalysed or his behaviour interpreted on psychoanalytic lines: the criteria, in short, are technical psychoanalytical ones. It is also common for psychoanalysts to describe mental health in loose general language: thus Karl Menninger says: 'Let us define mental health as the adjustment of human beings to the world and to each other with a maximum of effectiveness and happiness.' A more serious effort to grapple with the problem has been made by Ernest Jones. He lists three features of the normal or healthy mind: first, the 'internal freedom' of feelings of friendliness and affection towards others; secondly, mental efficiency, i.e., 'the fullest use of the given individual's powers and talents'; and finally, happiness which is 'probably the most important of the three'—a combination of the capacity for enjoyment with self-content. These criteria are approximately those which he applies to a practical matter—viz. determining whether, and when, treatment has been successful; 'The analytical success betokens the highest degree of the favourable results I described just now when speaking of the therapeutic criteria. One may then expect a confident serenity, a freedom from anxiety, a control over the full resources of the personality that can be obtained in no other way than by the most complete analysis possible.' Such language leaves room for honest but absurdly wide differences of opinion between a psychoanalyst and another person—say a psychiatrist, a general practitioner, or a relative of the patient—about whether a psychoanalysed patient, or indeed anybody at all, is mentally healthy. Yet this is no remote and theoretical matter. Partly because it has not been settled we are still without exact information about the comparative effects of psychoanalysis and other methods of psychotherapy, or of the indications that a successful outcome will ensue from psychoanalytical treatment of a particular patient. Yet a Health Service which promises adequate treatment to the whole population is in an awkward position when a demand that much more psychoanalytic therapy be provided is refused on the ground that such treatment is costly and its efficacy open to doubt. Every psychiatrist has seen patients who, he is told, have recovered after treatment of their mental disorder but who seem to him still ill. It is not a problem that affects only the assessment of psychoanalytic treatment: it comes up quite as often after physical methods of psychiatric treatment, like leucotomy. The inherent difficulty of the concept of mental health is underlined when we find the psychoanalyst, so expert in the microscopy of mental happenings, unable to dispense with equivocal and cloudy terms in stating his criteria of recovery.

Another psychoanalyst, Lawrence Kubie, has looked more closely than most into the social implications of health. Beginning with the assertion that 'psychoanalysis is uncompromising in its concept of mental health', he goes on to say that the analyst is not 'content to use conformity to the cultural mores of any time or place as his criterion of normality' . . .

. . . nor does the difference between normal and neurotic conduct depend upon the degree to which an act contributes either to the welfare of society or to its destruction, or on whether the behaviour is extravagant and fantastic or orderly and sedate. Certainly from the point of view of society all of these are important attributes of human behaviour; but they are neither constant nor explanatory as a basis for the distinction between the normal and the neurotic process. . . . The critical difference lies not in the act, nor in its setting, but in the psychological mechanisms which determine the act. . . . What passes for normality in our world to-day is not in any fundamental sense normal. It is rather the unstable equilibrium between conscious and unconscious phenomena. . . . The activities which result may not be peculiar or strange in themselves. They may be socially acceptable and even valuable; and they may meet all the demands of conscience. . . .

but they are residues of the unresolved neurotic problems of childhood, they are the 'veiled and universal neurotic component of "normal" human nature'. He concludes that on pragmatic grounds we may call any act normal if conscious processes predominate in it; he holds that every act is the product of biological forces and superimposed conscious, preconscious and unconscious psychological forces, all of which bear the imprint of many social pressures and are in a state of continuous unstable equilibrium. This is another way of looking at the efficiency of certain functions. But the functions are those which psychoanalysts emphasize in their account of mental organization. They are difficult functions to consider outside the psychoanalytical frame of reference, and the concept embodying them accordingly difficult to apply to the recognition of health and disease.

To deny a social content in the idea of health in no sense implies denying it a social context. Anthropologists and social psychologists have arrayed overpowering evidence showing how highly dependent we must be on knowledge of the social and cultural background when we would appraise conduct and the efficiency of psychological functions. No practising psychiatrist can be unmindful of this, and it is needless to cite the standard examples—Kwakutl and Shasta, Crow Indians and Ekoi, Yakuts and Dobuans—in order to underline it.

But in our own society the prevailing confusion about the quality and nature of health has begotten some dangerous errors. Thus during the last war many people assumed that a man who had neurotic illness would be less capable in social relations and work than a healthy man. A rather similar assumption is often made about would-be university students, and about entrants into a wide variety of careers and jobs. But the evidence for this is not conclusive, and much of what purports to be evidence is vitiated by the use of a concept of neurotic illness which takes account of occupational or social inadequacy, and a concept of occupational inadequacy which is much influenced by considerations of health. Unless the criteria of ill-health are independent and clear, it is difficult or unsafe to use data based on them for purposes of selection. [pp. 189–193]

24

Charles Rycroft:
A Critical Dictionary of Psychoanalysis

Reviewed by John Birtchnell

The renown of this book rests on the single word "critical." Had it simply been called *A Dictionary of Psychoanalysis*, it might never have featured in this series of outstanding books of their time. The introduction of the word "critical" implied that the book was going to tell the reader what was wrong with psychoanalysis; and this is what many nonanalysts would like to know. Four years after its first appearance it was published by Penguin, which was no doubt aware that the critical element was its main selling point. They emphasized this by displaying on the front cover an absurd and vulgar sketch combining the face of Freud with a large, protuberant breast.

On the first page of the book Rycroft acknowledged that it grew out of a notebook in which he had recorded his puzzlement and doubts about certain aspects of Freudian theory. I would like to suggest that reaching the point of publicly proclaiming one's disagreement with Freud represents a stage in the development of the psychoanalyst which is the equivalent of what Bowen, the family therapist, has called the differentiation of self from the family of origin. Many prominent theorists such as Jung, Adler, Reich, Klein, Suttie, Balint, Berne, Bowlby, Perls, and Laing reached and passed through such a stage. In fact, the Freudian system lends itself to such a process. The aspiring analyst must seek admission to the system and then submit himself to a rigorous and regressive training ritual, during which his analyst, I would suggest, becomes for him what Kohut has called a self-object. Only when he emerges on the far side of this experience can he decide how much of what he has been exposed to he is going to absorb into his own identity and how much he is going to reject.

We know from Peter Fuller's excellent biographical introduction to Rycroft's more recent *Psychoanalysis and Beyond* (1985) that Rycroft did not take easily to the Freudian system. He is quoted as saying, "If I had known about the psychoanalytic movement and its quasi-sectarian quality, I would certainly not have applied." He did apply, submitted himself to the training, and emerged a qualified psychoanalyst, at the age of 33, in 1947. At this time the ideological battle between Anna Freud and Melanie Klein was at its most intense. Initially he veered toward the Kleinian viewpoint, but subsequently he tried to maintain a middle-ground. He largely conformed, became a training analyst, sat on numerous committees, and held various offices within the British Psycho-Analytical Society, but he became progressively more disenchanted with the way that polemics were conducted within the society.

Shortly, however, he himself became caught up in disputes and controversies. In 1956 he caused a stir with the publication of his paper "Symbolism and Its Relationship to the Primary and Secondary Process." In this, he challenged the official view that symbolization was invariably unconscious, regressive, and defensive. This is a view which had been reemphasized by Ernest Jones, Freud's leading British disciple, in 1916, in an authoritative paper called "The Theory of Symbolism." During the next twenty years, in what I would consider to be his attempts to extricate himself from Freudian orthodoxy, he published a number of papers which were critical of Freud. He came to realise, however, that his voice carried little weight in the Society's affairs and that the real power was in the hands of those whose values he did not approve. As Fuller expressed it, "the weight of orthodoxy was such that any open confrontation with it inside the Society would have dragged him into precisely those rituals of polemic and pronouncement of anathemas that he was seeking to reject." He submitted his resignation, but he was persuaded to withdraw it. He was warned about how damaging it would be for the movement to have further splits. Eventually, in 1978, he let his membership lapse. Thereafter his two most important books were published, *The Innocence of Dreams* in 1979 and *Psychoanalysis and Beyond* in 1985.

The Critical Dictionary appeared, therefore, midway between the publication of his first critical paper and his final departure from the Society. In the first sentence of the book Rycroft appears to be struggling with his obvious ambivalence towards psychoanalysis. He explains that the book is not intended to be a dictionary of criticisms of psychoanalysis or to provide ammunition for those who may wish to demolish it. Instead, it is intended to help those who wish or need to inform themselves about it to do so intelligently and critically. Thus he intended to be constructively rather than destructively critical. In fact, he only allowed himself to be mildly critical and, for the most part, the book is a straightforward explanation of those psychoanalytic terms which had been in use up to the mid-sixties. The length of the explanations ranges from two lines to two pages, and in some of the longer explanations there are pointers to Rycroft's major disagreements with Freudian orthodoxy. To fully appreciate what those disagreements amount to the reader would need to refer to his longer texts.

The dictionary proper is preceded by an eighteen-page introduction which raises a number of interesting points about psychoanalysis. The reader is reminded that most of the psychoanalytic literature was originally thought out and subsequently written in German and that, although most of the translations are excellent, it seems likely that some ideas are not easily transported from one language to another. The German word *Angst*, for example, is more heavily laden with overtones of anguish and fear than is the English word *anxiety*, and this may lead to the incorrect assumption that the normally adjusted person does not become anxious. It is suggested that the German tendency to precede abstract nouns by a definite article, to write "the consciousness" rather than consciousness, and presumably "the unconsciousness" rather than unconsciousness, has the effect of implying that such abstractions have a real existence and may be invoked as explanatory agents. It is further explained that, in English, there is one vocabulary (derived from Anglo-Saxon) for describing everyday ideas and experiences and another (derived from Latin and Greek) for thinking and writing about abstract concepts. We use the Anglo-Saxon word *I* to refer to ourselves, and the Latin or Greek word *ego* to refer to the more abstract conception of the self. The equivalent German words are *ich* and *das Ich*. This, it is argued, causes the English reader to dissociate the more impersonal structure of the ego, with its characteristics and functions, from what is really nothing other than the person himself. I feel that here Rycroft is blurring a distinction which really does exist. Jacobson, for example, has argued in the reverse direction: that Freud himself sometimes used the term *ego* to refer to a psychic structure concerned with the ego functions and defences, and sometimes used it to refer to the self. The two concepts are, in fact, so distinct that there are now two separate psychoanalytic schools, the ego psychologists led by Anna Freud and Hartman and the self-psychologists led by Kohut and Kernberg. Ironically, in the main body of the dictionary Rycroft does draw a distinction between the ego and the self, and correctly draws attention to the preoccupation of the existential psychoanalysts with such a distinction. He makes no reference, however, to self-psychology or to any of the self-psychologists whose writings were not widely recognized in the mid-sixties.

From this point on, I will concern myself with various preoccupations of Rycroft's which are alluded to in the explanations provided in the dictionary but which are more fully examined in his longer texts. I will begin with his dissatisfaction with what he considers to be the implication of psychoanalysis, that man does not have a will of his own. He considers that it was Freud's belief that the human ego is a passive entity lacking energy or force of its own and only capable of action in so far as it is acted on by forces external to itself. These forces may be located either in the (unconscious) id or in the environment. This places man in the same category as the animals. Under the heading "Will" he maintains that the concept of will forms no part of psychoanalytic theory, being incompatible with the assumption of psychic determinism and with the idea that mental illnesses are caused by unconscious processes to which the notion of will is obviously inapplicable. Under the heading "Psychic Determinism" he explains that such an assumption leaves no place in analytic theory for a self or agent initiating action or defence, or for the use of explanations other than causal ones. He maintains that most analysts believe that the claims of psychoanalysis to be a science are based on its use of causal-deterministic assumptions. He further claims that psychoanalysts need to view the neuroses as being illnesses like physical illnesses in which the patient is a victim of circumstances which impinge on his body without his own will being in any way implicated. There are clearly other reasons why psychoanalysis can lay claim to being a science, and it is not necessary for the patient to be viewed simply as the passive recipient of forces in the way that a physical object is.

Somewhat unconvincingly, I feel, he tries to proffer the influence of early experiences to justify his belief that the ego is not a passive entity. Under the heading "Development" he states that psychoanalysts believe that adult behavior can be interpreted as an elaboration or evolution of infantile behavior and that complex "higher" forms of behavior can be interpreted as elaborations of simple, primitive behavior patterns and drives. The developmental process as a whole can be considered to result from the evolution of innate developmental processes and the impact of experience on these processes. In the introduction he explains that, in the neuroses, the patient appears to be suffering the consequences of relationships in which he must have been, to some extent at least, a willing agent. It is not entirely clear to me why this leads him to conclude that the ego is, in fact, an active agent, capable of initiating behavior, including those ultimately self-defeating forms of behavior we know as the neuroses. It seems to me that one could interpret Rycroft's preoccupation with free will as a manifestation of his own internal conflict over the extent to which he should allow himself to be a passive recipient of Freudian dogma and the extent to which he should exert his own free will in standing up against the orthodox psychoanalytic position.

He goes on to argue that if the ego is an active agent, rather than a passive entity, it cannot be possible to maintain that everything that goes on between analyst and patient is "a scrambled repetition of the patient's childhood," with the analyst acting as "completely detached, though benevolent observer." It is his belief that, although psychoanalysis was formulated as though it were based on the objective and detached scrutiny of "material" presented to the detached and uninvolved analyst by the analysand, its insights really arise out of the relationship that develops "when two people are gathered together in a psychotherapeutic setting." He considers that the raw material or basic data of his science is the relationship he is having with his patients. Any reference he might have made early in his career to the "psychic apparatus" was, in his opinion, "making kow-towing movements towards classical theory." It has often been observed that Freud's tendency to present his theory in terms of structure and apparatus was a continuation of his medical and neurological patient-centered orientation. Rycroft's prediction that, one day, psychoanalytic theory will have to be reformulated as a communication theory is very much in line with Szasz's long-held belief that psychiatry is really a science of communication and Sullivan's interpersonal approach both to psychoanalysis and to psychiatry as a whole. (The quotations in this paragraph are from Fuller.)

From the publication of his first critical paper in 1986, Rycroft continued to be preoccupied with the distinction between the primary and secondary processes, which he believed to be Freud's most important contribution to our understanding of mental functioning. There is, however, a fundamental difference between Freud's conception of these two processes and Rycroft's. Under "Processes, Primary and Secondary" he explains that Freud believed primary process to be ontogenetically and phylogenetically earlier than secondary process, that it was that mode of thinking that was operative in the id, and that it was characteristic of unconscious mental activity. Secondary process, on the other hand, was that mode of thinking that was operative in the ego, and it was characteristic of conscious mental activity. Primary process was governed by the pleasure principle, whereas secondary process was governed by the reality principle. Rycroft maintains that Freud considered the two processes to be mutually antagonistic, that secondary process was superior because it developed later, and that primary process was primitive and maladaptive. Rycroft explains that psychoanalytic observation and theorizing is involved in the paradoxical activity of using secondary process to observe, analyse, and conceptualise that form of mental activity (i.e., primary process) that scientific thinking has always been at pains to exclude. Rycroft believes that, in fact, the two processes complement each other and that they are equally adaptive and equally necessary for creativity. It is certainly the case that, in dreaming, primary process is most evident, but secondary process also occurs. Similarly, although the conscious thought of most adults is predominantly primary process, secondary process is also sometimes apparent.

Probably one of Rycroft's most important modifications of Freudian theory is his elevation of primary process to a status equal to that of secondary process. It seems highly probable that primary process does represent an earlier form of psychic functioning. It is a feature of the thinking and conceptualizing of primitive people and of ancient mythology. Children exhibit a great deal of primary process before they are taken over by an educational system which emphasises the importance of logic and precise grammatical expression. It is, however, and essential component of creative thinking, regardless of whether this be of an aesthetic or a scientific kind. Under "Creativity" Rycroft observes that psychoanalysis has always been tempted to demonstrate similarities between creative activity and neurotic processes. Freudian analysts, he claims, interpret the content of novels and paintings as an oedipal fantasy. Kleinian analysts have tried to prove that creative activity is either depressive or schizoid, that it either represents an attempt to make reparation for destructive fantasies or is in some way analogous to the delusional system-making of schizophrenics. He notes that since classical psychoanalysis designates imaginative activity as primitive, infantile, and a function of the id, writers such as Hartman and Kris have been driven to describe it in terms such as regression at the service of the ego. Creativity is individualistic and therefore, more than anything else, is difficult to include within a causal-determinist framework. At the end of his life Freud rejected the idea that psychoanalysis has anything to contribute to aesthetics. In contrast, Rycroft has constantly emphasised that imagination is a natural, normal activity of an agent or self. He has an acute awareness of the role played by the imagination at every level of mental functioning.

Not surprisingly, Rycroft has also challenged the Freudian attitude to dreams. His book *The Innocence of Dreams* (1979) represents an alternative to Freud's classic *The Interpretation of Dreams* (1900). Under the heading "Dreams" he explains that Freud's interest in dreams derived from the fact that they are normal processes, with which everyone is familiar, but which none the less exemplify the processes at work in the formation of neurotic symptoms. For Rycroft, dreams are not necessarily disguised expressions of repressed wishes, the royal road to the unconscious, nor analogies for psychopathological symptoms. He maintains that dreams are merely the form which the imagination takes during sleep and that there is no reason to suppose that symbolism is essentially a device by which dreamers deceive and obfuscate themselves, even though on occasion it may be used in this way. Freud considered dreaming to be essentially a visual rather than a verbal process, and that dream interpretation involves expanding the condensed, nondiscursive, mainly visual imagery of the dream into the discursive symbolism of language (i.e., of converting primary process into secondary process). Since Rycroft considers the two processes to be complementary, he would not be in favor of translating one into the other.

What appears to be behind most of Rycroft's criticism of Freud is his dissatisfaction with the concept of the unconscious and with the fact that the individual is helplessly and passively controlled and directed by instinctual forces and reactions that originate within the unconscious. Under the heading "Unconscious" he observed that patients with a speculative turn of mind may, if they have an unwary analyst, entertain an indefinite number of hypotheses about their unconscious motives without having any idea how to decide which of them are true. While he seems prepared to acknowledge that there are unconscious mental processes and also unconscious thoughts, he seems unable to accept the idea of entity called the unconscious which has a kind of autonomy of its own.

Where then does all this leave us? Rycroft is of interest because he is a psychoanalyst who rebelled against Freudian orthodoxy. Most psychoanalysts who rebel are able, through their rebellion, to make important contributions in their own right. Some rebel more strongly than others, and the originality of their contribution is a reflection of the intensity of their rebellion. Fritz Perls, who once wrote, "It took us a long time to debunk the whole Freudian crap . . . " rebelled a lot more strongly than Rycroft has and, in so doing, created the excitingly innovative Gestalt therapy. Rycroft's rebellion has been a relatively modest affair, but is no less valuable for that. Although no longer a member of the British Psycho-Analytical Society, he remains true to the psychoanalytic tradition.

Whatever critics may say of the efficacy of psychoanalysis as a form of treatment, there is no doubt that psychoanalysis has created a means of accommodating the subjective, the emotional and the irrational and provided a conceptual framework within which to generate theories about psychological development and human motivation. Along with all of this it has created a language, and all languages require a dictionary. Now that a dictionary exists it is capable of being expanded and updated and, now that Rycroft's has come of age, it is to be hoped that somebody, if not Rycroft himself, will come forward and take on this onerous but necessary task. Finally, it would be sad if all that Rycroft were remembered for was his dictionary. In the dictionary there are only pointers to his theoretical position. Hopefully, this brief review will stimulate the reader to seek out his more substantial contributions.

Selections from
A Critical Dictionary of
Psychoanalysis
by Charles Rycroft

ID

The Latin word for "it," used by Freud's translators to translate his "das Es," the term he borrowed from Groddeck and used to designate unorganised parts of the PSYCHIC APPARATUS. (Groddeck's translators prefer "the IT.") Historically the id is the descendent of the UNCONSCIOUS in the same way as the EGO is the descendent of the CONSCIOUS. According to CLASSICAL THEORY the id is developmentally anterior to the ego, i.e., the PSYCHIC APPARATUS begins as an undifferentiated id, part of which develops into a structured ego. The id "contains everything that is present at birth, that is fixed in the constitution—above all, therefore, the instincts, which originate from the somatic organization and which find a first psychical expression here [in the id] in forms unknown to us"—Freud. "It is the dark, inaccessible part of our personality; what little we know of it we have learnt from our study of the dream-work and of the construction of neurotic symptoms, and most of that is of a negative character and can be described only as a contrast to the ego. We approach the id with analogies; we call it a chaos, a cauldron full of seething excitations . . . it is filled with energy reaching it from the instincts, but it has no organization, produces no collective will, but only a striving to bring about the satisfaction of instinctual needs subject to the observance of the pleasure-principle"—Freud. The concept is one of many examples of Freud's passion for explaining mental phenomena in terms of the opposition of antithetical forces. The id is primitive, the ego civilized; the id is unorganized, the ego organized; the id observes the PLEASURE-PRINCIPLE, the ego the REALITY-PRINCIPLE; the id is emotional, the ego rational; the id conforms to the PRIMARY PROCESSES which ignore differences and are oblivious of contradictions and of space and time, the ego conforms to the SECONDARY PROCESSES which are analytical and respect the principles of contradiction and the categories of space and time.

OEDIPUS COMPLEX

Group of largely UNCONSCIOUS ideas and feelings centring round the wish to possess the parent of the opposite sex and eliminate that of the same sex. The complex emerges, according to CLASSICAL THEORY, during the oedipal phase of LIBIDINAL and EGO DEVELOPMENT, i.e., between the ages of three and five, though Oedipal manifestations may be present earlier—even, according to Melanie Klein (see KLEINIAN), during the first year of life. The complex is named after the mythical Oedipus, who killed his father and married his mother without knowing that they were his parents. According to Freud, the Oedipus complex is a universal phenomenon, built in phylogenetically (see PHYLOGENETIC), and is responsible for much unconscious GUILT. Resolution of the Oedipus complex is achieved typically by IDENTIFICATION with the parent of the same sex and (partial) temporary renunciation of the parent of the opposite sex, who is "rediscovered" in his (her) adult sexual object. Persons who are fixated at the Oedipal level are mother-fixated or father-fixated, and reveal this by choosing sexual partners with obvious resemblances to their parent(s). Oedipal rivalry with the father is a cause of CASTRATION ANXIETY.

Freud first mentioned the Oedipus complex in a letter to his friend Fliess in 1897, and the idea arose out of the self-analysis which he conducted after the death of his father. Its first published appearance was in the *Interpretation of Dreams*. It remained a cornerstone of psychoanalytical theory up to say, 1930, but since then psychoanalysis has become increasingly mother orientated and concerned with the pre-oedipal relationship to the mother, and the modern tendency is to regard the Oedipus complex as a psychic structure itself requiring interpretation in terms of earlier conflicts rather than as a primary source of neurosis itself. However, even the most enthusiastic supporters of psychopathological systems (see PSYCHOPA-THOLOGY) centring round the MOTHER have to take account of the fact that children have two parents, that in our society at least they grow up in close proximity to both and are confronted with intimations of their sexual life together and their own exclusion from it.

SYMBOL, SYMBOL-FORMATION, SYMBOLIZATION, SYMBOLISM

In general, a symbol is something that refers to or represents something else, in contrast to a SIGN, which indicates the presence of something. In this sense, WORDS, emblems, badges are all symbols since they derive their significance from the fact that they refer to something else, their referent, the connexion between them and their referents being based on association of ideas and, usually, established by convention. In all these instances, however, the connexion between symbol and referent is CONSCIOUS, whereas the psychoanalytical theory of symbolism concerns itself with the UNCONSCIOUS substitution of one image, idea, or activity for another. Jones distinguished between "true" symbolism and "symbolism in its widest sense," and wrote, "If the word symbolism is taken in its widest sense, the subject is seen to compromise almost the whole development of civilization. For what is there other than a never-ending series of evolutionary substitutions, a ceaseless replacement of on idea, interest, capacity, or tendency by another?" True symbolism, on the other hand, "arises as the result of intrapsychic CONFLICT [see also INTRAPSYCHIC] between the repressing tendencies [see REPRESSION] and the repressed . . . only what is repressed is symbolized; only what is repressed needs to be symbolized. . . . The two cardinal characteristics of symbolism in this strict sense are (1) that the process is completely unconscious . . . and (2) that the affect investing the symbolized idea has not, in so far as the symbolism is concerned, proved capable of that modification in quality denoted by the term "SUBLIMATION." According to this definition of symbolism, the substitutions involved in the creation of DREAM images and SYMPTOMS are examples of symbol-formation, while those involved in sublimation are not. "True" or psychoanalytical symbolism, in fact, resembles dreaming and symptom-formation in that they are private constructions, the meaning of which is discoverable only in terms of the individual experience of the subject and not by reference to dictionaries or social conventions. The apparent exceptions to this, the so-called universal symbols, encountered in dreams, mythology, and folklore, are explained by reference to "the uniformity of the fundamental and perennial interests of mankind" and to the uniformity of the human capacity for seeing resemblances between objects.

Symbolization is usually listed as one of the PRIMARY PROCESSES governing unconscious THINKING as exemplified in dreams and symptom-formation, though not by Freud himself, presumably on the ground that the processes involved in symbol-formation are DISPLACEMENT and CONDENSATION. He would also, it seems, not have agreed with the idea that words are not "true" symbols, since in his last work he wrote: "Dreams make an unlimited use of linguistic symbols, the meaning of which is for the most part unknown to the dreamer. Our experience, however, enables us to establish their sense. They probably originate from earlier phases in the development of speech." In his Introductory Lectures he also described symbolism as an "ancient but obsolete mode of expression." For the theoretical assumptions underlying both statements, see ONTOGENY AND PHYLOGENY. Jones's is, however, the "classical" analytical theory (see CLASSICAL THEORY) of symbolism. See Rycroft, for an attempt to reconcile the analytical and non-analytical usages on the basis of primary and secondary process symbolism, and Segal, for the distinction between symbols which represent instinctual processes and those which substitute for them.

Psychoanalytical theory asserts that the object or activity symbolized is always one of basic, instinctual, or biological interest, the substitution or displacement always being away from the body, i.e., and e.g., knives, aeroplanes, guns can be interpreted as phallic symbols, but the penis could never be a knife symbol. Displacements in the opposite, centripetal direction are "REGRESSIONS." An exception is the functional symbolism of Silberer, which occurs when a fatigued or sleepy person sets out to think about abstractions and instead finds visual images coming to mind.

TRANSFERENCE

1. The process by which a patient displaces on to his analyst feelings, ideas, etc., which derive from previous figures in his life (see DISPLACEMENT); by which he relates to his analyst as though he were some former object in his life; by which he projects on to his analyst OBJECT-REPRESENTATIONS acquired by earlier INTROJECTIONS (see PROJECTION); by which he endows the analyst with the significance of another, usually prior, object. 2. The state of mind produced by 1 in the patient. 3. Loosely, the patient's emotional attitude towards his analyst.

In the early days of psychoanalysis transference was regarded as a regrettable phenomenon which interfered with the recovery of repressed memories and disturbed the patient's objectivity. By 1912, however, Freud had come to see it as an essential part of the therapeutic process: "finally every conflict has to be fought out in the sphere of transference." It is not, of course, assumed that the analyst is the only person on to whom individuals tend to transfer feelings derived from the past, but that the detachment of the analyst—his refusal to play along with the patient's preconceptions or to respond in accordance with his expectations — creates a novel situation in which it is possible to interpret to the patient that he is behaving as though the analyst were his father, mother, brother, sister, or whatever (see INTERPRETATION). Such explicit statements made by the analyst are transference-interpretations; the patient's emotional involvement with the analyst is the transference-neurosis. The patient's relationship to the analyst qua father, mother, etc., is the transference-relationship, as opposed to the analytical relationship, as opposed to the relationship between analyst and patient including the latter's recognition of the actual nature of the contract and transaction between them and of the analyst's actual personality. Transference-resistance is the use of transference as a RESISTANCE against either remembering the past or facing ANXIETY connected with the prospect of ending treatment and having to forego the (in fact largely illusory) sense of security provided by being in treatment. Transference may be paternal, maternal, OEDIPAL, PRE-OEDIPAL, PASSIVE, DEPENDENT, ORAL, etc., according to the object transferred and the stage of DEVELOPMENT being recapitulated; OBJECT or NARCISSISTIC (identificatory, see IDENTIFICATION), according as to whether the patient conceives his analyst as an external person on whom he is dependent, whom he hates, etc., or as a part of himself; positive or negative, according as to whether he conceives the analyst as a benign or malevolent figure.

Most accounts of transference include the idea that early OBJECT-RELATIONSHIPS which the patient cannot possibly remember as such can none the less be reconstructed from the patient's transference-reactions. Instead of remembering his infancy and his relationship to the BREAST, the patient re-enacts it "in the transference." The work of Fairbairn, Klein, and Winnicott is inexplicable unless one realizes that they believe(d) that their patients' responses to themselves are valid evidence on which to base theories about the origin of object-relations in infancy (see FAIRBAIRNS'S REVISED PSYCHOPATHOLOGY; KLEINIAN). Most accounts also assume that the therapeutic effects of analysis are largely due to the opportunity provided by it to resolve "within the transference" conflicts dating from childhood and infancy, and attach little importance to novel aspects of the analytical relationship, such as the encounter with a person who combines interest with non-possessiveness and whose insight into the patient is probably more articulate and possibly actually greater than that of the actual parents.

25

Isaac M. Marks:
Fears and Phobias

Reviewed by C. P. Seager

A week may be a long time in politics, but how fares a book on an aspect of clinical psychiatry, published more than two decades ago? Isaac Marks wrote his book, *Fears and Phobias*, in 1969, at a time when a third intruder, behavioural psychotherapy, had intervened in the battle between physical treatment and psychodynamic psychotherapy as the two polarised options for correct care of the mentally ill and particularly for the neuroses. Eysenck had annoyed many by his study demonstrating that patients receiving dynamic psychotherapy did no better than those on the waiting list; psychoanalysis was an expensive way of passing the time until the condition resolved spontaneously. Clinical psychologists and a few psychiatrists began to take an interest in the work of Wolpe and looked back to the 1920s when William James and Mary Cover-Jones had demonstrated the induction and the treatment of fears in young children. No ethical committee would accept a research protocol on these lines today.

At the present time, the range of psychological treatments and the numbers of people who carry them out have been multiplied many times. The situation may be similar to the development of homeopathic medicine in the 1850s, at which time the available medical treatments were so horrific, with sometimes lethal, and usually toxic, accompaniments to the purging, bleeding and vomiting, that a search for alternative or complementary treatments was urgent.

Our present-day bewildering pharmacopoeia of highly effective and specialised drugs, each with its range of side effects for which there is a further range of medicaments, in their turn producing problems requiring further solutions, has resulted in the concept of iatrogenic disorder figuring

275

highly in the work of the diagnostic clerks of the Medical Records Department. It is no doubt a factor in the development of the wide variety of alternative therapies from Aromatherapy to Zen Buddhism. In psychiatry, there is the same pressure to avoid the use of "drugs" by the lay public, often without recognition of the very different indications for medication and the types of drugs in use.

Where does *Fears and Phobias*, published more than twenty-two years ago, fit into the changing pattern of psychiatric care of the neuroses? The book has a useful but dated review about the etiology of fear, which takes up the first 100 pages. Clinical syndromes are well set out in the next 80, with many fascinating personal reports of feelings and experiences. The final section, apart from the 18-page bibliography, deals with treatment, including comments on experimental design of studies and reports of appropriate controlled trials. It is interesting to note that mention of cognitive manipulation is confined to twenty lines, considering the major contribution this approach has made to recent treatment.

Marks himself says, "Knowledge in this area is advancing so rapidly that present views may need considerable modification in a few years time in the light of procedures currently being tested." In the preface to his subsequent book, *Fears, Phobias and Rituals*, published in 1987, he elaborated on this, pointing out that 1,000 articles a year have been appearing, and in the past seven years more than forty-six books have been published by professionals about fear and fear-related syndromes. He attempted in his first book to integrate the information from many different sciences and this approach has been continued in the second.

One important aspect of *Fears and Phobias* was the description of clinical studies rather than relying on experimental work with groups of psychology students complaining of "normal fears" such as those of snakes, spiders and heights. Undoubtedly, one can learn some aspects of etiology, symptomatology, and treatment from these individuals, who are leading a normal life by avoiding opportunities of encountering their relatively rare phobic situations. For someone to become a patient, this means that the problem is likely to be interfering with a major component of activities of living and sometimes interfering with earning capacity, family relationships and social enjoyment. Interestingly, it is probably true to say that many individuals who are ashamed and embarrassed by their "stupid fears" may gain the confidence to seek help after reading either the technical books of the kind discussed here or those for non-technical readers; perhaps more commonly now, they see the reports on television or radio during this era of enlightenment.

The book quotes a seventeenth-century author, highlighting the well-recognized fact that most treatments for phobias have been in use for centuries. The main contribution of modern behavioural psychotherapy is the introduction of controlled trials, with careful pretreatment assessment and measurement complemented by extensive follow-up rather than ex cathedra statements of what has been effected. The review of studies by Marks and Gelder, with patients drawn largely from the Maudsley Hospital, show undoubted, although not magical, benefits deriving from these controlled studies.

Reference is made to the value of drugs in the treatment of these disorders and there is a recognition of their palliative, but not curative, value. This was before the days when anything more than a short course of benzodiazepines for a specific problem is recognized as a potential direct line towards dependency. We had still to learn that any drug causing immediate and specific effect in relieving disabling anxiety symptoms was likely to be addictive, whether alcohol, barbiturates or benzodiazepines.

The publication of *Fears and Phobias* offered support to many therapists with differing professional backgrounds who saw opportunities to participate in treatment of conditions which, in the past, had been ignored because they were not sufficiently handicapping, or for which sedative drugs had been prescribed as a means of controlling the major symptoms without looking at the main disability. Most of these patients would not see themselves as suffering from psychiatric illness and would therefore reject any offer of in-patient treatment in a mental hospital, or even in the psychiatric unit of a general hospital, as an opportunity of tackling the problem. The move towards day hospitals, community mental health centres, and other "nonclinical" environments has seen the development of a range of community nurses, clinical psychologists, social workers, occupational therapists and counselors working from health centers and general practitioners' surgeries, offering an often behaviourally orientated treatment for the range of neurotic disorders that can be helped by such techniques.

Concentration on relatively minor neurotic disorders in the community, sometimes of a self-limiting nature, has led to the use of the pejorative term "the worried well." This unhelpful description is to ignore the degree of disability and discomfort occasioned by many conditions which are not likely to be admitted to a psychiatric unit but, nevertheless, need a period of continuing, systematic treatment offered by people trained and practiced in appropriate therapies. The issue has intensified because of the discharge into the community of people with "real psychiatric illness," by which is usually meant chronic schizophrenia, transferred from the long-stay wards of closing mental hospitals. These two groups are competing for scarce professional resources in the community and it is unfortunate that lack of management planning has, in the past, resulted in random allocation of resources on an ad hoc basis rather than assessing the needs of a particular community and deciding on the proportion of resources which can reasonably be allocated to the requirements of different patients. There is also a necessity to establish a hierarchy of professional skills, so that those who require relatively simple, nonspecific support can be seen by people with limited training and experience, leaving more complicated procedures for staff with specialist skills.

In summary, one has to recognize that this book is already of historical rather than present-day interest, and has been replaced by Marks's own updated account as well as a profusion of books and papers which give credence to the view that the broad group of treatments known as behavioural psychotherapy, together with the range of cognitive therapies now available, has offered effective treatment to a much wider range of people in need by a broader based group of professional therapists.

REFERENCES

Marks, I. M. (1969). *Fears and Phobias*. London: Heinemann.
_____ (1987). *Fears, Phobias and Rituals*. Oxford, England: Oxford University Press.

Selections from
Fears and Phobias
by Isaac M. Marks

INTRODUCTION

Nearly 2,000 years ago Celsus was probably the first person to use the word phobia in a medical context and to give a specific remedy for its treatment. Referring to hydrophobia, his term for rabies, he wrote:

> still there is just one remedy, to throw the patient unawares into a water tank which he has not seen beforehand. If he cannot swim, let him sink under and drink, then lift him out; if he can swim, push him under at intervals so that he drinks his fill of water even against his will; for so his thirst and dread of water are removed at the same time.

This drastic approach would be recommended today neither in the treatment of rabies nor of phobias proper. However, most other methods known to psychiatrists have been employed to alleviate genuine phobias. That many different techniques are currently in use is shown by the following passage which appeared in the newsletter of a phobic club whose members had answered a questionnaire (The Open Door, Nov. 1965). "HAVE YOU HAD ANY TREATMENT CONVENTIONAL OR OTHERWISE? Replies included: Drugs, Drugs and Drugs; Psychoanalysis; Narcoanalysis; Group therapy and other therapies including 'Heavy' Occupational Therapy (working in hospital kitchens and laundries!); Leucotomy; L.S.D.; Hypnosis; Autosuggestion; E.C.T. (Shock Treatment); Deep Relaxation; Yoga; Spiritual Healing; Acupuncture; Behavior Therapy; Psychology correspondence course; Homeopathy; Naturopathy, etc."

To this impressive list of treatments for phobias one could add the methods of ridicule, disuse by avoidance, "willpower", forced retraining, graduated retraining, social imitation of fearless models, individual and group psychotherapy, autogenic training, paradoxical intention, habituation, desensitisation, deconditioning, counterconditioning, relearning, reciprocal inhibition and aversion relief. The reader might well feel confused by the bewildering array of techniques which have been employed in the treatment of phobias. Until recently no procedures had been subject to controlled trial, and it was consequently difficult to evaluate the merits of different methods. The recent surge of controlled studies enables us now to say with more confidence what some of the procedures can do.

Prevention

Perhaps the most important measure to prevent the development of phobias is also the most difficult to put into practice. This measure is the provision of a milieu from infancy onwards in which the accepted mode of behavior is that of readiness to face difficulties and overcome frightening situations. A courageous attitude is easier to nurture in a child of naturally brave disposition than in one who is born timid, and we have to accept the limitations imposed on this attribute by genetic endowment. Nevertheless it is desirable that a child's models show a consistent readiness to master frightening situations and to reward a similar attitude in the child himself. The model's example "of fearlessness is not so likely to succeed, however, if it involves the use of abilities and techniques that are beyond the child's capacities. Nor does an example of courage help if it merely strengthens the child's conviction or fear that he himself is a coward" (Jersild 1950, p. 282).

When the child is sufficiently confident gentle encouragement should be given to enter mildly frightening situations until the child has lost all his fear. The child should not be ridiculed for being frightened, as shame reinforces fear. As a rule children should not be forced into frightening situations except under special circumstances where additional support is given until the fear has been overcome completely. Whatever happens the child should feel accepted and should not be rejected for appearing frightened, but praise and other rewards should be given freely for brave behaviour. This will be particularly necessary in a child who is naturally timid, whereas a tough child might require to be cautioned against excessive bravery when it amounts to foolhardiness.

Children and adults are more likely to show fear when debilitated by illness, fatigue or depression. Attempts should not be made to face fear while in such a state as this may enhance rather than allay fear. Such attempts are best encouraged when the subject is feeling well.

Management Immediately after Trauma

Sudden trauma is often followed by a lag phase before a phobia develops. Animal experiments suggest that immediate re-exposure to the original situation during this phase protects against the development of fear to that environment (Willmuth and Peters, 1964). It is in fact common lore that subjects should re-experience a traumatic situation again immediately after the original trauma. For example, during World War II treatment of combat neuroses was advocated within the sights and sounds of battle; "the acute phase is the crucial period in which therapy should be instituted in order to head off the organisation of the neurosis" (Kardiner and Spiegel 1947, pp. 76–77). Aeroplane pilots are encouraged to deliberately fly again as soon as possible after they have had a flying accident, and car drivers are recommended to drive once more as soon as they can after a car crash. It is sensible to help people face recently traumatic situations as soon as they can before the fear can be built into a phobia by the twin processes of first, repeated rehearsal of the trauma in the subject's mind and second, reinforcement by repeated avoidance.

While their phobias are still mild, patients can be helped to overcome their fear by warm reassurance and suggestion, and numerous stratagems have been employed successfully in selected cases to encourage them to face the feared situation, e.g., Frazier and Carr (1967) cite a patient who was bet $1,000 by his doctor that he would not die of heart attack should he venture forth from home, and promptly found himself able to go out alone for the first time in months. Prince (1898) described professional performers who were suddenly struck with stage fright, but who overcame this by constantly repeating aloud messages of reassurance written by the doctor on a piece of paper.

Treatment of Established Phobias

Once phobias are causing persistent avoidance of the phobic object then simple exhortations to bravery and willpower alone are not likely to help a patient. If anything they may aggravate his phobia by causing the patient to enter situations with which he cannot cope, he will get into a panic and escape from that situation, after which the phobia will increase. At this stage more specific techniques are necessary.

Many such techniques have been employed. In the past success has been claimed for a wide variety of techniques from faith healing and hypnosis to drugs and desensitisation. Most of these claims derive from isolated case reports or uncontrolled series of cases which are difficult to evaluate for two reasons. First, several kinds of phobias, especially those in children and in agoraphobics, fluctuate so much without treatment that improvement during administration of an uncontrolled technique might be due to this "spontaneous" change rather than to the technique itself.

Next, many psychological techniques are complex assemblies of several procedures, so that even if they do produce change in phobics it is by no means clear which aspects of the technique were responsible.

In the last decade a rash of controlled trials of treatment for phobias has appeared, so that some order is gradually emerging about which treatments work, in which patients they work, and what the effective ingredients are in these treatments. Most controlled trials in phobics have contrasted desensitisation with another procedure, but recently other techniques have also been subjected to controlled scrutiny. The claims for these and some uncontrolled methods will be discussed, after which results of all the different methods will be integrated together. However, knowledge in this area is advancing so rapidly that present views may need considerable modification in a few years' time in the light of procedures which are currently being tested.

DESENSITISATION

The procedure of desensitisation involves graduated exposure to phobic stimuli along a hierarchy while the patient simultaneously has a contrasting experience such as relaxation. Usually he is relaxed while he visualises a series of images of phobic situations, and later he also goes out to meet those situations in practice. Desensitisation is probably the commonest way in which phobias are treated today, and has been more thoroughly explored than any other technique. It is usually regarded as one of the many techniques which are called the behavioural psychotherapies. . . .

Techniques of Desensitisation

Most details of the technique have been elaborated by Rachman (1968). First a full history is essential to define the problems of the patient. The patient is then trained in progressive relaxation, the aim of which is to obtain a state of mental calm during subsequent presentation of phobic images. From 1 to 6 sessions may be needed to train the patient to the point where he can quickly achieve satisfactory relaxation. Jacobson's method is usually employed. This involves developing a "muscle sense", relaxing one muscle group (e.g., biceps) until a tingling sensation develops, relaxing consecutive muscle groups separately, relaxing various groups of muscles simultaneously. . . . [p. 185]

Difficulties During Desensitisation

Once the technique of desensitisation is given properly, the most important variable influencing results is the clinical status of the patient, how focal his problems are, how much anxiety there is at rest, how many compulsions and other neurotic symptoms there are. These will be reviewed. Even in suitable patients, however, progress in desensitisation can be hampered by many factors, most of which have been reviewed by Weinberg and Zaslove (1963), Wolpe and Lazarus (1966) and Rachman (1968). The problems are summarised in the following table. . . .

TABLE 25-1
Difficulties during Desensitisation

Difficulities during relaxation:
  Sleepiness
  Poor concentration
  Fear of losing control
  Muscular relaxation without mental relaxation
  Severe anxiety and depression

Problems of imagery:
  Inability to obtain images
  Dissociation of anxiety
  Dilution of image to more protective setting
  Intensification of image to panic proportions

Misleading hierarchies:
  Irrelevant hierarchies
  Fluctuating hierarchies

Relapse of desensitised phobias

Lack of cooperation

Life situation influences outside treatment

Studies of Desensitisation in Patients

For the psychiatrist it is crucial to know whether results obtained in volunteers are also applicable to patients in the clinic, because patients usually have much more distressing phobias and other problems than volunteers. So far the only investigations of desensitisation to include control groups of patients have been published from the Maudsley Hospital. Since results in patients are the acid test of the clinical value of desensitisation, these studies require description in some detail. . . .

TABLE 25-2
Controlled Studies of Desensitisation: Phobic Patients

Study	Fear treated	No. of pts. in des. group	Length of follow-up (months)	Control procedure
Cooper et al. (1965)	Mixed phobias	41	12	Mixed treatment without des.
Marks and Gelder (1965)	Mixed phobias	31	12	Mixed treatment without des.
Gelder and Marks (1966)	Agoraphobia	10	12	Hospitalisation
Gelder et al. (1967)	Mixed phobias	16	12	Insight psychotherapy
Marks et al. (1968)	Mixed phobias	14	9	Hypnotic suggestion

26

William H. Masters and Virginia E. Johnson:
Human Sexual Inadequacy

Reviewed by R. P. Snaith

Human Sexual Inadequacy is a unique research report: an account of a five-year follow-up of husbands and wives, here called "marital units," who went to St. Louis for the two-week rapid treatment course for sexual dysfunction at the Reproductive Biology Research Foundation. The report advanced, indeed promoted, therapeutic effort and provided guidelines for treatment. The advocacy of the male and the female co-therapist has become a standard principle, although the two-week residential course is rarely practicable.

The Foundation was established in 1954, and basic physiological observations of sexual intercourse were assembled, in 1966, in the authors' book *Human Sexual Response*. The Foundation's research program was based on the premise that the greatest handicap to successful treatment was the lack of reliable physiological information, and that basic knowledge could be turned to clinical account. The treatment service began in 1959, approximately five years after the physiological investigation started. The authors apologise for the "myriad shortcomings" of their report, which they admit is based on a motivationally biased sample with imperfect follow-up. They avoid dogmatic assertions, and freely admit to their unproved concepts of psychotherapy and their imprecise description of the complex nature of marital relationships, but in fact the very lack of psychotherapeutic jargon is an advantage.

Masters and Johnson were not psychiatrists and, without derogating psychiatric theories, they simply ignored them and applied what appeared to them to be the principles of common sense. Their investigation and report were conducted in the heyday of the innovations of behavior therapy but, although much of their therapeutic advice might be considered to be behavioural practice, they wisely avoided allying themselves with that or with any other psychotherapeutic school.

The elements of therapy are examination and discussion, education, decrease of anxiety, and "permission" to become sexually aroused. A principle of the Foundation's approach is that "there is no such thing as an uninvolved partner" and the marital unit, not the husband or wife, is the focus of therapeutic attention. Despite this principle, the report does refer to some single applicants and also to the provision of surrogate partners, but this is not further referred to and it is not stated whether they are included in the outcome statistics.

The professional qualifications of the co-therapists are not defined and neither counselling skills nor medical training are stipulated, although it is suggested that, ideally, one member of each team should have a background in social sciences and the other in biological sciences. Their personal qualifications, however, are defined: they must be able to convey an aura of comfort with the topic of sexual activity, dispense factual knowledge when appropriate, and create an atmosphere free of prejudice toward the sexual ideas, values, and practices discussed by the individual when seen alone and the marital unit when seen together.

On their arrival at the Foundation, the husband and wife (they are allowed separate identities, at least in the first two days) are introduced to their therapists, given an outline of the program, and informed of the local restaurants and places of entertainment — a nice touch which clarifies that they are to be exposed to an experience in communication and not to nonstop sexual training exercises. Introductions over and baggage unpacked, the husband and wife are seen separately for the first two days, the husband by the male and the wife by the female cotherapist. Before separating to these individual encounters, the couple are informed that they should not attempt sexual intercourse before instruction is given by the therapists.

An essential principle of the Masters and Johnson approach is that separate history-taking precedes mutual discussion. The wisdom of this procedure cannot be denied, for, although the authors and those who follow them insist that it is the marital unit which is the subject of treatment, therapy cannot commence in ignorance of the individual attitudes and problems of the man and woman who compose the unit. Although the authors advocate tape recording of the individual discussions, they also inform the person that nothing that he or she reveals about himself or herself will be discussed in subsequent joint sessions except with full permission. However, those who seek to follow the format of the Foundation approach may be forgiven for supposing that the procedure of tape recording may itself be a formidable barrier to the frank revelation of information.

The individual history-taking outline covers the sexual dysfunction of each partner, it being recognized that dysfunction frequently occurs in both the husband and the wife. They are asked how they have coped with the problem so far. Aspects of the marital relationship are discussed, followed by enquiry into the individual's development of general and sexual attitudes from childhood to the present time. Time and opportunity are allowed for the person to discuss attitudes to self and to partner, and also to reveal homosexual and other fantasies and practices. What is lacking from the proposed format of acquisition of information is any discussion of psychiatric disorder, either past or present, and this is a potential weakness of the model of enquiry. The authors are keen to deny that sexual dysfunction is necessarily based on psychopathology, and in this they are certainly correct, although there is a danger in missing those instances when it is a manifestation of psychiatric disorder. The possible basis of sexual dysfunction in somatic pathology is not overlooked, however, and a scheme for physical examination and laboratory investigation is included. Moreover, a later chapter titled "Dyspareunia" lists some of the somatic diseases that may cause or complicate sexual dysfunction and which it would be a gross error to ignore.

After the two-day period of individual discussion the co-therapists sometimes reach a conclusion that therapy is not a viable procedure, although the grounds on which a decision may be reached are not stated. For instance, the authors do not give their opinion of the likelihood of success of a heterosexual relationship when one or both partners are homosexual. They do however advise a tactful and face-saving formula for not proceeding in the following words: "If an adequately stable marriage is not defined by authority, termination of therapy is indicated. Every effort should be made to give an unrevealing, reasonable explanation for termination that would attempt to protect the marriage at current levels of psychosexual functioning." The report ends, as should all accounts of therapeutic endeavor, with an account of treatment failures; considering the profundity of the disaffection in some of the relationships in couples who *were* accepted for treatment, one can only speculate on the nature of the explanations which Foundation personnel devised for advising marital units not to continue in the quest for therapy.

The therapeutic instructions are based on the practice, between sessions with the co-therapist, of "sensate focus." This is the instruction to engage in mutual erotic arousal without attempting sexual intercourse. The Foundation philosophy is that anxiety about sexual intercourse—"performance anxiety"—is the basic cause of most sexual dysfunction and that therapy aims to overcome the severe inhibitions and fears that lead to this anxiety.

Terminology of the specific sexual dysfunctions follows the phases of the sexual response described in *Human Sexual Response*: arousal, vaso-congestive phase, orgasmic phase, and resolution. Since the major role of the co-therapists is the restructuring of personal attitudes toward sexual dysfunction, it comes as a surprise that the authors should use the derogatory phrase "sexual inadequacy" as a collective term. It is also surprising that they incorporate the word "incompetence" into one form of ejaculatory dysfunction and that they retain the pejorative word "impotence" instead of introducing the more exact term "erectile dysfunction." Their categorization of the specific forms of sexual dysfunction is primary and secondary impotence, premature ejaculation, ejaculatory incompetence (absence of intravaginal ejaculation) vaginismus, and primary and situational orgasmic dysfunction (the latter two terms referring to the female).

They considered the outcome statistics in terms of immediate outcome of the two-week course and a five-year follow-up assessment, usually undertaken at the home of the marital unit but sometimes by telephone. Considering that people came from all over North America, including Canada, for treatment at the Foundation, the tenacity of such a follow-up enterprise (carried out by the co-therapists themselves) is amazing. It is, however, an unavoidable criticism of the project that independent assessors were not employed, especially since the authors introduce their discussion: "For who is qualified to define with confidence the clinical success of any psychotherapeutic venture? The therapists?—inevitably prejudiced positively." The report also separated the outcome in young men and women from that in men and women in the age group above 50 years. First the initial outcome: this varied between no failures in 29 cases of vaginismus through to a 28 percent failure rate in 245 cases of primary and secondary impotence combined. Results in premature ejaculation were almost as good as in vaginismus: only four failures in 186 cases. Numbers in the older age groups were too small for confident statement of outcome, but nonetheless 75 percent of males and 60 percent of females overcame their dysfunction. The long-term follow-up outcomes were conducted only on those who had a successful immediate outcome. Overall, they found few reversals to the dysfunctional state.

Masters and Johnson were concerned at the overall high failure rate in impotence, but their appraisal of the clinical work of the Foundation led them to conclude that therapeutic intervention in sexual dysfunction was a rewarding endeavour. Few who have attempted to follow them have the facilities of a residential course, but there is little doubt that the straightforward guidelines provided by Masters and Johnson have inspired many others to reduce the distress which they termed "the crippling societal problem of human sexual inadequacy."

Selections from
Human Sexual Inadequacy
by William H. Masters and
Virginia E. Johnson

CONJOINT MARITAL-UNIT THERAPY

A basic premise of therapeutic approach originally introduced, and fully supported over the years by laboratory evidence, is the concept that there is no such thing as an uninvolved partner in any marriage in which there is some form of sexual inadequacy.

FEARS OF PERFORMANCE

Regardless of the particular form of sexual inadequacy with which both members of the marital unit are contending, fears of sexual performance are of major concern to both partners in the marital bed.

One of the most effective ways to avoid emphasizing the patient's fears of performance during any phase of the therapy program is to avoid all specific suggestion of goal-oriented sexual performance to the marital unit. Regardless of the length or the intensity of the psychotherapeutic procedures, at some point the therapist usually turns to his or her patient and suggests that the individual should be about ready for a successful attempt at sexual functioning. Immediately the fears of performance flood the psyche of the individual placed so specifically on the spot to achieve success by this authoritative suggestion. Rarely is this suggestion taken as an indication of potential readiness for sexual function, as intended, but usually is interpreted as a specific direction for sexual activity. If there is a professional suggestion that "tonight's the night," the individual feels that he has been told by constituted authority that he must go all the way from A to Z, from onset of sexual stimulation to successful completion. In many instances, regardless of the duration or effectiveness of the psychotherapeutic program, the fears of performance created by this authoritative suggestion for end-point achievement are of such magnitude that sensate input is blocked firmly, and there will be no effective sexual performance regardless of the degree of motivation. Removal of such goal-oriented concept, in any form or application, is necessary to secure effective return of sexual function. This can be achieved by moving the interacting partners, not the dysfunctional individual, on a step-by-step basis to mutually desirable sexual involvement.

. . . However, it must be reemphasized that the complaint of sexual dysfunction does not necessarily represent underlying psychopathology. It is possible to define those cases where sex-related inadequacy merely reflects too little sexual knowledge and/or unrealistic expectations in regard to sexual function. In these situations, sexual dysfunction consistently reflects the sexual partners' inability to communicate with one another. It frequently demonstrates inability of either or both marital partners to express their sexual identity without embarrassment, frustration, or fear of rejection. Most of them have never been able to share knowledge of those things that are sexually desired and those that distract from sexual responsivity.

In such situations, sexual dysfunction may not be the symptom but the "disease" itself.

THE HISTORY-TAKER

In taking a sexual history the interrogator should (1) convey an aura of comfort with the subject (and respond without embarrassment to unfamiliar material), (2) reflect factual knowledge when it is appropriate, and (3) create an atmosphere free of discernible prejudice toward the sexual values, ideas, or practices discussed by the patient. The fact that these requirements rarely are achieved with real consistency by professionals in the field must be acknowledged as a major factor in the clinical failure of various techniques of psychotherapy directed toward reversal of sexual dysfunction.

[B]y way of specific physical direction, the marital unit is requested to refrain from overt sexual activity until otherwise directed. This assumption of authoritative control over the marital unit's sexual functioning is established during the intake interview so that subsequent therapeutic direction can take into consideration individual need for sexual release.

By holding up the mirror of professional objectivity to reflect marital-unit sexual attitudes and practices, and by recalling constantly that the marital *relationship* is the focus of therapy, information necessary for marital-partner comprehension of the sexually dysfunctional status can be exchanged rapidly and with security.

27

Henri E. Ellenberger:
The Discovery of the Unconscious: The History and Evolution of Dynamic Psychiatry

Reviewed by D. Maediarmid

For nearly twenty years this 932-page gold mine of information about early psychotherapy (up to about ten years after Freud's death) has been available and has continued to sell steadily, now in paperback. I have only ever met one person who has read it all through.

Personally, I owe it a great deal. In the early 1970s it gave me, as a junior psychiatrist and trainee Jungian analyst, a truly liberating synoptic overview of psychodynamic psychiatry and psychotherapy, transcending the warring schools. "It lets you see where everything fits in," a friend put it when I rang round recently conducting a straw poll of opinions on the book. Hers was a common reaction. I have used it as a sourcebook and model for teaching trainee psychiatrists the historical bases of psychodynamics, and find that it does seem to make it much easier for trainees to understand both their own experiences in practice and the more sophisticated developments of theory. It has been helpful, for example, to follow Ellenberger's hint that psychotherapy was largely taught to doctors by patients, so our study of certain key and influential patients—like de Puysegur's Anton Race, Breuer's Anna O, Freud's Dora, or Jung's Helene Preiswerk—has been very illuminating, especially where modern understanding shows us how the doctor got the lesson a bit wrong. The book was once under consideration as a set book for the training of the Society of Analytical Psychology in London, but rejected as too long.

The early part of the book, dealing with primitive psychotherapy, Mesmer and his followers, the French hypnotists, and the phenomena of hysteria as observed in the late nineteenth century at the Salpetriere and elsewhere, is unexpectedly rich in useful clinical record. In fact, as one learns the history of psychotherapy one is struck by the repeated loss and later rediscovery of useful observations, due to the rapid changes of fashion in therapy. All those obscure doctors and practitioners one had never heard of—what interesting things they observed, and what good ideas they had about them, and how revealing when it is all put together! And going farther back, our kinship as psychotherapists with our medicine man and shaman colleagues among the primitive peoples, demonstrated by Ellenberger—are we to be uneasy or pleased about it? Ellenberger lists ten separate varieties of primitive healing, and it may be that we are selling our patients short in that not all of them are yet included in modern psychotherapy.

Like some other successful and useful books, the readers have valued it differently from the author. Ellenberger considered the crown and keystone of the whole book to be his tenth chapter, in which he summarizes the development of dynamic psychiatry in its relation to general psychiatry and the cultural and political background. No one I spoke to remembered that chapter best, and some had hardly read it. I had not read it. I did begin to read it when I started this reconsideration of the book, and found it fascinating. Ellenberger was specially equipped to write such a piece of history: born in South Africa, educated in German-speaking Switzerland, France, and various English-speaking countries, he studied medicine in France and Switzerland, taught at the Menninger School of Psychiatry in Kansas and at McGill University in Montreal, and at the time of writing was a professor of criminology in Montreal. To read a sketch of American-European history, with psychiatry and psychotherapy included, by such a man is truly educative and mind-expanding, but to an overworked practitioner and teacher like me with family responsibilities, too, it began to feel like what Henry James called "a princely expenditure of time." Guilt supervened and made me start skipping. I shall have to save the rest of it for a holiday.

I am told that it is in reaction against this almost ornamental effect of some of the historical context as presented by Ellenberger that the forthcoming *Yale Handbook of the History of Psychiatry* is differently conceived, by those who prefer to find actual causal links between political and social factors and the kind of psychiatry produced by a particular society.

Ellenberger did try to show how relations between psychiatrists and patients changed with changing social forms, and how, for example, the different treatment of Jews in the part of Europe Freud's family came from, and the part Adler's family came from, probably contributed to differences in their theories, and other links, too, between history and the development of psychotherapy. However, perhaps a different approach, a more neo-Marxist one for example, might be even more revealing.

But one central concern of the tenth chapter I did not skip, as it is of very practical significance for psychiatry. The chapter recapitulates and concentrates on a theme that runs through much of the book: How can the existence of mutually incompatible schools of thought within the discipline of dynamic psychiatry and psychotherapy be reconciled with the unity of science? The thrust of the book is toward an integrative resolution of this problem, which Ellenberger promotes in a number of ways.

For example, he gives a very full and sympathetic account of each of the four great systems: Janet's psychological analysis, Freud's psychoanalysis, Adler's individual psychology, and Jung's analytical psychology. Janet's writings are hardly available in this country, and Ellenberger's full account of the man and his work is a great service to us. It is a revelation how good a psychiatrist Janet was, and how much he had already found that was soon to be represented by Freud in different terminology. It is another revelation how good Adler was, and Ellenberger shows how often and in how many directions Adler's observations and ideas were quietly purloined without acknowledgment.

The effect is to present us with four alternative approaches, with more overlap between them than some of their own propaganda would suggest. Each has serious claims to psychiatric usefulness. Ellenberger has sought explanations for the differences between them. One is that each of the "big four" may have been taught different things by patients because each saw a different kind of patient. He quotes an earlier writer who pointed out that Adler's patients were less privileged and busy fighting for survival, while Freud's were better off and had leisure for sexual entanglement (even though they liked to remain unconscious of half of it). Ellenberger adds that Jung's early patients, for his first nine years as a psychiatrist, were severely ill schizophrenics. Again, each developed a theory arising out of his own personal experience: Jung and Adler did not have Oedipus complexes because their families of origin were so different from Freud's. Adler's childhood was characterised by competition with three brothers, and his earliest memory of sitting with his legs bandaged for rickets looking at his strong, ebullient older brother rings as relevant to his theories as Freud's early memory of his mother's naked body in the night train does to his. This agrees with Jung's observation that every original psychological theory is really autobiographical, a confession on the part of its inventor. Whoever may or may not have an Oedipus complex, Freud certainly had one, and whoever may or may not have an inferiority complex, Adler certainly had one. Generalizations are always true of the person who makes them.

But it is still a problem: Why should any particular system of psychology be supported with a loyal intensity surpassing the usual emotional investment in scientific debate? Janet is the honorable exception here—he is the one who assumed the unity of science and founded no school (and look what happened to him, one might cynically reflect). Ellenberger's answer to this question is his observation of what he calls the "creative illness"—another phenomenon to be found in primitive as in advanced societies. In a creative illness an intense preoccupation with a certain line of thought or experience, accompanied by somatic and psychological symptoms, passes through crisis to a permanent transformation of the personality, and the conviction that one has discovered a great and universal truth. Ellenberger cites as examples Mesmer, Fechner, Nietzsche, Freud (in his self-analysis), and Jung (in his self-induced controlled psychosis of 1913). He describes Janet as having something very like a creative illness at the age of 15, but somehow Janet did not emerge with an ideology to promote. Adler did not have one. So Freud and Jung were the two prophets. Such prophets pass on their vision, Ellenberger shows, by encouraging followers to have a similar creative illness to their own, and there spring up traditions, but each tradition has a certain narrowness: all trainee shamans have to have trances and travel in the land of spirits, but will never have the Nirvana experience of Tibetan monks, and vice versa. Hence arose the form of the training analysis, which meant in the early days that Freudian trainees had to have Freud's neurosis rather than their own, with the Oedipus complex in centre forefront, and trainees in Zurich had to have an encounter with the numinous archetypes, like Jung's.

It seems that Freud and Jung, then, stand out as the criminals who fragmented psychodynamic psychiatry. Ellenberger leans over backwards to be evenhanded, as he put it, "keeping a rigorously impartial outlook and abstaining from any kind of polemics." But one feels from the greater number of references that it is the embattled claim to exclusive truth on the part of Freud and his followers that is the harder nut to crack. Even though Ellenberger is careful to say that Jung, too, was left with an irrational certainty by *his* creative illness, I would have expected that some Freudians might have felt the book to be an attack on them. Yet although the book was published in six languages, and evoked 200 reviews in twelve languages, varying in length from one line to forty-five pages (none at all in the *British Journal of Psychiatry*), no hostility was expressed in any of them. The author's real impartiality must have been recognized.

Ellenberger painstakingly unravels falsifications of the early history of psychoanalysis by Ernest Jones and others, and seems to show that the trouble started when psychoanalysis became a *movement*, the *psychoanalytic movement*.

This was indeed a disturbing eventuality. What was psychiatry to make of a medical technique with its accompanying theory that mushroomed into a movement? Like the Boy Scout Movement, or the Student Christian Movement—almost like a religion? Freud was able to comment that Marxism had become uncannily like a religion, punishing criticism and doubt like heresy, but he did not seem to mind the same happening to psychoanalysis. Thank goodness the psychoanalytic movement, unlike Marxism or Christianity or Islam, had at least no political pretensions. But Freud did want to elevate the sexual theory into a dogma, and the movement did become a closely knit group of culturally motivated people, bound together by family libido aroused by the transference in the training analyses, and able to threaten dissidents (more so in America than here) with actual damage to their earning power as well as with the guilt and emotional isolation that would result from becoming a traitor to Freud and the artificially extended family. Hence loyalty to Freud outweighed scientific objectivity, and just as even cardinals have to swear assent to the fundamentals of the Christian creed, so a similar price was exacted from those who needed to continue to *belong* to this powerful, internally generous and supportive family with its exclusive possession of truth. As with all such groups, intellectual assent was the price of belonging, and for many it was a small price for a great reward. To wear a uniform is splendid, too, especially when it is somehow felt to express bold nonconformity (as with the uniform of the punks in London).

When psychiatry first had to deal with this problem, Freud was still like a god who had not yet been appropriately dismembered and eaten by his followers. Freud and the movement insisted that one swallow psychoanalysis whole. The British psychiatric establishment, led by Aubrey Lewis, simply spat it out, almost as though they had been taken in by Freud's presentation of psychoanalysis as a unitary, unanalysable package. American psychiatry behaved differently. Since Ellenberger's book we have learned more about psychotherapy, from many sources, and also more about the personal bases of the psychoanalytic movement from such books as the collection of Freud/Jung letters, Paul Roazen's *Freud and His Followers*, Susan Quinn's biography of Karen Horney, and Phyllis Grosskurth's of Melanie Klein. The nature of the psychoanalytic movement was such that only biography can make a sufficiently radical elucidation and critique of psychoanalysis. "Scientific" papers are not enough. Biography has made it more possible now for psychiatry to chew up and digest the phenomenon of psychoanalysis, instead of either swallowing whole or spitting out whole.

The first bites for psychiatry to take, I suggest, must separate the phenomenon of Freud into three digestible aspects: Freud as a doctor, as a genius, and as a person.

First as a doctor, Freud was a clinician of extraordinarily imaginative and penetrating powers of observation. He evolved techniques indispensable to psychiatry, and was a cornucopia of stimulating theories and hypotheses.

Second, as a genius, Freud helped on a certain slow and deep rhythm in the development of European culture. So did Jung. Both were expressing a need of the overcivilized Europeans to recover their vitality and freedom by rediscovering and reintegrating the instinctual, primitive, even animal roots of human life. This theme had been culturally present, linked with the Romantic movement from as far back as the eighteenth century, and expressed a need that is even now still insufficiently realized. Jung and Freud both expressed this need. The difference between them was that while Jung saw religion as an instinct also needing revitalization by the recovery of its primitive roots in modern man ("I am just an old bushman who finds his god in his dreams", he said), Freud saw religion as anti-instinct. Another, less important difference was that in contrast to Jung's now well-known sexual freedom in practice, Freud did not live out the integration of instinct that he preached—in his 80 years he only had ten years of normal heterosexual activity, as he married at 30 and gave up sex at 40. After his marriage failed he turned his needs and affections to sister-in-law and daughter. And compared with the freedom of attitude we now enjoy—and how much of that do we not owe to him?—he was himself a sexually prudish man. Maybe sexual frustration added passion to the utterance of his message. That message was a reaction to a long-established European attitude, the centuries-old official line of Christendom that love at its best ought to be spiritual. Freud had to say that love is essentially sensual. "Love suffereth long," said St. Paul to the Corinthians, "Love . . . makes thing wet," said Freud to teenage Dora (who did not need to be told, but only coaxed to admit what she already knew).

Freud's message was a necessary complementary truth whose time had come, but typical of a prophet he saw it as an absolute truth. Psychiatry needs to take cognisance of cultural trends, especially those that make for a healthier society, but it does not need to be carried away by a secular religion. The trick is to separate the useful insights from the dogma.

Third, as a man Freud was like all the rest of us, more or less neurotic. His Oedipus complex was analyzed, but his power complex was not. He had the schizoid trait of fearing the influence of other minds, and was most comfortable associating with those who wore the same mental uniform as he, as long as the uniform was designed by himself and was the creation of his own original thinking. We all tend to misuse leaders by making them an excuse for not thinking for ourselves, for not facing reality on our own two feet ("Let us our lives, our souls, our debts, our careful wives, our children, and our sins, lay on the King!" as Shakespeare's Henry V said). Freud actually needed that dependent tendency in his followers, and those who had little of it were rejected. His idea of a group was men taking on the superego of a leader—a happy, democratic, ideological pluralism was as unimaginable to him as to the Archduke Ferdinand. Geniuses are dangerous; their neuroses are infectious, and just as a Spanish prince's lisp changed the pronunciation of Spanish forever, Freud's neurosis permeated the psychoanalytic movement, and understanding how it did can help psychiatry to disentangle the observations and theories of a great man from the distortions caused by his unresolved anxieties.

Freud developed psychotherapy and used it to promote a certain significant cultural shift; admittedly a noble cause doing good to humanity, but it was an illegitimate use of medical science. It would have been better if he could have said that he personally wanted a world in which sexuality is valued not despised, rather than claiming to have scientifically proved that his vision of sex and psychology and life was true. Then his movement perpetuated aspects of his own neurosis, including clinging too defensively to good ideas out of fear that they might be adulterated by the good ideas of others. To look at that from a parochial, British point of view, he made psychotherapy and dynamic psychiatry into something unacceptable to most British psychiatrists, and so kept British psychiatry back half a century. That is, one can see it so if one wants to interpret that particular interaction in such a way as to put all the blame on Freud, which is, however, not good systems theory apart from being unfair to Freud.

A radical analytical critique of the various psychotherapies is what psychiatry still needs, and such a critique must not shirk the problem of the personal factors, including the very tricky one of personal charisma. Only such a critique will make a satisfactory integration possible. Most psychotherapists I think are by now impressed with the uselessness of shallow eclecticism, and there is a strong impression—and even perhaps some evidence—that it is the dogmatically assertive theories that work. Ellenberger's book was and is a great preparatory basis for integrating psychotherapy into one virile tool.

His last thought in the book is a hope that the philosophers may provide us with new concepts which will make it possible to reconcile academic experimental psychology with the psychology of the unconscious. Now, in fact, that reconciliation has already begun, as some academic psychologists have begun to feel their way into the unconscious from a base within their own discipline. Will a friendly hand be held out from the dynamic side? Here the difficulty in keeping up with the enormous literature from all the psychologies is a real handicap. How often in controversy the adversaries seem to be firing their shells at where the enemy fleet was five years ago. Or twenty-five.

I am not so hopeful about the philosophers myself. I believe that the great task of the integration of the psychologies and psychotherapies has to be largely a group or communal one, as science cannot make falsifiable statements until it has a language to make them in, which can only gradually be forged by people writing and talking. This important work is being done unwittingly and gradually in the myriad dialogues and discussions that take place daily in the case conferences, seminars, ward rounds, journal clubs, and so on, of NHS psychiatry, where psychodynamic observations and ideas, and many others, are well chewed over by different disciplines in a clinical context. Those trainee psychiatrists whom I know well, those in Bloomsbury and South East Thames, have formidably effective intellectual teeth and digestions for such a task. (I keep thinking that it must be the best of the young doctors who are coming into psychiatry nowadays.) I always recommend Ellenberger's book to them when I get the chance. Talking about it to colleagues has convinced me that it is a book that has already had much more real influence than public recognition in Britain. I shall be very surprised if the *Yale Handbook* supersedes it.

I have been in touch with Professor Ellenberger, and he says that as an 83-year-old man afflicted with Parkinson's disease he feels about the book as if it were written in a former life. I find that poignantly moving, as the book itself seems to me still after twenty years to be so alive with future, and it still has so much to say to young psychiatrists. Every time I go back to it I seem to see again that dynamic psychiatry is still in its confused beginning, but with a promise of help for humanity which I dare not now say anything about in case I seem to have got infected with "prophetitis," too. But whatever the future of dynamic psychiatry may be, Ellenberger's *The Discovery of the Unconscious* must surely remain a classic in its literature.

Selections from
The Discovery of the
Unconscious
by Henri E. Ellenberger

THE FIRST DYNAMIC PSYCHIATRY (1775-1900)

The Main Features

Throughout the innumerable variations of the first dynamic psychiatry, several main characteristics have remained constant:

1. Hypnotism was adopted as the main approach, the via regia to the unconscious. Supplementary approaches were added during the latter part of the century (mediumnism, automatic writing and crystal gazing).

2. Particular attention was devoted to certain clinical pictures (sometimes called magnetic diseases): spontaneous somnambulism, lethargy, catalepsy, multiple personality, and, toward the end of the century, interest came to focus more and more on hysteria.

3. A new model of the human mind was evolved. It was based on the duality of conscious and unconscious psychism. Later, it was modified to the form of a cluster of subpersonalities underlying the conscious personality.

4. New theories concerning the pathogenesis of nervous illness, which were based at first on a concept of an unknown fluid, were soon replaced by the concept of mental energy. In the latter part of the nineteenth century the concepts of the autonomous activity of split fragments of personality and of the mythopoetic function of the unconscious arose.

5. Psychotherapy relied mostly upon the use of hypnotism and suggestion, with special consideration given to the rapport between patient and magnetizer. . . .

Toward the end of the nineteenth century, attempts were made to combine the then current sexual theory of hysteria with that of dual personality emanating from the first dynamic psychiatry. Binet declared in 1887, "I believe it satisfactorily established, in a general way, that two states of consciousness, not known to each other, can co-exist in the mind of an hysterical patient." In 1889, he proclaimed, "The problem that I seek to solve is, to understand how and why, in hysterical patients, a division of consciousness takes place." An American gynaecologist, A. F. A. King, attempted to give an answer (in 1891). The key to the problem, he said, is that there are two departments of physiological government in the individual, the "department of self-preservation" and the "department of reproduction." Under certain circumstances, civilized life may deprive a woman of satisfaction in the "department of reproduction." The hysterical process expresses the automatic functioning of that need, and, seeing that this process does not reach its goal, it is bound to repeat itself over and over again, for months and for years. . . .

Models of the Human Mind

The study and practice of magnetism and hypnotism had led to reflections about the constitution of the human mind. Two models evolved: First, a concept of the duality of the human mind (dipsychism) and, later, a notion of the human mind as a cluster of subpersonalities (polypsychism).

Dipsychism

The first magnetizers were immensely struck by the fact that, when they induced magnetic sleep in a person, a new life manifested itself of which the subject was unaware, and that a new and often more brilliant personality emerged with a continuous life of its own. The entire nineteenth century was preoccupied with the problem of the coexistence of these two minds and of their relationship to each other. Hence the concept of the "double-ego," or "dipsychism." . . .

Polypsychism

This word seems to have been coined by the magnetizer Durand (de Gros). He claimed that the human organism consisted of anatomical segments, each of which had a psychic ego of its own, and all of them subjected to a general ego, the Ego-in-Chief, which was our usual consciousness. In this legion each subego had a consciousness of its own, was able to perceive and to keep memories and to elaborate complex psychic operations. The sum total of these subegos constituted our unconscious life. Durand (de

Gros) went so far as to say that when undergoing surgery under anesthesia, certain of these subegos suffered atrociously, although the conscious ego remained totally ignorant of those sufferings. In hypnosis, the main ego was pushed aside and the hypnotizer gained a direct access to a number of the subegos. The theory of polypsychism was taken up and given a philosophical elaboration by Colsenet, who linked it with Leibnitz's concept of a hierarchy of monads.

Magnetizers and others gathered numerous psychological data in favor of this theory. As early as 1803, Reil connected the phenomenon of dissociated personalities with a similar occurrence that is manifested in a certain type of normal dreams:

> The actors appear, the roles are distributed; of these, the dreamer takes only one that he connects with his own personality. All the other actors are to him as foreign as strangers, although they and all their actions are the creation of the dreamer's own fantasy. One hears people speaking in foreign languages, admires the talent of a great orator, is astounded by the profound wisdom of a teacher who explains to us things of which we do not remember ever having heard. . . .

One cannot overemphasize the influence that these two models of the mind, dipsychism and polypsychism, exerted on the systems of the new dynamic psychiatry. Dipsychism in its closed variety was the model from which Janet drew his concept of the subconscious and Freud his first concept of the unconscious as being the sum total of repressed memories and tendencies. Jung's theory of the unconscious was soon of the open variety, in that the individual unconscious is open to the collective unconscious of the archetypes. Both Freud and Jung evolved from a dipsychical to a polypsychical model of the human personality. With Freud, this occurred when he replaced his former model of the conscious-unconscious with his later three-fold model of the ego-id-superego, whereas Jung evolved a still more complex system. . . .

In 1889, Janet briefly mentioned this topic in his Automatisme psychologique. He emphasised the role of electivity in the rapport and the fact that the subject had a kind of negative hallucination for everything that was not connected directly with the magnetizer (in modern language a "scotoma"). The same factor was also stressed by Moll in 1892. At the International Congress of Psychology in Munich in 1896, Janet brought forth a fully elaborated theory of the rapport and of somnambulic influence. He had analyzed in detail what had occurred in his patients' minds in the intervals between hypnotic sessions and found that in a first phase (of influence proper), a vast improvement apparently occurred. A hysterical patient was freed of most of his symptoms; he felt happier, more active, and more intelligent, and did not think much about his hypnotist. This was followed by a second phase, that of somnambulic passion in which the symptoms receded, and the patient felt an increased need to see the hypnotist and to be hypnotized. This urge often assumed the form of passion. Depending on the case, this could develop into ardent love, jealousy, superstitious fear, or profound respect, and was accompanied by the feeling of having been accepted or rejected. The subject sometimes saw the hypnotist in dreams or in hallucinations. Janet discovered the very important fact that posthypnotic suggestions would be obeyed mainly during the period of somnambulic influence and much less during the phase of somnambulic passion. He stressed the therapeutic implications of these observations.

Janet enlarged this paper and published it again one year later, in 1897. On the basis of experiments with thirty patients, he confirmed the fact that posthypnotic suggestions would be carried out as long as the somnambulic influence lasted. Furthermore, Janet analyzed the subject's feeling toward the hypnotist during somnambulic passion and found it to be a mixture, differing from one patient to another, or erotic passion, filial or maternal love, and other feelings in which there was always a certain kind of love. However the main factor was the patient's *besoin de direction*, the need to be directed. The therapeutic implications were twofold: First, the therapist had to take complete command of the patient's mind. Once this was achieved, he had to teach the patient to do without him, which could be accomplished by gradually widening the intervals between sessions. The patient had also to be made aware of his own feelings. . . .

What Marcel Proust indefatigably analyzed were the many manifestations of polypsychism, the multiple shades of personality within us. He considered the human ego as being composed of many little egos, distinct though side by side, and more or less closely connected. Our personality thus changes from moment to moment, depending on the circumstances, the place, the people we are with. Events touch certain parts of our personality and leave others out. In a well-known description, the narrator told how, after being informed of the death of a woman, Albertine, the news was being understood successively by various parts of the personality. The sum of our past egos is a generally closed realm, but certain past egos may suddenly reappear, bringing forth a revival of the past. It is then one of our past egos that is in the foreground, living for us. Among our many egos, there are also hereditary elements. Others (our social ego, for instance), are a creation of the thoughts and influence of other people upon us. This explains the continuous fluidity in the mind, which is due to these metamorphoses of personality. Marcel Proust's work is of particular interest because its subtle analyses were not influenced by Freud and the other representatives of the new dynamic psychiatry. His academic sources went no further than Ribot and Bergson. It would be quite feasible to extract from his work a treatise on the mind, which would give a plausible picture of what the first dynamic psychiatry would have become had it followed its natural course. . . .

The Decline of the First Dynamic Psychiatry

The history of the first dynamic psychiatry shows a paradox: for an entire century (1784 to 1882), new discoveries struggled for recognition, and, after they were at long last acknowledged by "official medicine" with Charcot and Bernheim, they enjoyed a brilliant phase of success of less than twenty years, to be followed by a swift decline. The problem of these ups and downs puzzled many minds. Janet suggested that there are trends, not only in the style of life, but also in medicine. After 1882 the medical world became infatuated with hypnotism; publications on it reached the hundreds until a point of saturation was reached and the trend abandoned. This may be true; but there must also have been factors inherent to hypnotism that caused this rapid decline.

A perusal of the literature on hypnotism of that time shows what those factors might have been. Numerous hypnotists who had at first been enthusiastic about hypnotism soon discovered important drawbacks. Not everybody was able to become a good hypnotist, nor was the best hypnotist able to hypnotize everyone. . . . The rejection of the first dynamic psychiatry was as irrational and sudden as had been the fashion that had caused its rise to fame in the 1880s. It occurred in spite of great resistance on the part of certain adherents of the first dynamic psychiatry who were discovering new and promising facts. There were, for instance, the new methods of hypnotic catharsis, with which Janet experimented from 1886 on, and Breuer and Freud in 1893 and 1895, of which we will speak in other parts of this book. . . . But it is of course easier to reject en bloc a teaching that has incorporated errors than to undertake the difficult task of selecting the grain from the chaff, and, as Janet had to conclude, "hypnotism is dead . . . until the day it will revive."

Conclusion

The first dynamic psychiatry constituted a well-constructed body of knowledge, which, in spite of inevitable fluctuations, had been much more of an organic unit than is usually assumed. Common opinion states that the first dynamic psychiatry disappeared around 1900 to be replaced by wholly new systems of dynamic psychiatry. But a careful scrutiny of facts reveals that there was no sudden revolution but, on the contrary, a gradual transition from the one to the others, and that the new dynamic psychiatries took over far more from the first than has been realized. The cultural influence of the first dynamic psychiatry has been extremely persistent and still pervades contemporary life to an unsuspected degree.

The new dynamic psychiatries, having incorporated much from the first one, also assimilated a great deal of knowledge from other sources. The new dynamic psychiatries can be understood only if one first makes a survey of the entire sociological and cultural background throughout the nineteenth century.

28

Irvin D. Yalom:
The Theory and Practice of
Group Psychotherapy

Reviewed by Eric Crouch

This book first appeared in 1970 and has gone into two further editions, one in 1975 and this one in 1985. Yalom is also the author of *Existential Psychotherapy* (1980), *In-Patient Group Psychotherapy* (1983), the co-author with Liberman of *Encounter Groups: First Facts* (1973) and with Elkin of *Every Day Gets a Little Closer: A Twice-Told Therapy* (1974) (which recounts the course of therapy from the patient's and the therapist's viewpoint). The present book is the central work of the set and seems to me the most substantial. It is also one of the most readable of his works because of its straightforward style and the liberal use of clinical examples.

The book's first appearance followed the burgeoning of interest in all types of group treatment in the 1960s, when it seemed to some, especially in southern California, that groups could achieve anything. When I trained in the 1970s, group therapy was definitely "in" and Yalom was the guru. During the 1980s there was a swing away from all that. Advances in biological psychiatry and the considerable improvements in the understanding of behavioral psychotherapies, arising from solid research effort, have diverted elsewhere the interest of young psychiatrists. Within the psychotherapy field itself there is perhaps also a strengthening of theoretical approaches other than Yalom's.

A virtue of Yalom's book is that it brings to the written page some of the infectious excitement of its age. At the same time, it is a scholarly work in which research is critically reviewed and its lessons incorporated into guidance about clinical practice. In this respect, Yalom is one of the very best writers in the psychotherapy field. He recognizes that we are apt to deceive ourselves about the effects of what we do and that systematic research may be the only valid way of avoiding this. He points to those areas that are yet little explored by research; but he is also a careful and thoughtful clinician whose teaching is based on the many hours he has spent in groups of his own and on the observations of the many other therapists he has supervised. This balance between detailed guidance from clinical experience and an analysis of the clinical lessons to be learned from the research literature is rare in psychotherapy writing which seems, on the whole, not to be informed by research results—in contrast to the literature about behavioral therapies.

Readers may be familiar, as I am, with the second edition of this book. For the third edition Yalom has incorporated both new knowledge (such as work on pretherapy preparation), changes in fashion (such as the relative decline in encounter groups), and clearer guidance about the running of specialized groups (such as groups of in-patients). He has done this without lengthening the work significantly and without losing important material.

The book begins by raising the question of how group therapy helps patients to change, and introduces the concept of the "therapeutic factors." Yalom bows to recent usage by dropping his earlier use of "curative factors." There are certainly indications that these factors may help group members, but the term "curative" claims too much. Yalom spends four chapters looking at the nature of each therapeutic factor and how it might operate in groups. He summarizes most of the relevant research, and provides a particularly good introduction to thinking about how group therapy might help its participants.

Yalom could outline the historical development of the concept of therapeutic factors more fully, however. Essentially, the concept comes from a sampling of clinicians' ideas about what is therapeutic in groups. Different authors have developed their own lists of factors, although these are usually based on that by Corsini and Rosenberg (1956). It is difficult to know whether these lists exhaustively describe the therapeutic elements in an economical way that contains no overlap. My impression is that Yalom himself irritates some therapists by not listing "working through transference(s)" although his later chapter dealing with transference and transparency clearly shows that he regards transference as a very important element of therapy. A historical perspective would do more to show why this is so and why transference elements of therapy are mostly subsumed under "interpersonal learning."

Yalom describes how therapeutic factors may lead to change, and discusses the relative importance of the different factors. He puts most emphasis on interpersonal learning and group cohesiveness. For Yalom the group is a social microcosm in which the patient can experience relationships with a variety of types of people (hence the value of heterogeneity discussed later) including an authority figure (the therapist), express feelings about these relationships, receive feedback that may reveal how his or her perceptions contain distortions from reality, and practice new ways of behaving and relating which can later be used in the real world. Thus, interpersonal learning contains embedded within it elements of transference resolution, the gaining of insight and even graded practice. Clearly the group needs to be a safe and comradely place for the individual to feel free to experiment in this way. In the cohesive group, the patient feels accepted warts and all, and the esteem of his or her fellow patients may be the basis for increasing self-esteem.

Yalom moves on to deal with the responsibilities and tasks of the therapist in conducting therapy groups. The therapist creates and maintains the group, builds the group culture and sets norms of behaviour. Yalom emphasizes the importance for the therapist of working in the here and now. This is a reflection of his major focus on interpersonal learning. Here, as elsewhere in the book, he gives many relevant clinical examples taken from his own practice. The therapist should use the patient's past experience as a tool for illuminating the present; the "archaeological exploration of the past" has no place in the group.

Yalom discusses the therapist's responsibility for removing obstacles to progress that may arise and he/she may do this by using group-process commentary. Novice therapists often feel bewildered about process interpretation—experiencing either a confusing welter of contradictory ideas or a complete blank. Yalom provides excellent guidance by emphasizing the function of interpretation in relation to patients' presenting difficulties.

He discusses the work of Bion and what he refers to as the Tavistock approach, where the emphasis is on group as a whole interpretations. He points to outcome research which suggests that group as a whole interpretations are weak factors in producing change in individuals and that their sole use leads to ineffectual group therapy.

Chapter 7, entitled "The Therapist: Transference and Transparency" contains some of the most valuable material in the book. Certainly the beginning therapist will find the discussion of transparency of immense practical value. Yalom observes that transference is a powerful aspect of the group's reality, that the therapist must recognize and utilize aspects of transference and that there must be resolution of the distorted attitudinal set toward the leader as part of the work of the group. He discusses these issues in detail, but he parts company from the orthodox group-analytic line (if such exists), and makes it clear that the analysis of transference is not the major task of the group. Here Yalom shows his debt to Sullivan and his interpersonal theories, a debt that he acknowledges earlier in the book. In these views Yalom is by no means alone and there are other writers, such as Whitaker and Liberman (whom Yalom cites), who have developed similar ideas, although expressed in different terms (a familiar bugbear of psychotherapy writing).

My own feeling here is that Yalom could easily go a little further and build a bridge between the psychoanalytically based psychotherapies and the newer cognitive-behavioral therapies that are emerging from the behavioral tradition. The interactional focus of his work and the emphasis on interpersonal learning betray many of the same concerns that are addressed in cognitive-behavioral therapies. There would be value in tracing the similarities between these therapies, which have such diverse derivations, as well as clarifying what is different.

Transparency, or the degree to which the therapist reveals himself, is held to be of great importance. To Yalom, the analytic "blank screen" is not a productive element of group therapy. It is an appropriate degree of transparency that promotes resolution of the transference. The patient can check his projections onto the therapist with the therapist's actual reactions. A wide-ranging discussion here brings in both research results and references to Eugene O'Neill and Henrik Ibsen in order to illustrate both the advantages and the drawbacks of transparency and to help define its limits.

The three following chapters deal with preparatory elements of running a group—selection of patients, group composition, preparation of patients for therapy, and the setting for group sessions. Selection for therapy is dependent on the aims of the particular group, and the research evidence relating to selection is scanty. Therefore Yalom pulls together the consensus of clinical opinion on the topic and draws on his own clinical experience. He reports some of his own work on dropouts from group therapy which throws light on reasons for excluding some patients from out-patient therapy groups, but there is little to learn from research about inclusion criteria. Intensive heterogeneous out-patient groups should exclude brain-damaged, paranoid, hypochondriacal, addicted, sociopathic and acutely psychotic patients, although there is evidence that specialized and more homogeneous groups may produce benefits for patients in some of these categories.

He introduces his chapter on group composition with a section on predicting how patients will behave in therapy. Various types of intake interview procedure have attempted to make this prediction and Yalom's conclusion is that the more the intake procedure mimics the group situation itself then the more accurate will be its predictions. From clinical observation there seems to be a good deal of advantage in heterogeneity in group composition, at least for intensive out-patient group therapy. That is, the patients should not all be too alike in terms of problem type and areas of psychological conflict, although the heterogeneity needs to be within a fairly narrow range so that scapegoating does not occur.

The chapter on creating the group gives advice on the physical setting of the group and its boundaries in terms of duration, frequency of meetings, and group size. A section new to this edition deals with the controversy over whether patients should have preparatory sessions for group therapy or whether the group should be a mysterious place with an enigmatic, opaque therapist where the patient will rapidly develop transference to the therapist and to other patients. Yalom is clearly in favor of preparation on the basis of a fair amount of research evidence that suggests it enhances the work of groups.

There is a section on the marathon group or time-extended therapy session, proposed as a way of focusing and enhancing the work done in regular sessions. As Yalom states, this is a fashion that has come and gone. Perhaps he will drop this section from the next edition, but he leaves it in here as a way of illustrating the passing fads that affect group therapy, and he introduces his own research which throws doubt on the effectiveness of marathon sessions.

Two chapters deal with the evolution of the group from the first meeting to termination, setting out some of the events and stages of development that are commonly seen in groups, together with common developmental problems such as subgrouping. There is a section on membership problems, dropping out, adding new members—and how to throw out an unsuitable member! Naturally enough, these chapters end with a section on termination.

Chapter 13 deals with particular types of patient liable to cause difficulties in out-patient therapy groups. Some of these are presented in diagnostic terms (e.g., the schizoid patient, the borderline patient) and others in behavioral terms (the silent patient, the self-righteous moralist). Clinical examples are given illustrating how these difficulties may be overcome in a manner which has a chance of leading to therapeutic gain.

Chapter 14 is where Yalom writes about a number of topics he cannot fit in anywhere else. However, these are all important issues which are discussed among trainee therapists: concurrent individual and group therapy, the value of co-therapy, the leaderless group, the use of dreams, videotape feedback, written summaries and structured exercises (e.g., "warm-up" procedures).

Chapters 15 and 16 deal with other types of group than the intensive out-patient therapy group and are in some ways condensed versions of two of his other books, *In-Patient Group Therapy* and *Encounter Groups: First Facts*. Group work has been a popular feature of acute in-patient units in recent years and is often applied without clear goals, nor is there research evidence of its value. Thus Yalom's thoughtful analysis is very helpful. Encounter groups, on the other hand, have almost passed into history, but elements of the movement have transferred themselves into other fields, such as religious organizations, skills training workshops and self-help groups.

Yalom rounds off the book with a chapter on the training of group therapists and a comprehensive chapter-by-chapter bibliography.

This book was born twenty years ago, years that have seen great advances in other psychological therapies and changes of fashion on the group therapy scene. Nevertheless, the uniqueness of the book remains in providing a comprehensive introduction to group psychotherapy that spans both clinical experience and research results. Both the trainee who wants an idea of the nature of group therapy and the colleague who needs an introductory manual to supplement supervision in running his or her first group should read the work right through; for the academic interested in group therapy research and for the experienced group therapist it should be readily available on the shelf to dip into.

Selections from
The Theory and Practice of
Group Psychotherapy
by Irvin D. Yalom

1. Transference *does* occur in therapy groups; indeed, it is omnipresent and radically influences the nature of the group discourse.

2. Without an appreciation of transference and its manifestations, the therapist will often not be able to understand the process of the group.

3. The therapist who ignores transference considerations may seriously misunderstand some transactions and confuse rather than guide the group members; but if you see *only* the transference aspects of your relationships with members, you fail to relate authentically to them.

4. There are patients whose therapy hinges on the resolution of transference distortion; there are others whose improvement will depend upon inter-personal learning stemming from work not with the therapist but with another member around such issues as competition, exploitation, or sexual and intimacy conflicts; and there are many patients who choose alternate therapeutic pathways in the group and derive their primary benefit from other therapeutic factors.

5. Attitudes toward the therapist are not all transference based: many are reality based, and others are irrational but flow from other sources of irrationality inherent in the dynamics of the group. (As Freud knew, not all group phenomena can be explained on the basis of individual psychology.)

6. By maintaining flexibility, you may make good therapeutic use of these irrational attitudes toward you, without at the same time neglecting your many other functions in the group.

The most common charge that members levy against the leader is of being too cold, too aloof, too inhuman. In part, this charge is based on reality. For reasons, both professional and personal, that I shall discuss shortly, many therapists do keep themselves hidden from the group. Also, their role of process commentator requires a certain distance from the group. But there is more to it. Although the members insist that they wish you to be more human, they have the simultaneous counterwish that you be more than human. Freud often made this observation and eventually, in *The Future of an Illusion*, based his explanation for religious belief on the human being's thirst for a superbeing. It seemed to Freud that the group integrity depended upon the existence of some superordinate figure who, as I have discussed, fosters the illusion of loving each member equally. Solid group bonds become chains of sand if the leader is lost. If the general perishes in battle, it is imperative that the news be kept secret lest panic ensue. So, too, for the leader of the church. Freud was fascinated by a 1903 novel, *When It Was Dark*, in which Christ's divinity was questioned and ultimately disproved. The work depicted the catastrophic effects on Western European civilization; previously stable social institutions deconstituted like parts of a model airplane whose glue has suddenly deteriorated.

And so there is great ambivalence about the members' directive to the leader to be more human. They claim that you tell them nothing of yourself, yet they rarely make explicit inquiry. They demand that you be more human yet excoriate you for wearing a copper bracelet, mooching a cigarette, or forgetting to tell the group that you have conversed with a member over the phone. They prefer not to believe you if you profess puzzlement or ignorance. The illness or infirmity of a therapist always arouses considerable discomfort among the members; somehow the therapist should be beyond biological limitation. The followers of a leader who abandons his or her role are in deep distress. When Shakespeare's Richard II laments his "hollow crown" and gives vent to his discouragement and need for friends, his court bids him to be silent.

A group of psychiatric residents I once led put the dilemma very clearly. They often discussed the "big people" out there in the world—their therapists, group leaders, supervisors, and the adult community of senior practicing psychiatrists. The closer these residents came to completion of their training, the more important and problematic did the "big people" become. I wondered, Was it possible that they, too, would soon become "big people"? Could it be that even I had my "big people"? There were two opposing sets of concerns about the "big people," and both were equally frightening: first, that the "big people" were real, that they possessed superior wisdom and knowledge and would dispense an honest but terrible justice to the young, presumptuous frauds who tried to join their ranks; or, secondly, that the "big people" themselves were frauds, that the members were all Dorothys facing Oz's wizard. The second possibility had more frightening implications than the first: it brought them face to face with their intrinsic loneliness and apartness. It was as if, for a brief time, life's illusions were stripped away, exposing the naked scaffolding of existence—a terrifying sight, one that we conceal from ourselves with the heaviest of curtains. The "big people" are one of our most effective curtains: as frightening as their judgment may be, it is far less terrible than that other alternative—that there are no "big people," and that one is finally and utterly alone.

The leader is thus seen unrealistically by members for many reasons: true transference or displacement of affect from some prior object is one source; conflicted attitudes toward authority—dependency, autonomy, rebellion, and so on—which become personified in the therapist, are another; and still another source is the tendency to imbue the therapist with superhuman features so as to use him or her as a shield against existential anxiety. One further source lies in the members' explicit or intuitive appreciation of the great power of the group therapist. Your presence and your impartiality are, as I have already discussed, essential for group survival and stability. You cannot be deposed; you have at your disposal enormous power; you can expel members, add new members, mobilize group pressure against anyone you wish.

In fact, the sources of intense, irrational feelings toward the therapist are so varied and so powerful that transference will occur, come what may. I do not believe that a therapist need be unduly concerned with the task of generating or facilitating the development of transference. You need not, for example, assume a pose of unflinching neutrality. Better that you spend your time attempting to turn the transference to therapeutic account. A clear illustration of transference occurred with a patient who often attacked me for aloofness, deviousness, and hiddenness. He accused me of manipulation—of pulling strings to guide each member's behavior, of not being clear and open, of never really coming out and telling the group exactly what I was trying to do in therapy. It is striking that this patient was a member of a group in which I had been writing very clear, very honest, very transparent group summaries and mailing them to the members before the next meeting. Never has any therapist, I believe, made a more earnest attempt to demystify the therapeutic process. Yet earlier in the very meeting where he attacked me, he informed the group that he had not read the summaries and in fact had a large number of them unopened lying on his desk.

As long as a group therapist assumes the responsibility of leadership, transference will occur. I have never seen a group without a deep, complex underpinning of transference. The problem is, thus, not *evocation* but, on the contrary, *resolution* of transference. The therapist who is to make therapeutic use of transference must help patients to recognize, to understand, and to change their distorted attitudinal set toward the leader.

Two major approaches facilitate transference resolution in the therapy group: consensual validation and increased therapist transparency. The therapist may encourage a patient to validate his or her impressions of the therapist against those of the other members. If many or all of the group members concur in the patient's view of and feelings toward the therapist, you may conclude either that the reaction to you stems from global group forces related to your role in the group, or that the reaction is not unrealistic at all: the patients are perceiving you accurately. If, on the other hand, one member alone of all the group members possesses a particular view of you, then this member may be helped to examine the possibility that he or she sees the therapist, and perhaps other people, too, through an internal distorting prism.

Thus, one method of facilitating reality testing is to encourage patients to check out their perceptions with one another. The other major method calls for the use of the therapist's person; you allow the patient to confirm or disconfirm impressions of you by gradually revealing more of yourself. You press the patient to deal with you as a real person in the here-and-now. You respond to the patient, you share your feelings, you acknowledge or refute motives or feelings attributed to you, you look at your own blind spots, you demonstrate respect for the feedback the members offer you. In the face of the mounting data the patient has about you, it becomes increasingly difficult to maintain fictitious beliefs about you.

The group therapist undergoes a gradual metamorphosis during the life of the group. In the beginning you busy yourself with the many functions necessary in the creation of the group, with the development of a social system in which the many therapeutic factors may operate, and with the activation and illumination of the here-and-now. Gradually you begin to interact with each of the members; as the group progresses, you relate more personally to them, and the early stereotypes the patients cast onto you become more difficult to maintain. This process between you and each of the members is not qualitatively different from the interpersonal learning that ensues as a result of each member's relationship with other members. After all, you have no monopoly on authority, dominance, sagacity, or aloofness, and many of the members work out their conflicts in these areas not with the therapist (or not *only* with the therapist) but with other members who have these attributes.

This change in the degree of transparency of the therapist is by no means limited to group therapy; someone once said that when the analyst tells the analysand a joke, you can be sure the analysis is approaching its end. However, the pace, the degree, the nature of the therapist transparency and the relationship between this activity of the therapist and the therapist's other tasks in the group is problematic and deserves careful consideration. More than any other single characteristic, the nature and the degree of therapist self-disclosure differentiates the various schools of group therapy.

29

David J. Rothman:
The Discovery of the Asylum

Reviewed by J. L. T. Birley

Professor Rothman's book made a profound impression on me when I first read it. More to the point, perhaps, was the impression it made on his peers. The American Historical Association awarded it the Albert J. Beveridge prize for the best English language book published in American history. It is a beautifully written account of an exciting and ultimately tragic episode in American history: the attempt to use the institution as a means of reforming bad habits and curing mental illness.

Some may think that this is already a well told tale: the high hopes of "moral treatment" followed by the disappointment and pessimism at the end of the century. Professor Rothman's account covers a much wider field, encompassing the care not only of the mentally ill but of the poor, the orphan and the criminal.

In postcolonial America a wind of change blew from the same quarter over all these groups. It came from Europe and the libertarian ideas of the Enlightenment. Its message was that punishment often brutalized; instead the individual should be reformed. In colonial times, gaols were small, casual places where deviants of all sorts were kept for a short time to await a rough and at times brutal justice. Before independence there had been pressure for more humane legislation, but the Crown had disallowed it. In the postcolonial era, the nation's need to assert its independence added impetus to the movement for reform.

Reform of deviance and the cure of insanity could not really begin until their causes had been ascertained. This, however, was not a difficult task. The roots of the problem lay in faulty upbringing, bad company, and the structure and demands of society. These conclusions were based, not on guesswork, but on the findings of careful inquiries. For instance, Prisoner No. 315:

> A. N., born in Massachusetts; father was killed at Quebec when he was very young; family soon after scattered, and he was bound out to a farmer, with whom he lived till of age; was a wild, rude boy, and early addicted to some bad habits, drinking, swearing, etc.

The fact that he had committed forgery at the age of 55, after an apparently respectable life, did not alter the conclusion that the origins of his deviancy were laid down many years previously. Or, take another example:

> Of the 156 inmates recently admitted to Pennsylvania's Eastern State Penitentiary, 14 had been orphaned by the age of 12, 36 were missing one parent or another soon thereafter, 143 had received no religious instructions, and 144 never attended Sabbath school. "Such statistics," affirmed William Channing, one of the founders of the New York Prison Association, "tell at a glance that early neglect was certainly in part, probably in great part, the cause of after crime."

The same notions informed the cure of the insane, but with an extra emphasis on the temptations and strains afforded by a society whose aspirations were becoming limitless. Thus, Isaac Ray contended that youngsters contemplated life "not as a field of discipline and improvement, but a scene of inexhaustible opportunities for fulfilling hope and gratifying desire." Under this training, patience and perseverance "become distasteful to the mind which can breathe only an atmosphere of excitement. . . . It reels under the first stroke of disappointment, turns upon itself . . . and thus it is that many a man becomes insane."

To find the origins of poverty in a country with limitless opportunities was a harder task. Surveys, however, indicated that, to some degree, and particularly in the case of the chronic poor, that the problem lay with the individual's own bad habits. In New York, in 1821, the Society for the Prevention of Pauperism announced that "the paupers of this city are, for the most part, depraved and vicious, and require support because they are so." Drinking was a particularly common vice. Significantly, taverns were much commoner in the precincts of the lower classes. But it was totally wrong and unfair to blame only the poor. Society set all sorts of traps and temptations. Did it not license the taverns and permit the sale of liquor? The poor should be relieved, but also protected and removed from society to be reformed.

The same arguments applied, a fortiori, to children: orphans, runaways, those with poor or incompetent parents, and delinquents. What could be more important than to remove these unfortunates "from those baleful influences which inevitably tend to make them pests to society and ultimately the tenants of our prisons," and to provide them with "a healthy moral constitution, capable of resisting the assaults of temptations, and strong enough to keep the line of rectitude through the stormy and disturbing influences by which we are assailed"?

Professor Rothman emphasises that this general move towards reform and asylum was by no means a response to an overwhelming public clamor to remove problematic people. It arose from philanthropic and humanitarian concern. The regimes applied in the asylums were based on the latest theories, some of which were keenly debated. For instance, the total isolation of each inmate practiced at Pennsylvania Penitentiary, thus avoiding the contagion of vice, competed with the more partial separation advocated at Auburn, New York. Both were places of pilgrimage for the new penologists both at home and from Europe, and both had their passionate advocates and denigrators. The regimes of the children's asylums followed closely the prescriptions of current manuals in child care.

For the insane, the first stage, too, was removal, and visitors were to be strictly limited and preferably banned for, said Isaac Ray, "the patient might otherwise be as well at large as in the hospital for any good the latter may do him by way of seclusion." Within the asylum the emphasis was on orderliness and a predictable routine, regular occupation and nonrestraint.

The gradual change in the character of the asylums during the ensuing thirty years is graphically described, with illustrations of their increasing size. The Boston Almshouse and Blackwells Island Penitentiary in New York, built in 1849, were already vast, brooding buildings. Of greater concern to us, perhaps, is the gradual change in the claims and attitudes of the staff and the public toward these institutions. By the 1860s "the asylums were admitting great numbers of chronic patients, the poor houses were taking in the aged and decrepit, penitentiary cells filled up with hardened criminals and even the reformatories received teenagers surprisingly advanced in a life of crime." To be sure, the staff protested both at their new clientele, and at their inadequate funding, but the shift from reform to custody was not accompanied by any great demand that the system be dismantled. "The promise of reform had built up the asylums, the functionalism of custody perpetuated them." In the case of the insane asylum, the change to chronic containment was soon accepted by staff and public alike. Indeed, it was recommended. For, in addition to the dangerous effects of the family on the patient, Isaac Ray warned of the reverse risks "that the poor sufferer cannot receive the ministry of near relatives without endangering the mental integrity of those who offer them."

It is easy at this distance to criticise the enthusiasm and naivete of the reformers, and what seems like their sanctimonious hypocrisy and paternalism. But they were men of their time, and our own current views may appear equally naive to our descendants in 100 years. To avoid repeating history we have to try to learn its lessons. Large institutions are comparatively recent arrivals on the psychiatric scene. Compared to other examples of the architectural expression of a faith—cathedrals, for instance—they are very recent indeed. Their monumental size gives a misleading impression of permanence. Total solutions are always dangerous and often disastrous. "One cannot help but conclude this history," writes Professor Rothman, "with an acute nervousness about all social panaceas. Proposals that promise the most grandiose consequences often legitimate the most unsatisfactory developments."

Instead, surely, we require imaginative and varied contributions to what Karl Popper calls piecemeal social engineering. Reform is less exciting but more productive than revolution. Certainly there are moments when one wonders whether the "wheel of progress" is not even rotating on one spot but merely being rediscovered. 111 Denmark Hill, the Hospital Hostel at the Maudsley, and previously a private house, bears an uncanny resemblance to the building illustrated at the very beginning of Rothman's book—the New York Almshouse of 1735. "Built in the style of an ordinary residence, the almshouse followed, internally and externally, the organisation of the family." For a history of the 1980s it provides a promising first illustration. But what of the subsequent pictures? *Absit omen*.

Selections from
The Discovery of the Asylum
by David J. Rothman

THE INVENTION OF THE PENITENTIARY

Americans' understanding of the causes of deviant behavior led directly to the invention of the penitentiary as a solution. It was an ambitious program. Its design—external appearance, internal arrangement, and daily routine—attempted to eliminate the specific influences that were breeding crime in the community, and to demonstrate the fundamentals of proper social organization. Rather than stand as places of last resort, hidden and ignored, these institutions became the pride of the nation. A structure designed to join practicality to humanitarianism, reform the criminal, stabilize American society, and demonstrate how to improve the condition of mankind, deserved full publicity and close study.

In the 1820s New York and Pennsylvania began a movement that soon spread through the Northeast, and then over the next decades to many midwestern states. New York devised the Auburn or congregate system of penitentiary organization, establishing it first at the Auburn state prison between 1819 and 1823, and then in 1825 at the Ossining institution, familiarly known as Sing-Sing. Pennsylvania officials worked out the details of a rival plan, the separate system, applying it to the penitentiary at Pittsburgh in 1826 and to the prison at Philadelphia in 1829. In short order, the Connecticut legislature stopped using an abandoned copper mine to incarcerate offenders, and in 1827 built a new structure at Wethersfield. Massachusetts reorganized its state prison at Charlestown in 1829; that same year, Maryland erected a penitentiary, and one year later New Jersey followed suit. Ohio and Michigan built penitentiaries in the 1830's, and so did Indiana, Wisconsin, and Minnesota in the 1840's.

The results of all this activity deeply concerned Americans, so that annual reports to state legislators and popular journals as well contained long and detailed discussions and arguments on the merits of various enterprises. Europeans came to evaluate the experiment and the major powers appointed official investigators. France in 1831 dispatched the most famous pair, Alexis de Tocqueville and Gustave Auguste de Beaumont; in 1832 England sent William Crawford, and in 1834, Prussia dispatched Nicholas Julius. Tourists with no special interest in penology made sure to visit the institutions. Harriet Martineau, Frederick Marryat, and Basil Hall would no more have omitted this stop from their itinerary than they would have a southern plantation, a Lowell textile mill, or a frontier town. By the 1830's, the American penitentiary had become world famous.

The focus of attention was not simply on whether the penitentiary accomplished its goals, but on the merits of the two competing modes of organization. The debate raged with an incredible intensity during these decades, and the fact that most prisons in the United States were modeled after the Auburn system did not diminish it. Even more startling, neither did the basic similarity of the two programs. In retrospect they seem very much alike, but nevertheless an extraordinary amount of intellectual and emotional energy entered the argument. The fervor brought many of the leading reformers of the period to frequently bitter recriminations, and often set one benevolent society against another. Periodicals regularly polled foreign visitors for their judgment or printed a vigorous defense by one school and then a critical rejoinder by the other. The roster of participants in this contest was impressive, pitting Samuel Gridley Howe (a Pennsylvania advocate) against Matthew Carey (for Auburn), Dorothea Dix against Louis Dwight, Francis Lieber against Francis Wayland. Every report from the New York and Pennsylvania penitentiaries was an explicit apology for its procedures and an implicit attack on its opponents. And as soon as a state committed its prison organization to one side or the other then it too entered the controversy with the zeal of a recent convert.

The content of the debate between the Auburn and Pennsylvania camps points to the significance of the ideas on the causes of crime to the creation of the penitentiary, and the zeal reflects the expectations held about the innovation. To understand why men became so passionate about internal questions of design is to begin to comprehend the origins and popularity of institutionalization in this era. Under the Auburn scheme, prisoners were to sleep alone in a cell at night and labor together in a workshop during the day for the course of their fixed sentences in the penitentiary. They were forbidden to converse with fellow inmates or even exchange glances while on the job, at meals, or in their cells. The Pennsylvania system, on the other hand, isolated each prisoner for the entire period of his confinement. According to its blueprint, convicts were to eat, work, and sleep in individual cells, seeing and talking with only a handful of responsible guards and selected visitors. They were to leave the institution as ignorant of the identity of other convicts as on the day they entered. As both schemes placed maximum emphasis on preventing the prisoners from communicating with anyone else the point of dispute was whether convicts should work silently in large groups or individually within solitary cells.

To both the advocates of the congregate and the separate systems, the promise of institutionalization depended upon the isolation of the prisoner and the establishment of a disciplined routine. Convinced that deviancy was primarily the result of the corruptions pervading the community, and that organizations like the family and the church were not counterbalancing them they believed that a setting which removed the offender from all temptations and substituted a steady and regular regimen would reform him. Since the convict was not inherently depraved, but the victim of an upbringing that had failed to provide protection against the vices at loose in society, a well-ordered institution could successfully reeducate and rehabilitate him. The penitentiary, free of corruptions and dedicated to the proper training of the inmate, would inculcate the discipline that negligent parents, evil companions, taverns, houses of prostitution, theaters, and gambling halls had destroyed. Just as the criminal's environment had led him into crime, the institutional environment would lead him out of it.

The duty of the penitentiary was to separate the offender from *all* contact with corruption, both within and without its walls. There was obviously no sense to removing a criminal from the depravity of his surroundings only to have him mix freely with other convicts within the prison. Or, as Samuel Gridley Howe put it when composing a prisoner prayer: "In the name of justice, do not surround me with bad associates and with evil influences, do not subject me to unnecessary temptation, do not expose me to further degradation. . . . Remove me from my old companions, and surround me with virtuous associates." Sharing this perspective, officials in the 1830's argued that the great mistake of the prisons of the 1790's had been their failure to separate inmates. Lacking an understanding of the forces of the environment and still caught up with the idea that humane and certain punishment would eradicate deviancy, they had neglected to organize or supervise the prisoners' immediate surroundings. Consequently their institutions became seminaries of vice. Now, however, reformers understood the need to guard the criminal against corruption and teach him the habits of order and regularity. Isolation and steady habits, the right organization and routine, would yield unprecedented benefits.

As a result of this thinking, prison architecture and arrangements became the central concern of reformers of the period. Unlike their predecessors, they turned all their attention inward, to the divisions of time and space within the institution. The layout of cells, the methods of labor, and the manner of eating and sleeping within the penitentiary were the crucial issues. The most influential benevolent organization devoted to criminal reform, the Boston Prison Discipline Society, appropriately considered architecture one of the most important of the *moral* sciences. "There are," the society announced, "principles in architecture, by the observance of which great moral changes can be more easily produced among the most abandoned of our race. . . . There is such a thing as architecture adapted to morals; that other things being equal, the prospect of improvement, in morals, depends, in some degree, upon the construction of buildings." Those who would rehabilitate the deviant had better cultivate this science.

As with any other science, the advocates of moral architecture anticipated that the principles which emerged from the penitentiary experiment would have clear and important applications to the wider society. An arrangement which helped to reform vicious and depraved men would also be effective in regulating the behavior of ordinary citizens in other situations. The penitentiary, by its example, by its discovery and verification of proper principles of social organization, would serve as a model for the entire society. Reformers fully anticipated that their work behind prison walls would have a critical significance beyond them. Since crime was symptomatic of a breakdown in traditional community practices, the penitentiary solution would point the way to a reconstitution of the social structure.

Tocqueville and Beaumont appreciated how significant both of these purposes were to the first penologists. The institutions, Americans believed, would radically reform the criminal and the society. "Philanthropy has become for them," observed the two visitors, "a kind of profession, and they have caught the *monomanie* of the penitentiary system, which to them seems the remedy for all the evils of society." Proponents described the penitentiary as "a grand theatre, for the trial of all new plans in hygiene and education, in physical and moral reform." The convict "surrendered body and soul, to be experimented upon," and the results, as the Boston Prison Discipline Society insisted, would benefit not only other custodial institutions like almshouses and houses of refuge, but also "would greatly promote order, seriousness, and purity in large families, male and female boarding schools, and colleges." Perhaps the most dramatic and unabashed statement of these views appeared in a memoir by the Reverend James B. Finley, chaplain at the Ohio penitentiary. "Never, no never shall we see the triumph of peace, of right, of Christianity, until the daily habits of mankind shall undergo a thorough revolution," declared Finley. And in what ways were we to achieve such a reform? "Could we all be put on prison fare, for the space of two or three generations, the world would ultimately be the better for it. Indeed, should society change places with the prisoners, so far as habits are concerned, taking to itself the regularity, and temperance, and sobriety of a good prison," then the grandiose goals of peace, right, and Christianity would be furthered. "As it is," concluded Finley, "taking this world and the next together . . . the prisoner has the advantage."

It is no wonder, then, that Auburn and Pennsylvania supporters held their positions staunchly, eager to defend every detail. With the stakes so high and the results almost entirely dependent upon physical design, every element in penitentiary organization assumed overwhelming importance. Nothing less than the safety and future stability of the republic was at issue, the triumph of good over evil, of order over chaos. Intense partisanship was natural where the right program would reform the criminal and reorder the society, and the wrong one would encourage vice and crime.

30

A. Bandura:
Principles of Behavior Modification

Reviewed by Paul Lelliott

Reading this book for the first time, I was reminded of an occasion when I was asked by an examiner what I would do if a patient offered me a gift. When I replied that I would receive it with thanks, the examiner asked in an irritated way, "But what I mean is what would you say?" Wishing to pass the examination, I recited an acceptable reply along the lines of interpreting the transference. My examiner demonstrated that twenty years after Bandura's advocacy of social learning principles as a means of therapy, many mental health workers still persist in distancing themselves from their patients by adopting interpretative responses to their actions and words. I might have answered the question by saying that in my experience, patients offer me gifts when I have helped them; it serves to reinforce the mode of therapy they have found beneficial, and indicates that if further treatment is necessary it should be along similar lines. The giving and receiving of gifts is an acceptable and often desirable part of a human relationship, and generally to be encouraged. Refusing to accept a gift or qualifying acceptance with an interpretation that invariably alludes to some character failing or unpleasant early experience would not only be impolite, but would probably suppress this appropriate human behavior in the future. Bandura maintained that it is the *social* relationship between therapist and patient that is the vehicle for therapy, an approach that takes patients' complaints at face value, sharing their distress, failures, and successes, openly expressing opinions, and demonstrating alternatives.

Although Bandura's description of social learning theory extends beyond its application in modifying individuals' maladaptive behavior, addressing wider issues of public education, racial and cultural integration, the effects of advertising, and television violence, it is to mental health that it is primarily addressed.

Bandura allied himself with the antipsychiatrists in opposing the application of medical models to deviant behavior. He suggested, "Had Hippocrates represented behavioral anomalies as products of idiosyncratic social-learning experiences rather than as expressions of a somatic illness, the conceptualization and treatment of divergent response patterns might have taken an entirely different course."

Bandura satirized psychoanalytical thinking by inventing the "zoognick," an intrapsychically functioning agent which could be inferred from the presence of antisocial and assaultative behavior. He imagined tests being devised to measure "zoognick strength" and more and more people's behavior coming to be attributed to underlying "zoognicks." A charismatic zoognick therapist emerges, with attendant disciples, who teaches that it would be dangerous to attempt to directly modify the antisocial behavior due to the reemergence of the zoognick in other forms through symptom substitution.

Bandura's argument that psychiatric illnesses are merely abstract concepts inferred from deviant types of behavior is as relevant today as it was then. Perhaps all that has changed in the past twenty years is that these abstract concepts tend to be couched in terms of biological rather than psychoanalytical terms. Although more psychiatrists now share Bandura's views on psychoanalysis, behavior is still often only attended to the extent that it allows inferences to be drawn about internal processes which are held to be causal. Today these inferences are likely to be about abnormalities in neurotransmission in brain nuclei. The failure, despite years of searching, to identify sensitive and specific biological markers of psychiatric illness or to demonstrate convincingly structural or biochemical abnormalities in the hypothesised sites has not shaken the belief that the symptoms (invariably behavioral) can be explained by such paradigms. Bandura directed his contention that "theoretical models of dubious validity persist largely because they are not stated in refutable form" at psychoanalysis. However, it could equally apply to neurotransmitter theory which is capable of accommodating data that would appear to directly contradict a hypothesis by invoking such mechanisms as inhibitory or facilitatory presynaptic stimulation.

Bandura believed that this emphasis on inferring underlying causes (diseases) from deviant behavior had led to an unremitting search for drugs as quick and easy cures. This search has accelerated enormously since *Principles of Behavior Modification* was written. Despite the vast expenditure in time and money, we have not discovered more effective antidepressants, mood stabilizers, or antipsychotics than imipramine, lithium, or chlorpromazine, whose effects were discovered serendipitously. One wonders how much suffering could have been relieved had the same time and money been invested in exploring behavioral and social treatments, and a sum equivalent to the expenditure on psychotropic drugs used to train nonprofessional behavior therapists.

There is now evidence that the symptoms of depression may be alleviated as effectively by cognitive/behavioral therapy as by tricyclic antidepressants, and that the former may even be more likely to "cure" the condition in the sense of producing lower rates of relapse after therapy has been discontinued. However, even in disorders where there is general consensus that behavior therapy is the treatment of choice, such as phobic and obsessive-compulsive disorders, time may pass before effective treatment is offered. Most general practitioners and even psychiatrists are unwilling or unable to organize a behavioral treatment. Many patients with agoraphobia and obsessive-compulsive disorders are prescribed benzodiazepines before exposure is offered.

Two decades after Bandura argued that a medical training does not necessarily equip one to understand or treat psychological disorders, psychiatrists have largely retained their monopoly over their management. Although it has now been shown that nurses can deliver behavioral treatments as effectively as psychiatrists at a fraction of the cost, we are still some way short of Bandura's dream of psychological centers offering "brief and highly efficacious treatments for specific behavioral dysfunctions."

Community surveys have confirmed Bandura's belief that there is a vast reservoir of minor psychological disturbances, and have shown that anything up to one-third of the population is suffering from minor neurotic disorder. Bandura suggested that many of this group do not seek treatment through not wishing to incur the label of mental illness. Those that do are in danger of receiving treatments that at best do not help and at worst can cause problems worse than the initial complaint (e.g., benzodiazepine dependence). Perhaps it is time for doctors to admit to these patients that they do not necessarily have the skills or the time to help them and for this service to be provided by nonprofessional counsellors trained in behavioral techniques.

Principles of Behavior Modification was written at a time when behavioral researchers were moving out of the laboratory and into the clinic. It still serves as a valuable source of references to the animal work and analogue studies that demonstrated learning principles, and to early case reports and open studies of behavioral techniques in psychiatric disorders. Bandura anticipated many of the developments of the past twenty years,

during which controlled group studies using sensitive measures of behavior change have repeatedly proven the success of behavior therapy in
a variety of psychiatric disorders and extended psychological treatments
into new fields (notably behavioral medicine). He also predicted the
development of self-managed behavioral programs, the rise of cognitive
therapy, and the advent of specialist behavior therapists.

Not surprisingly, sections of the book are dated. The debates concerning
the value of relaxation and modeling, the optimal gradient of stimulus
presentation, and anxiety evocation in exposure are now settled. The
time-consuming technique of imaginal desensitization has now been
replaced by a simple package of exposure in vivo the pace of which is
determined by the patients' willingness to face feared stimuli and the bulk
of which is performed without a therapist as exposure-homework. Ad-
juncts such as relaxation and modeling have been found to be redundant.
Aversive counterconditioning has largely fallen into disuse for ethical
reasons.

Progress in developing behavioral and social treatment for schizophrenia has been patchy over the past twenty years. Little can be added to
Bandura's description and critique of token economies for increasing
socialisation in chronic schizophrenic patients: although they are effective,
difficulty still remains in transferring the gains into wider community
living. There has also been little further work in developing nonpharma-
cological methods of modifying delusions and hallucinations in acute
schizophrenia; only a few case reports and small uncontrolled studies can
be added to Bandura's review. Psychiatrists remain convinced that psychotic symptoms cannot be modified other than by physical treatments.
The greatest advance in the behavioral treatment of schizophrenia has been
in an area that Bandura did not predict, with the demonstration that
altering the social environment (particularly the family) in which patients
in remission live is as important in preventing relapse as medication.

Despite the passage of time, *Principles of Behavior Modification* continues
eloquently to question our attitudes to the genesis and treatment of mental
disorders and the way in which mental health care is delivered. Unlike
other antipsychiatrists, Bandura's claims are supported by carefully conducted studies, and many of his conclusions have been strengthened over
the years by numerous controlled trials of behavioral treatments in patient
groups.

Selections from
Principles of Behavior
Modification
by A. Bandura

The earliest conceptions of psychopathology viewed behavioral anomalies as external manifestations of evil spirits that entered the victim's body and adversely affected his behavior. Treatment accordingly was directed toward exorcising demons by various methods, such as cutting a hole in the victim's skull, performing various magical and religious rituals, or brutally assaulting—physically and socially—the bearer of the pernicious spirits. Hippocrates was influential in supplanting the demonological conceptions of deviant behavior by relabeling it disease rather than demonic manifestations. Wholesome diets, hydrotherapy, bloodletting, and other forms of physical intervention, some benign, others less humane, were increasingly employed as corrective treatments.

Although psychological methods gradually replaced physical procedures in modifying deviant response patterns, the analogy of physical health and disease nevertheless continued to dominate theories of psychopathology. In this conceptualization, behavioral patterns that depart widely from accepted social and ethical norms are considered to be derivatives or symptoms of an underlying disease. Modification of social deviance thus became a medical specialty, with the result that persons exhibiting atypical behavior are labeled "patients" suffering from a "mental illness," and they generally are treated in medically oriented facilities. The disease concepts are likewise indiscriminately applied even to social phenomena, as evidenced by the frequent designation of cultural response patterns as "healthy" or "sick". Had Hippocrates represented behavioral anomalies as products of idiosyncratic social-learning experiences rather than as expressions of a somatic illness, the conceptualization and treatment of divergent response patterns might have taken an entirely different course.

A quasi-disease model is still widely employed in explanations of grossly deviant behavior, but the underlying pathology is generally considered to be psychic rather than neurophysiological in nature. This conceptual scheme became further confused when the appropriateness of the disease analogy to social behavior was increasingly challenged. Most personality theorists eventually discarded the notion that deviant behavior is a manifestation of an underlying mental disease, but they nevertheless unhesitatingly label anomalous behaviors as symptoms and caution against the dangers of symptom substitution. In these theories, the conditions supposedly controlling behavior continue to function analogously to toxic substances in producing deviant responses; however, the disturbing agents comprise a host of inimical psychodynamic forces (for example, repressed impulses, energized traits, psychic complexes, latent tendencies, self-dynamisms, and other types of energy systems) somewhat akin to the pernicious spirits of ancient times. Many contemporary theories of psychopathology thus employ a quasi-medical model fashioned from an amalgam of the disease and demonology conceptions, which have in common the belief that deviant behavior is a function of inimical inner forces. Consequently, attention is generally focused, not on the problem behavior itself, but on the presumably influential internal agents that must be exorcised by "catharsis," "abreaction," and acquisition of insight through an extended interpretive process. Indeed, direct modification of so-called symptomatic behavior is considered not only ineffective but actually dangerous, because, it is held, removal of the symptom has no effect upon the underlying disorder, which will manifest itself again in a new, possibly more debilitating symptom.

The questions raised concerning the utility and validity of the concept of "symptom" apply equally to the psychopathology presumed to underlie the troublesome behavior. From the focusing of attention on inner agents and forces, many fanciful theories of deviant behavior have emerged. The developmental history of social behavior is rarely known, and its reconstruction from interview material elicited by therapists or diagnosticians is of doubtful validity. In fact, the content of reconstruction is highly influenced by the interviewer's suggestive probing and selective reinforcement of content that is in accord with his theoretical orientation. Heine, for example, found that clients who were treated by client-centered, Adlerian, and psychoanalytic therapists tended to account for changes in their behavior in terms of the explanations favored by their respective interviewers. Even a casual survey of interview protocols would reveal that psychotherapists of different theoretical affiliations tend to find evidence for their own preferred psychodynamic agents rather than those cited by other schools. Thus, Freudians are likely to unearth Oedipus complexes and castration anxieties, Adlerians discover inferiority feelings and compensatory power strivings, Rogerians find compelling evidence for inappropriate self-concepts, and existentialists are likely to diagnose existential crises and anxieties. It is equally true that Skinnerians, predictably, will discern defective conditions of reinforcement as important determinants of deviant behavior. In the latter explanatory scheme, however, the suspected controlling conditions are amenable to systematic variation; consequently the functional relationships between reinforcement contingencies and behavior are readily verifiable.

Theoretical models of dubious validity persist largely because they are not stated in refutable form. The lack of accurate knowledge of the genesis of behavioral deviations further precludes any serious evaluation of suggested determinants that are so involved that they could never be produced under laboratory conditions. When the actual social-learning history of maladaptive behavior is known, principles of learning appear to provide a completely adequate interpretation of psychopathological phenomena, and psychodynamic explanations in terms of symptom-underlying disorder become superfluous. The spuriousness of the supposition that psychodynamic forces produce symptomatic behavior can be best illustrated by cases in which the antecedents of aberrant response patterns are known. Such examples are hard to obtain since they require the production of deviant behavior under controlled conditions. Ayllon, Haughton, and Hughes furnish a graphic illustration of how a bizarre pattern of behavior—which was developed, maintained, and subsequently eliminated in a schizophrenic woman simply by altering its reinforcing consequences—was interpreted erroneously as a symptomatic manifestation of complex psychodynamic events by diagnosticians who were unaware of the specific conditions of reinforcement regulating the patient's behavior.

Unfortunately, the exact antecedents of deviant behavior are rarely known, and in the absence of powerful techniques that permit adequate control over behavioral phenomena, clinical endeavors have until recently lacked the self-corrective features necessary for eliminating weak or invalid theories of psychopathology. As a consequence, rival interpretations of social behavior have for decades retained a secure status with little risk that any one type of theory might prove more cogent than another.

In recent years there has been a fundamental departure from conventional views regarding the nature, causes, and treatment of behavioral dysfunctions. According to this orientation, behavior that is harmful to the individual or departs widely from accepted social and ethical norms is viewed not as symptomatic of some kind of disease but as a way that the individual has learned to cope with environmental and self-imposed demands. Treatment then becomes mainly a problem in social learning rather than one in the medical domain. In this conceptual scheme the remaining vestiges of the disease-demonic model have been discarded. Response patterns are not viewed as symptoms and their occurrence is not attributed to internal, pernicious forces.

Social learning and psychodynamic theories differ not only in whether they view deviant behavior as a quasi disease or as a by-product of learning, but also in what they regard to be the significant controlling factors, and in the status assigned to internal events. As will be shown later, social-learning approaches treat internal processes as covert events that are manipulable and measurable. These mediating processes are extensively controlled by external stimulus events and in turn regulate overt responsiveness. By contrast, psychodynamic theories tend to regard internal events as relatively autonomous. These hypothetical causal agents generally bear only a tenuous relationship to external stimuli, or even to the "symptoms" that they supposedly produce.

The conceptualization of deviant behavior as manifestations of disease has, in several ways, impeded development of efficacious methods of behavioral change. In the first place, it led to heavy reliance upon physical and chemical interventions, unremitting search for drugs as quick remedies for interpersonal problems, and long-term neglect of social variables as influential determinants of deviant response patterns. Secondly, the mislabeling, partly by historical accident, of social deviations as symptoms of mental illness established medical training as the optimal preparation for psychotherapeutic work. In fact, such training, because of its primary concern with somatic processes and pathologies, leaves one ill-prepared for devising and implementing methods that are successful in promoting favorable social change. Had educational processes, which also depend upon neurophysiological functioning, been historically misconstrued as principally medical phenomena, our society would undoubtedly be faced with the same critical shortage of educational-facilities and well-trained instructional personnel that characterizes our current "mental health" enterprises.

Although the designation of behavioral eccentricities as manifestations of disease initially resulted in more humane treatment, as Szasz cogently points out, continued adherence to this analogy has become a serious hindrance. Many people who would benefit greatly from psychological treatment avoid seeking help because they fear being stigmatized as mentally deranged, which often carries deleterious social consequences. Those who are compelled by chronic distress to seek a solution to their interpersonal problems are typically ascribed a sick role and are regarded as relatively helpless, dependent, and incompetent in managing their daily lives.

When individuals are labeled mentally ill, this often results not only in suspension of customary response consequences essential for change, but in substitution of contingencies that foster maladaptive tendencies. Moreover, as will be shown later, for people who undergo long-term institutionalization, the attendant stigmatization, the patient-role requirements of the mental hospital culture, the limited opportunities to perform behaviors that are necessary in community life, and the development of institutional dependency produce further impediments to successful readjustment to typical environmental demands.

The medical orientation toward deviant behavior has resulted also in a disinterest in, and lack of facilities for, the modification of lesser, but nevertheless troublesome, forms of psychological problems. People with circumscribed behavioral difficulties are justifiably unwilling to label themselves mentally deranged and to enter into a protracted expensive treatment that offers no guarantee to success. Thus, for example, people who suffer from snake phobias may be unable to perform their work under certain conditions, to participate in camping and other outdoor activities, or to reside in locales inhabited by harmless snakes. Treatments derived from social-learning principles are now available that can effectively eliminate such phobias in any person in a few sessions. Psychological centers that offer brief and highly efficacious treatments for specific behavioral dysfunctions would provide valuable therapeutic services to many persons who would otherwise endure unnecessary restrictions in certain areas of their psychological functioning.

31

C. M. Parkes:
Bereavement:
Studies of Grief in Adult Life

Reviewed by David A. Alexander

When he submitted his dissertation on *Morbid Grief Reactions: A Review of the Literature* to the University of London in 1959, Parkes made his first major contribution to the study of grief and bereavement. There followed a series of publications (e.g., Parkes 1965, 1971) which culminated in the first edition of the book reconsidered here. On my first reading of this book, I was reminded of Samuel Johnson's comment that "the two most engaging powers of an author are to make new things familiar, and familiar things new." Parkes's descriptions of unusual reactions to loss are presented in a fashion which makes them feel reassuringly familiar, and those reactions which are more commonplace are described in a way which requires us to consider them anew.

Bereavement is not an unusual event in life: death and other forms of loss are ubiquitous features of the life style. However, until fairly recently, bereavement was not regarded as a legitimate or even attractive topic of scientific inquiry. Because of the vulnerability and sensitivities of the bereaved, many researchers have felt intimidated from pursuing the topic. Others may have felt that dealing with grief was the province of our spiritual advisors, or have feared that working in an area characterized by suffering and distress would be too daunting a challenge. However, this book offers much reassurance and confirms Parkes's own claim that "grief, like any other aspect of human behavior, is capable of description and study, and when studied it turns out to be as fascinating as any other psychological phenomenon" (Parkes 1972, p. xi). One might add that compared with some phenomena, grief is an even more attractive one because of its ubiquity and because of the opportunities there are to ease the suffering of our fellow men and women after bereavement.

When reviewing the second edition of this book in 1987, I was struck by the fact that relatively few changes had been made apart from the incorporation of about seventy more references. This, however, is not an indictment of the efforts of Parkes but rather a confirmation of the durability of his earlier findings and observations. There are now available a number of excellent comprehensive texts on this subject (e.g., Raphael 1984, Stroebe and Stroebe 1987), but Parkes' first book could justifiably claim to be a landmark in our exploration of the origins, nature, and significance of grief.

Although psychoanalysts including Freud, Abraham, and Klein, had accorded bereavement an etiological and theoretical role in their formulations, they were not concerned with conducting a systematic study of the subject. However, a major tragedy in America—the Coconut Grove Fire Disaster—was to inspire the first such study (Lindemann 1944). After that, there were a number of helpful descriptive accounts of the impact of bereavement, including those by Langer (1957), Maddison and Walker (1967), and Averill (1968).

Nonetheless, these early forays into the field left many questions unanswered and many issues were ignored. The relationship between "normal" and "pathological" grief was unclear, and there were few prescriptions (other than nonsecular ones) for helping the bereaved. Such efforts did, however, foster a growing awareness that bereavement was a highly significant life event with important implications for the health and welfare of those who experienced it. An authoritative contribution to the topic was called for to further our understanding of the effects of bereavement, and to provide purpose and direction to the efforts of those whose job it was to help the bereaved through their period of transition. The first edition of Parkes's book, based on carefully collected data, emerged therefore as a timely and influential text.

Although he refers to some of the limited research findings available at that time, Parkes relies mainly on the information derived from the Bethlem and London studies, and from work carried out later by his American colleagues and himself in Boston. The London work involved a follow-up of twenty-two widows, under the age of 65 years, to find out how they would react to and cope with the loss of a spouse. In the Bethlem study, the aim was to explore the nature of atypical reactions to bereavement shown by twenty-one individuals (four men, seventeen women). The American study involved a higher proportion of men (nineteen widowers, forty-one widows), and aimed to determine why some individuals negotiate quite successfully the problems imposed by a bereavement whereas others do not do so and may require professional assistance. Clearly, the identification of those factors which put specific individuals at risk of adverse reactions after bereavement is a valuable contribution, particularly because it provides an opportunity for prophylactic intervention.

Highlighted by reference to his case material, Parkes details how individuals commonly react to bereavement (and other kinds of loss such as amputation). Special attention is given to distinctive features such as pining and searching, and anger and guilt. Familiarity with such reactions is important for doctors and others who have to deal with the bereaved in order that they can reassure those whose reactions are within the normal range, and can identify those who require specialized help (the fact that such individuals are in a minority is emphasized). However, because we are social beings, it is the provision of help within conventional social settings that Parkes believes can be helpful to most of those burdened by their grief. Basic social and practical help may be provided by lay groups, such as Cruse or the Society for Compassionate Friends, but Parkes's approach to the subject confirms that we can all do something to ease the suffering of the bereaved. We can help by attending to basic practical matters on their behalf, and we can show a willingness to try to understand and share this suffering without resorting to trite comments, clichés, and empty reassurances—and without being overwhelmed by their grief.

Religious convention and ceremonies, including funerals, are regarded by the author as serving a very useful function. Not only do they legitimize emotional expression and provide communal opportunities for this, but they also offer the bereaved a sense of direction and purpose. Whether the abbreviation and dilution of the previously extensive funerary rituals is in the best interests of the bereaved is questioned by Parkes, and consequently the Church is urged to assume its responsibility in providing direction and guidelines for those who are in grief.

Perhaps prescient of the concerns to be expressed later in the 1970s about benzodiazepine dependence and other consequences of regarding medication as a panacea for a person's suffering and discontents, Parkes has reservations about the extent to which psychotropic medication should be used to alleviate the pain of normal grief—although he does not deny the value of the selective use of night sedation. The problem of dependence however is not confined, as Parkes himself points out, to medication because he declares that Cruse (the organization to which he has devoted so much of his time and energies) is "an organization for transition rather than a perpetual refuge . . ." (Parkes 1972, p. 177).

The book does not just contain a series of descriptive accounts or a set of prescriptions; Parkes has attempted to establish his findings and ideas within a theoretical framework. Concepts and principles, deriving from the work of Klein, the ethologists, and from psychoanalysis, play a part in shaping Parkes's theoretical position. However, it is not to detract from his own work to say that it was fortuitous and invaluable that Bowlby (1969) had already laid an excellent foundation for an understanding of human relationships and of the consequences of their termination. The debt to Bowlby is certainly considerable, as Parkes himself recognizes.

This is not a text, however, for the confirmed academic who has an exclusive appetite for a theoretical perspective. Nor does it provide a comprehensive review of the contemporary literature. Moreover, it is not even a practitioner's manual, providing a detailed outline of practical counselling and psychotherapeutic skills (a contribution later to be made by Worden 1982). One could also point out that there is a biased concentration of the reactions of widows rather than widowers in Parkes's empirical studies, and it is grief and bereavement only from an adult's perspective.

Why then has this book become such an influential text, securing an unimpeachable place in the literature on grief and bereavement? I think several factors help to answer this question. First, it was written by a practicing clinician who has been able to combine methodological rigor with a compassionate approach to this subject. Second, it is written in a clear and simple style that gives it an appeal to professional and lay helper alike. Third, the method of data collection was systematic and extensive, thereby giving the reader some confidence in the validity of the observational claims and findings. Fourth, because of the relatively undeveloped nature of the field at that time, the book fostered an interest in the subject and served a propaedeutic role. It was certainly an early confirmation that Parkes was to become an outstanding teacher, researcher, and clinician in this field of work. It is a fitting tribute to Parkes's contribution that his name is the most commonly indexed in two recent and influential books (Stroebe and Stroebe 1987, Worden 1982) and, in what is possibly the most comprehensive book on the subject (Raphael 1984), his name is second only to Raphael's in terms of frequency of citation. Finally, despite the inevitable pain that follows a bereavement, Parkes tries to offer hope and foster a positive attitude by regarding loss as an opportunity for change and development.

In conclusion, this first edition is a highly commendable and readable book which was welcomed by professionals and laymen who sought a compassionate but empirically justified approach to the bereaved. It is a capably researched account of the impact of and reactions to bereavement by an academic clinician, who has an unchallenged pedigree in terms of his interest in the welfare of those who have suffered the loss of a loved one.

Because of this book, I suspect, many individuals will have resisted the temptation of turning away from grief: a reaction that Parkes himself indicates "will only add to the fear, perpetuate the problems, and miss an opportunity to prepare ourselves for the changes that are inevitable in a changing world" (Parkes 1972, p. 195).

REFERENCES

Averill, J. (1968). Grief: its nature and significance. *Psychological Bulletin* 70:721-748.

Bowlby, J. (1969), *Attachment and Loss. Vol. 1: Attachment*. New York: Basic Books.

Langer, M. (1957). *Learning to Live as a Widow*. New York: Gilbert Press.

Lindemann, E. (1944). Symptomatology and management of acute grief. *American Journal of Psychiatry* 101:141-148.

Maddison, D. C. and Walker, W. L. (1967). Factors affecting the outcome of conjugal bereavement. *British Journal of Psychiatry* 113:1057-1067.

Parkes, C. M. (1965). Bereavement and mental illness. Part 1. A clinical study of the grief of bereaved psychiatric patients. *British Journal of Medical Psychology* 38:1-12.

_____ (1971). Psychosocial transitions: a field for study. *Social Science and Medicine* 5:101-115.

_____ (1972). *Bereavement: Studies of Grief in Adult Life*. New York: International Universities Press.

Raphael, B. (1984). *The Anatomy of Bereavement*. London: Hutchinson.

Stroebe, W. and Stroebe, M. S. (1987). *Bereavement and Health*. Cambridge, England: Cambridge University Press.

Worden, J. W. (1982). *Grief Counselling and Grief Therapy*. London: Tavistock.

Selections from
Bereavement: Studies of Grief in Adult Life
by C. M. Parkes

Whether the bereaved person chooses a drink or a drug he will try to select a 'therapist' who will give him the type of treatment he wants. Society permits him a greater measure of control over his alcohol intake than it does over other drugs, but it also provides a system whereby he can obtain some of the time of a highly trained professional, whose skills should include a greater understanding of psychosocial problems than is to be expected from the average barman. He is likely, therefore, to feel safer if his drugs are being prescribed by a doctor, who will tell him when he has had enough and who can supply a variety of medications to suit his special needs, than if alcohol is his only drug and he must repeatedly choose between a hangover and a good night's rest.

Apart from their use as night sedatives, drugs (including alcohol) are taken to reduce anxiety and tension by day. There is now a wide range of tranquillizers on the market which can be expected to take the edge off feelings of panic and excessive anxiety. Similarly, anti-depressive drugs have been used to damp down depression.

While I do not doubt the efficacy of these drugs in reducing the intensity of the unpleasant features of grief, the appropriateness of their use after bereavement is questionable. If, as we suppose, grief is a process of 'unlearning', if it is necessary for the bereaved person to go through the pain of grief in order to get the grief work done, then anything that continually allows the person to avoid or suppress this pain can be expected to prolong the course of mourning. Admittedly we have little empirical evidence that drugs have this effect and their use is so widespread that any serious consequences would probably have become apparent already if they were at all frequent. But the fact remains that until the effects of tranquillizing drugs and anti-depressives have been properly assessed they should be used with caution following bereavement.

32

Otto Kernberg:
Borderline Conditions and Pathological Narcissism

Reviewed by Salman Akhtar and Alan M. Gruenberg

Less than ten years after its release in 1975, Otto Kernberg's *Borderline Conditions and Pathological Narcissism* was declared by 138 prominent American psychiatrists to be a seminal publication of the decade (Strauss et al. 1984). And now, after only seventeen years of being in print, his book is included in this volume dedicated to reevaluating psychiatric classics. The enormous prestige and popularity of the book are due to both the nature and the timing of its message. To psychoanalysts, Kernberg's message was that it is necessary to enrich their theory by assimilating into ego psychology the work done within the Kleinian and independent British psychoanalytic traditions. By integrating the contributions of Fairbairn and Klein with those of Hartmann, Erikson, and Jacobson, Kernberg offered a new and complex theoretical infrastructure to the clinical phenomena of severe character pathology. At the same time, his book represented a striking effort to bring psychoanalytic principles to the descriptive, and increasingly biologically oriented general psychiatric community. It demonstrated that psychoanalysis is far from an ideological relic, that it and descriptive psychiatry do not have to remain conceptual adversaries, and that psychoanalysts do not deal with the "worried well" but with really disturbed and disturbing psychiatric patients.

The timing of Kernberg's message was crucial for both psychoanalysis and psychiatry. American psychoanalysis especially had begun to experience "a diminution of scientific productivity and the loss of intellectual excitement" (Cooper 1983, p. 4). Although theoretical purists (Calef and Weinshel 1979, Klein and Tribich 1981) did not readily warm to it, Kernberg's work eventually proved to be a much needed, rejuvenating stimulus for the field. General psychiatry too seemed ripe to receive his systematic presentation of the diagnosis, differential diagnosis, treatment, and prognosis of severe personality disorders. The appearance of his work paralleled burgeoning nosological refinements in this realm, especially the pioneering works of Grinker et al. (1968), Grinker and Werble (1977), Gunderson and Singer (1975), and Gunderson and Kolb (1978). Growing out of the Menninger Foundation Psychotherapy Research Project and striving toward descriptive criteria that are ordinarily minimized by psychoanalysts, Kernberg's work had a scientific ring. It appealed to empirical researchers (e.g., Perry and Klerman 1978), who included this, a psychoanalytic work, in their comparison of various sets of criteria for the borderline syndrome. Over the subsequent years, Kernberg's "borderline personality organization" and Gunderson et al.'s "borderline personality disorder" became a conceptual pair, with a dialectical tension optimal for scientific advance.

With this as a backdrop, let us now turn to a closer scrutiny of the book. It is a compendium of ten chapters divided into two parts: Borderline Personality Organization and Narcissistic Personality.

PART I: BORDERLINE PERSONALITY ORGANIZATION

This part of the book (chapters 1–7) deals with the phenomenology and treatment of borderline personality organization. Chapters 1 and 7 consider phenomenology; chapters 2, 3, and 6 deal with treatment; chapter 5 comments on both; and chapter 4 focuses on prognosis.

Phenomenology

Delineation of the borderline syndrome is the focus of the first chapter. This chapter—a reprint of Kernberg's (1967) seminal paper on the topic—synthesizes the preceding psychoanalytic literature on severe character pathology and seeks to establish a common psychic substrate to diverse character constellations. Kernberg labels this substrate *borderline personality organization*, emphasizing that it is a stable condition and not a fluctuating state between neurosis and psychosis. He offers descriptive, psychostructural, genetic (developmental), and dynamic characteristics of their shared psychic organization. Among the *descriptive* features, he includes chronic anxiety, polysymptomatic neurosis, pansexuality, "prepsychotic" (schizoid, paranoid, and hypomanic) and "lower level" (narcissistic, infantile, antisocial, and as-if) personalities, impulse neuroses, and many individuals presenting with alcohol or drug addiction. Among the *structural* characteristics, he includes generalized ego weakness (manifesting in lack of impulse control, sublimation, and anxiety tolerance), heightened propensity for primary process thinking, primitive defenses (splitting, denial, projective identification, primitive idealization, omnipotence, and devaluation) and, most importantly, pathological internal object relations. Kernberg portrays these patients as lacking an integrated self-concept, and continuing to have infantile all bad and all-good views of themselves and others. They also display an incapacity to understand others in depth, and a chameleon-like quality of superficial adaptability. Actually "identity diffusion is a typical syndrome of borderline personality organization" (p. 39). Among the *genetic-dynamic* features, Kernberg lists a history of extreme frustrations and aggression during the first few years of life, resulting in a specific condensation between pregenital and genital conflicts; an aggressively tinged and premature Oedipus complex is a frequent consequence.

Returning to phenomenological aspects in chapter 7, Kernberg describes these patients' subjective sense of emptiness. They often experience a peculiar loss of contact with other people, who appear distant and automaton-like to them, while the patients themselves feel similarly. "Life no longer seems to make sense, there is no hope for any future gratification or happiness, there is nothing to search for, or aspire to" (p. 214). Kernberg distinguishes such inner deadness from mournful loneliness resulting from unavailability of objects due to reality constraints or superego dictates. He also describes various defensive maneuvers against emptiness, including frantic socializing, ingestion of drugs or alcohol, impulsive sexuality, and overeating.

The strength of Kernberg's description lies in its derivation of clinically observable phenomena, without losing anchor in an object relations point of view. Use of primitive defenses, for instance, is described in detail (pp. 25–34) with an eye toward their behavioral manifestations. Splitting, the central defensive operation in borderline organization, is seen as resulting in a selective and ego-syntonic impulsivity, incapacity for ambivalence, and extreme and repetitive oscillation between contradictory self-concepts. Similar reconciliation between description and meaning is also evident in Kernberg's delineation of other defenses and in his comments upon the ill-consolidated identities of these patients.

Kernberg also highlights the distinctions between hysterical and infantile personalities (pp. 13–16), and between borderline and schizophrenic conditions (pp. 177–182). The former distinction is valuable for clarifying the "hysterical-histrionic confusion" (Gorton and Akhtar 1990) in current psychiatric nosology. "Infantile" (histrionic) personalities resemble hysterical individuals, but are more suggestible, dependent, crudely seductive, and masochistic. Borderline patients who have had transient psychotic reactions, have received sustained psychopharmacological treatment, or have become socially withdrawn, raise the question of whether schizophrenia is present. Their distinction depends not only upon descriptive symptomatology, but also upon the manner in which the patient responds to being confronted with his use of primitive defenses. In borderline patients, such confrontation tends to strengthen ego functioning and increase reality testing. In psychotic patients, confrontation brings about further regression. The two types of patients develop different kinds of psychotic transferences. In borderline patients, such loss of reality testing has little effect upon the patient's functioning outside the treatment hours. In contrast, psychotic patients experience themselves as one with the therapist at all times, although such oneness may dramatically change from raw aggression and frightening engulfment to a euphoric, near mystical experience of goodness and love.

While these are illuminating phenomenological details, their understandability and use by psychodynamically less sophisticated psychiatrists remain debatable. Moreover, the inclusion of generalized ego weakness as a criterion of borderline personality organization poses problems, since this feature is characteristic of only the most severe form of such psychopathology (borderline personality disorder) and not of the better integrated narcissistic and paranoid characters. Its inclusion, therefore, adds ambiguity to the otherwise useful distinction between borderline personality organization (a psychostructural substrate) and borderline personality disorder (its flagrant manifestation).

Treatment

Kernberg states that borderline patients are unable to tolerate the regression and abstinent ambience of psychoanalysis: they tend to develop severe and intractable transferences. Supportive psychotherapy, as traditionally understood, also fails to help them; such treatment prevents regression and avoids a transference psychosis. However, it often leads to splitting up of the negative transference, with persistent acting out outside the treatment and either clinging idealization or emotional shallowness in the therapeutic situation. Most such patients should therefore be treated with a judicious mixture of the two extreme approaches.

This therapeutic strategy is comprised of: (1) elaboration of negative transference and its deflection, through examination of it in the patient's relations with others, (2) confrontation and interpretation of pathological defenses, (3) active blocking of the acting out of the transference within the therapy itself, (4) environmental structuring, (5) utilization of positive transference for maintaining therapeutic alliance, and (6) fostering appropriate expressions of sexual conflicts interfering with the patient's adaptation. Kernberg goes on to provide specific strategies to deal with the primitive defenses of borderline patients (pp. 94–103) and with certain special problems that tend to develop in the early stages of their treatment (pp. 201–210). These include conscious withholding of information, devaluation of the help being offered, meaninglessness in the therapeutic interaction, paranoid control, early and severe acting out, misuse of previous knowledge regarding psychotherapy, intense separation reactions, and difficulties in the psychotherapist's relationship with the hospital staff, if any are involved. Kernberg emphasizes that not all patients can be treated in this manner, and that certain realistic conditions must be met for such work to be undertaken. He also comments about hospital management of borderline patients and discusses the extent to which the psychotherapist needs to appear as a "real person" to them.

In a related vein, Kernberg provides a succinct overview of countertransference manifestations in the treatment of borderline patients. He delineates the features of both acute and persistent or chronic countertransference, including the therapist's emotional discontinuation of the treatment, his unrealistic "total dedication," and "microparanoid" attitudes toward the patient. While these clearly interfere with the treatment, emotional reactions of the therapist may also help in evaluating the degree of regression in the patient and in clarifying the chief transference paradigms. The therapist's concern is a paramount issue here. Such concern implies ongoing self-criticism by the therapist and a willingness to review difficult situations with a consultant or a colleague.

Prognosis

Kernberg sees the prognosis of borderline personality organization as depending upon (1) descriptive diagnosis, (2) ego strength, (3) superego consolidation, (4) object relations, and (5) the therapist's skills and personality. Ominous prognosis is usually associated with antisocial, severely sadomasochistic, and hypomanic personalities. Markedly withdrawn individuals whose sexual life has become restricted to masturbation with perverse fantasies also have a bad prognosis. In contrast, narcissistic and infantile personalities can be expected to have a better outcome with treatment. Non-specific manifestations of ego weakness, absence of internalized value systems, and impaired capacity to experience guilt and sadness are also negative prognostic indicators. Honesty, concern, presence of at least some nonexploitative relationships, and inborn talents, on the other hand, render the prognosis favorable. The stability, depth, and capacity for "individualization" (p. 145) in object relations also favorably affect prognosis. Finally, the therapist's skill, which includes "his capacity to integrate creatively his personality traits and countertransference reactions into the technique, is the most crucial factor in the outcome of the treatment of patients with low level of psychic functioning, that is, ego weakness" (p. 147).

PART II: NARCISSISTIC PERSONALITY

This part of the book consists of individual essays (chapters 8–10) on the treatment of narcissistic personality, its clinical manifestations, and the distinction between normal and pathological narcissism. A reverse order of their arrangement would have better assured a step-by-step elucidation of the issues involved. This weakness of editing, however, does not detract from the profound nature of the material contained herein. This can be broadly summarized under three headings.

Phenomenology

Kernberg portrays narcissistic individuals as displaying inordinate self-absorption, intense ambition, grandiosity, over-dependence on tributes from others, and an unremitting need for power, brilliance, and beauty. He emphasizes the pathology of their inner worlds. This manifests in their shallow emotional life, defective empathy, and inability to love and to experience sadness and mournful longing when facing separation and loss. Kernberg also points out that the narcissistic person lacks genuine sublimation; his work is in the service of exhibitionism, done in order to receive praise. In addition, there are subtle superego defects and tendencies toward corruptibility and cutting ethical corners. Kernberg emphasizes the paranoid substrate of the syndrome, and regards mistrust, hunger, rage, and guilt about this rage to be the basic cause of the self-inflation and not merely reactive phenomena. He also gives a special place to the narcissist's chronic envy and his defenses against such envy, particularly devaluation, omnipotent control, and narcissistic withdrawal.

Kernberg differentiates three levels of social functioning among narcissistic personalities. First, there are narcissistic individuals who, possessing superior intelligence and talents, may achieve outstanding social success. The constant admiration they receive keeps them going and they may never seek treatment. "One might say that their gains from their illness often compensate for the disturbances that stem from the pathology of their object relations" (p. 333). Second, there are the narcissistic patients who seek treatment for impaired capacity for long-term relationships and a nagging aimlessness despite reasonable success. This group constitutes the majority of narcissistic individuals. The third group comprises the narcissistic patients who display ego weakness and, therefore, exist as dreamers and futile schemers.

Pathogenesis

In his formulation of the etiology of narcissistic personality, Kernberg differs sharply from Kohut (1971), the other major contemporary theoretician in this realm. Kohut suggests that the exhibitionistic and worshiping tendencies of narcissistic individuals (and the corresponding "mirror" and "idealizing" transferences) reflect fixations at archaic levels of normal development. Kernberg, however, views these phenomena as pathological developments in the first place. He emphatically distinguishes between normal and pathological narcissism (pp. 315–327). Normal narcissism is associated with reasonable goals, inner confidence, integrated sense of ideals, instinctually gratifying life, and capacity to love, give, and have concern for others. Pathological narcissism, on the other hand, is associated with fantastic goals, undue reliance on external sources for self-esteem regulation, poorly internalized superego functions, and incapacity for love and concern.

Kernberg differentiates the normal narcissism of children (and adults), which retains a realistic quality, from the early development of pathological narcissism, which creates megalomanic fantasies. He believes that narcissistic patients were treated by their parents in a cold, even spiteful, but nonetheless "special" manner. In addition, the quality of their early introjections was altered by age-specific misperceptions as well as by paranoid distortions of parental figures due to their own aggression toward their parents. Using Kohut's (1971) term with a different structural formulation, Kernberg proposes that the "grandiose self" is formed by a fusion of aspects of the real self, the idealized self, and an idealized object representation. Associated with such fusion, which permits a greater overall cohesion than is evident in other forms of borderline pathology, is the disowning of the needy-hungry self-representations, the depriving object representations, and the rage, envy, and fear that bind them together. Such a state of affairs leads to a condensation of preoedipal and oedipal conflicts under the overriding influence of pregenital, especially oral, aggression. This has deleterious effects on the oedipal experience and on the salutary identifications that, under ordinary circumstances, follow from its resolution. These effects include intense castration anxiety on the one hand, and an orally derived greedy promiscuity and perverse tendencies on the other.

Treatment

Kernberg believes that well-functioning narcissistic personalities, despite their underlying borderline organization, should be treated with psychoanalysis. Narcissistic personalities with overt ego weakness, however, need a long preparatory period of supportive psychotherapy before in-depth treatment. Once an analytic treatment is underway, narcissistic patients display tenacious resistance to acknowledging any attachment to the analyst. They devalue the analytic process, deny the reality of their own emotional life, and assert the fantasy that the analyst is not an autonomous individual separate from them. Their lack of curiosity about the analyst is striking and renders their sessions monotonous, empty of affect, and dull.

The analyst faced with such a situation must: (1) relentlessly focus upon the transference and counteract the patient's efforts toward omnipotent control and devaluation, (2) consistently search for the hidden intent of the patient's behavior in the countertransference, (3) refuse to let sudden switches in the patient's attitude (reflecting splitting or attempts at devaluation) go unquestioned, and (4) keep in mind that these patients often require very long psychoanalytic treatments. Kernberg also warns against treating many such patients simultaneously because they put great stress on the analyst.

After the defensive narcissism of these patients is worked through, their primitive hunger and rage come to the surface. "The deep aspiration and love for an ideal mother and the hatred for the distorted, dangerous mother, have to meet at some point in the transference, and the patient has to become aware that the feared and hated analyst-mother is really one with the admired longed-for analyst-mother (p. 257). At this point, the patient must acknowledge his own aggression and go through a period of profound guilt and sadness; this stage contrasts strikingly with the previous emptiness in the treatment.

Kernberg compares (pp. 284–306) his approach with that espoused by Kohut (1971), and points out the neglect of the intimate connections between narcissistic and object relations conflicts in the latter's theory. Kohut regards the narcissistic individual's insistence on being mirrored and/or provided an idealized support as expressing unmet developmental needs from childhood. Kernberg, in contrast, views these with suspicion, and emphasizes their function as a shield against angry fantasies. He stresses that narcissistic transferences are multilayered structures that include in them early wishes, defenses, real experiences, and unconscious distortions of them. He also differs from Kohut in not regarding these patients' rage as merely a reaction to the analyst's empathic failures. Indeed, he proposes that a full exploration, interpretation, and working through of negative transference is the only way to diminish the patient's envy and resolve his pathological grandiose self.

CONCLUDING REMARKS

This summary does not do justice to the book's enormous complexity, depth, and richness. It may, however, demonstrate the breadth of its scope and highlight the reasons for its remarkable status and world-wide readership. To be sure, the book has its weaknesses, mostly in the realm of editing. Being largely a collection of previously published papers, it suffers from some repetitiveness. Also, the papers could have been arranged in a more meaningful order. More important is the regretful reversal in striving toward clarity caused by the simultaneous use of terms such as *borderline personality organization*, *borderline conditions*, *borderline features*, and *borderline level of functioning*. A similar difficulty results from the inclusion of generalized ego weakness as a diagnostic criterion for the entire group of disorders associated with borderline personality organization. There is also an occasional slippage in sustaining the "principle of multiple function" (Waelder 1930), with the resulting tendency to attribute only one meaning to a particular phenomenon. These soft spots, however, neither diminish the book's value nor negate its profound impact on subsequent psychoanalytic and psychiatric understanding of personality disorders.

Kernberg's own work in this realm has not ceased with this book. His ideas about the diagnostic and therapeutic issues involving severe personality disorders continue to evolve. In this later work (Kernberg 1976, 1984, 1992; Kernberg et al. 1990), he has shown greater rapprochement with both American ego psychology and contemporary descriptive psychiatry, without sacrificing his own unique style of theorizing. Kernberg's work has also stimulated much further investigation and research into severe personality disorders. He was reported to be the second most frequently cited author and the most frequently cited psychoanalyst in the current psychiatric literature on personality disorders (Blashfield and McElroy 1987). Examples of work influenced by Kernberg's views include the delineation of descriptive correlates of splitting and identity diffusion (Akhtar 1984, Akhtar and Byrne 1983), the analysis of diagnostic criteria sets for the borderline syndrome (Perry and Klerman 1978), the overt and covert phenomenology of severe personality disorders (Akhtar 1992), and the detailed descriptions of psychoanalytic psychotherapy techniques for such patients (Volkan 1976, 1987). Kernberg's influence is also discernible in certain revisions of *DSM-III* criteria, for instance, the inclusion of chronic envy as a diagnostic criterion of narcissistic personality disorder in *DSM-III-R*. His emphasis on the negative prognostic valence of antisocial features and the positive prognostic valence of inborn talents, intelligence, and neurotic symptoms in the context of borderline personality organization has been upheld by later investigations (Stone 1990). His cautious approach to safeguarding the therapeutic framework has been reiterated by more recent investigators (Adler 1989, Selzer et al. 1987, Waldinger and Gunderson 1987), who also emphasize the importance of an initial contract and appropriate goal setting in the treatment of borderline patients.

In view of its conceptual depth, panoramic scope, synthesizing power, and tremendous import as a catalyst for further thinking, Kernberg's *Borderline Conditions and Pathological Narcissism* has truly earned the status of a classic. To extend Freud's favorite analogy of a chess game for psychoanalytic treatment, this is certainly the work of a grand master.

REFERENCES

Adler, G. (1989). Psychodynamic psychotherapies in borderline personality disorder. In *Review of Psychiatry*, vol. 8, ed. A. Tasman, R. E. Hales and A. J. Frances, pp. 49–64. Washington, DC: American Psychiatric Press.

Akhtar, S. (1984). The syndrome of identity diffusion. *American Journal of Psychiatry* 141:1381–1385.

———— (1992). *Broken Structures: Severe Personality Disorders and Their Treatment*. Northvale, NJ: Jason Aronson.

Akhtar, S. and Byrne, J. P. (1983). The concept of splitting and its clinical relevance. *American Journal of Psychiatry* 140:1013–1016.

Blashfield, R. K. and McElroy, R. A. (1987). The 1985 journal literature on personality disorders. *Comprehensive Psychiatry* 28:536–546.

Calef, V. and Weinshel, E. (1979). The new psychoanalysis and psychoanalytic revisionism. *Psychoanalytic Quarterly* 48:470–491.

Cooper, A. M. (1983). The place of self psychology in the history of depth psychology. In *The Future of Psychoanalysis*, ed. A. Goldberg, pp. 3–17. New York: International Universities Press.

Gorton, G., and Akhtar, S. (1990). The literature on personality disorders, 1985–88: trends, issues, and controversies. *Hospital and Community Psychiatry* 41:39–51.

Grinker, R., and Werble, B. (1977). *The Borderline Patient*. New York: Jason Aronson.

Grinker, R., Werble, B., and Drye, R. C. (1968). *The Borderline Syndrome: A Behavioral Study of Ego Functions*. New York: Basic Books.

Gunderson, J. G., and Kolb, J. E. (1978). Discriminating features of borderline patients. *American Journal of Psychiatry* 135:792–796.

Gunderson, J. G., and Singer, M. (1975). Defining borderline patients: an overview. *American Journal of Psychiatry* 133:1–10.

Kernberg, O. F. (1967). Borderline personality organization. *Journal of the American Psychoanalytic Association* 15:641–685.

―――― (1976). *Object-Relations Theory and Clinical Psychoanalysis*. New York: Jason Aronson.

―――― (1984). *Severe Personality Disorders*. New Haven, CT: Yale University Press.

―――― (1992). *Aggression in Personality Disorders and Perversions*. New Haven, CT: Yale University Press.

Kernberg, O. F., Selzer, M. A., Koenigsberg H. W., et al. (1990). *Psychodynamic Psychotherapy of Borderline Patients*. New York: Basic Books.

Klein, M., and Tribich, D. (1981). Kernberg's object-relations theory: a critical evaluation. *International Journal of Psycho-Analysis* 63:27–43.

Kohut, H. (1971). *The Analysis of the Self*. New York: International Universities Press.

Perry, J. C., and Klerman, G. L. (1978). The borderline patient. *Archives of General Psychiatry* 35:141–150.

Selzer, M. A., Koenigsberg, H. W., and Kernberg, O. F. (1987). The initial contract in the treatment of borderline patients. *American Journal of Psychiatry* 144:927–930.

Stone, M. H. (1990). *The Fate of Borderline Patients*. New York: Guilford Press.

Strauss, G. D., Yager, J., and Strauss, G. E. (1984). The cutting edge in psychiatry. *American Journal of Psychiatry* 114:38–43.

Volkan, V. D. (1976). *Primitive Internalized Object Relations*. New York: International Universities Press.

―――― (1987). *Six Steps in the Treatment of Borderline Personality Organization*. Northvale, NJ: Jason Aronson.

Waelder, R. (1930). The principle of multiple function: observations on multiple determination. *Psychoanalytic Quarterly* 5:45–62.

Waldinger, R., and Gunderson, J. G. (1987). *Effective Psychotherapy with Borderline Patients*. New York: MacMillan.

Selections from
Borderline Conditions and
Pathological Narcissism
by Otto Kernberg

There exists an important group of psychopathological constellations which have in common a rather specific and remarkably stable form of pathological ego structure. The ego pathology differs from that found in the neuroses and the less severe characterological illnesses on the one hand, and the psychoses on the other. These patients must be considered to occupy a borderline area between neurosis and psychosis. The term *borderline personality organization*, rather than "borderline states" or other terms, more accurately describes these patients who do have a specific, stable, pathological personality organization; their personality organization is not a transitory state fluctuating between neurosis and psychosis.

The presenting symptoms of these patients may be similar to the presenting symptoms of the neuroses and character disorders; therefore, without a thorough diagnostic examination the particular characterological organization of these patients may be missed, with the result of a poor prognosis for treatment. Borderline personality organization requires specific therapeutic approaches which can only derive from an accurate diagnostic study.

Transient psychotic episodes may develop in patients with borderline personality organization when they are under severe stress or under the influence of alcohol or drugs. Such psychotic episodes usually remit with relatively brief but well-structured treatment approaches. When classical analytic approaches are attempted with these patients, they may experience a loss of reality testing and even develop delusional ideas which are restricted to the transference. Thus, they develop a transference psychosis rather than a transference neurosis. These patients usually maintain their capacity for reality testing, except under these special circumstances—severe stress, regression induced by alcohol or drugs, and a transference psychosis. In clinical interviews the formal organization of the thought processes of these patients appears intact. Psychological testing, particularly with the use of nonstructured projective tests, will often reveal the tendency of such patients to use primary-process functioning.

The main characteristics of this proposed modification in the psychoanalytic procedure are: (i) systematic elaboration of the manifest and latent negative transference without attempting to achieve full genetic reconstructions on the basis of it, followed by "deflection" of the manifest negative transference away from the therapeutic interaction through systematic examination of it in the patient's relations with others; (ii) confrontation with and interpretation of those pathological defensive operations which characterize borderline patients, as they enter the negative transference; (iii) definite structuring of the therapeutic situation with as active measures as necessary in order to block the acting out of the transference within the therapy itself (for example, by establishing limits under which the treatment is carried out, and providing strict limits to nonverbal aggression permitted in the hours); (iv) utilization of environmental structuring conditions, such as hospital, day hospital, foster home, etc., if acting out outside of the treatment hours threatens to produce a chronically stable situation of pathological instinctual gratification; (v) selective focusing on all those areas within the transference and the patient's life which illustrate the expression of pathological defensive operations as they induce ego weakening and imply reduced reality testing; (vi) utilization of the positive transference manifestations for maintenance of the therapeutic alliance, and only partial confrontation of the patient with those defenses which protect the positive transference; (vii) fostering more appropriate expressions in reality for those sexual conflicts which, through the pathological condensation of pregenital aggression and genital needs, interfere with the patient's adaptation; in other terms, "freeing" the potential for more mature genital development from its entanglements with pregenital aggression.

33

Edward O. Wilson:
Sociobiology, the New Synthesis

Reviewed by Edward Hare

Sociobiology was published in 1975. Four years earlier its author had published "an enormous and definitive book" on social insects, a work which established him as the world authority on that subject. In *Sociobiology*, Wilson set out to apply evolutionary theory to social behavior not only in insects but throughout the animal kingdom. As a biologist he naturally included man among the animals, but it was this which caused the uproar. Had he omitted his last thirty-three pages—the chapter on "Man: From Sociobiology to Sociology"—his book would probably have led a quiet life as a well-written semipopular textbook on social animals.

Sociobiology was praised as opening a new field in social study, a biological basis for a science of sociology. It was dismissed as the popularization of a subject outside its author's field of competence, the term sociobiology being "merely a grand word for one branch of evolutionary ethology." And it was attacked with a surprising degree of virulence, not only by creationists and left-wingers but by a host of respectable academics as well (e.g., Rose et al. 1984; Sahlins 1976). To a psychiatrist concerned with the vagaries of human nature, it is the virulence which is interesting; for as Oliver Wendell Holmes said of the indignation aroused by his remark about the pharmacopoeia and the fishes, "a loud outcry at a slight touch reveals the weak spot in a profession as well as in a patient."

The most acrimonious criticism of *Sociobiology* was that it used spurious biological analogy to give pseudo-scientific respectability to sexism and the capitalist ethic of the middle classes. Wilson had argued: that there was strong evidence of genetic factors in the social behavior of animals (the social behavior of chimpanzees, for example, is everywhere very similar, even among widely separated groups); that the social behavior of apes and of present-day hunter-gatherer societies had much in common—including aggressive dominance-seeking males and docile females; and that, as these features most probably had a genetic basis, it was reasonable to presume similar genetic traits in civilized mankind, even if these were now largely overlaid by culture. But, said the critics, animals are not human, and to suppose their behavior had anything in common with human behavior was to be guilty of naive anthropomorphism. So *Sociobiology* was derided as mere myth-making, as a just-so story, as a piece of bourgeois thought; and its author's suggestion that his new synthesis might provide "an enduring set of first principles of sociology" [page 579] was considered absurd or offensive, not only by orthodox sociologists but also by philosophers who held ethics to be outside the scope of science.

What these criticisms imply, I think, is that Wilson stirred up the never-ending conflict between science and religion (or the secular counterparts of religion). The stability of most societies depends on the general acceptance of a moral code, whose authority derives from myths enshrined in holy writ. Ideas or discoveries that might undermine the credibility of these myths will threaten social stability; and the rulers of society, who derive their power from its stability, will naturally wish to suppress such dangerous knowledge—and have done so down history with a violence exemplified by the fate of Prometheus, Galileo, the Christian heretics, and the Russian dissidents. In 1690 the physician and philosopher John Locke argued that since civilized behavior depended on a belief in God, the protection of the State should be withdrawn from atheists; and in the early nineteenth century the progress of geology was retarded by the fear that if God's special intervention in the course of nature were denied, it would lead to free-thinking and so to revolution (Gillespie 1951). Wilson's contribution to dangerous knowledge was to support the idea that human social behavior is partly under genetic control. The idea is dangerous (to those in power) because it implies a person cannot be held entirely responsible for his behavior. If that were so, then society would be without a moral sanction against those who broke its rules. This explains why the Church disapproved of astrology, why Stalin disapproved of genetics (as shown by his support for Lysenko), and why the predestination of Calvin was of a kind "not to be enquired into."

The dominance of nurture over nature has been upheld not only by those wielding religious power but also by philosophers and sociologists fiercely opposed to religion. Hume, who defined a clergyman as "a person appropriated to teach hypocrisy and inculcate vice" (Brady 1984), and who, on his deathbed, told Boswell that "when he heard a man was religious he concluded he was a rascal," nevertheless believed the mind is a tabula rasa at birth and that a person's character and behavior are formed entirely from what happens to him thereafter. John Stuart Mill (1873), whose father taught him that religion was not merely a mental delusion but a moral evil opposed to the progress of the human mind, deplored "the prevailing tendency to regard all marked distinctions of human nature as innate." He held this idea to be "one of the chief hinderances to the rational treatment of great social questions," and believed there were "irresistible proofs" that "by far the greater part" of natural differences between men were produced by "differences in circumstances." Darwin on the other hand, although also a freethinker, concluded that the greater part of human attributes were inborn (Barlow 1958); and Galton (1883), who had found that both the physical and mental attributes of identical twins were strikingly similar even when they had been reared apart, considered this clear evidence of "the vastly preponderating effect of nature over nurture." Maudsley (1919), always biologically minded, took the same view: "civilised nature doesn't mean the vital (brutish) nature is any less."

There was still another criticism of *Sociobiology*. This was directed against its reductionist view that human attributes are all understandable in biological terms and therefore, ultimately, in terms of physics and chemistry. Maudsley was a reductionist, defending himself on the general ground that matter is more wonderful than you think (Maudsley 1913). In recent years reductionism has been made respectable by the support of eminent physicists and biologists (Atkins 1981, Dawkins 1986, Jaynes 1976, Smith 1985). But this opinion, which would have been considered blasphemous in a religious age, is still emotionally or intellectually unacceptable to many. Even Alfred Wallace, Darwin's codiscoverer of the origin of species, never believed that evolution applied to Man. Evolutionary reductionism, first attacked by Samuel Butler in his *Luck or Cunning?*, has been criticized on the general ground that evolution is not a passive process but implies at every stage the presence of individual learning and purposive exploration (Granit 1977, Popper 1974), and on the particular ground that human mental powers are so much greater than other creatures' as no longer to be comparable, the influence of culture now quite outweighing that of genetics (Crook 1980).

These multifarious criticisms of *Sociobiology*, and particularly the virulence of some of them, surely indicate the importance of the subject raised in its final chapter. Wilson did not deny the large part played by culture in shaping human society: he simply pointed out that there were probably some genetic factors, too, and that it would be useful to enquire further into the nature and strength of such factors since, in so far as they were present, they would exert a constraint on the range of cultural possibilities:

"the genes hold culture on a lease" (Wilson 1978). The gain to sociology from accepting a more biological basis might be that this would involve taking a long-term evolutionary view of human nature in addition to the short-term cultural view. Darwin noted that there are animal species (e.g., the emu and the cassowary) where the usual sexual patterns of courtship and care of offspring are reversed—a phenomenon that might remind one, for instance, of that German tribe noted (and deplored) by Tacitus—and an interesting parallel has been drawn between the genetic variations of behavior in animal species and the cultural variations of behavior in human societies. But Darwin also believed in capitalism, in the innate superiority of men's minds over women's (his opinion was similar to that of Mill) (Darwin 1871) and of the white races over the black (Dawkins 1986); and Maudsley (1919) held that "democracy is in no wise lovely." The fact that we now tend to think differently illustrates the rapidity with which cultural values may change, and this suggests there is a risk in basing sociological theory on what may prove to be transient aspects of human thought and behavior. "All sensible biologists," said Bonner (1975; see also Andreski 1972), "are apprehensive of human sociology" because it seems such a "murky mixture of the obvious and the obscure." Wilson's book reinforced what is perhaps a growing opinion that if sociology is to become a science it must be based on biology (Berghe 1979, Pugh 1978, Symons 1979). My own hope is that the furor over *Sociobiology* will represent an instance of today's outrageous idea becoming the commonplace of tomorrow.

REFERENCES

Andreski, S. (1972). *Social Sciences as Sorcery*. Harmondsworth, England: Deutsch.
Atkins, P. (1981). *The Creation*. London: Freeman.
Barlow, N. (1958). *The Autobiography of Charles Darwin 1809–1882*. London: Collins.
Bonner, T. J. (1975). Review of E. O. Wilson's *Sociobiology*. *Scientific American* 244:129–132
Brady, F. (1984). *James Boswell: The Later Years 1769–1795*. London: Heinemann.
Crook, J. H. (1980). *The Evolution of Human Consciousness*. Oxford: Clarendon.
Darwin, C. (1871). *The Descent of Man*. 2nd ed. London: Murray.
Dawkins, R. (1986). *The Blind Watchmaker*. Harlow: Longmans.
Galton, F. (1883). *Inquiries into Human Faculty*. London: Everyman.
Gillespie, C. C. (1951). *Genesis and Geology*. New York: Harper & Row.
Granit, R. (1977). *The Purposive Brain*. London: MIT.
Jaynes, J. (1976). *The Origin of Consciousness in the Breakdown of the Bicameral Mind*. New York: Houghton Mifflin.
Maudsley, H. (1913). Mental organization: an introductory chapter. *Journal of Mental Science* 59:1–14.
_____ (1919). War psychology: English and German. *Journal of Mental Science* 65–87.
Mill, J. S. (1873). *Autobiography*. World Classics edition. Oxford: Oxford University Press, 1958.

Popper, K. (1974). *Unended Quest: An Intellectual Autobiography*. London: Fontana-Collins.
Pugh, G. E. (1978). *The Biological Origin of Human Values*. London: Routledge & Kegan Paul.
Rose, S., Lewontin, R. C., and Kamin, L. J. (1984). *Not in Our Genes*. London: Penguin.
Sahlins, M. (1976). *The Use and Abuse of Biology*. Ann Arbor, MI: University of Michigan Press.
Smith, C. G. (1985). *Ancestral Voices: Language and the Evolution of Human Consciousness*. New York: Prentice Hall.
Symons, D. (1979). *The Evolution of Human Sexuality*. New York: Oxford University Press.
Van Den Berghe, P. L. (1979). *Human Family Systems: An Evolutionary View*. Oxford: Elsevier.
Wilson, E. O. (1978). *On Human Nature*. London: Harvard University Press.

Selections from
Sociobiology, the New Synthesis
by Edward O. Wilson

The following extracts from Wilson's book illustrate very briefly some of its main themes. The book assumes a high school knowledge of zoology and thus assumes the reader is familiar with such biological concepts as natural selection, genes, chromosomes, the gene pool and altruism, the Darwinian theory of evolution, and the major groups of the vertebrates and invertebrates.

These extracts concern:

1. *Natural Selection*. Natural Selection is the biological basis of evolution. It is the process whereby certain genes gain representation in the following generations superior to that of genes located at the same chromosomal position. This section defines *sociobiology* and explains how it differs from *sociology*.

2. *Societies*. Wilson describes the four main types of society in the animal world. Human society is so different from all others as to be unique.

3. *Human Social Evolution*. Its three main stages are described in terms of biology and evolution.

4. *Sexual Selection*. One important factor in the uniqueness of human society has been sexual selection (female choice of mate) for particular traits and abilities in men.

5. *The Future*. Wilson briefly reflects on how sociobiology may develop during the next hundred years.

Note: Some of the passages are slightly abridged from Wilson's original text.

Natural Selection

Natural Selection is the process whereby certain genes gain representation in the following generations superior to that of other genes located at the same chromosome positions.

In the process of natural selection, any device that can insert a higher proportion of certain genes into subsequent generations will come to characterize the species. One class of such devices promoted prolonged individual survival. Another promotes superior mating performance and better care of offspring. As more complex social behaviour by the organism is added to the genes' technique for replicating themselves, *altruism* becomes increasingly prevalent and eventually appears in exaggerated forms: Wilson defines "altruism" as "self-destructive behavior for the benefit of others." (p. 578) This brings us to the central theoretical problem of Sociobiology: how can altruism, which by definition reduces personal fitness (p. 578), possibly evolve by natural selection? The answer is *kinship*: if genes causing altruism are shared by two organisms because of common descent, and if the altruistic act by one organism increases the *joint* contribution of these genes to the next generation, the propensity to altruism will spread through the gene pool.

Sociobiology is defined as the systematic study of the biological basis of all social behaviour. Here, it focuses on animal societies, their population structure, castes and communication, together with all the physiology underlying the social adaptations. But the discipline is also concerned with the social behaviour of early man and the adaptive features of organisation in the more primitive contemporary human societies. *Sociology, sensu strictu*, is the study of human societies at all levels of complexity. It stands apart from Sociobiology because of its largely structuralist and *non-genetic* approach. One of the functions of Sociobiology is to reformulate the foundations of the Social Sciences in a way which draws them into the *modern synthesis* (of Darwinian Evolutionary theory). The new sociobiology should be composed of roughly equal parts of invertebrate zoology, vertebrate zoology and population biology. Biologists have always been intrigued by comparisons between societies of invertebrates, especially insect societies, and those of vertebrates. They have dreamed of identifying the common properties of such disparate units in such a way as would provide insight into all aspects of social evolution, including that of man.

This may seem an impossibly difficult task, but in my own studies I have become impressed more with the similarities than with the differences between invertebrate and vertebrate societies.

Societies

To visualise the main features of social behavior in all organisms, at once, from colonial jellyfish to man, is to encounter a paradox. Social systems have originated repeatedly in one major group of organisms after another, achieving widely different degrees of specialization and complexity. Four groups occupy pinnacles high above the others: the colonial invertebrates, the social insects, the non-human mammals and man. Each has basic qualities of social life unique to itself. Here, then, is the paradox. Although the sequence just given proceeds unquestionably from more and older forms of life to more advanced and recent ones, their key properties of social existence, including cohesiveness, altruism and cooperativeness, *decline*. It seems as though social evolution has slowed as the body plan of the individual organism became more elaborate.

The 4 groups of societies are:

1. *The colonial invertebrates,* including the corals, the jellyfish, the siphanophores and the bryozoans, have come close to producing perfect societies. The individual members, or zooids as they are called, are in many cases fully subordinated to the colony as a whole—not just in function, but more literally, through close and fully interdependent physical union. So extreme is the specialization of the members, and so thorough their assembly into physical wholes, that the colony can equally well be called an organism.

2. *The higher social insects,* comprised of ants, termites and certain wasps and bees, form societies that are much less perfect. To be sure, they are characterized by sterile castes that are self-sacrificing in the service of the mother queen. Also the altruistic behavior is prominent and varied. The castes are physically modified to perform particular functions and are bound to one another by tight, intricate forms of communication. Furthermore, individuals cannot live apart from the colony for more than short periods. They can recognise castes but not individual nest mates. In a word, the insect society is based upon impersonal intimacy.

Social insects are physically separate entities. Some aggressiveness and discord may occur. Bumble bee queens control their daughters by aggression, attacking them if they attempt to lay eggs. If the queen is removed from the relatively simple wasp and bumble bee societies, certain of the workers fight among one another for the right to replace her.

3. *In invertebrate societies,* aggressiveness and discord are carried much further. Selfishness rules the relationship between members. Sterile castes are unknown, and acts of altruism are infrequent. Each member of the society is a potentially independent, reproducing unit. Cooperation is usually rudimentary. It represents a concession whereby members are able to raise their personal survival and reproductive rates above those that would accrue from a solitary life. The death of a dominant male is usually followed by nothing more than a shift in the dominance hierarchy, perhaps

accompanied, as in the case of langurs and lions, by the murder of the leader's youngest offspring.

4. *Human beings* remain essentially vertebrate in their social structure. But they have carried it to a level of complexity so high as to constitute a distinct, fourth pinnacle of social evolution. They have broken the old vertebrate restraints: not by reducing selfishness, but rather by acquiring the intelligence to consult the past and to plan the future. Human beings establish long-remembered contracts and profitably engage in acts of reciprocal altruism that can be spaced over long periods of time, indeed over generations. Men intuitively introduce kin selection into the calculus of these relationships. They are preoccupied with kinship ties to a degree inconceivable in other social species. Their transactions are made still more efficient by a unique syntactical language. Human societies approach the insect societies in cooperativeness and far exceed them in powers of communication. They have reversed the downward trend in social evolution that prevailed over one billion years of the previous history of life. When placed in this perspective, it perhaps seems less surprising that the human form of social organisation has arisen only once, whereas the three other peaks of evolution have been scaled repeatedly by independently evolving lines of animals.

Human Social Evolution

[Wilson describes three main stages:]

1. *The first stage*, to 3 million years ago (Australopithecus stage), when brain capacity was increasing at an accelerating rate. Simultaneously, erect posture, striding, and bipedal locomotion were perfected and the hands moulded for the precision grip. These early men undoubtedly used tools to a much greater extent than do modern chimpanzees.

2. *The second stage*. A much more rapid phase of acceleration began about 100,000 years ago. It consisted primarily of a cultural evolution building upon the genetic potential in the brain that had accumulated over the previous millions of years. The brain had reached a threshold, and a wholly new, enormously rapid form of mental evolution took over.

[Of this second stage we may ask: "What environmental features cause this unique evolutionary path: and once started, why did the hominids go so far"?]

It should be noted that very little can be inferred directly from comparisons with other living primates—the manlike traits of chimpanzees could be due to evolutionary convergence. The best procedure is to extrapolate backward from living hunter-gatherer societies.

What we can conclude with some confidence is that primitive man lived in small territorial groups, within which males were dominant over females. There is no compelling reason to conclude that men did the hunting while women stayed at home. In chimpanzees males do the hunting, which may be suggestive. But in lions, the females are the providers, often working in groups while the males usually hold back. In the African wild dog both sexes participate. The prevailing theory of the origin of human sociality may be termed the *Autocatalysis Model* (i.e., a process of positive feedback).

3. *The third stage. Later social evolution. Homo sapiens* appeared in Europe about 40,000 years B.C. Agriculture was invented about 10,000 years ago, after which population increased enormously. Finally, after A.D. 1400, European civilisation shifted gear again, and knowledge and technology grew not just exponentially but super exponentially.

Sexual Selection

Seed eating is a plausible explanation to account for the movement of hominids from the forests to the savannah, and big-game hunting might account for their advance to *Homo erectus*. But to carry evolution all the way to the *Homo sapiens* grade and further (to agriculture and civilisation), additional factors were probably needed. One of these was *sexual selection*.

Polygyny is a general trait in hunter-gatherer bands and may also have been the rule in early hominid societies. Sexual selection would be enhanced by the constant mating provocation that arises from the females' nearly continuous sexual receptivity. Because of the existence of a high level of cooperation within the band, sexual selection would tend to be linked with hunting prowess, leadership, skill at tool-making and other visible attributes that contribute to the success of the family and the male band. Aggressiveness was constrained and the old forms of overt primate dominance replaced by complex social skills. Young males found it profitable to fit into the group, controlling their sexuality and aggression and awaiting their turn at leadership. As a result the dominant male in hominid societies was most likely to possess a mosaic of qualities that reflect the necessities of compromise: controlled, cunning, cooperative, attractive to the ladies, good with children, relaxed, tough, eloquent, skilful, knowledgeable and proficient in self-defence and hunting. Since positive feedback occurs between these most sophisticated social traits and breeding success, social evolution can proceed indefinitely without additional selective pressures from the environment.

The Future

When mankind has achieved an ecological steady state, probably by the end of the 21st Century, the internalisation of social evolution will be nearly complete. About this time, biology should be at its peak with the Social Sciences maturing rapidly. Some historians of science will take issue with this projection arguing that the accelerating pace of discoveries in these fields implies a more rapid development. But historical precedents have misled us before: the subjects we are talking about are more difficult than physics and chemistry by at least two orders of magnitude.

It seems that our autocatalytic social evolution has locked us onto a particular course which the early hominids still within us may not welcome. To maintain the species indefinitely we are compelled to drive toward total knowledge, right down to the level of the neuron and the gene. When we have progressed enough to explain ourselves in these mechanistic terms and the Social Sciences come to full flower, the result may be hard to accept.

[Wilson concludes with a foreboding quotation from Camus: of the kind that perhaps naturally flows from a fully reductionist view.]

A world that can be explained even with bad reasons is a familiar world. But on the other hand, in a universe divested of illusions and lights, man feels an alien, a stranger. His exile is without remedy since he is deprived of the memory of a lost home or the hope of a promised land.

This, unfortunately, is true. But we still have another hundred years.

34

Robin Skynner:
One Flesh: Separate Persons

Reviewed by Stan Ruszczynski

There are probably few practitioners of marital and family psychotherapy who are not aware of the work of Dr. Robin Skynner. In his own unique style, he has been part of the vanguard of the development of thinking and practice in these fields. Together with colleagues he was instrumental in setting up the Group Analytic Practice, the Institute of Group Analysis, and the Institute of Family Therapy. He is a teacher and a prolific writer, and many of his papers, articles, and lectures have recently been collected and published in two books (Skynner 1987, 1989).

Dr. Skynner is also widely known to a lay audience, largely through his excellent book co-written with actor and author John Cleese (Skynner and Cleese 1983). In this book in particular, Skynner demonstrates his capacity to translate complex theoretical and clinical concepts into ideas accessible to a general reader. The sequel to this book, currently being co-written, is keenly awaited.

Much of what Skynner is known for, and what underlies much of his work, was set down in *One Flesh: Separate Persons* in 1976. As the subtitle indicates, this book outlines his "Principles of Family and Marital Psychotherapy." In the opening sentences of the book, Skynner puts marital and family psychotherapy into context. He writes:

> The institution of the family stands in a peculiarly central, crucial position. It faces inward to the individual, outward toward society, preparing each member to take his place in the wider social group. . . . Our needs for physical, emotional and intellectual exchange, and for nurturance, control, communication and genital sexuality, can all exist side by side and find satisfaction in harmonious relationship to one another. . . . It [the family] has

367

enormous creative potential . . . and it is not surprising that, when it becomes disordered, it possesses an equal potential for terrible destruction.

It is exactly because marital and family life is so central to public and personal mental health, either in promoting it, stunting it, or, at worst, damaging it, that it is rightly the concern of the mental health profession. Marital psychotherapy and family psychotherapy should therefore stand alongside individual and group therapies as potential treatments of choice.

In his introduction to the book, Skynner writes of this text being an attempt to provide a review of the various theories of marital and family psychotherapy, with practical guidance and clinical illustrations that may enable professionals to apply the ideas to their own practice. At the time of writing, no such introductory general text was available. What did exist tended to concern itself with either family psychotherapy or marital and sexual therapy, and took either a psychoanalytic orientation or a systemic one.

What is of particular interest and value in this book is the attempt Skynner makes to relate and integrate family, marital and sex therapy viewed from a range of theoretical and conceptual positions. He refers to this himself when, in his chapter on "Developmental Sequences" (Chapter 2), he writes:

> A generally useful classification (of the sequences of events in childhood development) is based on a combination of Freudian and Kleinian developmental concepts, modified in the light of elaborations by other individual-centred therapists such as H. S. Sullivan and E. Erikson, and also by researchers in group dynamics and development, including, Bion, Bennis, Schutz and Durkin.

He goes on to acknowledge that followers of any one of these schools may justifiably feel that some violence has been done to their conceptual schemes. He specifies, for example, that there may well be real differences between Klein's positions of emotional development and Freud's stages. However, he justifies his integrative approach by saying that he is attempting to find the common patterns which must underpin all these various theories.

This lack of theoretical purity, this eclecticism, is one aspect of the book which some readers may find difficult, particularly when many of the clinical illustrations which pepper the book tend towards the anecdotal and personal and so do not readily avail themselves of critical theoretical and clinical examination. However, this criticism, although probably valid, misses Skynner's purpose in writing the book, and also the value that the book still has today. Skynner wanted to introduce the relative beginner, be he/she a psychiatrist, social worker, counselor, or psychologist, to an overview of the variety of approaches to thinking about and working clinically with couples and families. He was clear in the book that an integrated, eclectic approach is the one he finds most useful for his clinical work. The value of the book goes beyond that: it allows the practitioner to discover, from his own experiences, which of the conceptual and technical models he finds most therapeutically valuable. It is this that I personally found most satisfying when I first read the book on its publication, and still do now on rereading it. It has always remained a textbook to dip into.

The book is written in two parts, theory and practice. Or, as Skynner writes, concepts and applications.

In the first part, he systematically goes through general systems theory, a developmental scheme (eclectic, as outlined above, but heavily influenced by ego psychology), psychoanalytical theories, modelling and social learning theories. Throughout, there is a constant attempt to show the overlap and similarities between these different models. Three of the nine chapters in this first part concentrate on the marital relationship. This, I believe, is appropriate as the couple are at the heart of the family. Children internalize not just models of their parents in isolation but also, probably more importantly, of their parents in relation to each other and in relation to them. These internalized images then become part of the blueprint that, largely unconsciously, is taken not only into their own marriages and families, but into all their social interactions and relationships.

Skynner gives a very clear and concise outline of the psychoanalytic object-relations model of marital interaction, and specifies the developmental and defensive aspects of unconscious partner choice. He also discusses with conviction the view that in the case of most children and adolescents who are referred for psychotherapeutic help, the level of the child's developmental arrest, or the nature of the symptom being presented, relates very closely to pathology in the parental relationship. Whether understood in systemic terms or in terms of psychoanalytic notions of projection and projective identification, the child may be said to become the victim of the emotional conflicts of the parental couple.

In the final chapter in this first part, Skynner addresses "The Ethics of Change." He asks such questions as what right we (as practitioners) have to attempt to change others; what the motivations of referrers may be; whether change is possible; and, if so, whether it is desirable. It is a thought-provoking chapter and addresses issues which are often taken for granted or overlooked.

In the second part of the book, the author turns to clinical practice. He outlines different therapeutic models and distinguishes between them. He then describes his own clinical practice, across the range of his clinical work including that of couples groups which he often co-ran with his wife. Throughout, there are many clinical examples and vignettes to illustrate what is being discussed.

I was particularly interested to read his views on transference. He writes that he does not encourage the transference by drawing it onto himself, and only interprets it if it is getting in the way. He also says that the wide spacing of the interviews, and his more natural, active, and spontaneous behavior diminish the development of transference phenomena. Finally, he says that as the therapist he offers himself explicitly as an expert and this, too, limits the development of the transference.

How much these factors actually do limit the development of the transference is open to debate, and Skynner seems to imply this when he goes on to say that, despite all his best efforts, marked transferences to the therapist do develop. He sees this as usually being concerned with defensive needs, either in the family or in the therapist. This view is in sharp contrast to a purer psychoanalytic understanding which would view transference as inevitable and unavoidable, and would value the transference feelings and enactments evoked by the psychotherapeutic encounter as being a rich source of information about the family members and their images and expectations of relationships. This view is not one simply held by individual psychoanalytic psychotherapists, but one that family and marital psychotherapists would hold (e.g., Box et al. 1981, Scharff 1982). However, this may be an unfair observation since the application and adaptation of psychoanalytic theory and practice to marital and family work has gone on since the publication of Skynner's book. I suspect, however, that he would still hold to his original view.

The next five chapters discuss a variety of technical issues such as indications and contraindications for marital and family work; the use of multifamily and couples groups; and training and teamwork. This second section finishes with a chapter outlining the family therapy with a particular family carried out over sixteen sessions at three or four weekly intervals by Dr. Skynner and a female cotherapist.

Without doubt, exactly as intended, this book remains an excellent introduction to marital and family psychotherapy. In its 400-plus pages it is informative, provocative, practical, and always lucid and accessible. Although an introductory text, it is ambitious in its aims and raises many issues for debate and discussion. Like a good therapist or teacher, Skynner makes the reader pause and think for himself, and come to his own conclusions.

I would like to raise two further thoughts. The first is a criticism, the second is a point of interest.

To take the criticism: There are points in the book when Skynner could be accused of sexism and chauvinism. Sometimes his descriptions of the wives and mothers in the families he is writing about are rather clumsy. It seems particularly unfortunate to use expressions such as "shrewishly" (p. 75) and "bitchiness" (p. 77). There is a danger that such clumsiness may distract some readers from utilizing the book to the degree it deserves.

This may be compounded by Skynner's clearly stated view that for some families it is optimal for the father to accept ultimate responsibility and authority for all important matters. What he is referring to is something that most marital and family psychotherapists are familiar with, particularly in relation to working with the more severely disturbed relationships and chaotic families: that is, the lack of structure, boundaries, and authority which such families display. The therapeutic solution is of course the development of benevolent boundaries and authority, but there is no reason why this should necessarily be in the domain of the male. Most appropriately, this should be carried jointly by the parental couple in the case of a family, and by both spouses in the case of a marriage. Without denying appropriate differentiation, clinical experience demonstrates quite clearly that it is the capacity to share power and authority that produces healthy marriages and families.

The final thought is simply one of interest. There has recently been a lot of interest, at least among those more inclined towards a psychoanalytic framework, in Bion's concept of container-contained (Bion 1962, 1967), developed out of Klein's concept of projective identification (Klein 1946). Bion's model of containment suggests how personal relationships can be so beneficial and therapeutic. The other's capacity to be sensitive to, process and make some sense of tensions and anxieties evoked by the self, all usually unconsciously, allows the tensions and anxieties to be experienced less persecutorily. It also allows for the self to internalize the notion that such containment is possible and so begin to better manage inevitable feelings of conflict and fear.

This framework is very useful for thinking about the nature of marital and family interaction; about what the marriage and the family naturally fulfill for the individual members. It also offers a model for psychotherapeutic intervention. It may be that when a couple or a family seek psychotherapeutic help, it is because their natural containment capacity has broken down; the psychotherapist is sought to offer a temporary containment in the psychotherapeutic relationship, which allows the now unmanageable tensions and conflicts to be reflected upon.

Inherent in Dr. Skynner's book is the attempt to think about what is happening between the couple in a marriage or between family members. His personal openness, and his willingness to use whatever concepts and theories prove of value, suggest that he would find Bion's framework at least familiar.

When I started to think about writing this review, I wrote to Dr. Skynner to tell him of my project. He wrote back a very generous letter of some length. I am sure that he will not mind if I quote his final paragraph:

> I never intended to write a book at all! At the time I began, it was impossible to get American text books on family therapy in Britain, and I decided to write a long paper or pamphlet of about 50 pages for the seminars I was doing then. However, 50 became 100, 100 became 200, 200, 400 and even then I realised it was all just an outline summary of what I had to say.

I, for one, am very pleased and grateful that Dr. Skynner wrote this "outline summary." It proved substantial food for thought and reflection when published in 1976, and still does today. It remains an introduction of some substance, and I for one continue to use it, not uncritically, and to recommend it. The publishers are quite right to keep it in their lists and to republish it.

REFERENCES

Bion, W. (1962). *Learning from Experience*. London: Karnac Books.
_____ (1967). *Second Thoughts*. London: Karnac Books.
Box, S., (ed). (1981). *Psychotherapy with Families: An Analytic Approach*. London: Routledge.
Klein, M. (1946). Notes on some schizoid mechanisms. In *The Writings of Melanie Klein*, vol. 3. London: Hogarth.
Scharff, D. E. (1982). *The Sexual Relationship*. London: Routledge.
Skynner, A. C. R. (1976). *One Flesh: Separate Persons. Principles of Family and Marital Psychotherapy*. London: Constable.
_____ (1987) *Explorations with Families: Group Analysis and Family Therapy*. Ed. J. Schlapobersky. London: Methuen.
_____ (1989) *Institutes and How to Survive Them: Mental Health Training and Consultation*. Selected Papers. Ed. J. Schlapobersky. London: Methuen.
Skynner, A. C. R., and Cleese, J. (1983). *Families and How to Survive Them*. London: Methuen.

Selections from
One Flesh: Separate Persons
by Robin Skynner

In Chapter 1, where we looked at the world in terms of systems theory, living organisms were seen as part of larger organizations – the supra-systems which include, at different levels, the group to which a given individual belonged, its species, animal life, living beings generally and so on; at the same time the parts of a given organism were seen as subsystems which could be further divided into smaller and smaller meaningful assemblies, the whole being interrelated in a hierarchy whereby the greater dominated and controlled the lesser, within certain degrees of freedom.

But with living organisms we find a seeming contradiction, for the lesser is not only contained within the greater, but in some degree the lesser also contains the greater as part of its own structure. The organism includes within itself a model, map or representation, however abstract, incomplete or distorted, of its environment and also of itself.

Bowlby's use of the phrase "working model" is intended to remind us that such images, models or objects are not to be thought of as static, like pictures in a photograph album. Studies of an individual's inner life, under psychoanalysis, show that the models are dynamic, interacting, changing, more like a family movie. Yet even this dynamic image is not fluid and creative enough, for an actual family movie merely reproduces events from some of the limited behaviour and interaction which were actually witnessed. The inner models do more than this: They appear to be made up not only of a set of perceptions but also of associated attitudes beliefs, tendencies and types of relationships which are recombined into new syntheses all the time.

The models are alive in the sense that they continue to form new combinations and to have a life of their own in this inner world, within the limited scope of the original information absorbed about them. By experimenting or playing with the models internally (a process expressed in actual play in the case of children, and made use of in play therapy), patterns of behaviour appropriate to different situations are worked out.

The subject identifies with one inner figure and casts a real person he has to deal with in the role of another, subsequently reproducing in his behaviour actions which have their roots in past experiences. The source may be relationships he has witnessed, in which case he will be playing a role learned from another person, or he may reproduce a relationship in which he was actually one of the participants. In the latter case, it is important to remember that he may identify with, and play or enact, not only his own previous part, but also that of the person who interacted with him in the first place, casting his present companion in the role that he himself played earlier.

Normal, healthy development is characterized, as we have seen, by a progressive capacity to relinquish the original relationship of egocentricity, total dependency and expectation of gratification without return, in favor of a more equal, mutual relationship where the needs of others and of the group as a whole are increasingly considered and respected, at the cost of greater self-discipline and restraint or delay in personal gratification.

Leaving on one side those malevolent relationships which have their *raison d'être* in the infliction of pain and suffering, marriage can, it will be clear, be either a process facilitating growth (when the partners cherish and respect each other as individuals and have no desire to possess or restrict one another), a substitute for personal growth (when the partner is used to contain the lost aspects of the self, without attempt at reintegration), or a defense against growth (where they rely on each other's defenses to maintain the *status quo* and seek comfort and security only).

If, as has been suggested, each individual's capacity for relationships, including love, marriage and parenthood, is determined by the repertoire laid down or programed in the internalized relationship-models or object-relationships, and if these are derived from early experience in the family of origin, the attitude of the parents to each other, as experienced in childhood, will be of vital importance. In particular, the parent's sexual relationship will be crucial, for this interaction, which involves the most total and profound relating—intellectually, emotionally and bodily, integrating what is most animal, earthy and lusty with the most tender, spiritual and altruistic of human qualities—can be viewed as a paradigm for all other fruitful and creative human interactions. Though, like all things that are fully formed and perfected, it is not easily won and demands effort and work before it can become effortless and spontaneous, sexuality should reach an expression where it can be a model for, and illuminate and transform all other aspects of the family relationship.

To express this principle briefly, it is useful to introduce the concept of the Minimum Sufficient Network; in any situation this is the psychological or social structure containing enough of the three subsystems—superego, ego and id—for autonomous function to be possible. In cases which respond well to individual psychotherapy or casework, the three subsystems are adequately developed within the individual to permit communication within the intrapsychic network to a sufficient degree, without much need to involve others. But where developmental arrest, due to deprivation or trauma, has led to these structures remaining dispersed among a number of people, the only autonomous system will be the group containing those individuals, and treatment must go beyond intrapsychic exploration and interpretation to facilitate communication between the persons involved.

I have already outlined Klein's developmental concepts in Chapter 2. What I began to notice was a kind of "sandwich" distribution regarding suitability for group therapy, whereby the most primitive levels of development and the more sophisticated levels could use group situations fruitfully, though in different ways, while the level intermediate between these "top" and "bottom" levels required a dyadic relationship.

Individuals and families representing the "bottom layer of the sandwich" make extensive use of paranoid/schizoid functioning. Boundaries are vague and fluctuating. Parts of the self are readily projected into others, who as easily accept them and perform certain functions for other members. These mutual projections may change repeatedly, so that roles change and the problem appears in different members at different times. Pleasurable and painful feelings are split and kept apart, often by projecting the former into a "good" child and the latter into a "bad" scapegoat. At this level the members forming a group or family are thus not true individuals with separate identities and boundaries, but rather functions, roles or part-objects which are located in particular physical bodies on any one occasion.

Such individuals feel comfortable in a group, not because they are having true relationships with others as separate people, but because the relationships are essentially on a part-object basis to the group as a mass, as in the infant in the first three months who is little harmed by multiple mothering and can accept changing nurses because he cannot yet recognize his mother as a person.

At this level families relate to organizations rather than to particular individuals within them, and are not unduly disturbed by changes of staff provided the unit as a whole remains available to them. To be allowed to enter the building and sit on the stairs may be as supportive as a formal interview, even a great deal more supportive if the former is available on demand and the latter involves delay. At this level conjoint therapy is not only possible but essential if progress is to be made, since only then will the overt problem be visible as the function it is connected with passes from one member to another. Only then, too, will there be a minimum sufficient network capable of autonomous functioning and able to use constructively the help provided.

The "middle layer of the sandwich" is made up of families whose functioning corresponds in some measure to that of a child who has developed some capacity to contain its negative feelings without projecting them, who is able to integrate love and hate and tolerate the ambivalence and depressive anxiety which results, and who is able to perceive others as separate individuals with needs of their own who also require concern and care. This layer corresponds, in other words, to Klein's depressive position, but to the earlier stages in the emergence of such capacities where the synthesis is still insecure and the capacity to keep the image of the loved ones present and intact is precarious and easily threatened by arousal of frustration and rage through absence and rejection. Such individuals and families, like infants between about six months and two years of age, are deeply dependent on positive relationships with each other and with the therapist, and are made severely anxious by any threat of loss, separation or rejection. Uncovering of strong negative feelings in the course of family sessions can lead such families to flee, and even the awareness of differences of attitude and of separate identities can be experienced as a threat of abandonment.

At this level, the emphasis needs to be on secure, reliable dyadic relationships. Conjoint diagnostic interviews are possible if used with care, and conjoint therapy sessions can still be utilized if they are accompanied by individual sessions for all the members or for a key figure (usually the mother) who is thereby helped to play this supportive role in the family as a whole. If the individual therapists attend the family or marital sessions they should maintain their personal relationships to their own family members, each representing his point of view rather like a legal advocate and letting other therapists support their own family members in the same way. A compromise is also possible, whereby the individual relationship is provided in the conjoint session itself without separate individual interviews, through the co-therapists' acting in a similar partisan way. Gradually, as the family members mature and gain in capacity to preserve their inner models or objects in the face of frustration and loss, the individual contact becomes less necessary and ordinary conjoint techniques can be utilized.

This middle layer is more difficult to recognize than the others, but a history of loss of loved ones in infancy or other evidence of deprivation or separation, or of depressive episodes, or a clinging "babes-in-the-wood" mutual supportiveness, or other obvious inability to sustain loss and separation should make one alert to the possible need for individual contact.

The "top layer of the sandwich" represents all those other individuals and families in which the capacity for relationships represented by the depressive position is securely established. Ambivalence, aloneness and separateness can now be faced squarely, so that the emergence of negative affect or of difference and conflict in the family sessions can be coped with and used constructively. Individual, family, or stranger-group methods can be used at this level, depending on other factors such as time available and other resources, treatment goals, problems over attendance, and so on.

Most family therapists have been curiously uninterested in this question of the most favourable interval between meetings, seemingly taking it for granted that weekly sessions represent a minimum frequency, as in individual analytic therapy, and appearing very glad to get good results from as little as that. However, Bowen has recently reported similar findings to my own claiming to achieve more rapid therapeutic effects in couples' group and couple therapy with monthly as compared with weekly meetings. It may be that the optimum spacing is dependent on the technique used, and that longer intervals are more appropriate where the therapy catalyzes family interaction which is then carried on as "homework," rather than focusing interaction around the therapist by encouraging transference fantasy.

However, the "failures" described by Solomon and myself make it particularly necessary to stress that such spaced-out sessions may be undesirable or harmful where there is a history of deprivation or depression against which family members are successfully defending themselves. As stressed in earlier chapters, these families require (in order of ascending need) either more frequent family meetings, perhaps with multiple therapists maintaining a primary relationship to their "own" family members, or separate individual sessions at least for key members for key members and, above all, for the mother.

35

A. T. Beck:
Cognitive Therapy and the Emotional Disorders

Reviewed by E. S. Paykel

Beck's original book on cognitive therapy was published in the United States in 1976 but not reviewed in the *British Journal of Psychiatry* until December 1979. The review was favorable. A second book (Beck et al. 1979) was not reviewed, although by then there was a substantial and growing literature on cognitive approaches to treatment.

Beck is a psychiatrist and former psychoanalyst who came to be increasingly dissatisfied with psychoanalytic theories and the results of therapeutic interpretations based on them. His earlier book on depression, published in 1967, was one of the first modern works concerned with the disorder. In it he reviewed the literature and some studies of his own, with an emphasis on symptom phenomenology. He also reported work with a symptom inventory which he had developed earlier and which has since been used widely.

Subsequently, his cognitive theories evolved from a more direct look at the depressive thought content, with considerable therapeutic contributions from behavior therapy. In the late 1960s in the United States, moves away from psychoanalysis were gaining momentum, but were still not easy for the committed; I can remember the cool reception which a rather muted lecture at Yale around 1970 from Dr. Beck (a kindly and courteous man) evoked in the senior figures in the audience.

The 1976 book set out the theoretical structure evolved by Beck and his group. The 1979 work, larger but very readable, is more a treatment manual. The theories center around conscious ideation, moving away, as

Beck pointed out, both from the unconscious thought processes of the psychoanalysts and from the neglect of thought content by the behavior therapists. Beck directed attention to the presence of automatic thoughts, negative in content. These thoughts were regarded as preceding and giving rise to negative moods. He made a detailed analysis of what he described as systematic logical errors in thinking, such as arbitrary inferences and over-generalization. He postulated underlying cognitive schemes that might give rise, when activated, to disorders such as depression. A method of therapy focusing on thought processes was described, aimed at recognition and control of the negative thoughts. The therapy uses techniques such as recording of thoughts, reality testing, and cognitive rehearsal. It is verbal, but in its structure and use of techniques such as homework exercises and self-monitoring has a clear behavioral component.

The 1976 book ended with the forthright claim that in comparison with psychoanalysis, cognitive therapy was readily comprehensible to patients, economical with regard to therapists' time, testable in research, and easily teachable to others.

On rereading this book one is struck by the clear, economical style. It consists of firm statements by a man who knows what he wants to say, and who is conscious of setting out for others an authoritative statement of a new theory that will have a memorable impact. Also, it is apparent that Beck was not just talking about depression. He deals with thoughts in relation to the normal emotions of sadness, euphoria, anxiety, and anger, and to the full gamut of emotional disorders: depression, anxiety, phobic and obsessional states, psychosomatic disorders, and hysteria. Only when he moves to treatment does he focus on depression.

It is not yet easy to assess the place of Beck's work: it has not reached a final point of equilibrium. It certainly took off with great success. By the late 1970s a vigorous group of young therapists and researchers were attending conferences and presenting data with some fervor. More recently, cognitive therapy has become part of the general armamentarium of the clinical psychologist. A number of controlled trials in depression have been carried out, which show the treatment to be at least as effect as drug therapy. It has led to further books, by various authors, to at least one journal, and to some distinguished research by psychologists in this country, clustering in Cambridge, Edinburgh, and Oxford.

However, its practical place in depression is still far from clear, and it is possible that reaction will set in. The treatment is intensive in its use of therapist time: drug treatment is considerably cheaper. On the other hand, there are early hints that cognitive therapy may reduce relapse rates. Studies have largely been confined to the milder range of depression, particularly general practice patients and outpatients. There has been little comparison of cognitive therapy with drugs or ECT in more severe depression. Most cognitive therapists are reluctant to tackle chronic and resistant depressions, although it is here that the need for alternative treatments is greatest. It is not certain whether the therapeutic effects are specific or reflect nonspecific effects of the considerable therapeutic contact. Most studies do not show the effects particularly on thought content rather than other aspects of depression. Results so far available from the recent large American collaborative trial comparing cognitive therapy, interpersonal psychotherapy, drug therapy, and placebo suggest that all active treatments have approximately equal and similar effects but that cognitive therapy may have less effect in the severe depressions. Comparisons of recovered depressive patients with controls do not show the proposed abnormalities of thinking that might predispose to depression. This has led to a greater emphasis on the latent nature of the depressive schemas: a dangerous move toward the unverifiability of unconscious processes. Beck's own position appears to have changed over the years from regarding negative cognitions as causing depression to the view that they are not necessarily causal but part of the depressive syndrome and a convenient point of leverage for effecting change in it.

These are more than mere cavils, but less than fatal flaws: they are current hesitations. The real place of cognitive hypotheses and of cognitive therapy in depression will take longer to establish. Meanwhile, there is no doubting that the impact has been enormous. We have seen the birth of a modern movement. Others, particularly among clinical psychologists, were moving towards cognitive approaches at the same time as Beck, but it was his early work and his formulation that brought the therapy into being. Whatever its ultimate place as a treatment in depression, it has brought thought content back to centre stage in concepts of disorder. It has produced a new acceptance that psychological treatments can have major effects in a disorder where biological mechanisms appear important. It is also rapidly extending outside depression, for instance in the treatment of appetite disorders, and in a common disorder where alternative treatments are not satisfactory: generalized anxiety. Cognitive approaches are a major part of the currently evolving packages of anxiety management programs. The approach itself may turn out to be the greatest contribution.

REFERENCE

Beck, A. T., Rush, A. J., Shaw, B. L., and Emery, G. (1979). *Cognitive Therapy of Depression.* New York: Guilford.

Selections from
Cognitive Therapy and the
Emotional Disorders
by A. T. Beck

INTRODUCTION

Paradoxically, the popularization of emotional disorders and the prodigious efforts to mass-produce professional services have occurred in the context of increasingly sharp disagreements among authorities regarding the nature and appropriate treatment of these disorders. With intriguing regularity, new theories and therapies have captured the imagination of both the layman and the professional and have then gradually drifted into oblivion. Moreover, the most durable schools devoted to the study and treatment of emotional disturbances—traditional neuropsychiatry, psychoanalysis, and behavior therapy—still retain their original differences in theoretical framework and experimental and clinical approaches.

Despite the striking differences among these dominant schools, they share one basic assumption: The emotionally disturbed person is victimized by concealed forces over which he has no control. Emerging from the nineteenth-century doctrine of physicalism, traditional neuropsychiatry searches for biological causes such as chemical or neurological abnormalities, and applies drugs and other physical measures to relieve the emotional disorder. Psychoanalysis, whose philosophical underpinnings also were formed in the nineteenth century, attributes an individual's neurosis to unconscious psychological factors: The unconscious elements are sealed off by psychological barriers that can only be penetrated by psychoanalytic interpretations. Behavior therapy, whose philosophical roots can be traced to the eighteenth century, regards the emotional disturbance in terms of involuntary reflexes based on accidental conditionings that occurred previously in the patient's life. Since, according to behavioral theory, the patient cannot modify these conditioned reflexes simply by knowing about them and trying to will them away, he requires the application of "counterconditioning" by a competent behavior therapist.

Because these three leading schools maintain that the source of the patient's disturbance lies beyond his awareness, they gloss over his conscious conceptions, his specific thoughts and fantasies.

Suppose, however, that these schools are on the wrong track. Let us conjecture, for the moment, that a person's consciousness contains elements that are responsible for the emotional upsets and blurred thinking that lead him to seek help. Moreover, let us suppose that the patient has at his disposal various rational techniques he can use, with proper instruction, to deal with these disturbing elements in his consciousness. If these suppositions are correct, then emotional disorders may be approached from an entirely different route: *Man has the key to understanding and solving his psychological disturbance within the scope of his own awareness.* He can correct the misconceptions producing his emotional disturbance with the same problem-solving apparatus that he has been accustomed to using at various stages in his development.

These assumptions converge on a relatively new approach to emotional disorders. Nevertheless, the philosophical underpinnings of this approach go back thousands of years, certainly to the time of the Stoics, who considered man's conceptions (or misconceptions) of events rather than the events themselves as the key to his emotional upsets. This new approach—cognitive therapy—suggests that the individual's problems are derived largely from certain distortions of reality based on erroneous premises and assumptions. These incorrect conceptions originated in defective learning during the person's cognitive development. Regardless of their origin, it is relatively simple to state the formula for treatment: The therapist helps a patient to unravel his distortions in thinking and to learn alternative, more realistic ways to formulate his experiences.

The cognitive approach brings the understanding and treatment of the emotional disorders closer to a patient's everyday experiences. The patient can regard his disturbance as related to the kinds of misunderstandings he has experienced numerous times during his life. Moreover, he has undoubtedly had previous successes in correcting misinterpretations, either through acquiring more adequate information or by recognizing the logical fallacy of his misunderstandings. The cognitive approach makes sense to a patient because it is somehow related to his previous learning experiences and can stimulate confidence in his capacity to learn how to deal effectively with present misconceptions that are producing painful symptoms. Furthermore, by bringing emotional disorders within the purview of everyday experience and applying familiar problem-solving techniques, the therapist can immediately form a bridge to the patient.

PARADOXES OF DEPRESSION

The Clue: The Sense of Loss

In exploring the theme of loss, we find that the psychological disorder revolves around a cognitive problem. The depressed patient shows specific distortions. He has a negative view of his world, a negative concept of himself, and a negative appraisal of his future: the cognitive triad.

The distorted evaluations concern shrinkage of his domain, and lead to sadness (Chapter 3). The depressive's conception of his valued attributes, relationships, and achievements is saturated with the notion of loss—past, present, and future. When he considers his present position, he sees a barren world; he feels pressed to the wall by external demands that cheat him of his meager resources and keep him from attaining what he wants.

A Synthesis of Depression

After experiencing loss (either as the result of an actual, obvious event or insidious deprivations) the depression-prone person begins to appraise his experiences in a negative way. He overinterprets his experiences in terms of defeat or deprivation. He regards himself as deficient, inadequate, unworthy, and is prone to attribute unpleasant occurrences to a deficiency in himself. As he looks ahead, he anticipates that his present difficulties or suffering will continue indefinitely. He foresees a life of unremitting hardship, frustration, and deprivation. Since he attributes his difficulties to his own defects, he blames himself and becomes increasingly self-critical. The patient's experiences in living thus activate cognitive patterns revolving around the theme of loss. The various emotional, motivational, behavioral, and vegetative phenomena of depression flow from these negative self-evaluations.

The patient's sadness is an inevitable consequence of his sense of deprivation, pessimism, and self-criticism. Apathy results from giving up completely. His loss of spontaneity, his escapist and avoidance wishes, and his suicidal wishes similarly stem from the way he appraises his life. His hopelessness leads to loss of motivation: Because he expects a negative outcome from any course of action, he loses the internal stimulation to engage in any constructive activity. Moreover, this pessimism leads him ultimately to suicidal wishes.

The various behavioral manifestations of depression, such as inertia, fatigability, agitation, are similarly the outcomes of the negative cognitions.

Inertia and passivity are expressions of the patient's loss of spontaneous motivation. His easy fatigability results from his continuous expectations of negative outcomes from whatever he undertakes.

The continuous downward course in depression may be explained in terms of the feedback model. As a result of his negative attitudes, the patient interprets his dysphoria, sense of loss, and physical symptoms in a negative way. His conclusion that he is defective and cannot improve reinforces his negative expectations and negative self-image. Consequently, he feels sadder and more impelled to avoid the "demands" of his environment. Thus, the vicious cycle is perpetrated.

ANXIETY NEUROSIS

Thinking Disorder in Anxiety Neuroses

We have already noted that a thinking disorder is at the core of neuroses. The interference with realistic thinking is readily observed by the anxious patient himself. The characteristic manifestations are:

1. Repetitive thoughts about danger. The patient has continuous verbal or pictorial cognitions about the occurrence of harmful events ("false alarms").

2. Reduced ability to "reason" with the fearful thoughts. The patient may suspect that his anxiety-producing thoughts are not reasonable; however, his capacity for objectively evaluating and reappraising is impaired. Even though he may be able to question the reasonableness of his anxiety-producing thoughts, he believes predominantly in their validity.

3. "Stimulus generalization." The range of anxiety-evoking stimuli increases so that almost any sound, movement, or other environmental change may be perceived as a danger. For example, a woman in an acute anxiety attack had these experiences: She heard the siren of a fire engine and thought, "My house may be on fire." At the same time, she visualized her family trapped at home in the fire. Then she heard an airplane flying overhead and had a pictorial image of herself in the airplane and the airplane's crashing. As she imagined the crash, she experienced anxiety.

Some of the characteristics of anxiety such as blocking on words and interference with short-term recall may be explained superficially in terms of the disruption of voluntary control over focusing attention. When an anxious person has difficulty in concentrating on an immediate task (for example, taking a test, giving a speech), one might conjecture, initially, that attention has become too scattered to remain attached for long to a specific object or subject. Similarly, easy distractibility by irrelevant stimuli could be readily ascribed to the erratic nature of his attention.

On further investigation, however, a more precise way of understanding these phenomena emerges. The patient's problem stems not so much from the mercurial nature of his attention as from the involuntary fixation of his attention. We find that most of the patient's attention is stuck, as it were, on the concept of danger and the perception of "danger signals." This attention-binding is manifested by his involuntary preoccupation with danger, overvigilance for stimuli relevant to danger, and overscanning of his subjective feeling. The amount of attention remaining for focusing on specific tasks, recall, or self-reflection is greatly restricted. In other words, because of the fixation of most of his attention on concepts or stimuli relevant to danger, the patient loses most of his ability to shift his voluntary awareness to other internal processes or external stimuli. This loss of voluntary control over concentration, recall, and reasoning may make the patient believe he is losing his mind—a phenomenon that enhances his anxiety.

TECHNIQUES OF COGNITIVE THERAPY

Recognizing Maladaptive Ideation

As pointed out in previous chapters, emotional reactions, motivations, and overt behavior are guided by thinking. A person may not be fully aware of the automatic thoughts that influence to a large extent how he acts, what he feels, and how much he enjoys his experiences. With some training, however, he may increase his awareness of these thoughts and learn to pinpoint them with a high degree of regularity. It is possible to perceive a thought, focus on it, and evaluate it just as one can identify and reflect on a sensation (such as pain) or an external stimulus (such as a verbal statement).

The term "maladaptive thoughts" is applied to ideation that interferes with the ability to cope with life experiences, unnecessarily disrupts internal harmony, and produces inappropriate or excessive emotional reactions that are painful. In cognitive therapy, the patient focuses on those thoughts or images that produce unnecessary discomfort or suffering or lead to self-defeating behavior. In applying the term "maladaptive," it is important that the therapist be wary of imposing his own value system on the patient. The term is generally applicable if both the patient and the therapist are able to agree that these automatic thoughts interfere with the patient's well-being or with the attainment of his important objectives.

STATUS OF COGNITIVE THERAPY

To summarize, cognitive therapy meets the basic requirements of a psychotherapeutic system in that it presents a comprehensive, plausible *theory* of psychopathology: (a) The formulations are comprehensible and explain with simple concepts the phenomena of the neuroses. (b) The theory is internally consistent. (c) The theory of psychopathology meshes with the principles of therapy so closely that it is fairly easy to determine how the treatment procedures are derived from the theory. (d) The rationale and mode of operation of the therapy are apparent in the theory. For example, since specific cognitive distortions are responsible for the neuroses, it is logical to attempt to ameliorate the neurosis through helping the patient form more realistic concepts in order to eliminate the cognitive distortions. (e) New techniques consistent with the theory are easily developed. (f) The principles of the theory are easily operationalized and have been supported by numerous systematic studies.

The specific requirements for a uniform, empirically-based *therapy* have also been met: (a) The procedures are well-defined and explicitly described in treatment "packages" consisting of procedural manuals and transcripts of interviews. (b) The same therapeutic program used by different therapists does not differ substantially from one to the other.[1] (c) Neophyte therapists can adopt the techniques and apply them in a humanistic (as opposed to mechanical) way. (d) Experimental and correlational studies support the principles associated with the therapy. (e) The efficacy of cognitive therapy has been substantiated by analog studies; single case studies; and well designed therapeutic trials, including control groups.

We can now turn to the question: Can a fledgling psychotherapy challenge the giants in the field—psychoanalysis and behavior therapy? I believe on the basis of my experience in conducting psychoanalytic therapy and behavior therapy that cognitive therapy combines the most valuable features of the older systems within the framework of its own conceptual system and principles of therapy.

---

[1] As part of our research project on the cognitive psychotherapy of depression, we have tape-recorded each session of the participating therapists. Comparisons of the transcribed sessions confirm the basic similarities in procedures used by different therapists.

TREATMENT OF DEPRESSION

The cognitive approach involves, first of all, separating the syndrome of depression into its specific components. Conceivably, the therapist could start with any of the symptoms—emotional, motivational, cognitive, behavioral, or physiological—and concentrate his efforts on changing that symptom cluster. Each symptom cluster may be conceptualized as a problem and as a potential target for intervention. Since each of the components of depression contributes to other components, it might be anticipated that improvement in any one problem area would lead to improvement in others, and would finally spread to include the entire syndrome of depression.

The specific problems under consideration are complex and consist of more than the particular difficulty verbalized by the patient. A problem generally can be formulated in terms of three "levels": (a) The observable abnormal behavior or symptom, for example, easy fatigability, crying spells, suicidal threats; (b) the underlying motivational disturbances (if any), such as the wish to avoid activities or to escape from life; (c) underlying the motivation, a cluster of cognitions, such as the belief that striving toward a goal is futile, that there are no satisfactions ahead, and that he is defeated, deprived, and defective.

36

Murray Bowen:
Family Therapy in Clinical Practice

Reviewed by Michael E. Kerr

Family Therapy in Clinical Practice is a collection of Murray Bowen's most important papers written between 1957 and 1977. These represent the evolution of Bowen family systems theory from the earliest descriptive work, to the first formal presentation of the theory in 1966, to refinements in therapy and extensions of theory over the next ten years. Since the specifics of Bowen's research, theory, and therapy are not widely known in psychiatry, this review will summarize the information contained in the twenty-two papers of his volume.

RESEARCH

Although he began in psychoanalysis, Bowen eventually departed almost completely from psychoanalytic ideas. His odyssey began around 1950, while he was a staff psychiatrist at the Menninger Clinic. Interested in the symbiotic attachment between mothers and adult schizophrenic offspring, he was doing individual psychotherapy with both the patients and their mothers (and other family members). His observations led him to conclude that phenomena such as maternal deprivation, hostility, rejection, seduction, and castration were secondary manifestations of an underlying intense attachment. This insight helped set Bowen on the road toward a new theory.

To further study symbiosis as seen in schizophrenia, Bowen initiated a unique research project at the National Institute of Mental Health (NIMH) in 1954. This study began with three chronic schizophrenic women and their mothers, living on an inpatient unit. Direct observation of mother–patient interactions revealed their attachment to be more intense than originally thought. Each pair consisted of two people living, acting, and being for each other, neither having the strength to differentiate into an autonomous person. More importantly, contact with other family members helped the researchers recognize that the symbiosis was a fragment of a larger family process, so that new families admitted to the project included fathers and siblings. In the five years of the project, three mother–patient pairs and four mother-father-patient-sibling families lived on the ward for 6 to 36 months. The average stay was 18 months. In addition, seven outpatient families were seen for up to 2 years and twelve other families were evaluated.

When the family was observed in action as a whole, it provided a radically new perspective. It was like watching a football game from the top of the stadium rather than from the sideline: broad patterns of movement in the family came into view. Individual functioning was seen to be determined as much by relationships between family members as it was by internal forces, so that people often functioned very differently outside the family than in it.

Observations of the schizophrenic person in the family context were consistent with schizophrenia being a *functional* disorder, rather than constitutional helplessness. The functional helplessness or underfunctioning of the patient is reciprocal to the overfunctioning of the parents. Anxiety is an important element in the process: in the mother, it signals the schizophrenic one to act more like a baby than he really is. This allows the mother to control her immaturity by caring for the "baby." Thus, the schizophrenic one's helplessness makes a less anxious adjustment in the mother possible. A father's passivity and withdrawal reinforce the intensity between mother and child. The parents appear to be equally immature; this is reflected in the distance between them (emotional divorce) and in their focus on the schizophrenic adult child. The schizophrenic one thus absorbs more parental immaturity than his sibling, which allows the sibling to grow freer of the parents.

Bowen further developed family psychotherapy in 1955 to treat the family unit, since his observations all supported a conclusion that the *family functions as a unit* rather than as a collection of emotionally autonomous people. The therapy was consistent with his theory, and changed only on the basis of theory, not on the basis of clinical judgment or feelings. At the beginning of therapy, neither spouse was responsible for self, but each was caught up in being for and demanding of the other. When one spouse could be more of a self in the face of such pressure, and without demanding of the other, the family changed. For example, if a father became "less soluble" in his wife's tears, he could think and act more out of self. This would at first lead to intense anxiety in the mother, but if he withstood the pressure to pacify her, she eventually relaxed and moved into a more comfortable closeness with him. Predictably, the schizophrenic patient would then make moves to win mother back. The patients often got more disturbed when the parents gave in less to their infantile clinging. If the parents held their ground, the patients would then function better. The families were not really helpless, but had become functionally helpless from years of relating to each other in this way and from continually seeking answers outside themselves.

A therapeutic principle was to keep intense relationships within the family, in other words, not to foster transference relationships with the therapist and staff. This emotional detachment makes it easier to focus on family process rather than on individuals, but is difficult to maintain. In daily experience, people participate emotionally by identifying with the victim, applauding the hero, and hating the villain. Staff could easily lose objectivity in this way, and family members were constantly seeking allies. To facilitate detachment, Bowen made some unconventional rules for the research team. For example, staff were not to talk about the families behind their backs, and family members could read nursing and progress notes. Words from individual theory, particularly diagnostic labels, were not used. If therapist and staff lost objectivity and attempted to influence the family through interpretations and directives, the family remained a functionally helpless, anxious organism without a leader. But if the therapist stayed outside the process, it required the parents to function responsibly, and leadership could emerge from within the family.

Bowen left NIMH in 1959 and moved to the Department of Psychiatry, Georgetown University School of Medicine. There, he expanded informal outpatient studies that he had begun in 1956 on families with emotional problems less severe than schizophrenia. By 1966, he had completed 12 years and 10,000 hours of observing families in family psychotherapy. After NIMH, the effort was to extend his theoretical orientation from a family concept of schizophrenia to a family theory of emotional illness, and to adapt family psychotherapy to the entire range of emotional illness. *The recognition that patterns of functioning in families with schizophrenia were present in a less intense form in better functioning families led to the new theory.*

THEORY

A scientific theory is an abstract formulation about verifiable natural events. In attempting to develop a scientific theory about human behavior,

Bowen had to separate nonverifiable subjectivity, which dominates man's thinking about himself, from verifiable events. He used functional facts to accomplish this. For example, although love is a subjective concept, it is factual that many family members react predictably to statements regarding it and these reactions are functional facts. Functional facts are defined by describing how, what, when, and where events occur, not by focusing on why events occur, which invites subjective speculation and cause-and-effect thinking.

Bowen's theory assumes that man is a product of evolution and that his behavior is governed by the same natural forces that govern all life. A corollary assumption is that clinical dysfunctions (physical, psychiatric, and social) are linked to the *emotional system*, which is that part of man he has in common with other species. Emotional functioning includes the automatic responses necessary to sustain life, together with the interplay of instinctual and learned responses, feeling states, and subjectivity. Forces governing relationships are anchored in the emotional system, which is deep — in contact with cellular and somatic processes, which means that disturbances in relationships can be reflected at these deeper levels. Thinking, reasoning, and the perception of feeling states are functions of the *intellectual system*. Thus, feelings permit an individual to be aware of at least superficial aspects of the functioning of the emotional system.

Bowen introduced the term *system* in the mid-1960s to describe the predictable automatic behavior that occurs between family members. Family relationships have the quality of systems, in that a change in the functioning of one family member is followed by compensatory changes in the functioning of other members. Bowen's family systems theory consists of the following eight interlocking concepts:

1. *Differentiation of self*: Individuals differ in their ability to maintain a self in relationship systems. At one extreme are people with so little self that they can only be for others and demand from others, or, at times, be oppositional to them. At the other extreme are people with enough self such that, while they can sacrifice for and be realistically dependent on others, they are also responsible for themselves and do not foster irresponsibility in others. People exist at many gradations between these extremes. Poorly differentiated people are dominated by their emotionality. Well differentiated people can use factual knowledge, principles, and a long-term view to counterbalance anxiety, emotional reactivity, and subjectivity. Poorly defined people are more chronically anxious than better defined people, and are more vulnerable to severe and chronic psychiatric, physical, or social dysfunctions. Compared to the consistency of those who are better differentiated, the functioning of poorly differentiated people

fluctuates widely in reaction to changes in the emotional environment. The self is composed of biological and psychological elements interacting as a unit.

2. *Triangles*: A two-person system tolerates little anxiety before involving a third person. The resulting three-person system or triangle is the smallest stable relationship unit. The activity of a triangle reflects the level of differentiation of its members and the level of anxiety. Anxiety is generated by the way each person in a triangle functions in relationship to the other two, but the anxiety is absorbed unevenly. The uneven absorption results from people maneuvering to gain and hold positions in the triangle that are most comfortable: for example, two comfortable insiders excluding an uncomfortable outsider. A consequence of this process is that two people may enhance their functioning at the expense of a third person. When the anxiety level exceeds the capacity of one triangle, it overflows to interlocking triangles.

3. *Nuclear family emotional process*: The emotional process in triangles and interlocking triangles determines which family relationships absorb more anxiety. Anxiety in relationships manifests itself in one or more of four patterns of emotional functioning: (1) emotional distance, (2) marital conflict, (3) dysfunction in a spouse, and (4) impairment of one or more children. The more anxious a family is (the level of anxiety being related to differentiation, life events, and cutoff from extended family and social networks), the more severe or numerous are the manifestations of that anxiety. Given the presence of other necessary variables (e.g., a genetic predisposition or infectious agent), an anxiety-driven clinical dysfunction can be physical, psychiatric, or social.

4. *Family projection process*: The transmission of parental immaturity and anxiety to a child (impairment of a child) involves three steps: (1) a feeling in the parent merges into thinking about defects in the child, (2) the parent searches for and diagnoses a defect in the child that best fits the parent's feeling state, and (3) the parent acts toward and treats the child as though the parent's diagnosis is accurate. As the child chronically accepts the projection, he becomes more infantile and more vulnerable to dysfunction. The projection process reflects the parents' overinvolvement with a child, which can have either a positive or a negative emotional tone. An overly focused-on child grows up more emotionally appended to the parents than a less focused-on sibling.

5. *Emotional cut-off*: Everyone has some degree of unresolved emotional attachment to his family of origin, but poorly differentiated people have the most unresolved attachment. People often manage problems associated with the attachment by reducing contact with parents and extended family, either through physical distance or emotional withdrawal. The

more people are cut off from their families, the more they focus on their spouse and children, which exaggerates the tendency to replicate the problems of the past in the present.

6. *Multigenerational transmission process*: Each generation's emotional functioning so profoundly affects the emotional functioning of the next generation that children develop levels of differentiation close to their parents' levels. If a nuclear family's emotional process tends to contain the family problem in the parental generation (through marital conflict or spouse dysfunction), the children develop differentiation levels somewhat higher than those of their parents. In contrast, if the family problem tends to be projected onto one or more children, those children develop levels somewhat lower than their parents. Less involved siblings can develop levels similar to or higher than those of the parents. The children marry spouses with levels of differentiation identical to their own, and the process repeat itself. Gradually, some generational lines decrease in differentiation, while others increase. Within eight to ten generations, every family produces people at all levels of differentiation.

7. *Sibling position*: Children are born into functioning positions in families that program them into ways of relating; these ways are played out in family, work, and social relationships throughout life. For example, regardless of culture or socioeconomic background, oldest children (like other positions) have predictable functioning characteristics, but the projection process can alter these characteristics. For example, if the projection process focuses on an oldest child, his tendency toward leadership may become exaggerated to the point of rigid authoritarianism or else undermined to the point of marked indecisiveness.

8. *Societal emotional process*: Families can undergo periods of anxiety-driven regression in emotional functioning that are marked by serious clinical symptoms. A regression results from a family's inability to adapt to real or imagined stressors without a prolonged escalation of anxiety. Societies can undergo similar anxiety-related shifts in emotional functioning that are marked by phenomena such as increased civil unrest, crime, divorce, drug abuse, and an overall emphasis on rights rather than responsibilities. Society has been in a gradually deepening regression for three to four decades that is likely to continue and worsen well into the next century. The population explosion, disappearance of new frontiers, and depletion of resources are some of the factors fueling the process.

THERAPY

Developments in Bowen's therapeutic approach generally paralleled developments in his theory: theoretical thinking about the nature of a

problem determines a therapeutic approach. Bowen's theory conceptual-
izes symptoms as reflecting a disturbance in family functioning, so that the
goal of therapy is to improve the family system. Reduction of anxiety will
improve family functioning and reduce symptoms in the short term, but
long-term change depends on at least one family member improving his
basic level of differentiation. Raising a basic level is a slow process,
requiring two main changes: (1) more differentiation between emotional
and intellectual functioning, and (2) more control over automatic emotional
functioning. If one family member functions with more self, others will
predictably oppose it; if the differentiating one resists this pressure to
conform to the emotionality, others, including the symptomatic one, will
eventually improve their functioning.

Bowen characterizes the therapy developed at NIMH, involving the
whole nuclear family, as *family group therapy*. However, this approach
proved to be the least effective for fostering differentiation. The two
approaches that eventually proved to be the most effective were family
psychotherapy with two spouses seen conjointly or therapy with one
family member. Because change in one member is followed predictably by
changes in others, it is unnecessary to treat the symptomatic one directly,
whether it be the other spouse or a child.

A major innovation in therapy, differentiation of self in one's own family
of origin, came to fruition in 1967. After twelve years of trying to think
theoretically about his own family, and to become more objective and
neutral about it, Bowen was able to maintain emotional detachment while
relating actively to his family. Detachment depends on developing the
ability to act based on factual knowledge about family emotional process
and one's part in it, rather than on feelings and subjectivity. Over time, the
ability to be detached while in contact with the family results in some
resolution of the emotional attachment to one's parents. Resolution of the
attachment to the past generations increases a person's ability to function
with more differentiation in his nuclear family and other systems. Following the success with his own extended family, Bowen began coaching
others in similar efforts in their families.

The term *coach* derived from the recognition that people can change in
psychotherapy without the change being based on a conventional therapeutic relationship. The internal and behavioral change stems from acting
with more self in the nuclear and extended families, not from a process
between the patient and the therapist. Critical elements in this approach
are the coach representing theory (particularly differentiation of self) in his
words and actions, which both communicates a way of thinking and
reduces transference, and the family member being willing to think for
himself and take on emotionally difficult situations in his family. Differen-

tiation of self in one's own family has become a central component of training family psychotherapists.

CONCLUSION

Bowen's volume also includes some topical papers concerning death and the family, the role of the family in alcoholism, and the application of Bowen theory to administrative systems. Parts of other papers describe the family movement and its influence on psychiatry, as well as the relationship of Bowen theory to other bodies of knowledge. A particularly important clarification is that Bowen theory is not derived from general systems theory; it is a *natural systems theory* or a specific theory about the functional facts of one living system, the human family.

Bowen died on October 9, 1990, at the age of 77. At the time of his death, he was still active in research and clinical practice, and director of the Georgetown Family Center. He regarded his theory as incomplete: each concept requires amplification and new concepts will be added. Bowen believed the human race would eventually shift from cause-and-effect to systems thinking, in reference to its own behavior, and that it would comprehend the connection of this thinking to all life. A change of such magnitude, however, would inevitably occur slowly.

Selections from
Family Therapy in Clinical Practice
by Murray Bowen

FAMILY SYSTEMS THEORY

The evolution of my own theoretical thinking began in the decade before I started family research. There were many questions concerning generally accepted explanations about emotional illness. Efforts to find logical answers resulted in more unanswerable questions. One simple example is the notion that mental illness is the result of maternal deprivation. The idea seemed to fit the clinical case of the moment, but not the large number of normal people who, as far as could be determined, had been exposed to more maternal deprivation than those who were sick. There was also the issue of the schizophrenogenic mother. There were detailed descriptions of schizophrenogenic parents, but little to explain how the same parents could have other children who were not only normal, but who appeared supernormal. There were lesser discrepancies in popular hypotheses that linked emotional symptoms to a single traumatic event in the past. This again appeared logical in specific cases, but did not explain the large number of people who had suffered trauma without developing symptoms. There was a tendency to create special hypotheses for individual cases. The whole body of diagnostic nomenclature was based on symptom description, except for the small percentage of cases in which symptoms could be connected to actual pathology. Psychiatry acted as if it knew the answers, but it had not been able to develop diagnoses consistent with etiology. Psychoanalytic theory tended to define emotional illness as the product of a process between parents and child in a single generation, and there was little to explain how severe problems could be created so rapidly. The basic sciences were critical of psychiatric explanations that eluded scientific study. If the body of knowledge was reasonably factual, why could we not be more scientific about it? There were assumptions that

emotional illness was the product of forces of socialization, even though
the same basic emotional illness was present in all cultures. Most of the
assumptions considered emotional illness as specific to humans, when
there was evidence that a similar process was also present in lower forms
of life. These and many other questions led me to extensive reading in
evolution, biology, and the natural sciences as part of a search for clues that
could lead to a broader theoretical frame of reference. My hunch was that
emotional illness comes from that part of man that he shares with the lower
forms of life.

From this discussion of the family as a system, I have avoided saying what
kind of a "system." The family is a number of different kinds of systems.
It can accurately be designated a social system, a cultural system, a games
system, a communication system, a biological system, or any of several
other designations. For the purposes of this theoretical-therapeutic system,
I think of the family as a combination of "emotional" and "relationship"
systems. The term *emotional* refers to the force that motivates the system
and *relationship* to the ways it is expressed. Under relationship would be
subsumed communication, interaction, and other relationship modalities.
    There were some basic assumptions about man and the nature of
emotional illness, partially formulated before the family research, that
governed the theoretical thinking and the choice of the various theoretical
concepts, including the notion of an "emotional" system. Man is viewed as
an evolutionary assemblage of cells who has arrived at his present state
from hundreds of millions of years of evolutionary adaptation and maladaptation, and who is evolving on to other changes. In this sense, man is
related directly to all living matter. In choosing theoretical concepts, an
attempt was made to keep them in harmony with man as a protoplasmic
being. Man is different from other animals in the size of his brain and his
ability to reason and think. With his intellectual ability he has devoted a
major effort to emphasizing his uniqueness and the "differences" that set
him apart from other forms of life, and he has devoted comparatively little
effort to understanding his relatedness to other forms of life. A basic
premise is that what man thinks about himself, and what he says about
himself, is different in many important ways from what he is. Emotional
illness is seen as a disorder of man's emotional system, and man's
emotional system is seen as basically related to man's protoplasmic being.
I view emotional illness as a much deeper phenomenon than that conceptualized by current psychological theory. There are emotional mechanisms
as automatic as a reflex and that occur as predictably as the force that
causes the sunflower to keep its face toward the sun. I believe that the laws
that govern man's emotional functioning are as orderly as those that

govern other natural systems and that the difficulty in understanding the system is governed more by man's reasoning that denies its existence than by the complexity of the system. In the literature there are discrepant views about the definition of and the relatedness between emotion and feelings. Operationally I regard an emotional system as something deep that is in contact with cellular and somatic processes, and a feeling system as a bridge that is in contact with parts of the emotional system on one side and with the intellectual system on the other. In clinical practice, I have made a clear distinction between feelings, which have to do with subjective awareness, and opinions, which have to do with logic and reasoning of the intellectual system. The degree to which people say, "I feel that . . ." when they mean, "I believe that . . ." is so commonplace that many use the two words synonymously. However valid the ideas behind the selection of these concepts, they did play a major part in the choice of concepts.

When any family member makes a move toward differentiating a self, the family emotional system communicates a three-stage verbal and nonverbal message: (1) You are wrong. (2) Change back. (3) If you do not, these are the consequences. Generally, the messages contain a mixture of subtle sulks, hurt feelings, and angry exchanges, but some communicate all three stages in words. The differentiating one responds in two ways. The first kind of response is within self and can include almost any emotional or psychological symptom or even symptoms of physical illness. The second kind of response is to the family. A high percentage of differentiating ones merge back into the family togetherness within hours. The merger may be to allay one's own distress, or it may come in response to a family accusation of indifference or of not loving. Or the differentiating one may fight back, which is still part of the family reaction-response system. The family emotional system has an automatic response for any emotional stimulus. The differentiating one may react with silence and withdrawal, another emotional reaction to which the family has the balancing response. A family member may run away, never to return—another emotional reaction. Predictably, the member then fuses into another receptive family and duplicates old patterns in the new emotional field. This emotional complex is much deeper than superficial angry retaliation. If one can conceive of the emotional triangle in constant balancing motion, inter-locked with a complex of other triangles in the family and with still others in the extended family and social network, with the balances operating within each person and between each one and all the others, it is easier to conceptualize the total system in which each is dependent on the others, and the variety of gyroscopic balancing always operates to maintain emotional equilibrium.

This therapeutic system defines an Achilles' heel of the emotional system and provides one predictable answer to breaking through the emotional barrier toward differentiation. There is one major secret: an emotional system responds to emotional stimuli. If any member can control his emotional response, it interrupts the chain reaction. The most important factors in successful differentiation are a knowledge of triangles and the ability to observe and predict the chain-reaction events in the family. This knowledge and ability provide some help in controlling one's own responses in the system. The next important factor is an ability to maintain reasonable emotional control in one's responses to the family and within self during the hours or days of the family's attack and rejection — while remaining in constant emotional contact with the family. This last point is important. Silence or withdrawal from the emotional field is a signal of emotional reaction to the others.

In broad terms, a differentiating step requires long and careful deliberation to define a life principle secure enough to become a firm belief that can be stated as such without anger or debate or attack—all of which are emotional stimuli. The life energy that goes into defining a principle for self goes in a self-determined direction, which detracts from the former energy devoted to the system, especially to the important other. When this self-determined position is presented, the system reacts emotionally to win back the differentiating one into the togetherness. The family uses any mechanism to achieve this. There are calm arguments to favor the rightness of togetherness, fervent pleading, accusations, solicitousness, and threats of the consequences in terms of hurt to the family and the family's rejection if this course is continued. A high percentage of differentiating ones, fairly sure of beliefs and principles, can go into a session with the family, be won over by the logical argument of the family, and forget the principles that were carefully thought out before the session. Most people require several attempts to get through the first step.

The therapist can help the differentiating one when family pressure is great. He must do this without being perceived as against the family. At moments when the differentiating one develops such symptoms as stomach distress, the therapist may help with a comment such as: "You may have convinced your head to stand for what you believe, but you have not yet convinced your stomach."

When the differentiating one can finally control self throughout the step without fighting back or withdrawing, the family usually reaches a final showdown session with maximal attack and feelings. If the differentiating one can maintain a calm stand through this, the family anxiety suddenly subsides into a new and different level of closeness, with open appreciation and a higher regard for the differentiating one as a person. This step is usually followed by a calm period, until the other spouse or another family member starts on a similar step of defining self, which repeats the same pattern as the first. The process goes back and forth between the spouses in successive small steps. If one person in a family system can achieve a higher level of functioning and he stays in emotional contact with the others, another family member and another and another will take similar steps. This chain reaction is the basis for the principle that change in a central triangle is followed by automatic change throughout the family system. The change in all the others takes place automatically in the living situations of everyday life. Change is most rapid when the initial triangle involves the most important people in the system.

37

Alice Coleman:
Utopia on Trial

Reviewed by Hugh Freeman

There has been a surprising lack of interest in—and an even greater lack of worthwhile research on—the relationship between the physical environment and human life in its psychological-behavioral aspects. Following up the outcome of interventions is a basic investigatory task for psychiatrists, but has had little attraction for planners or architects, any more than for lawyers. It is ironic, though, that psychiatry should so often be attacked for taking too clinical or mechanistic a view, considering that hardly any other discipline (except social work) devotes so much attention in everyday practice to the objective circumstances of peoples' lives. Perhaps this bad press has something to do with the failure of social psychiatry to construct a coherent environmental offshoot, or to intervene usefully in that kind of public issue—a gap which I tried to start filling in *Mental Health and the Environment* (Freeman 1985).

A very unusual architect, Oscar Newman, shifted the subject's paradigms by a series of naturalistic experiments which showed that design features of public housing could actually affect people's behavior. This work related to one of the overwhelming concerns of New Yorkers (and increasingly, now, of other city dwellers)—crime and violence—although in fact it has much wider implications for urban living in general. Newman demonstrated that making public space more "defensible" could both reduce crime rates and improve the local quality of life, yet only limited use has since been made of this knowledge, and he has been labeled an "architectural determinist," as if that were the end of the matter. (Interestingly enough, *determinism* was a concept that grew out of American research which at first was largely concerned with environments for the mentally ill and, as Mechanic and Aiken (1987) have pointed out, encouraged the community care ideology). Newman, though, provided the starting point of important British work by Alice Coleman.

Like Newman's *Defensible Space* (Newman 1972), *Utopia on Trial* (Coleman 1985) is a heady mixture of polemic, research reports, policy analysis, and practical recommendations; each book has a scientific basis, but each also reveals the author's strong feelings. Coleman believes that postwar British housing policy and other large-scale redevelopments have not only been failures, but have created a whole set of new and overwhelming social problems. Whereas Newman recorded mainly crime, Coleman has measured environmental disadvantage or social malaise in public housing through a number of indices, and has done so on a much bigger scale than anyone before. These social indicators were all found to have a direct relationship (of worsening) against five increasing design variables: dwellings per entrance, dwellings per block, number of storeys, number of overhead walkways, and adverse spatial organisation; crime levels also showed a similar relationship. It is made clear, though, that "bad design does not determine anything, but it increases the odds against which people have to struggle." No determinist label for her, then, if she can help it.

There is such a massacre here of the sacred cows of architecture and planning that their bleached bones lie scattered throughout: high-rise blocks "are not only financial disasters; they are also human disasters"; "the combination of high-rise with low density has produced the worst possible result"; "in a flat [apartment], a mother (of young children) has a range of options—all unpalatable"; "the demand for more play areas in estates is misconceived"; "inter-war semis [semi-detached houses] were cheap without being nasty, while post-war buildings may be nasty without being cheap"; "estates have been designed on the basis of false prophecies of movement patterns, and encourage abuses"; and "the worst designs bring out the worst behavior in children." Most trenchant of all: "people have been denied the right to choose their own kind of housing, and have then had disastrous designs chosen for them, creating a needless sense of social failure." All these statements are supported by direct evidence, and all ought to be taken most seriously.

One instance where the methodology does seem most open to criticism, though, is in using the number of children in social service care as one of the measures of social malaise of a public housing area, together with litter, graffiti, vandal damage, and presence of urine or feces. Apart from its sensitivity to the effects of local ideologies or administrative policies (particularly in some of the areas that were mapped), this variable is inherently too different from the others to be conflated with them, and its

place in the chain of causality is uncertain. Like psychiatric morbidity—
which failed to enter the model because of lack of data—the rate of children
in public care is a multifactorial product that raises complex questions, for
instance about incidence versus prevalence, length of time spent living in
a particular environment, or the age and sex structure of the local
population. Counting the number of pieces of litter per square yard is
simply not comparable, although it may be equally important in its own
way.

Coleman maintains that where families are given a genuine choice—and
this applies as much to council tenants as to owner-occupiers—they will
most often choose the now traditional semi. This form of living environment does very well on the indicators of social malaise, and also tends to
discourage crime, through the much greater defensibility of its space,
compared with tower blocks for instance. Equally important is the fact that
it restores to people the responsibility of caring for their homes, and
(within limits) the important power to make their mark on territory which
is identifiably their own. Correspondingly, they are freed from the shackles
of vast, unresponsive, grossly inefficient, and outrageously expensive
bureaucracies—which is "democratically controlled public housing" in
Marxist terminology. From the mental health perspective, it would be
reasonable to predict that this liberation from the prison of high-rise or
other megastructures would result in residents experiencing much lower
levels of stress, whatever other problems they may have to continue facing
in different homes. It is generally accepted that such stress is a determinant
of psychiatric morbidity, although in ways which still remain almost
entirely undefined (see below).

"The lady doth protest too much," some might say. What has been most
remarkable, in fact, is the relative silence of those who might have been
expected to deny this message most vehemently—whether trendy architects, municipal bosses, or high-technology builders. Here and there,
high-rise blocks are actually being demolished now, notwithstanding that
their often shoddy construction has incurred debts lasting far into the
future, while small-scale housing is appearing even in inner cities. Although Coleman evidently hit the nail on the head, her pioneering work
now needs to be developed so that the relationship of building forms with
behavior or psychological well-being is investigated in more sensitive
ways. Professor Coleman has mostly discounted housing management as
being able to contribute positively to the quality of residents' lives, in
comparison with building structure, but it is more likely that both are
important.

It would be wrong to imagine that her lessons have been generally
learnt. The Maiden Lane estate in Camden was completed in 1983 and

described then by the *Architectural Review* as "representing the very best in British housing lore and as civilised as any recent European solution." Within four years, though, it had attained social breakdown; its "references to ocean liners" had produced dangerously steep staircases, a mugger's paradise of tunnels, and rubbish collections which eluded the dustmen. So much for the legacy of Le Corbusier (Stamp 1988).

The environment, though, can be approached from many different directions – all relevant, if difficult to integrate. Costs in one may need to be traded off against benefits in another, through highly complex maneuvers. Yet all too often this fails to happen, whether through ignorance, political obduracy, or the overwhelming attraction of short-term economic returns. Rodwin and Hollister (1984) (not the psychiatrist of that name) therefore did a useful service in assembling a collection of images of the city, as seen by a great variety of disciplines, from law to economics. Among these, the anthropologist points out that, following long-term market failures, what at first seem to be technocratically soluble problems turn out to contain intractable social and political dimensions, relating to the fact that the most disadvantaged groups bear the biggest brunt of difficult readjustments. Hence the "inner-city" morass, in which the chronic mentally ill are often caught; this view provides a useful contrast to that of defensible space, although it does not undermine the Newman–Coleman thesis.

Sociological and psychological approaches today remain influenced by Georg Simmel's prediction, early in this century, of the possible effects of continuous contacts with innumerable people in cities; "one would be completely atomized internally and come to an unimaginable psychic state" (Simmel 1908). Hence, city dwellers have "the right to distrust" others and the need to be selective in their responses – both of which attitudes can also be harmful to everyday life. Later, Wirth showed that the impersonality and arbitrariness of the city was reduced through the creation of subcommunities, within which each person could establish some control over his immediate environment at least.

One of the most important contributors to Radwin and Hollister's *Cities of the Mind* was Kevin Lynch. His *Image of the City* (Lynch 1960) has been endlessly quoted over the past thirty years, yet he had to regret that it has actually had very little effect in changing the way in which cities are shaped, or in making them more responsive to their inhabitants' wishes – which was its main motive. "Decision makers," he says, "often base their choices on a strong personal image of the environment, but this image is implicit and not tested against others." As for the individual in the city, he should feel delight "in ambiguity, mystery, and surprise, so long as they are contained within a basic order and as long as we can be confident of weaving the puzzle into some new, more intricate pattern." One of the tragedies of large-scale redevelopment and of present-day architectural doctrines is that they destroy all possibility of experiencing these environmental pleasures; the city becomes nothing more than a collection of huge, inhuman structures, surrounded by dereliction.

It was not ever thus. Early nineteenth-century Manchester may have been, as de Tocqueville put it, a filthy sewer from which pure gold flowed—and Engels said something similar a decade later—but the city was also "an urban and industrial prodigy, a phenomenon of a new age." That was John Archer's description, in his editorial introduction to *Art and Architecture in Victorian Manchester* (Archer 1985), a collection of ten superbly illustrated essays. Certainly, the human costs were great to the immigrants who poured in—just as they are today in the burgeoning cities of the Third World—but on the other hand, the potential rewards seemed infinite. The city's atmosphere, described by Girouard as "of relentless activity and money being made in heaps," left an unforgettable impression on visitors. Embodying it all was the Town Hall, an achievement which Archer claims was "of a scale, significance and permanence" that outstripped those of all other provincial cities and even rivaled most of what London had to offer. Around it were the warehouses, built mainly in the Italian palazzo style, so that it did not seem ridiculous to compare Manchester with a city of the Italian Renaissance. (It still has as many canals as Bruges, although one wouldn't think so).

No British writer has so far even attempted a synthesis of the meaning of Victorian Manchester and its society, but Gary Messinger (1986) saw it as "the first predominantly industrial city of the world." He scrupulously collected the comments on Manchester of writers from Disraeli ("as great a human exploit as Athens") to J. B. Priestley ("an Amazonian jungle of blackened bricks"), but perhaps most important was his emphasis that detailed statistical inquires into the health and living conditions of populations began there. This trail leads from James Kay and the Manchester Statistical Society of 1832 to today's high-rise blocks, and awaits new explorations.

If Britain gave the world industrial cities in the last century, in the present one it can show what has been described as a unique social experiment—the new towns. No other country has produced a comparable scale of deliberately planned large communities, with a theoretical basis which certainly changed over thirty years but was always clear and coherent. Their origins were in Ebenezer Howard's "garden city," which he conceived as a single answer to the human problems of both crowded megalopolises and culturally impoverished rural populations. By 1945, British planners were confident that they could prescribe the conditions in which most people could live satisfactorily—such hubris!

In fact, no one had thought of collecting data which might have thrown light on the relationship between these new environments and their inhabitants. This vast national investment was unaccompanied by even the smallest efforts at evaluation, and we shall never know whether it was all worthwhile, in comparison with other ways in which the money might have been spent—the opportunity costs. But many years after it was established, the largest new town—Milton Keynes—decided to consult its residents, and the results of this appeared under the questioning title *The Best of Both Worlds?* (Bishop 1986).

Milton Keynes residents mostly see their community as a series of villages, although they use the whole area extensively and in a citylike way; their top priority, though, is their own house and its immediate surroundings, rather than the wider setting. They do not see the new city as anything very special or even unique, but rather as being a little better than usual environments; at the same time, they would not like it to develop into just another anonymous suburb. They want a house to look like a house and reject the imagery of contemporary architects, who are mostly fixated on some overall design rather than on peoples' needs for living space. Like many grand designs, though, Milton Keynes seems to have passed into a phase of disillusionment: psychiatrists there report marital and family breakdown in almost epidemic proportions. Perhaps this was predictable from the fact that the 80,000 immigrants to it were mostly separated from their networks of family and social support. However, the whole story could only be revealed by large-scale epidemiological study, and there is no indication that the funding for this will ever be available. An "experiment" it wasn't.

But if study of the environment–person relationship is ever to gain the dignity and utility of a scientifically valid discipline, it will need better theories, more valid methodology, and eventually a respectable body of empirical data. Cohen et al. (1986) made a helpful contribution to this daunting task in their report of an extensive study of children in Los Angeles schools who either were or were not exposed to high levels of aircraft noise. The results were not outstanding—exposed children had higher blood pressures (although still within the normal range) and some relative cognitive impairment—but much more important is the authors' exhaustive and very honest examination of the methodological and theoretical problems associated with this field of work. For one thing, there have been few attempts to examine the interplay between multiple environmental stressors and the effect this may have on health, although direct effects of stressors on behavior or physiology may be less detrimental than the costs of coping responses to them.

A significant contribution to the empirical data from Birtchnell et al.

(1988): screening a large sample of young married women on a London housing estate, they found a disproportionate number of those with high depression scores in dwellings with the highest scores for environmental disadvantage. These high scores also had homes with interiors that were significantly poorer in appearance than were the homes of the low scorers. When trying to interpret relationships of this kind, the direction of causality may not be clear, and the location of these women in the worst areas of the estate might have been influenced by their own inherent vulnerability. Nevertheless, it does seem reasonable to suggest that "the accommodation itself also played a part in the development and maintenance of their depression."

Perhaps related to this pervading depression is the apathy and hopelessness that seems to characterize environmentally impoverished areas. While there is no panacea for this problem, community action projects can be important ingredients of regeneration, and in *How Green Is Your City?*, Joan Davidson provided a valuable account of these in Britain. Although there is a tendency to interpret "environment" largely in visual terms, she points out that this should be more holistic, including the efficiency with which local resources are used. Rehabilitation of buildings, recycling of waste, energy-saving, and greening schemes can bring back vitality to jobless and disheartened people. Among other things, this revitalization of communities is very important for the resettlement of people leaving psychiatric and mental retardation hospitals, who tend to be resettled in inner-city areas because those are the only ones that have both empty accommodation and an absence of community resistance to such incomers. Both of these features, though, also indicate the poor level of social integration in such environments, which is unlikely to be helpful to the handicapped as they seek to reestablish their lives. As Alice Coleman pointed out, this is no Utopia, even when most of its structures are relatively new.

REFERENCES

Archer, J. H. G., ed. (1985). *Art and Architecture in Victorian Manchester*. Manchester, England: Manchester University Press.

Birtchnell, J., Masters, N., and Deahl, M. (1988). Depression and the physical environment: a study of young married women on a London housing estate. *British Journal of Psychiatry* 153, 56–64.

Bishop, J. (1986) *Milton Keynes—The Best of Both Worlds?* Bristol, England: SAUS.

Cohen, S., Evans, G. W., Stokols. D., and Krantz, D. S. (1986). *Behavior, Health and Environment Stress*. New York: Plenum.

Coleman, A. (1985). *Utopia on Trial*. London: Hilary Shipman.

Davidson, J. (1988). *How Green Is Your City?* London: Bedford Square Press.

Freeman, H. L., ed. (1985). *Mental Health and the Environment.* London: Churchill Livingston.

Lynch, K. (1960). *The Image of the City.* Cambridge, MA: MIT Press.

Mechanic, D., and Aiken, L. H. (1987). Improving the care of patients with chronic mental illness. *New England Journal of Medicine* 317, 1634–1638.

Messinger, G. S. (1986). *Manchester in the Victorian Age: The Half-Known City.* Manchester, England: Manchester University Press.

Newman, O. (1972). *Defensible Space.* New York: Macmillan.

Rodwin, L., and Hollister, R. M. (1984). *Cities of the Mind.* New York: Plenum.

Simmel, G. (1908). *Conflict in Sociology.* 3rd ed. Glencoe, NY: The Free Press.

Stamp, G. (1988). Modern estate nears "complete breakdown." *The Independent.* May 30.

Selections from
Utopia on Trial
by Alice Coleman

JANE JACOBS–AN AMERICAN VIEW

Jane Jacobs demonstrated the essential falsity of planning theory by instancing areas possessed of all the supposed virtues, which were nevertheless disintegrating, and supposedly unviable areas which were spontaneously upgrading. Impressed by this contrary evidence, she advocated the most basic of all scientific principles: the need to observe the facts and to discard theories at variance with them. She also argued that it was not enough to observe what was bad about cities and then invent what might be a good substitute. The existing good should also be observed, to act as a constructive model, and 'good' should not merely be equated with aesthetic appearance but should focus upon what actually worked to promote a stable social structure.

Practising what she preached, Jane Jacobs observed successful city neighbourhoods and distilled the essence of what they shared in common. They proved to be close-textured, high-density assemblages of mixed land uses, where many people live within walking distance of many destinations and there is constant coming and going on foot along a dense network of streets. This pattern works naturally to ensure the emergence of a firm social structure. People passed on the sidewalk (pavement) come to be known by sight, and this leads to a web of public acquaintanceship, in which roles are known and talents can be called upon by the community without invading people's private lives. Degrees of congeniality can be savoured and personal friendships can mature naturally, without forcing the pace. The overall result is a complex system of interlocking levels and circles of acquaintanceship, which gives the community a clear knowledge of its accepted mores, and hence practical guidelines for behaviour—an essential framework for stability.

A strong, stable social structure is also the aim for new planned developments, but Jane Jacobs showed the very designs that are alleged to create it are the barriers that preclude its emergence. The segregation of land uses into large units, . . . with spacious grounds, extensive parks, huge schools, big shopping precincts, industrial estates and cultural complexes, means that few destinations are within walking distance. Cars are needed for most purposes, but people passing each other at high speed behind glass are deprived of natural opportunities to build up a web of public acquaintanceship. Housewives, in particular, may become very lonely, but in order to develop friendships they have to take the risk of inviting strangers into their homes; gradualism is largely eliminated. In these circumstances the circle of contacts tends to remain small and the prevailing atmosphere is one of anonymity. There is no accepted set of social mores, which means that some people agonise over what is acceptable behaviour while others, at the opposite end of the scale of temperaments, find no constraints to curb their excesses.

Jane Jacobs believed that the contrast between these two extreme types of area makes a striking impact upon the bringing up of children. In the successful areas the streets are peopled with friends and acquaintances who know the accepted mores and keep a responsible eye on children playing on the sidewalk. Their involvement is reinforced by 'eyes on the street' from the windows of the buildings—people who find it interesting to watch a busy scene full of familiar figures. Such a neighbourhood is self-policing and mothers do not fear to allow their children out into it as they grow beyond the toddler stage. This gives them a wide range of adult examples on which to model their behaviour, and helps them to become successfully integrated into the adult community.

Social breakdown, like charity, begins at home. Psychologists have long stressed the importance of the home, as a family, during the child's formative years, and we now stress its importance as a *place*. Shared nests, however lovingly designed by experts, can interfere with the quality of parenting and colour the attitudes of the generations reared in them. . . .

We have identified 15 design variables in blocks of flats which affect the behaviour of at least some residents, especially children, and also of other people using the building. Litter-dropping behaviour, for example, becomes more frequent as buildings and grounds increase in size and interconnectedness, and also where residents cannot see or control the approach to their dwellings. The results are strengthened by the fact that all six of the test measures used—litter, graffiti, vandal damage, children in care, urine pollution and faecal pollution—become more common as the design values worsen within each variable. . . .

The 3,893 houses surveyed show far less sign of social breakdown than purpose-built flats, while 279 houses converted into flats are intermediate between the two. Litter is less common, graffiti extremely rare, and excrement virtually unheard of. Vandal damage may occur where houses are adjacent to flats, but children are taken into care much less often. Litter is therefore the main test measure for houses. It varies in frequency according to a number of design features which are different from those of flats, and proves that less stabilising house designs have become more common over time. This means that some new estates of houses may be more problem-ridden than some of the better purpose built blocks.

Our main practical recommendations are:

1. No more flats should be built.
2. House designers should renounce the unstabilising layouts of the last decade.
3. Existing flats should be modified to remove their worst design features.

Two design guides follow. The first outlines our recommendations for houses, listing features to be incorporated or avoided in order to minimise social problems. The second summarises the modifications which we advocate to reduce the disadvantagement scores of existing flats. . . .

WIDER INSIGHTS

As each design variable worsens, there is an increasing probability that more families will fail, in more ways, to develop their children's capacity for adjusting to civilised life, and the probability becomes a smoother progression when it is related to the combination of all designs together.

The mildest form of social deviance is litter. It is rare in traditional houses with all the design safeguards that have evolved over time, but the more these safeguards have been abandoned, the more likely is a copious and obnoxious accumulation of garbage. As design worsens, litter is joined by graffiti, and then successively by vandal damage, by family breakdown necessitating the placing of children in care, and by excrement. Each of these increases in a classic S-shaped growth curve, which begins slowly, then accelerates and finally slows down towards saturation point. The later any form of abuse appears, the more slowly it grows. Litter and graffiti have already reached saturation point in the worst existing blocks, but the other measures have not. They would do so, however, if even worse blocks were to be built in the future.

The amount of public money spent on cleaning, repairing and administering design-disadvantaged buildings . . . is a total waste, since all these functions would be carried out by the inhabitants themselves if post-war housing had been styled to facilitate self-tending by occupiers. . . .

Crime is related to design in much the same way as vandalism, children in care and excrement and, consequently, that design-disadvantaged areas cause higher public expenditure for policing, courts and prisons, higher private and insurance losses, and higher social costs in the sufferings of crime victims.

As well as the broad agreement between our six social malaise measures and the several categories of crime, we also have preliminary evidence that arson rates and some kinds of psychiatric illness are related to the malign effect of Utopian designs. There is no reason to think that the list of design-induced ills has been fully explored. They certainly appear to be wide ranging, which emphasises range of benefits that design modification could bring. . . .

Some rather cherished ideas have been found to be totally irrelevant: population density and the amount of nearby public open space. Other equally cherished ideas prove to have an effect that is completely opposite to that claimed. Various measures of poverty are associated with less rather than more social breakdown. Unemployment is not associated with increased vandalism. More residential green space brings more intensive abuse, and so does the presence of shops, services or community halls, located inside the estate. . . .

Other explanatory factors involve the existence of unused areas, whether in the form of derelict or wasteland sites, abandoned buildings or 'voids' (empty, boarded-up flats). These are due partly to misconceived policies, but also partly to inefficiency in recycling idle land or re-letting empty dwellings.

Child density definitely contributes to high levels of abuse in badly designed dwellings. . . . There should not be more than one child under 15 per six adults aged 20 or more in a block of flats. . . . Where ownership is independent of design it does not exert such a strong influence as the design variables do.

All these discoveries add up to the fact that it is the Utopian design that has been imposed upon post-war Britain that appears to be the chief factor in many aspects of social decline in new or redeveloped areas.

WHY?

Why should Utopia have been such an all-pervading failure, when it was envisaged as a form of national salvation? It was conceived in compassion but has been born and bred in authoritarianism, profligacy and frustration. It aimed to liberate people from the slums but has come to represent an even worse form of bondage. It aspired to beautify the urban environment, but has been transmogrified into the epitome of ugliness. Its redemption, after 40 years, is not only a matter of improving the buildings, but also of winning the hearts and minds of those who create and control them.

. . . It is the natural condition of human beings to make progress by trial and error, and it is the misfortune of our age that the trial and error have been both large-scale and prolonged, with only minimal attention to the question of progress. Planners, architects, developers and housing managers have all been drawn into the same huge plausible vortex—so plausible, indeed, that none of them can be blamed for lacking the foresight to see where it would lead.

. . Housing officers at the design workface have become well aware that Utopia has proved disastrous and some housing authorities are opening their minds to more effective methods of improvement. Architects are engaged on a quest for a 'post-Modern' approach, and a few developers are breaking away from the established mould. . . .

John F. C. Turner's book *Housing by People* (1976) has demonstrated that the much reviled shanty towns of the Third World are actually a constructive housing solution, because people are free to build their own homes and then progressively improve them, according to their means. The inhabitants' control of the design, construction and management of their own dwellings is a process which stimulates individual and social well-being. If they are denied control and responsibility, the dwelling environment becomes a barrier to personal fulfilment and a burden on the economy—a judgement which applies just as aptly to the concrete jungles of Britain.

In his preface to Turner's book, Colin Ward, author of *The Child in the City* (1978), summarises its philosophy as follows: The important thing about housing is not what it *is*, but what it *does* in people's lives. Dweller satisfaction is not necessarily related to the imposition of standards, and people find deficiencies in housing infinitely more tolerable if they are their own responsibility than if they are someone else's. . . .

CREDITS

The editors gratefully acknowledge permission to reprint material from the following sources:

From *Suicide: A Study in Sociology* by Emil Durkheim. Reprinted with permission of The Free Press, a division of Macmillan Inc. Translated by John A. Spaulding and George Simpson. Copyright © 1950, 1978 by The Free Press (Canada) and Routledge and Kegan Paul.

From *The Interpretation of Dreams* by Sigmund Freud. Translated from the German and edited by James Strachey. Published in the United States by Basic Books, Inc. (copyright © 1956) by arrangement with George Allen & Unwin, Ltd. and the Hogarth Press, Ltd. Reprinted by permission of HarperCollins Publishers, Inc., Unwin Hyman, and Sigmund Freud Copyrights, The Institute of Psycho-Analysis and the Hogarth Press. From *New Introductory Lectures*, copyright © 1966 by W. W. Norton & Company and reprinted by permission.

From *General Psychopathology* by Karl Jaspers. Copyright © 1963 by Manchester University Press and reprinted by permission.

From *The Ego and the Mechanisms of Defence* by Anna Freud. Copyright © 1966 by International Universities Press and reprinted by permission.

From *The Psychoanalytic Theory of Neurosis* by Otto Fenichel. Reprinted with permission of W. W. Norton & Company, Inc. Copyright © 1945 by W. W. Norton & Company, Inc. Renewed 1972 by Hanna Fenichel.

INDEX

Abraham, K., 252, 336
Adler, A., 263, 293, 294, 330, 331
Adler, G., 350
Adrian, E. D., 57
Aiken, L. H., 404
Akhtar, S., 341–351
Alexander, D. A., 335–339
Alexander, F., 43
Allport, G. W., 54
Anderson, E. W., 20, 95, 123, 124
Andreski, S., 358
Archer, J. H. G., 407
Arnold, 119
Aschaffenburg, G., 64
Atkins, P., 357
Augustine, Saint, 238
Aveline, M., 145–154
Averill, J., 336
Avery-Jones, 57
Ayllon, 331

Babinski, J. F. F., 248
Bacal, H. A., 108, 109
Baglivi, G., 240
Bailey, P., 237

Balint, E., 104, 105
Balint, M., 39, 103–111, *112–114*,
    203, 204, 263
Bandura, A., 325–328, *329–333*
Barlow, N., 357
Bateson, G., 216
Beaumont, G. A. de, 320, 322
Beck, A. T., 379–381, *382–388*
Benjamin, L. S., 170
Berghe, 358
Bergson, H. 77, 79, 80
Berkowitz, R., 218
Berne, E., 225–229, *230–235*, 263
Bernheim, H., 303
Berrios, G. E., 1, 25, 27
Binet, A., 299–300
Binswanger, O., 76
Bion, W., 42, 307, 368, 371
Birley, J. L. T., 315–318
Birtchnell, J., 163–170, 263–269, 408
Bishop, J., 408
Blackmore, R., 241
Blashfield, R. K., 350
Bleuler, E., 63–70, *71–73*, 75, 76,
    77, 79, 83

Bleuler, M., 63–70
Bleuler, R., 63–70
Bloch, S., 193
Blum, K., 139
Bonner, T. J., 358
Boswell, J., 356
Bowen, M., 377, 389–396, *397–401*
Bowlby, J., 87–89, *90–91*, 154, 263,
    338, 373
Box, S., 370
Boyle, 241
Braceland, F., 237
Brachet, 241
Brady, F., 356
Brain, R., 57, 93–94, 241
Breuer, J., 303
Brockman, B., 205, 207
Brodie, B. C., 240
Brown, G. W., 217
Brown, M., 229
Burton, 189
Burton, R., 238
Butler, S., 357
Byrne, J. P., 350

Calef, V., 342
Calvin, J., 356
Camus, A., 365
Carey, M., 320
Carr, A., 281
Carter, R. B., 241, 242
Celsus, A. C., 254, 279
Chapple, 196
Charcot, J.-M., 64, 176, 239, 240,
    248, 303
Chaslin, 83
Churchland, P. M., 27
Churchland, P. S., 27
Cleese, J., 367
Cohen, S., 408
Coleman, A., 403–410, *411–415*
Colsenet, 301

Coltart, N., 207
Cooper, A. M., 342
Cooper, D., 218
Cooper, 284
Cope, Z., 57
Corsini, R. J., 225, 306
Cover-Jones, M., 275
Cramer, D., 185–189, 225–229
Crawford, W., 320
Crook, J. H., 357
Crouch, E., 193–197, 305–310
Crown, S., 53–59, 237, 238
Cullen, W., 240
Cutting, J., 75–81

Darwin, C., 357, 358
Davanloo, H., 207
David, A. S., 215–220
David, T., 218
Davidson, J., 409
Davison, K., 93–96
Dawkins, R., 357
Demetrius, 241
Descartes, R., 241
Dilthey, W., 21
Disraeli, B., 407
Dix, D., 320
Dubois d'Amiens, 240
Duehrssen, 131
Dunlap, 119n
Durand (de Gros), 300–301
Durkheim, E., 1–6, *7–8*, 57
Dwight, L., 320
Dymond, 211

Edwards, G., 137
Elder, A., 106
Elkin, 305
Ellenberger, H. E., 291–298,
    299–304
Ellman, S. J., 9–12
Engels, F., 407

Erasistratus, 241
Erikson, E. H., 341, 368
Esterson, A., 215–220, *221–224*
Eysenck, H. J., 53–59, *60–61*, 197,
     203, 252

Fairbairn, W. R. D., 147, 341
Fallon, I. R. H., 218
Fechner, G. T., 294
Fenichel, O., 39–44, *45–51*
Ferenczi, S., 103, 203
Finley, J. B., 322, 323
Fish, F., 27
Fliess, W., 271
Forel, A., 64
Foulkes, S. H., 194
Frank, J. D., 145–154, *155–161*
Frazier, S., 281
Freeling, P., 109
Freeman, H., 121, 403–410
Freud, A., 33–34, *35–38*, 39, 194,
     264, 265
Freud, S., 1, 9–12, *13–17*, 22, 26,
     35, 40, 41, 42, 43, 44, 45, 48,
     57, 66, 67, 77, 80, 94, 98, 99,
     149, 152, 164, 167, 168, 176,
     185, 195, 207, 239, 242, 248,
     252, 255, 263, 264, 266, 267,
     268, 270, 271, 273, 293, 294,
     295, 296, 297, 301, 303, 311,
     312, 336, 350, 368
Fuller, P., 264

Galen, 238, 241, 245, 254
Gallagher, J. M., 109
Galton, F., 357
Garfield, S. L., 205
Gath, A., 87–89
Gay, P., 9
Gelder, 277, 284
Gellhorn, 120
Gillespie, C. C., 356

Girouard, 407
Glass, G. V., 146
Goldfarb, 91
Goldstein, M. J., 217
Gorton, G., 344
Granit, R., 357
Griesinger, 21, 242
Grinker, R., 342
Groddeck, G., 270
Gross, M. M., 137, 139, 140
Grosskurth, P., 295
Gruenberg, A. M., 341–351
Gruhle, 93
Gunderson, J. G., 342, 350
Guntrip, H., 147
Gurland, B., 149
Gurman, 188
Guttman, E., 55
Guze, 95

Halbwachs, M., 5
Hall, B., 320
Hamilton, M., 123, 124, 125
Hare, E., 355–359
Harrison, P. J., 24–28
Hartman, 265, 268
Hartmann, 341
Haughton, 331
Heather, N., 135, 137, 138
Heine, H., 330
Heron, J., 109
Hippocrates, 238, 326, 329
Hirsch, S. R., 217
Hoehn-Saric, R., 149
Hoenig, J., 123
Hollender, M. H., 240
Hollister, R. M., 406
Holmes, G., 57
Holmes, J., 203–208
Holmes, O. W., 355
Hooley, J. M., 217
Hopkins, P., 106

Hore, B. D., 133–140
Horney, K., 295
Howard, E., 407
Howard, K. I., 206
Howe, S. G., 320, 321
Hughes, 331
Hume, D., 356
Hundert, E., 25
Hunter, R., 238, 240
Husserl, E., 21

Ibsen, H., 308
Imber, S., 149

Jacobs, J., 411–415
Jacobson, E., 120, 265, 341
James, J., 229
James, W., 275
Janet, P.-M.-F., 82, 242, 248, 293,
    294, 301, 302, 303
Jaspers, K., 19–23, 24–28, *29–32*,
    93, 128, 216
Jaynes, J., 357
Jeanneret, C.-E. (Le Corbusier),
    406
Jellinek, E. M., 133–140, *141–143*
Jersild, 280
Johnson, S., 335
Johnson, V. E., 285–288, *289–290*
Jones, E., 260, 264
Jorden, 239, 246, 247
Jousset, 2
Julius, N., 320
Jung, C. G., 64, 77, 255, 263, 293,
    294, 296, 301

Kahn, 131
Kant, I., 21
Kardiner, A., 281
Kay, J., 407
Keithly, L. J., 205
Keller, M., 137

Kelly, G., 147
Kernberg, O., 147, 265, 341–351,
    352–353
Kerr, M. E., 389–396
Keynes, M., 408
Kierkegaard, S., 21
Kiesler, D. J., 170
Kincaid, J., 245
King, A. F. A., 300
King, T., 88
Klein, M., 39, 43, 147, 263, 264,
    271, 295, 336, 338, 341, 342,
    368, 371, 375, 376
Klerman, G. L., 95, 342, 350
Kline, P., 33–34
Koch, 129, 130
Kohut, H., 147, 263, 265, 347, 349
Kolb, J. E., 342
Kolle, K., 22
Kosslyn, S. M., 76
Kraepelin, E., 21, 66, 67, 75, 93,
    98, 123, 165, 248, 252
Kräupl Taylor, F., 25, 27
Kretschmer, E., 21, 26, 248
Kris, E., 268
Kubie, L., 260

Laing, R. D., 57, 58, 76, 115,
    215–220, *221–224*, 263
Landouzy, H., 240
Langer, M., 336
Larkin, P., 203
Latham, R. G., 241, 247n10
Laycock, 241
Lazarus, 283
Leary, T., 164, 165, 170
Leavy, S. A., 237
Le Corbusier (C.-E. Jeanneret), 406
Leff, J. P., 217, 218
Leibnitz, G. W., 301
Leigh, D., 239
Lelliott, P., 325–328

LePois, C., 239, 240
Leschke, 120
Levine, H. G., 133
Lewis, A., 53, 58, 60, 123, 193,
    249–257, *258–261*, 295
Lewis, J. B. S., 55
Liberman, B., 149, 308
Lieber, F., 320
Lieberman, S., 115–117
Lindemann, E., 336
Littré, E., 244n
Locke, J., 356
Lucas, R., 39–44
Lurie, M. J., 109
Lynch, K., 406
Lysenko, T. D., 356

Maddison, D. C., 336
Maediarmid, D., 291–298
Mahler, M., 154
Malan, D. H., 106, 151, 153,
    203–208, *209–214*
Mapother, 252, 255
Marinker, M., 109
Marks, I. M., 275–278, *279–284*
Marryat, F., 320
Marshall, H., 256
Martineau, H., 320
Marx, K., 1, 2, 295, 405
Marziali, E., 206
Masters, W. H., 285–288, *289–290*
Maudsley, H., 255, 357, 358
Mayer-Gross, W., 93–96, *97–101*,
    124, 255
McCarthy, 142
McElroy, R. A., 350
McGinley, E., 218
McHugh, P. R., 27
McKay, C., 245n3
McLemore, C. W., 170
Mechanic, D., 404
Menninger, K., 259–260

Merskey, H., 237–243
Mesmer, F., 294
Messinger, G. S., 407
Meyer, A., 252
Meyer, 94
Mezger, 128
Mill, J. S., 163, 357, 358
Miller, T. I., 146
Minkowski, E., 75–81, *82–86*
Minuchin, S., 218
Moebius, P. J., 248
Mohanna, M., 1
Moll, 301
Moran, Lord, 104
Moreno, J., 196

National Schizophrenia
    Fellowship, 218
Newman, O., 403, 404
Nietzsche, F., 21, 294
Norell, J., 106

O'Neill, E., 308
Orlinsky, D. E., 206

Paré, A., 239
Parkes, C. M., 335–339, *340*
Parloff, M., 149
Pathman, 121
Paykel, E. S., 379–381
Peaston, J., 245
Perls, F., 263, 269
Perry, J. C., 342, 350
Peters, 281
Piaget, J., 171, 177
Pichot, P., 75
Pietroni, P. C., 103–111
Pinel, P., 255
Pirandello, L. 181–182
Pitcairn, 245
Plutarch, 241
Pomme, 241

Popper, K., 177, 318, 357
Priestley, J. B., 407
Prince, M., 281
Proust, M., 302
Pugh, G. E., 358

Quinn, S., 295

Rachman, 282, 283
Raphael, B., 336, 338
Ray, I., 316, 317
Razin, 188
Reich, W., 263
Reil, 255, 301
Reynolds, J. R., 240
Roazen, P., 295
Robertson, I., 135, 137, 138
Robins, 95
Rodwin, L., 406
Rogers, C. R., 185–189, *190–192*,
    211, 227, 331
Rose, S., 355
Rosenberg, 306
Rosenfeld, 44
Roth, M., 93–96, *99–101*
Rothman, D. J., 315–318, *319–323*
Rund, B. R., 217
Rush, B., 133
Russell, B., 77, 177
Ruszczynski, S., 367–372
Rutter, M., 87
Rycroft, C., 263–269, *270–274*
Ryle, 205

Sahlins, M., 355
Samuel, O., 106
Sarton, G., 245n2
Scharfetter, C., 27
Scharff, D. E., 370
Schmideberg, M., 43
Schneider, K., 21, 123–127,
    128–132
Schultz-Hencke, 131

Schwartz, M. A., 27
Selzer, M. A., 350
Senger, C. P., 275–278
Shakespeare, W., 297, 312
Shepherd, M., 19–23, 24, 76, 255
Sherlock, S., 57
Shneidman, E. S., 5
Simmel, E., 40
Simmel, G., 406
Sims, A. C. P., 27
Singer, M., 342
Skinner, B. F., 115, 331
Skynner, R., 367–372, *373–377*
Slater, E., 93–96, *99–101*, 215, 242
Slavney, P. R., 27
Smith, A. C., 176–179, 215
Smith, C. G., 357
Smith, M. L., 146
Snaith, R. P., 285–288
Solomon, 377
Soranus, 245n2
Sowerby, P., 109, 110
Spearman, C. E., 54
Spiegel, 281
Spitzer, M., 24, 95
Stalin, J., 356
Stamp, G., 406
Standage, K., 123–127
Stengel, E., 249, 250, 256
Stern, W., 129
Stewart, 142
Stone, A., 149
Stone, M. H., 350
Strauss, G. D., 341
Stroebe, M. S., 336, 338
Stroebe, W., 336, 338
Strupp, H. H., 149
Sullivan, H. S., 165, 169, 177, 267,
    308, 368
Suttie, 263
Sydenham, T., 239, 240, 241, 247,
    248
Symonds, R. L., 1–6

Symons, D., 358
Szasz, T. S., 163–170, *171–175*, 176–179, *180–183*, 267

Tacitus, 358
Taylor, F. K., 193–197, *198–202*, 249–257
Thines, G., 24
Thurstone, L. L., 54
Tocqueville, A. de, 320, 322, 407
Todd, 133
Tours, M. de, 2
Trachtenberg, M. C., 139
Tribich, D., 342
Trotula of Salerno, 238
Tuke, D. H., 248
Turner, J. F. C., 415

Veith, I., 237–243, *244–248*
Vogel, 142
Volkan, V. D., 350
von Gebsattel, 21
von Gudden, 64

Waelder, R., 349
Waldinger, R., 350
Walker, C., 24
Walker, W. L., 336
Wallace, A., 357
Walshe, F. M. R., 57
Walters, A., 240
Ward, C., 415
Wayland, F., 320

Weber, M., 21
Weinberg, 283
Weinshel, E., 342
Weinstein, L. N., 11
Wender, P. H., 217
Werble, B., 342
Werlinder, H., 123, 124
Wernicke, C., 21, 26
Weyer, 239
Whitaker, C., 308
Whytt, R., 240
Wiggins, O. P., 27
Willis, T., 239, 240, 247
Willmuth, 281
Wilson, E. O., 355–359, *360–365*
Wing, J. K., 216
Winnicott, D. W., 39, 147
Wolpe, J., 115–117, *118–122*, 185, 275, 283
Wood, P., 57
Woollams, S., 229
Wootton, Baroness, 254
Worden, J. W., 338
World Health Organization, 135, 136
Wright, J. P., 241
Wynne, L. C., 217

Yalom, I. D., 305–310, *311–314*
Yates, 119n

Zaslove, 283
Ziehen, 130